THE SPIRIT OF CONTR

AND OTHER ESSAYS

WILLIAM HAZLITT was born in Maidstone in 1778, the second son of a radical, Unitarian minister. After a brief period in the United States, the family settled in Shropshire, where Hazlitt lived until he went to Hackney College in London in 1793. Here he came into contact with some of the leading radical thinkers of the period. To the disappointment of his father, he decided against becoming a Unitarian minister. Over the next few years, when he first met the poets Coleridge and Wordsworth, he tried to make a career as a portrait painter and wrote philosophy, but his *Essay on the Principles of Human Action* (1805) failed to make an impact. It was during this period also that he met his great friend Charles Lamb, who, with Coleridge and William Godwin, helped him find work. Charles and Mary Lamb also introduced him to his first wife Sarah Stoddart, who he married in 1808. In 1812 he started work as a political reporter for the *Morning Chronicle*. In the decade that followed, Hazlitt established a reputation as an essayist and reviewer, especially at Leigh Hunt's *Examiner*. His staunchly radical politics made him a hate-figure for conservatives, but when the *London Magazine* was launched in 1820 he was among its star contributors. By this time he had started gathering his essays and reviews into collections, including *The Round Table* and *Characters of Shakespeare's Plays* in 1817, *Political Essays* in 1819, *Table Talk* in 1821, and *The Spirit of the Age* in 1825.

Hazlitt's marriage ended in divorce in 1822 after he became infatuated with Sarah Walker, an episode thinly disguised in his *Liber Amoris* (1823). The following year, he married Isabella Bridgewater, but their relationship broke up in 1827. An air of melancholy and disappointment suffuses his brilliant late essays, but his radicalism remained undimmed. He died in poverty in a lodging-house in Frith Street, Soho in 1830.

JON MEE is Professor of Eighteenth Century Studies at the University of York. He was previously Professor of Literature at the Universities of Warwick and Oxford, and Margaret Candfield Fellow in English Literature at University College, Oxford. He has worked at the Australian National University and held visiting professorships at ANU, the University of Chicago, and the H. E. Huntington Library.

JAMES GRANDE is Lecturer in Eighteenth-Century Literature and Culture at King's College London. He was previously a research assistant on the Leverhulme-funded Godwin Diary Project at Oxford, a British Academy Postdoctoral Fellow at KCL, and a post-doctoral research fellow on the ERC project 'Music in London, 1800–1851'. He is a trustee of Keats-Shelley House in Rome.

OXFORD WORLD'S CLASSICS

*For over 100 years Oxford World's Classics have brought
readers closer to the world's great literature. Now with over 700
titles—from the 4,000-year-old myths of Mesopotamia to the
twentieth century's greatest novels—the series makes available
lesser-known as well as celebrated writing.*

*The pocket-sized hardbacks of the early years contained
introductions by Virginia Woolf, T. S. Eliot, Graham Greene,
and other literary figures which enriched the experience of reading.
Today the series is recognized for its fine scholarship and
reliability in texts that span world literature, drama and poetry,
religion, philosophy, and politics. Each edition includes perceptive
commentary and essential background information to meet the
changing needs of readers.*

To the memory of
Roy Park
scholar of gusto
1936–2019

ACKNOWLEDGEMENTS

THE editors are extremely grateful to Professor Kevin Gilmartin, who was in at the beginning of this project, and to Sarah Drago, who did so much wonderful work on the notes and other aspects of preparing this edition. The introduction and notes have benefited greatly from the advice of Paddy Bullard, Greg Dart, Uttara Natarajan, Gillian Russell, John Stevenson, Jim Watt, John Whale, Susan Wolfson, and Duncan Wu. Any errors that remain are, of course, the responsibility of the editors.

James Grande would like to thank Natasha, Morwenna, and Gwendolen Grande for their love and support. Jon Mee's greatest debt is to Jane Huyg.

CONTENTS

INTRODUCTION

I wish [Hazlitt] would not quarrel with the world at the rate he does; but the reconciliation must be effected by himself, and I despair of living to see that day. But, protesting against much that he has written, and some things which he chooses to do; judging him by his conversation which I enjoyed so long, and relished so deeply; or by his books, in those places where no clouding passion intervenes—I should belie my own conscience, if I said less, than I think W. H. to be, in his natural and healthy state, one of the wisest and finest spirits breathing.[1]

Written by Charles Lamb in 1823 in a public response to the Poet Laureate Robert Southey, this defence of William Hazlitt captures the ambivalence even his closest friends felt about the great critic and essayist, an ambivalence in many ways founded not only in the excesses and oddities of Hazlitt's behaviour, but also in the contrarian principles of his prose. His tendency towards taking a stance against 'the world' was also often expressed as contradiction within himself, as he constantly tested his own positions in his writing. Throwing out a provocation, he was habitually arguing against it vigorously by the end of an essay, a principle that can make quoting from Hazlitt hazardous, especially if it matters to you what he really thought. Lamb's defence also captures something else about Hazlitt that is sometimes forgotten. He wrote in the glare of public debate, about politics, about literary tastes, and about people. Hazlitt presented himself as a man of principle, especially when it came to his refusal to accept the political order of his day, but constantly questioned those principles on the basis of the utility of dissent. 'The Spirit of Controversy' lends its name to this collection, because it seems to us to be the temper of so much of Hazlitt's own writing.

If Hazlitt was a contrarian, then the contradictions within himself were manifold. He loved London, but delighted in the natural world; blasted William Wordsworth, but thought him the great poet of the age; he perpetuated a strain of misogyny, especially against women writers, shared by many male romantics, but celebrated the age's great actress Sarah Siddons and the feminist writer Mary

---

[1] 'Letter of Elia to Robert Southey, Esquire', *London Magazine* 8 (October 1823), 405.

Wollstonecraft; he cherished the poetry of Robert Burns, but could be insulting about Scotland, especially its philosophers and economists. Hazlitt thought the theatre one of the defining cultural institutions of his day, and worked as a critic for *The Examiner* and the daily papers, but perpetuated the anti-theatrical prejudice that favoured reading Shakespeare over seeing the plays performed. He was a popular lecturer and performer, but seemed against anything that suggested fashion and show. He aspired to be a philosopher, but made his name as a journalist who spoke to the multifarious spirit of his age. His political writing looked to reform and mocked those who wished to return Britain and Europe to the days before the French Revolution, but his essays contain within them a rich vein of nostalgia, especially focused on his father and the oppositional heritage of Protestant Dissent, which he feared was ebbing away from his world. Hazlitt's self-presentation as the man of unwavering principle, who continues to pursue the ideals of the French Revolution, even unto a lifelong veneration of Napoleon, is constantly running into his sense of what he called 'our limited, imperfect, and mixed being'.[2] Indeed, for all his association with the great period of English Romantic poetry, one of Hazlitt's greatest achievements was to incorporate the fleshly eighteenth-century comedy of the novelists Henry Fielding, Tobias Smollett, and Laurence Sterne into his essay writing and to celebrate London as the capital city of a new kind of urban culture.

Hazlitt's background in Protestant nonconformity stayed an important shaping influence throughout his life. His father—the Reverend William Hazlitt senior—had been born into a Calvinist family in Ireland, but moved away from stricter versions of Presbyterian puritanism when he became attracted to anti-trinitarian ideas at university in Glasgow.[3] Unitarians like Hazlitt's father could not square the mysteries of the Holy Trinity with their idea of a rational Christianity. Denial of the Trinity was illegal under the terms of the 1697 Blasphemy Act and remained prohibited by law until 1813. Protestant Dissenters more generally had been excluded from full civil rights by the Test and Corporation Acts passed in the late seventeenth century. Unless they were willing to swear to the thirty-nine

---

[2] 'On the English Novelists', in *Complete Works*, ed. P. P. Howe, 21 vols (London: Dent, 1930–4), vi. 132.

[3] See Stephen Burley's account of Hazlitt's father in *Hazlitt the Dissenter: Religion, Philosophy, and Politics, 1766–1816* (Basingstoke: Palgrave, 2014), chapter 1.

articles of the Church of England, Dissenters could not enter Oxford or Cambridge and were excluded from many public roles. Despite the partial respite from persecution granted by the Act of Toleration (1689), a series of campaigns for repeal were an important part of Hazlitt junior's early life, but they remained unsuccessful until 1828.

Unitarian ministers like Hazlitt's father allowed considerable freedom to their congregations in terms of theology: liberty of conscience was a prized value in these circles. Whether Hazlitt remained a Christian remains unclear, but he always respected the broad commitment to civil rights associated with Dissent. Hazlitt senior appears in many of his son's most moving essays, often as a sincere and humane foil to the foibles of their ostensible subject. Asked to write his father's obituary, Hazlitt came up instead with the brilliant essay 'On the Pleasure of Painting'. Placed at its heart is a remarkable account of painting his parent's portrait, with its palpable sense not just of a personal loss but of a whole world suffering a raw absence:

The picture is left: the table, the chair, the window where I learned to read Livy, the chapel where my father preached, remain where they were; but he himself is gone to rest, full of years, of faith, of hope, and charity. (pp. 142–3)

William Hazlitt senior's liberal ideas extended to politics. Like many Dissenters, he was sympathetic to the American colonists, but hostile reaction to his opinions drove him out of his Irish pulpit into an American one in 1783. The family's stay in the new republic was relatively brief, they returned to Britain in 1787, and Hazlitt's father took over the congregation at the small village of Wem in Shropshire, disappointed—so his son claimed in 'My First Acquaintance with Poets'—not to be given the more significant ministry in nearby Shrewsbury. Chagrined his father may have been, but he remained very much engaged in circles committed to liberal religious and political causes. These connections carried the young William to Liverpool in the summer of 1790, where he was tutored by friends of his father and felt the excitement of the campaigns to repeal the Test and Corporation Acts and abolish the slave trade.[4]

---

[4] Hazlitt's Latin tutor in Liverpool, John Yates, had delivered a famous sermon in January 1788 that confronted his congregation with their own complicity in the trade. See the first-hand account in the diary of Hannah Lightbody, published as a special issue of *Enlightenment and Dissent*, 24 (2008), 57–8.

William's background is there for all to see in his first published writing, a letter to the *Shrewsbury Chronicle* in November 1791, where young Hazlitt expressed his outrage at the Church-and-King riots that had destroyed the home and laboratory of Joseph Priestley, whom he would later remember as the 'Voltaire of the Unitarians' and 'certainly the best controversialist of his day, and one of the best in the language'.[5] Probably with the connivance of the local authorities, Priestley had been targeted by a loyalist mob because of his sympathies for the French Revolution and vocal antipathy to the compact of Church and State. Hazlitt's relationship with rational dissent was further cemented when his father sent him to be educated for the ministry at the New College, Hackney, in November 1793, supported by a scholarship from the Presbyterian Fund. Regarded by its opponents as '*the slaughterhouse of Christianity*', the College provided Hazlitt with freedom enough to decide against a career as a minister, and he left in 1795, to the deep dismay of his father.[6]

Among the other freedoms Hazlitt enjoyed at Hackney were contacts with some of the leading lights of progressive middle-class opinion. His tutors encouraged an atmosphere of intellectual sociability at the college that extended out into the city at large. William was to have most of his life shaped by these networks, and their later iterations. Among his tutors at Hackney were Priestley on history; Thomas Belsham, on Hebrew, Latin, and logic; and the mathematician Abraham Rees. All these men had literary connections and wrote for the press. The reviews, newspapers, and pamphlets on topical issues that swirled around Hazlitt's student days were attracting increasing numbers to the idea of writing as a career. Uncertain though the fortunes of authorship were, Hazlitt was drawn to the circles around William Godwin and Thomas Holcroft, both of whom he probably met in 1795.[7] Godwin

---

[5] See Burley, *Hazlitt the Dissenter*, 47–8; 'The Late Dr. Priestley' (*The Atlas*, 14 June 1829), Howe, *Complete Works*, xx. 237.

[6] See *Gentleman's Magazine*, 63 (1973), 412, and the discussion in Burley, *Hazlitt the Dissenter*, 86–7. Burley provides an excellent account of Hazlitt's time at Hackney, including some of the philosophical differences he developed with Priestley's brand of materialism.

[7] See Duncan Wu, *William Hazlitt: The First Modern Man* (Oxford: Oxford University Press, 2008), 64, and *The Diary of William Godwin*, ed. Victoria Myers, David O'Shaughnessy, and Mark Philp (Oxford Digital Library 2010). <http://godwindiary.bodleian.ox.ac.uk>. The name Hazlitt first appears in the diary in 1794, both as singular and plural. At this early stage the singular probably identifies William's brother John. The diary editors take the plural to apply to the brothers.

was the darling of liberal intellectuals in this period, both for his hefty *Political Justice* (1793), with its philosophical justification for reform, and for his novel *Caleb Williams* (1794) and its account of 'things as they are', to use its full title. Holcroft—whose autobiography Hazlitt later completed—was Godwin's closest friend. Best known as a novelist and playwright, Holcroft was arraigned for his political opinions at the Treason Trials of 1794, but released after the acquittal of John Thelwall. Hazlitt also got to know Thelwall, the most popular orator of the radical movement, whose style seems to have influenced his own bravura performances at the lectern. Many of these writers were associated with the Unitarian publisher Joseph Johnson. A supportive friend to Godwin and Wollstonecraft, publisher of Hazlitt's own father, Johnson was imprisoned in 1798 for publishing an anti-war pamphlet. Perhaps, though, the most life-changing of the meetings provided to him by these liberal networks came after Hazlitt had left London and returned to Wem, where in 1798 he met the young poet and apprentice minister Samuel Taylor Coleridge.

To Hazlitt in 1798, Coleridge seemed destined to carry forward the torch of poetic genius allied to liberal principles. The poet had come to preach at Shrewsbury with the prospect of taking over the Unitarian congregation there. Hazlitt's encounter with him is described at length in 'My First Acquaintance with Poets'. Written in 1823, the essay communicates in equal measure the passionate hopes for the future Hazlitt felt at the time and the sense of betrayal he felt twenty-five years later. The hope and the betrayal are both centred on the figure of Coleridge. It is a slippery essay that to some extent obscures the successes of Hazlitt's own middle period between the bedazzled hopefulness of his early years and the melancholia of the later 1820s. Its tone readily mixes his sense of the sublimity of poetic genius ('with longings infinite and unsatisfied', p. 220); sly and funny personal barbs ('his nose, the rudder of the face, the index of the will, was small, feeble, nothing—like what he has done', p. 222); and nostalgia for what still seemed a seed time of liberty ('a spirit of hope and youth in all nature, that turned every thing into good', p. 221). A crossroads appears, given full dramatic—even comic—effect in the essay, when Coleridge receives news, just as Hazlitt comes down to breakfast, of the stipend from Thomas Wedgwood, son of the potter Josiah, that will free him from the need to seek the security of a ministry. Hazlitt narrates this as a moment of release into a world of poetry—which he enjoyed too via an invitation to visit Coleridge in Somerset—but also a prospective fall from the integrity of Dissent captured in the counter-portrait of his father who lives in 'a dream of infinity and eternity, of death, the resurrection, and a judgment to come!' (p. 223). Compared with the hard-won purposefulness of Hazlitt senior, Coleridge is a flimsy kind of visionary, a man who 'seemed to make up his mind to close with this proposal in the act of tying on one of his shoes' (p. 225). Nevertheless, Hazlitt gives a full sense of the transformative experience of visiting Coleridge, not to mention his introduction to Wordsworth, a few months later in Nether Stowey. Encountering the poetry that was to become the duo's *Lyrical Ballads* (1798), 'the sense of a new style and a new spirit in poetry came over me' (p. 230). Hazlitt makes this moment of discovery an epiphany against which the rest of his life is judged in all its disappointments in his own failings; in the backsliding poets; and in politics: 'As we taste the pleasures of life, their spirit evaporates, the sense palls; and nothing is left but the phantoms, the lifeless shadows of what *has been*!' (p. 230).

In 1798, though, Hazlitt was still thrilled by the myriad possibilities of the life of genius that Coleridge's example seemed to offer. First, Hazlitt tried for the career in painting followed much more successfully by his brother John, but reluctantly accepted he had no genius there. He then tried for a metaphysician, expanding ideas he had first explored at Hackney into *An Essay on the Principles of Human Action* (1805), predictably published by Joseph Johnson. Hazlitt always claimed it contained an important 'metaphysical discovery'.[8] Against the idea of human beings as innately selfish, put into mechanical motion by their own self-interest, Hazlitt argued that the imagination was a faculty that continually moves us beyond our own immediate interests, even in the way it imagines future versions of the self as the basis for present action. From this perspective, the human mind was continually engaging in acts of sympathy with beings beyond the present self. The mind is 'naturally disinterested', Hazlitt argued, not bound to slavishly follow the dictates of self-interest.[9] The war between his sense of humans as creatures of a mixed and imperfect being and his equally strong faith in the capacity for

---

[8] 'A Letter to William Gifford, Esq.' (1819), Howe, *Complete Works*, ix. 51.
[9] Ibid. i. 1.

a rational benevolence is a feature of many of his essays. His idea of our sympathies as embodied and deeply mediated always made him sceptical of reformers like Jeremy Bentham whose faith in rational judgement refused to acknowledge the drag of personal attachments, custom, and habit: 'The moralist can no more do without the intermediate use of rules and principles, without the 'vantage-ground of habit, without the levers of the understanding, than the mechanist can discard the use of wheels and pulleys, and perform every thing by simple motion' (p. 254). This way of looking at the world influenced John Keats in his faith that 'axioms in philosophy are not axioms until they are proved upon our pulses'.[10]

While struggling as a painter and metaphysician, Hazlitt was extending the metropolitan networks he had first encountered at Hackney. Coleridge and Godwin—despite their differences—tried to help him with commissions, including an abridgement of Abraham Tucker's weighty and labyrinthine philosophical tome *The Light of Nature Pursued*, eventually published in 1807, again by Johnson. The year before he first met his friend and loyal supporter Charles Lamb, at a dinner party with Coleridge and Godwin. Hazlitt became a regular at the Wednesday Club that Lamb hosted with his sister Mary. Intimate and convivial gatherings of writers and artists, with drink in plentiful supply, these sociable get-togethers could become boisterous, even to the point of violence. Lamb's brother John once punched Hazlitt in the face for mocking his opinion of the renaissance painter Hans Holbein as a colourist. 'I am a metaphysician, and do not mind the blow; nothing but an *idea* hurts *me*,' Hazlitt reportedly replied.[11] From this period, too, comes the first essay in this volume, the opening volley in a lifelong fusillade against the political economist Thomas Malthus, published not in the middle-class periodical press, but in the hard-hitting pages of William Cobbett's *Political Register* with its enormous circulation. Malthus had first laid out his *Essay on the Principle of Population* (1798) against the progressive ideas on human improvement found in Godwin and the French *philosophe* Condorcet. Hazlitt's sense of the mixed nature of human being and the importance of imaginative sympathy to any plan of improvement

[10] John Keats to J. H. Reynolds, 3 May 1818, in *Selected Letters*, ed. Robert Gittings and Jon Mee (Oxford World's Classics, 2002), 88.

[11] See Thomas Moore, *Memoirs, Journal, and Correspondence of Thomas Moore*, ed. Lord John Russell (Boston: Little, Brown & Co., 1853), iii. 146.

always made him only ever an uncomfortable ally of Godwin's rational perfectibility, but he could not abide Malthus's claim that the poor had to be left to bear the weight of the iron laws of population growth. It was a theme he returned to many times, not least in his essay on Malthus in *The Spirit of the Age*, but the fact that it first appeared in Cobbett's *Political Register* hints at the way Hazlitt bridged so many different parts of the print culture of his time. Cobbett's robust populist radicalism was worlds away from Godwin's tight rationalism or the allusive literary style of Leigh Hunt's *Examiner*, where Cobbett nearly always appears as an anti-Shakespearean philistine. Devotee of Shakespeare Hazlitt may have been, but he could celebrate Cobbett's writing in *Table Talk* (1821) as much for its style as its content: 'He is not only unquestionably the most powerful political writer of the present day, but one of the best writers in the language' (p. 152). When reform really revived after the defeat of Napoleon, Hazlitt's flexibility stood him in good stead: he wrote in many different kinds of opposition organ, from the cheap radical press to Francis Jeffrey's lofty Whig *Edinburgh Review*, always insisting that he had kept to the principles of 1789 abandoned by so many others.

Hazlitt only really settled in London in 1812, and entered into his first regular employment (already in his mid-30s) as a parliamentary reporter at the *Morning Chronicle*. Lamb's recommendation—staked on Hazlitt's 'singular facility in retaining all conversations at which he has ever been present'—convinced the editor James Perry to take him on.[12] He also worked for the *Chronicle* as a theatre critic. The second review printed here—on Edmund Kean—appeared in various guises, but we have taken the one fresh from the pages of the newspaper. Similarly, with Hazlitt's 'Why the Arts Are Not Progressive?', which we have taken as it appeared in the *Chronicle* as 'A Fragment', not so much a lofty reflection on timeless truths, but part of a more urgent contemporary debate about the diffusion of knowledge and the claims of genius. The essay is sharply self-aware of its situation in a literary culture being formed by Thomas Campbell's poetry, Frances Burney's latest novel, the painting of Benjamin West, Maria Edgeworth's fashionable tales, and the influential criticism of *The Edinburgh Review*. The Kean essay was a timely one. Drury Lane had only recently reopened in 1812 after the disastrous fire of 1809

---

[12] Quoted in Wu, *William Hazlitt*, 144.

and was struggling to re-establish itself. With the theatre on the verge of bankruptcy on Kean's opening night, Hazlitt was there, to the actor's great good fortune, as the author's advocacy of his style over the new few years was to make his career, just as Kean's ceaseless energy was to become a touchstone for the critic's ideas on artistic power. This energy was soon encapsulated by Hazlitt in a single critical term, 'gusto', which he understood as 'power or passion defining any object' (p. 24). Never precisely defined, Hazlitt used the term both to define the intensity of artistic expression and the active identification with it on the part of the reader or viewer.

Hazlitt was becoming a successful journalist at the *Chronicle*, and supplemented his income over the autumn and winter of 1814 working at the *Champion* for John Scott, later his editor at the *London Magazine*, but the real breakthrough came at the *Examiner*, where he came as close to being part of a group as he ever did in his career. At a time when many commentators were increasingly alarmed at the growth of 'the Reading Public', to use the ubiquitous contemporary term, the rapid expansion of print was nowhere more obvious than in the welter of periodicals, journals, and newspapers appearing in the marketplace. Hazlitt made his name as a writer in the rapidly expanding print ecology. The 1810s were dominated by the grand reviews: the liberal Whig *Edinburgh*, where Hazlitt was delighted to appear occasionally, and the Tory *Quarterly*, both of which reached peaks of circulation in the decade.[13] Around these twin peaks appeared a new generation of monthly and weekly magazines, each trying to find its niche. The *Examiner* began in 1808, but relaunched in 1813, after Hunt's imprisonment; now with Hazlitt on the team. At the other end of the political spectrum was *Blackwood's Edinburgh Magazine*—founded in October 1817—with Hunt in its sights from the very first issue. If its new style of personal attack was a *succès de scandale*, *Blackwood's* had at least partly learned its method from Hazlitt's robust reviews of Coleridge, Southey, and Wordsworth in *The Examiner*. To *Blackwood's*, Hunt and 'pimply Hazlitt', as it loved to call him, were 'Cockneys', harbouring literary ambitions beyond their status as mere jobbing hacks. Their tastes were unsupported either by education or breeding. Anyone associated with them was liable to be included in the general

---

[13] William St. Clair, *The Reading Nation in the Romantic Period* (Cambridge: Cambridge University Press, 2004), 573.

assault, including John Keats, most famously in a contemptuous review that appeared in August 1818, wrongly blamed for his death by some contemporaries. Ironically, what brought *The Examiner* and *Blackwood's* together, although they may not have liked the idea, was their literary ambition: precisely the idea that they might offer judgements of taste beyond the buying and selling of books.[14]

Theatre reviews Hazlitt wrote for *The Examiner*, including 'Mrs. Siddons', 'Mr. Kemble's King John', and 'Coriolanus', were later collected, sometimes rewritten, in *A View of the English Stage* (1818). Adopting the more substantial medium of the book form embodied his own ambition to be an author rather than a hack, however routinely the idea was ridiculed in *Blackwood's*. For all his aspirations to a more permanent form of authorship, though, Hazlitt developed some of his most familiar ideas as he went about his work as a theatre reviewer, reporting on particular performances on specific days. Out of this writing emerges his sense of Shakespeare's chameleon nature, increasingly contrasted with the perceived egotism of Wordsworth's poetry. Hazlitt's first theatre criticism for the *Examiner* appeared in spring 1815, but he seems to have met its editor Leigh Hunt earlier and visited him in Horsemonger Lane prison in 1813. Hunt was serving time for libelling the Prince of Wales, enough in itself to earn him Hazlitt's respect. There are various accounts, including some by Hazlitt himself, of him hanging back from the crowd that had come to see the celebrity martyr in his cell, with its rose trellis wallpaper. Hazlitt acted as the theatre reviewer at *The Examiner* until 1817, when Hunt more or less took over, but the two collaborated in other areas, including 'The Round Table' series of essays, first announced on New Year's Day 1815, that included 'On Imitation', 'On Gusto', and 'Actors and Acting'. The two-volume book that came out of the collaboration in 1817 was largely managed by Hazlitt, and contained only five contributions by Hunt. In their exchanges in the newspaper, though, both developed the idea of a conversational and informal style that reached out to *The Examiner*'s readers—'all persons not actually admitted to the said Table, must write to us in the form of a Letter'—but always with Hazlitt the more pugnacious and Hunt the more mollifying voice.[15] Among the avid readers of the exchanges

[14] The point is adroitly made in David Stewart's *Romantic Magazines and Metropolitan Literary Culture* (Basingstoke: Palgrave Macmillan, 2011), 12.

[15] *The Examiner*, 366 (1 January 1815), 14.

between Hazlitt and Hunt in *The Examiner* was Keats, who clearly developed many of his own key ideas from what he read. Hazlitt's view of Shakespeare as the supreme embodiment of the disinterested, self-annihilating imagination ('the least of an egotist that it was possible to be') fed into Keats's famous definition of the 'quality . . . which Shakespeare po[s]sessed so enormously—I mean *Negative Capability*, that is when man is capable of being in uncertainties, Mysteries, doubts, without any irritable reaching after fact & reason'. Keats later incorporated this idea into his distinction between the properly 'camelion Poet' and 'the wordsworthian or egotistical sublime'.[16]

Hazlitt's successes at *The Examiner* created new opportunities for him in the expanding circuit of lectures on the arts and sciences attracting large audiences to the venues springing up around London, most notably at the Royal and the Surrey Institutions. The Surrey had Hazlitt as a star turn. William Bewick reported his lectures 'to be the finest . . . that ever were delivered'.[17] He had lectured earlier and less successfully on philosophy in 1812 at the Russell Institution, but from January 1818 he delivered three series of literary lectures that became the hot ticket in town: on the English Poets; on the English Comic Writers; and on Elizabethan Drama. The first was in direct competition with Coleridge, already established on the circuit; 'the disciple', to use James Chandler's terms, becoming 'the rival'.[18] Richard Holmes suggests that the final lecture—'On the Living Poets'—was an attempt to 'bury Coleridge, by praising him'. 'His voice rolled on the ear like the pealing organ, and its sound alone was the music of thought,' recalled Hazlitt of their early years. Then came the typical *bouleversement*: 'And shall I, who heard him then, listen to him now? Not I! . . . That spell is broke; that time is gone for ever...'[19] The lecture certainly sustained the recent demolition of his former heroes in his review of Wordsworth's *The Excursion* in *The Examiner*. It also returned to the arguments of the fragment on 'Why the Arts Are Not Progressive?' to insist that his

[16] 'On Shakespeare and Milton', Howe, *Complete Works*, v. 47; Keats to George and Tom Keats, 21, 27 (?) December 1817 and to Richard Woodhouse, 27 October 1818, in *Selected Letters*, 41–2, 148, and 147.

[17] Quoted in Sarah Zimmerman, *The Romantic Literary Lecture in Britain* (Oxford: Oxford University Press, 2019), 133.

[18] James Chandler, *England in 1819: The Politics of Literary Culture and the Case of Romantic Historicism* (Chicago: University of Chicago Press, 1998), 13.

[19] Richard Holmes, *Coleridge: Darker Reflections* (London: Flamingo, 1999), 471; 'On the Living Poets', Howe, *Complete Works*, v. 167.

contemporaries were losing touch with what was valuable and natural in the poetic tradition. The theme appeared as a more general reflection on commercial culture in his *Edinburgh Review* essay 'On Fashion', but there characteristically turns at the end from praise of Frances Burney's *Evelina* to attack the disposition of monarchs to associate 'only with the worst and weakest' (p. 120).

For younger writers of a liberal disposition, like Keats and his friends, Hazlitt was becoming a guru. As a reader of *The Examiner*, Keats had already delighted in Hazlitt's reviews of Kean and the associated idea of gusto, but he also became a devoted listener to the lectures. They confirmed his sense that Hazlitt's 'depth of Taste' was one of the wonders of the age.[20] In the lecture theatre, Hazlitt's style was characteristically provoking, setting himself up aslant to his listeners, many of whom were respectable Dissenters, sympathetic to reform, but unused to hearing their faith in the diffusion of knowledge mocked. One member of Hazlitt's audience, Mary Russell Mitford, wrote that 'Mr Hazlitt is really the most delightful lecturer I ever heard—his last, on modern poetry was amusing past all description to everybody but the parties concerned'.[21] But sometime friends, like the Unitarian Henry Crabb Robinson, were discomposed: in February 1818 he found Hazlitt 'so very contemptuous towards Wordsworth . . . that I lost my temper and hissed'.[22] Robinson never liked the way—whether in his essays and reviews or in the lecture halls—that Hazlitt exploited his personal knowledge of their mutual friends.

The personal, though, was nearly always political for Hazlitt, especially in these years when the campaign for radical reform was intensifying after the end of the long war against Hazlitt's hero Napoleon. Unusually, Hazlitt had continued to look to Napoleon as the embodiment of revolutionary principles through the long years from 1793, during which Britain was at war with France, even after he became Emperor. The brief cessation of hostilities at the Peace of Amiens allowed Hazlitt a visit to Paris over the winter of 1802–3. He took copies of the Old Masters in the Louvre and caught a glimpse of Napoleon that he never forgot. After the Emperor's final defeat in 1815, the lawyer and author Thomas Noon Talfourd described Hazlitt

---

[20] Keats to George and Tom Keats, 13, 19 January 1818, in *Selected Letters*, 47.

[21] Quoted in Stanley Jones, *Hazlitt: A Life from Winterslow to Frith Street* (Oxford: Oxford University Press, 1989), 284.

[22] Quoted in Zimmerman, *The Romantic Literary Lecture in Britain*, 146.

'staggering under the blow of Waterloo . . . as if he had sustained a personal wrong'; the painter Benjamin Robert Haydon wrote that 'it is not to be believed how the destruction of Napoleon affected him; he seemed prostrated in mind and body; he walked about, unwashed, unshaved, hardly sober by day, and always intoxicated by night, literally, without exaggeration, for weeks'.[23] From this moment of crisis, however, Hazlitt set about making himself into an important political journalist. It is to this period that we owe his brilliant 'What is the People?' with its direct questioning of the reader in its memorable opening followed by the sly modulation from 'you' to 'we', binding his readers into his own quest to give a shape and voice to the political nation beyond the Church and State, but also creating space for them to give their assent or disagree with him. Critics like Philip Harling and Kevin Gilmartin have recently demonstrated how important Hazlitt was to the radical reform movement, and vice versa.[24] Their work has modified the influential contrast E. P. Thompson made between Hazlitt's literary radicalism and Cobbett's directness.[25] The ringing passage from 'What is the People?'—quoted by Thompson—is replete with Shakespearean allusion and peals the bells of parallelism: 'The wine they drink is made of grapes: the blood they shed is that of their subjects: the laws they make are not against themselves: the taxes they vote, they afterwards devour' (p. 81). Nevertheless, for all the literariness of Hazlitt's style here, the passage has all the visceral hatred of traditional authority associated with popular radicalism. Whatever his reservations about Cobbett himself, Hazlitt shared his antagonism to 'Old Corruption', admired his inveterate oppositionism ('wherever power is, there is he against it') and recognized him as 'a kind of *fourth estate* in the politics of the country' (pp. 156 and 152)—the first recorded use of this phrase to describe the new status of the press as a power in the land. Hazlitt's brilliant essay 'On Court Influence', first published in John Hunt's *Yellow Dwarf* in January 1817, takes a familiar trope into a very unfamiliar territory:

[23] Thomas Noon Talfourd, *Final Memorials of Charles Lamb*, 2 vols (London, 1848), ii. 170; *Life of Benjamin Robert Haydon*, ed. Tom Taylor, 3 vols (London, 1853), ii. 279.

[24] Philip Harling, 'William Hazlitt and Radical Journalism', *Romanticism* 3 (1997), 53–65, and Kevin Gilmartin, *William Hazlitt: Political Essayist* (Oxford: Oxford University Press, 2015).

[25] E. P. Thompson, *The Making of the English Working Class* (Harmondsworth: Penguin, 1980), 820–1.

But the air of a Court is the concentrated essence of the opinion of the world. The atmosphere there is mephitic. It is subtle poison, the least exhalation of which taints the vitals of its victims. It is made up of servile adulation, of sneering compliments, of broken promises, of smiling professions, of stifled opinions, of hollow thanks, of folly and lies. (p. 107)

Predictably, perhaps, the essay does turn to attack his old adversaries Coleridge and Southey as amplifiers of this corrosive influence, but the linguistic fizz of Hazlitt's writing provides new energy to the old idea that power corrupts.

Little Hazlitt wrote on any topic was not shaped by his political sympathies. Take his 'Character of Burke', a topic he discussed many times, but which is represented here from an excursus within his review of Coleridge's *Biographia Literaria* (1817) in the *Edinburgh Review*. For Hazlitt, admiring Burke's writing and oratory from across the political divide was a measure of critical disinterestedness. In 'My First Acquaintance with Poets' he repeated his view that 'speaking of him with contempt might be made the test of a vulgar democratical mind. This was the first observation I ever made to Coleridge, and he said it was a very just and striking one' (p. 224). Hazlitt valued Burke as a stylist, but perhaps more as a figure who brought the imagination into politics, able to touch his readers rather than simply reason with them. His regret was the great orator's role in turning British opinion against the French Revolution: 'it was Mr. Burke who, at this giddy, maddening period, stood at the prow of the vessel of the state, and with his glittering, pointed spear *harpooned* the Leviathan of the French Revolution, which darted into its wild career, tinging its onward track with purple gore.'[26] Burke's *Reflections on the Revolution in France* (1790) pre-dated Hazlitt's own writing career, but the revolution controversy that raged around it while he was a student was as important as that visit to Nether Stowey to his literary identity, not least his sense of the role writers could have in forming public opinion. In the late 1810s, his insistence on seeing corruption as a pervasive part of the culture as a whole won him the undying animosity of conservative organs like the *Quarterly* and *Blackwood's*. Hazlitt was the dangerous maverick in Hunt's 'Cockney' gang, and he was attacked on these grounds for the rest of his life.

[26] *Life of Napoleon* (1828), Howe, *Complete Works*, xiii. 51–2.

Pierce Egan represented Hazlitt as one of the sights of the town in the vivid panorama of his *Life in London* (1821). He appears there as a man who has the measure of high and low cultures, as comfortable with fashionable slang as the language of the fine arts, embodying a new kind of urban taste, with 'all the qualities of a barometer . . . in the evening lolling at his ease upon one of *Ben Medley's* elegant couches, enjoying the reviving comforts of a good *tinney*, smacking his *chaffer* over a glass of old hock, and topping his *glim* to a *classic* nicety, in order to throw a *new light* upon the elegant leaves of ROSCOE'S Life of Lorenzo de' Medici, as a *composition* for a NEW LECTURE at the Surrey Institution'.[27] Opening the 1820s as a star in the literary firmament, Hazlitt naturally joined the writers on John Scott's *London Magazine*. First published in January 1820, the London soon joined in the Cockney war with *Blackwood's*. Hazlitt also took with him from *The Examiner* the conversational motif of 'the Round Table', developed into the 'Table Talk' essays in the *London Magazine*. After Scott's death in February 1821, from wounds sustained in a duel over the feud with *Blackwood's*, Hazlitt began to dissociate himself from *The London*, and started to contribute to other magazines, most notably the *New Monthly Magazine*, where he placed the 'Bentham' essay as part of a series on 'Spirits of the Age'. In Hazlitt's absence, Lamb became the *London Magazine*'s mainstay, developing his persona as 'Elia' there, but mourned the loss of his friend from the team: 'I cannot but think the *London* drags heavily . . . And O how it misses Hazlitt.' Hazlitt, who had applied for the editorship after Scott's death, thought it lacked 'unity of purpose', but in essays like 'Minor Theatres' and 'The Indian Jugglers' he had conveyed his sense of the magazine's engagement with the energies— and disappointments—of London life celebrated by Egan.[28] The great sweep of 'The Indian Jugglers' across his contemporary culture—high and low—perhaps inevitably settles down to questions of greatness and genius: 'A really great man', he tells us, 'has always an idea of something greater than himself' (pp. 170–1). A reader might prepare here for an attack on Wordsworth's egotism, but instead the essay ends with a eulogy to the fives player Jack Cavanagh, filched

[27] Pierce Egan, *Life in London, or the Day and Night Scenes of Jerry Hawthorn, Esq., and his Elegant Friend Corinthian Tom* (London, 1821), 31–2.

[28] Quoted in Tim Chilcott, *A Publisher and his Circle: The Life and Work of John Taylor, Keats's Publisher* (London: Routledge, 1972), 150 and 156.

from an earlier essay in *The Examiner*, which takes the ministers Canning and Castlereagh in its way, but not without swipes at Wordsworth's 'lumbering' epic poetry and Coleridge's 'wavering' lyric prose.

The early 1820s were a period of personal turmoil for Hazlitt, not least because of the disturbing obsession with Sarah Walker, his landlady's daughter, that ended with him divorcing his wife and losing the goodwill of many of his friends. His political enemies were delighted with the proof, as they saw it, of the moral consequences of his liberal ideas, especially when the episode was written up by Hazlitt for all to see in the thinly disguised *Liber Amoris* (1823). Nevertheless, his greatest triumph as an essayist was yet to come with the gathered collection of essays in *The Spirit of the Age* (1825); the phrase perhaps still most readily associated with his name. This gallery of portraits defines not so much the essence of his age as his sense of its contradictory energies, very much developing his staple themes and issues, as is easily seen by comparing its essays on Godwin, Byron, and Wordsworth with the earlier work gathered here. In one sense, the pressures of writing for the periodical press inevitably made him a serial recycler of his own work; from another perspective he was continuing to advocate and develop signature ideas like the importance of habit and local attachments to human life, and the sense of betrayal that fixed to the figures of Coleridge, Wordsworth, and Southey.

Both these themes inform the celebration of the metropolis in 'On Londoners and Country People' with its faith that the city was not just a place of alienation, but somewhere that an idea of community might be developed within the urban experiences of literary talk, theatre going, and coffee-house politics. By the end, the 'go-cart of local prejudices and positive illusions' (p. 240) that makes up the Londoner's life transforms into a sense of 'a *public*; and each man is part of it'. The essay is a great demonstration of the way Hazlitt could start with an aphoristic assertion and use the medium to work through to a very different position. Out of his sense of the limited effects of custom and habit, he retrieves his abiding vision of the democratic possibilities inherent to city life: 'There is here a visible body-politic, a type and image of that huge Leviathan the State. We comprehend that vast denomination, the *People*, of which we see a tenth part daily moving before us' (p. 248). He is singularly dismissive of the implicitly Wordsworthian version of the relationship between local attachments and the sense of community: 'In the country, men are no better than a herd of cattle or scattered deer. They have no idea but of individuals, none of rights or principles—and a king, as the greatest individual, is the highest idea they can form' (p. 248).

The idea of the London playhouse as 'a school of humanity, where all eyes are fixed on the same gay or solemn scene...where a thousand hearts beat in unison' (p. 248), an idea given a more directly political expression in 'What is the People?', becomes in 'Our National Theatres' a late essay from *The Atlas*, a complaint against social 'exclusion'—'the motto of the English nation' (p. 309). 'The Spirit of Controversy', on the other hand, insists on the importance of dissent in the broadest sense as a vivifying element of public culture. In his final decade or so, Hazlitt with De Quincey and Lamb developed the periodical essay, long associated with conversational informality, towards a more intimate and self-reflexive medium. The tides of Hazlitt's own mind are often at the centre of the writing, especially in the final decade, but if there is a strong and powerfully lyrical sense of nostalgia in essays like 'The Free Admission' and 'The Letter-Bell', then the sense of faded opportunities, of a life worn thin amid 'the ebb and flow and restless agitation of the human mind' (p. 317), plays its own part in developing a sense of alternatives within the present state of things. 'The postman's double-knock at the door the next morning' pierces 'to the heart', in 'The Letter-Bell'; a sign not only of time passing, but of 'the useful and mechanical' replacing 'the picturesque and dramatic', as the mail coach had replaced the post-boy, and the telegraph had replaced the beacons that announced the fall of Troy (p. 329). But the new-fangled optical telegraph has also lately communicated the news of the Revolution of 1830 to all France. Hazlitt's good old cause has revived, and, just as the mood seems to settle into melancholy, introduces a characteristic counter-current that refuses any lapse into either solipsism or despair.

Out of the reviews and opinion-pieces he wrote in *The Examiner* and elsewhere, Hazlitt developed his own distinctive version of the essay. Hunt had launched the 'Round Table' series as a self-conscious continuation of the easy sociability long associated with Joseph Addison and Richard Steele in *The Spectator*. Their conversational style had been intrinsic to the development of the literary essay for over a century. For the *Quarterly Review*, the very idea of Hazlitt and Hunt laying claim to this inheritance was laughable. Their style reduced Addison's conversational ease to 'vulgar descriptions, silly paradoxes, flat truisms, misty sophistry, broken English, ill humour and rancorous abuse'. Clearly, what constituted familiar style was up for grabs. Hazlitt praised Hunt's 'gay and conversational style' in *The Spirit of the Age*, but it was very different from his own, as their exchanges in the pages of *The Examiner* reveal. Hazlitt always tended to the side of the conversational ideal that valued the frank collision of minds.[29] His lectures on the English comic tradition included a survey of the periodical essayists that made his own tastes clear. He preferred Steele to Addison, because his essays were less like lectures and more conversational. Johnson he thought too pompous as an essayist, although his conversation itself—as reported by James Boswell's *Life of Johnson*—he praised, revealingly because there 'his natural powers and undisguised opinions were called out . . . he unsheathed the sword of controversy'.[30] The essay 'On Familiar Style', included here, explores his own sense of the ambition 'to write as any one would speak in common conversation' (p. 199). Lamb he praises, as always, but he rounds on those contemporaries who sacrificed passion to the appearance of ease: 'A thought, a distinction is the rock on which all this brittle cargo of verbiage splits at once' (p. 203). As Hazlitt warms to his theme in the essay, so the rhythm of his own version of the conversational style becomes clear. He takes aim at a target, and takes pleasure in the sharp aphorism to communicate his personal thoughts, but the sharp phrase never precludes the change of course, or a sense that the essay is a form where thoughts can be developed in contrary ways and in association with the reader, who is hailed as an active participant in the process. Hazlitt the essayist is a daring performer, walking the tightrope—like the Indian Jugglers—for the pleasure of his audience.

Hazlitt has often been brought forward as the practitioner of a particularly 'romantic' form of essay writing, defined by introspection at one pole and a rousing sense of the power of the imagination at the other. From this perspective he has often been celebrated in a triad of Romantic critical essayists with Lamb and De Quincey, his sometime

---

[29] See Jon Mee, *Conversable Worlds: Literature, Contention, and Community, 1762–1830* (Oxford: Oxford University Press, 2011), chapter 6, for a discussion of Hazlitt and Hunt in this tradition, and *Quarterly Review* 17 (April 1817), 155.

[30] 'On the Periodical Essayists', Howe, *Complete Works*, vi. 103.

collaborators at the *London*.[31] This tradition traces in Hazlitt a deeply personal development of the 'literary' essay, focused on imaginative insight, and the personal nature of his judgements, grounded in a lifetime of associations burnished by books, painting, and the company of the geniuses of his age, but his manner was always more conflictual than either De Quincey or Lamb's. Nor was he only someone who argued stoutly for the freedom of judgement in matters of taste, rather his idea of literary criticism remained affiliated to an idea of 'the struggle against the absolutist state' that Terry Eagleton and others have seen as its foundational moment.[32] Hazlitt himself regularly invoked the idea of the freedom of mind brought with the Reformation and the printing press, not to mention the Glorious Revolution of 1688. These have been indices of English 'liberty' to many writers, but to Hazlitt they are most useful to bring before his readers the present travesty of what they were supposed to have promised. Recently scholars have made us more aware of Hazlitt's power as a political journalist, creating a space for independent criticism of authority, but ready to use the language made available on the anvil of Cobbett and his colleagues. Increasingly, too, a new sense of metropolitan Hazlitt has been celebrated: the frequenter of lodging houses, of cider cellars, of the theatres, of the whole panoply of London life in the early nineteenth century.[33] P. G. Patmore remembered Hazlitt holding court in the Southampton coffee house, with the caricaturist George Cruikshank and the radical satirist William Home, 'till a very *un*certain hour in the morning'.[34] Many of the essays included here offer a marvellous commentary on this world. 'He has', as Virginia Woolf pointed out, 'an extraordinary power of making us contemporary with himself.'[35] All these different aspects of Hazlitt's mind often appear in the same essay, whatever its ostensible topic, producing a literary-political mode that would be taken up by Woolf and George Orwell in the twentieth century. His flexible use of

[31] See *Romantic Critical Essays*, ed. David Bromwich (Cambridge: Cambridge University Press, 1987) for an excellent introduction to this tradition.
[32] Terry Eagleton, *The Function of Criticism* (Verso: London, 1984), 9.
[33] See, especially, Gregory Dart, *Metropolitan Art and Literature, 1810–1840: Cockney Adventures* (Cambridge: Cambridge University Press, 2012) and the anthology *William Hazlitt: Metropolitan Writings*, ed. Dart (Manchester: Carcanet Press, 2005).
[34] P. G. Patmore, *My Friends and Acquaintance*, 3 vols (London, 1854), ii. 316.
[35] Virginia Woolf, 'William Hazlitt', in *The Common Reader. Second Series* (London: Hogarth Press, 1932), 180.

the essay to create the appearance of thinking the issues through in
the act of writing lives on perhaps in the work of essayists such as
Andrew O'Hagan and Zadie Smith today, as well as such avowed
Hazlitt fans as the poet and critic Tom Paulin and late Labour Party
leader Michael Foot. Hazlitt's essays also speak to a broader resur-
gence of long-form journalism in the digital and social media age, as
a form that is at once conversational and expansive, reflective and
combative, a space to think with and in.

Hazlitt repeatedly gathered his essays into books, including *The*
Round Table (1817), *A View of the English Stage* (1818), *Political Essays*
(1819), *Table Talk* (1821–2), *The Spirit of the Age* (1825), and *The*
Plain Speaker (1826)—a decade-long sequence that mirrors the
'Great Decade' of Wordsworth twenty years earlier (so often Hazlitt's
standard and target). The present edition prints the essays not as
Hazlitt revised them for book publication, but as they reached their
widest contemporary audience, embedded in the newspapers and
magazines of the day. In his revisions, Hazlitt polished, took out some
of the more topical allusions, and in a few cases even pulled his
punches. These innumerable small changes produced essays that can
sometimes lack the tang of earlier versions, as well as their allusive
range. A saltier Hazlitt emerges from knowing that the angry shopkeeper on the Strand is 'the ham-shop keeper' in the *Yellow Dwarf*'s
version of 'What is the People?' (p. 91); such details were intrinsic to
the familiar style that made him a 'slang-whanger' in the disapproving eyes of the *Quarterly Review* (see p. 374). More substantially, perhaps, an important distinction was dropped in *The Round Table* from
the first version of 'Why the Arts Are Not Progressive?':

We judge of science by the number of effects produced—of art by the
energy which produces them. The one is knowledge—the other power.
(p. 14)[36]

Likewise, Hazlitt's account of the Parthenon Marbles appears here as
part of the controversy over Lord Elgin's removal of the sculptures,
in response to a House of Commons select committee report, not as
a later reflection on Romantic aesthetics. To give one final example,
'On Court Influence' is printed here as it appeared in the pages of the

---

[36] See David Bromwich, *Hazlitt: The Mind of a Critic* (Oxford: Oxford University
Press, 1983), 288, who claims this was the first statement of the distinction between the
literature of knowledge and the literature of power, anticipating Thomas De Quincey.

Yellow Dwarf, including a rousing peroration that Hazlitt cut before the essay was reprinted in *Political Essays*:

Happy are they, who live in the dream of their own existence, and see all things by the light of their own minds; who walk by faith and hope, not by knowledge; to whom the guiding-star of their youth still shines from afar, and into whom the spirit of the world has not entered! They have not been 'hurt by the archers,' nor has the iron entered their souls . . . The world has no hold on them. They are in it, not of it; and a dream and a glory is ever about them. (p. 114)

This was a paragraph that Hazlitt recycled more than once, but it perhaps best belongs here, as a tribute to the character of the dissident—once again, modelled on his father—and a polemical contrast to the craven conformity of the 'whirligig Court poet'. What seems characteristic of Hazlitt here is not the personal note of nostalgia, or even the dramatic sense of expressive depth, but the way he provides a yardstick against which the present might be measured. If his father cast a shadow, it was not to a dampening effect, but to rouse him to continual endeavour. Virginia Woolf's judgement stands as a neat counterpoint to his friend Lamb's estimation of him with which this introduction began:

There is a stir and trouble, a vivacity and conflict in his essays, as if the very contrariety of his gifts kept him always on the stretch. He is always hating, loving, thinking, and suffering. He could never come to terms with authority or doff his own idiosyncrasy in deference to opinion.[37]

If Woolf ranked Lamb and Montaigne above him as essayists for their completeness, perhaps she also valued something of herself in his restless sense of engagement, the refusal to accept that things had to be as they were, and his endless thirst for the animating spirit of controversy.

---

[37] Woolf, *Common Reader*, 181.

NOTE ON THE TEXT

THE texts of the essays and reviews included in this edition are taken from the first published version, usually from a newspaper or periodical, rather than the later iterations Hazlitt collected into volumes: *Characters of Shakespeare's Plays* (1817), *The Round Table* (1817), *A View of the English Stage* (1818), *Lectures on the English Poets* (1818), *Lectures on the English Comic Writers* (1819), *Political Essays* (1819), *Lectures on the Dramatic Literature of the Age of Elizabeth* (1820), *Table Talk* (1821–2), *The Spirit of the Age* (1825), and *The Plain Speaker* (1826). The reasons for this choice are explained in the Introduction. Some of the essays made their first appearance in the books listed above, and we have taken our versions from these first editions. Where there was no title as such in the original publication, we have introduced each essay with the title by which it became best known, and omitted any place or date line that introduced them originally and any byline or signature that ended them. The 'Character of Mr. Burke' is taken from Hazlitt's review of Coleridge's *Biographia Literaria*, which later became an essay in its own right in *Political Essays*. In each instance, all publication details are included at the head of the relevant notes at the end of this volume. Where essays were published in multiple parts, over successive weeks or months of a periodical, breaks between parts have been signalled by three asterisks. Original spellings have been retained in most cases to keep the flavour of the originals, but printer's errors silently corrected and most punctuation modernized, such as the change from double to single quotation marks and the removal of quotation marks from indented quotations.

SELECT BIBLIOGRAPHY

Collected Editions

THE standard edition of Hazlitt remains *The Complete Works of William Hazlitt*, ed. P. P. Howe, 21 vols (London: J. M. Dent, 1930–4). See also *The Selected Writings of William Hazlitt*, ed. Duncan Wu, 9 vols (London: Pickering & Chatto, 1998). New attributions to Hazlitt have been made in *The New Writings of William Hazlitt*, ed. Duncan Wu, 2 vols (Oxford: Oxford University Press, 2007).

See also *The Letters of William Hazlitt*, ed. Herschel Sikes, assisted by W. H. Bonner and Gerald Lahey (London and Basingstoke: Macmillan, 1979).

Two very useful thematic selections are *Hazlitt on Theatre*, ed. William Archer and Robert Lowe (New York: Hill and Wang, 1957), and *William Hazlitt: Metropolitan Writings*, ed. Gregory Dart (Manchester: Carcanet Press, 2005).

Biographies and Useful Sources

Baker, Herschel, *William Hazlitt* (Cambridge, MA: Harvard University Press, 1962).

Chilcott, Tim, *A Publisher and his Circle: The Life and Work of John Taylor, Keats's Publisher* (London: Routledge, 1972).

Grayling, A. C., *The Quarrel of the Age: The Life and Times of William Hazlitt* (London: Weidenfeld & Nicolson, 2000).

The Diary of William Godwin, ed. Victoria Myers, David O'Shaughnessy, and Mark Philp (Oxford: Oxford Digital Library, 2010). <http://godwindiary.bodleian.ox.ac.uk>

Hazlitt, W. Carew, *Memoirs of William Hazlitt, with Portions of his Correspondence*, 2 vols (London: Richard Bentley, 1867).

Jones, Stanley, *Hazlitt: A Life. From Winterslow to Frith Street* (Oxford: Oxford University Press, 1989).

Wu, Duncan, *William Hazlitt: The First Modern Man* (Oxford: Oxford University Press, 2008).

Criticism

(Books on Hazlitt, or with substantial chapters on him.)

Albrecht, W. P., *Hazlitt and the Creative Imagination* (Lawrence: University of Kansas Press, 1965).

Bainbridge, Simon, *Napoleon and English Romanticism* (Cambridge: Cambridge University Press, 1995).

Barrell, John, *The Political Theory of Painting from Reynolds to Hazlitt* (New Haven and London: Yale University Press, 1986).

Bate, Jonathan, *Shakespearean Constitutions: Politics, Theatre, Criticism, 1730–1830* (Oxford: Clarendon Press, 1989).

Bromwich, David, *Hazlitt: The Mind of a Critic* (Oxford: Oxford University Press, 1983).

Burley, Stephen, *Hazlitt the Dissenter: Religion, Philosophy, and Politics, 1766–1816* (Basingstoke: Palgrave, 2014).

Carlson, Julie, 'Hazlitt and the Sociability of Theatre', in Gillian Russell and Clara Tuite (eds), *Romantic Sociability: Social Networks and Literary Culture in Britain, 1770–1840* (Cambridge: Cambridge University Press, 2002), 145–65.

Chandler, James, *England in 1819: The Politics of Literary Culture and the Case of Romantic Historicism* (Chicago: University of Chicago Press, 1998).

Connell, Philip, *Romanticism, Economics and the Question of 'Culture'* (Oxford: Oxford University Press, 2001).

Cox, Jeffrey, *Poetry and Politics in the Cockney School: Keats, Shelley, Hunt and their Circle* (Cambridge: Cambridge University Press, 1998).

Dart, Gregory, *Metropolitan Art and Literature, 1810–1840: Cockney Adventures* (Cambridge: Cambridge University Press, 2012).

Eagleton, Terry, 'William Hazlitt: An Empiricist Radical', *New Blackfriars* 54 (1973), 108–17.

Epstein, James, *Radical Expression: Political Language, Ritual, and Symbol in England, 1790–1830* (New York: Oxford University Press, 1994).

Fairclough, Mary, *The Romantic Crowd: Sympathy, Controversy and Print Culture* (Cambridge: Cambridge University Press, 2013).

Foot, Michael, 'The Shakespeare Prose Writer: William Hazlitt', in *Debts of Honour* (London: Davis Poynter, 1980).

Franta, Andrew, *Romanticism and the Rise of the Mass Public* (Cambridge: Cambridge University Press, 2007).

Fulford, Tim, *Romanticism and Masculinity: Gender, Politics and Poetics in the Writings of Burke, Coleridge, Cobbett, Wordsworth, De Quincey and Hazlitt* (Basingstoke: Macmillan, 1999).

Gilmartin, Kevin, *Print Politics: The Press and Radical Opposition in Early Nineteenth-Century England* (Cambridge: Cambridge University Press, 1996).

Gilmartin, Kevin, *William Hazlitt: Political Essayist* (Oxford: Oxford University Press, 2015).

Harling, Philip, 'William Hazlitt and Radical Journalism', *Romanticism* 3 (1997), 53–65.

Henderson, Andrea K., *Romanticism and the Painful Pleasures of Modern Life* (Cambridge: Cambridge University Press, 2008).

Hessell, Nikki, *Literary Authors, Parliamentary Reporters: Johnson, Coleridge, Hazlitt, Dickens* (Cambridge: Cambridge University Press, 2012).

Higgins, David, *Romantic Genius and the Literary Magazine: Biography, Celebrity and Politics* (New York: Routledge, 2005).

Hofkosh, Sonia, *Sexual Politics and the Romantic Author* (Cambridge: Cambridge University Press, 1998).

Holmes, Richard, *Coleridge: Early Visions* (New York: Viking, 1989).

Holmes, Richard, *Coleridge: Darker Reflections* (London: Flamingo, 1999).

Jackson, Noel, *Science and Sensation in Romantic Poetry* (Cambridge: Cambridge University Press, 2008).

Jarrells, Anthony, *Britain's Bloodless Revolutions: 1688 and the Romantic Reform of Literature* (New York: Palgrave Macmillan, 2005).

Keen, Paul, *The Crisis of Literature in the 1790s: Print Culture and the Public Sphere* (Cambridge: Cambridge University Press, 2006).

Kinnaird, J. W., *William Hazlitt: Critic of Power* (New York: Columbia University Press, 1978).

Klancher, Jon, *The Making of English Reading Audiences* (Madison: University of Wisconsin Press, 1987).

Klancher, Jon, *Transfiguring the Arts and Sciences: Knowledge and Cultural Institutions in the Romantic Age* (Cambridge: Cambridge University Press, 2013).

McGann, Jerome J., *The Romantic Ideology: A Critical Investigation* (Chicago: University of Chicago Press, 1983).

Manning, Peter J., 'Manufacturing the Romantic Image: Hazlitt and Coleridge Lecturing', in James Chandler and Kevin Gilmartin (eds), *Romantic Metropolis: The Urban Scene of British Culture, 1780–1840* (Cambridge: Cambridge University Press, 2005), 227–45.

Mee, Jon, *Conversable Worlds: Literature, Contention, and Community, 1762–1830* (Oxford: Oxford University Press, 2011).

Milnes, Tim, *Knowledge and Indifference in English Romantic Prose* (Cambridge: Cambridge University Press, 2003).

Milnes, Tim, *The Testimony of Sense: Empiricism and the Essay from Hume to Hazlitt* (Oxford: Oxford University Press, 2019).

Natarajan, Uttara, *Hazlitt and the Reach of Sense: Criticism, Morals, and the Metaphysics of Power* (Oxford: Oxford University Press, 1998).

Natarajan, Uttara, Tom Paulin, and Duncan Wu (eds), *Metaphysical Hazlitt: Bicentenary Essays* (London: Routledge, 2005).

Newlyn, Lucy, *Reading, Writing, and Romanticism: The Anxiety of Reception* (Oxford: Oxford University Press, 2000).

Park, Roy, *Hazlitt and the Spirit of the Age* (Oxford: Oxford University Press, 1971).

Parker, Mark, *Literary Magazines and British Romanticism* (Cambridge: Cambridge University Press, 2000).

Paulin, Tom, *The Day-Star of Liberty William Hazlitt's Radical Style* (London: Faber, 1998).

Roe, Nicholas, *John Keats and the Culture of Dissent* (Oxford: Clarendon Press, 1997).

Russell, Gillian, 'Keats, Popular Culture, and the Sociability of Theatre', in Philip Connel and Nigel Leask (eds), *Romanticism and Popular Culture in Britain and Ireland* (Cambridge: Cambridge University Press, 2009), 194–213.

Stewart, David, *Romantic Magazines and Metropolitan Literary Culture* (Basingstoke: Palgrave Macmillan: 2011).

Thompson, E. P., *The Making of the English Working Class* (1963; revised edition Harmondsworth: Penguin, 1980).

Tomalin, Marcus, *Romanticism and Linguistic Theory: William Hazlitt, Language and Literature* (Basingstoke: Palgrave Macmillan, 2009).

Whale, John, *Imagination under Pressure, 1789–1832: Aesthetics, Politics and Utility* (Cambridge: Cambridge University Press, 2000).

White, Daniel E., *Early Romanticism and Religious Dissent* (Cambridge: Cambridge University Press, 2006).

Wolfson, Susan, *Romantic Shades and Shadows* (Baltimore: Johns Hopkins University Press, 2018).

Zimmerman, Sarah, *The Romantic Literary Lecture in Britain* (Oxford: Oxford University Press, 2019).

See also *The Hazlitt Review* (2008–), the annual peer-reviewed journal of the Hazlitt Society.

A CHRONOLOGY OF WILLIAM HAZLITT

1778 Born in Maidstone, the fourth child of William and Grace Hazlitt. Only three of the seven children survive.

1780 Hazlitt's father supports the Americans in the War of Independence. The family is forced to move to Bandon, near Cork in Ireland.

1783 The family relocates to America. Hazlitt's father establishes the first Unitarian church in Boston.

1787 The family returns to England. Hazlitt's father takes up a ministry in Wem, Shropshire. Hazlitt's brother John stays in London to study painting under Sir Joshua Reynolds.

1790 Hazlitt spends part of the summer in Liverpool tutored in Classics by the Unitarian minister John Yates and in French by John de Lemprière.

1793 Hazlitt attends New College Hackney in London. Reads Godwin's *Political Justice*, Hume, Berkeley, Hartley, and the French philosophers Condorcet, D'Holbach, and Helvetius.

1794 Hazlitt continues at the New College Hackney. He sees Sarah Siddons perform for the first time in October.

1795 Hazlitt withdraws from Hackney and abandons the idea of becoming a minister, to his father's disappointment, and returns to Wem. He moves back to London, where he meets Godwin.

1796 Hazlitt meets Wollstonecraft. Reads Burke and Rousseau as well as English poets. By the end of the year painting in Liverpool, where he meets William Roscoe and his circle.

1798 Meets Coleridge in January at Wem. In May, he takes up the invitation to visit Coleridge in Somerset, where he meets Wordsworth. Reads *Lyrical Ballads* in manuscript. Decides to become a painter, and stays with his brother John at Bury St Edmunds. Hazlitt attends an exhibition of Italian Renaissance painting at the Orleans gallery in London in December.

1799 Hazlitt is based in London, but travels around England in search of portrait commissions.

1802 Hazlitt's portrait of his father is exhibited at the Royal Academy. Takes advantage of the Peace of Amiens to visit Paris and begins to study paintings at the Louvre. Sees Napoleon and meets Charles James Fox.

1803 Hazlitt returns to England, where he revisits Coleridge. He meets Charles Lamb at Godwin's in March. Joins Coleridge and Wordsworth in the Lake District and paints their portraits.

1805 Living in London and Wem. Publication of his first book, *An Essay on the Principles of Human Action*, with Joseph Johnson, thanks to Godwin's help.

1806 Publication of *Free Thoughts on Human Affairs*.

1807 Publication of *An Abridgement of the Light of Nature Pursued by Abraham Tucker*, *A Reply to the Essay on Population*, and the *Eloquence of the British Senate*.

1808 Marries Sarah Stoddart in May. Moves to Winterslow, near Salisbury, in November. Sarah is pregnant.

1809 Death of Sarah and William's baby son. Hazlitt's *New and Improved Grammar of the English Tongue* published in Godwin's Juvenile Library.

1811 Birth of son, William.

1812 Hazlitt delivers his first series of lectures at the Russell Institution. James Perry takes him on as parliamentary reporter for the *Morning Chronicle* on Lamb's recommendation. Probably meets Leigh Hunt at the Lambs'.

1813 Moves to York Street and becomes Jeremy Bentham's tenant. Writes short essays and drama reviews for the *Morning Chronicle*. Visits Leigh Hunt in prison.

1814 Sees Edmund Kean on the London stage for the first time. Leaves the *Morning Chronicle* after disagreements with James Perry. The *Examiner* publishes his review of Wordsworth's *Excursion*. He begins writing for John Scott at the *Champion*, and is asked to write a review of Frances Burney's *The Wanderer* for *The Edinburgh Review*.

1815 Writes on drama and painting for the *Champion* and miscellaneous essays for the *Examiner*. Publishes with the *Edinburgh Review*.

1816 Completes *Memoirs of Thomas Holcroft* for publication after several years of dispute with Godwin over the content. Meets Keats in Benjamin Robert Haydon's studio.

1817 Discusses monarchy and republicanism with Shelley after meeting the poet through Hunt in January. Publication of *The Round Table* and *Characters of Shakespeare's Plays*.

1818 Gives two lecture series, on the English poets and on English Comic Writers, at the Surrey Institution. Publication of *A View of the English Stage* and *Lectures on the English Poets*. Attacked by *Blackwood's Edinburgh Magazine*, Hazlitt sues for libel.

1819 Publication of a *Letter to William Gifford*, *Lectures on the English Comic Writers*, and *Political Essays*. *Morning Chronicle* describes Hazlitt as 'one of the ablest and most eloquent critics of our nation'. Lectures on Elizabethan drama at the Surrey.

1820 Begins writing for the *London Magazine*. Publication of *Lectures on the Dramatic Literature of the Age of Elizabeth*.

1821 Infatuation with Sarah Walker begins. Publication of *Table Talk*.

1822 Divorces his wife in Edinburgh; Sarah Walker refuses his proposal of marriage.

1823 Publication of *Liber Amoris*. Briefly arrested for debt. Lives in London and Winterslow.

1824 Marries Isabella Bridgwater. Publication of *Sketches of the Principal Picture Galleries in England*; edits *Select British Poets*. Relieved from debt by his wife's income, they travel to France and Italy. Meets Stendhal in Paris.

1825 Publication of *Table Talk* in Paris and of *The Spirit of the Age* in London. Returns to England in October.

1826 Publication of *The Plain Speaker* and *Notes of a Journey through France and Italy*. Hazlitt returns to Paris to work on his biography of Napoleon.

1827 Lives in Paris for part of the year. Separates from Isabella on his return to England. Lives in Winterslow. Suffers ill health.

1828 First volumes of *The Life of Napoleon*.

1830 Publication of *Conversations with James Northcote*. Dies in his lodgings at Frith Street, Soho, on 18 September. Buried in the churchyard of St Anne's, Soho, on 23 September. *The Life of Napoleon* is published in its entirety posthumously.

THE SPIRIT OF CONTROVERSY
AND OTHER ESSAYS

1

REPLY TO MALTHUS

A swaggering paradox, when once explained, soon dwindles into
an unmeaning common-place.*

BURKE.

THIS excellent saying of a great man was never more strictly applicable to any system than it is to Mr. Malthus's paradox, and his explanation of it. It seemed, on the first publication of the Essay on
Population,* as if the whole world was going to be turned topsy-turvy;
all our ideas of moral good and evil were in a manner confounded, we
scarcely knew whether we stood on our head or our heels; but, after
exciting considerable expectation, giving us a good shake, and making
us a little dizzy, Mr. M. does, as we do when we shew the children
London—sets us on our feet again, and every thing goes on as before.
The common notions that prevailed on this subject, till our author's
first population scheme tended to weaken them, were, that life is
a blessing, and that the more people could be maintained in any state
in a tolerable degree of health, comfort, and decency, the better: that
want and misery are not desirable in themselves, that famine is not to
be courted for its own sake, that wars, disease, and pestilence are not
what every friend of his country or his species should pray for in the
first place: that vice in its different shapes is a thing that the world
could do very well without, and that if it could be got rid of altogether,
it would be a great gain. In short, that the object both of the moralist
and politician, was to diminish as much as possible the quantity of
vice and misery existing in the world: without apprehending that by
thus effectually introducing more virtue and happiness, more reason
and good sense, that by improving the manners of a people, removing
pernicious habits and principles of acting, or securing greater plenty,
and a greater number of mouths to partake of it, they were doing
a disservice to humanity. Then comes Mr. M. with his octavo book,*
and tells us there is another great evil, which had never been found
out, or at least not sufficiently attended to till his time; namely, excessive population; that this evil was infinitely greater and more to be
dreaded than all the others put together; and that its approach could

only be checked by vice and misery;* that any increase of virtue or
happiness was the direct way to hasten it on; and that in proportion as
we attempted to improve the condition of mankind, and lessened the
restraints of vice and misery, we threw down the only barriers that
could defend us from this most formidable scourge of the species,—population. Vice and misery were indeed evils, but they were
absolutely necessary evils; necessary to prevent the introduction of
others of an incalculably and inconceivably greater magnitude; and
that every proposal to lessen their actual quantity, on which the measure of our safety depended, might be attended with the most ruinous
consequences, and ought to be looked upon with horror. I think, Sir,
this description of the tendency and complexion of Mr. M.'s first
Essay is not in the least exaggerated, but an exact and faithful picture
of the impression which it made on every one's mind. After taking
some time to recover from the surprise and hurry into which as great
a discovery would naturally throw him, he comes forward again with
a large quarto,* in which he is at great pains both to say and unsay all
that he had said in his former volume; and upon the whole concludes,
that population is in itself a good thing, that it is never likely to do
much harm, that virtue and happiness ought to be promoted by every
practicable means, and that the most effectual as well as desirable
check to excessive population is *moral restraint*.* The mighty discovery thus reduced to, and pieced out by common sense, the wonder
vanishes, and we breathe a little freely again. Mr. M. is however by no
means willing to give up his old doctrine, or *eat his own words*: he
stickles stoutly for it at times. He has his fits of reason and his fits of
extravagance, his yielding and his obstinate moments, fluctuating
between the two, and vibrating backwards and forwards with a dexterity of self-contradiction which it is wonderful to behold. The following passage is so curious in this respect that I cannot help quoting
it in this place. Speaking of the reply of the author of the Political
Justice* to his former work, he observes, 'But, Mr. Godwin says, that
if he looks into the past history of the world, he does not see that
increasing population has been controuled and confined by vice and
misery *alone. In this observation I cannot agree with him.* I will thank
Mr. Godwin to name to me any check that in past ages has contributed to keep down the population to the level of the means of subsistence, that does not fairly come under some form of vice or misery,
except indeed the check of moral restraint, which I have mentioned in the

course of this work; and which, to say the truth, whatever hopes we may entertain of its prevalence in future, has undoubtedly in past ages operated with very inconsiderable force.'[1]* When I assure the reader that I give him this passage fairly and fully, I think he will be of opinion with me, that it would be difficult to produce an instance of a more miserable attempt to reconcile a contradiction by childish evasion, to insist upon an argument, and give it up in the same breath. Does Mr. M really think that he has such an absolute right and authority over this subject of population, that, provided he mentions a principle, or shews that he is not ignorant of it, and cannot be caught *napping* by the critics, he is at liberty to say that it has or has not had any operation, just as he pleases, and that the state of the fact is a matter of perfect indifference? He contradicts the opinion of Mr. G. that vice and misery are not the only checks to population, and gives as a proof of his assertion, that he himself truly has mentioned another check. Thus after flatly denying that moral restraint has any effect at all, he modestly concludes by saying that it has had some, no doubt, but promises that it will never have a great deal. Yet in the very next page he says, 'On this sentiment, whether virtue, prudence, or pride, which I have already noticed under the name of moral restraint, or of the more comprehensive title, the *preventive check*, it will appear, that in the sequel of this work, I shall lay considerable stress,' p. 385. This kind of reasoning is enough to give one the headache. But to take things in their order.—The most singular thing in this singular performance of our author is, that it should have been originally ushered into the world as the most complete and only satisfactory answer to the speculations of Godwin, Condorcet* and others, or to what has been called the modern philosophy. A more unaccountable piece of wrong-headedness, a total perversion of reason could hardly be devised by the wit of man. Whatever we may think of the doctrine of the progressive improvement of the human mind, or of a state of society in which every thing will be subject to the control of reason, however absurd, unnatural or impracticable, we may conceive such a system to be, certainly it cannot, without the grossest inconsistency, be objected to it, that such a system would necessarily be rendered abortive, because, if reason should ever get this mastery over all our

---

[1] The prevalence of this check may be estimated by the general proportion of virtue and happiness in the world, for if there had been no such check, there could have been nothing but vice and misery.

actions, we should then be governed entirely by our physical appetites
and passions, without the least regard to consequences. This appears
to me a refinement on absurdity. Several philosophers and specu-
latists had supposed that a certain state of society, very different from
any that has hitherto existed, was in itself practicable; and that if it
were realised, it would be productive of a far greater degree of human
happiness than is compatible with the present institutions of society.
I have nothing to do with either of these points. I will allow to any one
who pleases that all such schemes are 'false, sophistical, unfounded in
the extreme.'* But, I cannot agree with Mr. Malthus that they would
be *bad* in proportion as they were *good*; that the true and only
unanswerable argument against all such schemes is that very degree
of *happiness*, virtue, and improvement, to which they are supposed to
give rise. And I cannot agree with him in this, because it is contrary to
common sense, and leads to the subversion of every principle of
moral reasoning. Without perplexing himself with the subtle arguments of his opponents, Mr. M. comes boldly forward, and says,
'Gentlemen, I am willing to make you large concessions. I am ready to
allow the practicability and the desirableness of your schemes, the
more desirable and the more practicable, the better; the more happiness, the more virtue, the more knowledge, the more refinement, the
better; all these will only add to the exuberant strength of my argument. I have a short answer to all objections, (to be sure, I found it in
an old political receipt-book, called Prospects, &c. by one Wallace,*
a man not much known, but no matter for that '*finding is keeping*, you
know') and with one smart stroke of his wand, on which are inscribed
certain mystical characters, and algebraic proportions, he levels the
fairy enchantment with the ground. For, says Mr. M. though this
improved state of society were actually realised, it could not possibly
continue, but must soon terminate in a state of things pregnant with
evils far more insupportable than any we at present endure, in consequence of the excessive population which would follow, and the
impossibility of providing for its support. This is what I do not
understand. It is, in other words, to assert that the doubling the
population of a country, for example, after a certain period, will be
attended with the most pernicious effects, by want, famine, bloodshed, and a state of general violence and confusion; that this will
afterwards lead to vices and practices still worse than the physical
evils they are designed to prevent, &c. and yet that at this period

those who will be the most interested in preventing these consequences, and the best acquainted with the circumstances that lead to
them, will neither have the understanding to foresee, nor the heart to
feel, nor the will to prevent the sure evils, to which they expose themselves and others; though this advanced state of population, which
does not admit of any addition without danger, is supposed to be the
immediate result of a more general diffusion of the comforts and con-
veniences of life, of more enlarged and liberal views, of a more refined
and comprehensive regard to our own permanent interests as well as
those of others, of correspondent habits and manners, and of a state
of things, in which our gross animal appetites will be under the constant control of reason. The influence of rational motives, of refined
and long-sighted views of things is supposed to have taken place of
narrow, selfish and merely sensual motives: this is implied in the very
statement of the question. 'What conjuration and what mighty
magic'* should thus blind our philosophical descendants on this single subject in which they are more interested than in all others, so that
they should stand with their eyes open on the edge of a precipice, and
instead of retreating from it, should throw themselves down headlong. I am unable to comprehend; unless indeed, we suppose that the
impulse to propagate the species is so strong and uncontroulable, that
reason has no power over it. This is what Mr. M. was at one time
strongly disposed to assert, and what he is at present half inclined to
retract. Without this foundation to rest on, the whole of his reasoning
is utterly unintelligible. It seems to me a most preposterous way of
answering a man who chuses to assert, that mankind are capable of
being governed entirely by their reason, and that it would be better
for them if they were to say no; for, if they were governed entirely by
it, they would be much less able to attend to its dictates than they are
at present; and the evils which would thus follow from the unrestrained increase of population, would be excessive. Almost every little miss who has had the advantage of a boarding-school education, or
been properly tutored by her mamma, whose hair is not of an absolute
flame colour, and who has hopes in time, if she behaves prettily, of
getting a good husband, waits patiently year after year, looks about
her, rejects or trifles with half a dozen lovers, favouring one, laughing at another, 'chusing among them, as one picks pears,' saying,
'This I like, that I loathe,'* with the greatest indifference, as if it were
no such very pressing affair, and *all the while behaves very prettily*;

till she is at last smitten with a handsome house, a couple of footmen
in livery, or a black servant, or a coach with two sleek geldings, with
which she is more taken than with her man. Why, what an idea does
Mr. M. give us of the grave, masculine, genius of our Utopian philosophers, their sublime attainments, and gigantic energy, that they
will not be able to manage these matters as decently and cleverly as
the silliest women can do at present! Mr. M. indeed, endeavours to
soften this absurdity by saying, that moral restraint at present owes its
strength to selfish motives; what is this to this purpose? If Mr. M.
chuses to say, that men will always be governed by the same gross
mechanical motives that they are at present, I have no objection to
make to it, but it is shifting the question; it is not arguing against the
state of society we are considering from the consequences to which it
would give rise, but against the possibility of its ever existing. It is to
object to a system on account of the consequences which would follow if we were to suppose men to be actuated by entirely different
motives and principles from what they are at present, and then to say,
that those consequences would necessarily follow, because men would
never be what we suppose them. Or it is to alarm the imagination by
deprecating the evils that must follow from the practical adoption of
a particular scheme, yet to allow that we have no reason to dread those
consequences, but because the scheme itself is impracticable.—I am
ashamed of wasting your readers' time and my own in thus beating
the air. It is not, however, my fault, that Mr. Malthus has written
nonsense, or that others have admired it. It is not Mr. M.'s nonsense,
but the opinion of the world respecting it, that I would be thought to
compliment by this serious refutation of what, in itself neither
deserves nor admits of any reasoning upon it. If, however, we recollect
the source from whence Mr. M. borrowed his principle, and the
application of it to improvements in political philosophy, we must
allow that he is merely *passive* in error. The principle itself would not
have been worth a farthing without the application, and he accordingly
took them as he found them, lying snug together; and as Trim, after
having converted the old jack-boots into a pair of new mortars, immediately planted them against which ever of my Uncle Toby's garrisons
the allies were then busy in besieging,* so the public spirited gallantry
of our modern engineer, directed him to bend the whole force of his
clumsy discovery against that system of philosophy, which was the
most talked of at the time, but to which it was the least applicable of

all others. Wallace, I have no doubt, took up his idea either as a paradox or a *jeu d'esprit*; or, because anything, he thought, was of weight
enough to overturn what had never existed any where but in the
imagination, or he was led into a piece of false logic by an error we are
very apt to fall into, of supposing, because he had never been struck
himself by the difficulty of population in such a state of society, that
therefore, the people themselves would not find it out when it came, nor
make any provision against it. But, though I can in some measure
excuse a lively paradox, I do not think that the same favour is to be
shewn to the dull, dogged, heavy repetition of absurdity.—Mr. M.
might have taken as the motto of his first edition, 'These three bear
record on earth, Vice, Misery, and Population.'*—In the answer to
Mr. G. this principle was represented as an evil, for which no remedy
could be found but in evil: that its operation was mechanical, necessary, unceasing; that it went strait forward to its end, unchecked by
fear, or reason, or remorse; that the evils which it drew after it could
only be avoided by other evils, by actual vice and misery. Population,
was in short the great devil, the untamed Beelzebub, that was only
kept chained down by vice and misery; and which, if it were once let
loose from these restraints, would go forth and ravage the earth. That
they were therefore, the two main props and pillars of society, and
that the lower and weaker they kept this principle, the better able they
were to contend with it: that, therefore, any diminution of that degree
of them which at present prevails, and is found sufficient to keep the
world in order, was of all things chiefly to be dreaded.—Our author
is fully aware of the force of the stage maxim,* to elevate and surprise.
Having once healed the imaginations of his readers, he knows that he
can afterwards mould them into what shape he please. All this bustle,
and terror, and stage effect, and theatrical mummery, was only to
serve a temporary purpose; for all of a sudden the scene is shifted,
and the storm subsides. Having frightened away the boldest champions of modern philosophy, this monstrous appearance, full of
strange and inexplicable horrors, is suffered quietly to shrink back to
its natural dimensions, and we find it to be nothing more than
a common-sized, tame-looking animal; which, however, requires
a chain and the whip of its keeper to prevent it from becoming mischievous. Mr. M. then steps forward, and says, the evil we were all in
danger of was not population, but philosophy. Nothing is to be done
with the latter by mere reasoning. I, therefore, thought it right to

make use of a little terror to accomplish the end. As to the principle of population itself, you need be under no alarm: only leave it to me, and I shall be able to manage it very well. All its dreadful consequences may be easily prevented by a proper application of the motives of common prudence and common decency. If any one should be at a loss to conceive how Mr. M. can reconcile such contrary opinions, I should be inclined to suggest to Mr. M. Hamlet's answer to his friend Guildenstern, ''Tis as easy as lying; govern those ventiges' (the work-houses, and charitable donations) 'with your fingers and thumb; and this very instrument will discourse most excellent music: look you, here are the stops.'* (Mr. M.'s, Essay, and Mr. Whitbread's Poor Bill*.)

2

WHY THE ARTS ARE NOT PROGRESSIVE?

It is often made a subject of complaint and surprise, the arts in this country and in modern times have not kept pace with the general progress of society and civilization in other respects, and it has been proposed to remedy the deficiency by more carefully availing ourselves of the advantages which time and circumstances have placed within our reach, but which we have hitherto neglected, the study of the antique, the imitation of the best models, the formation of academies, and the distribution of prizes.

First, the complaint itself, that the arts do not attain that progressive degree of perfection which might reasonably be expected from them, is not well-founded, for the general analogy appealed to in support of the regular advances of art to higher degrees of excellence, totally fails; it applies to science, not to art.—Secondly, the expedients proposed to remedy the evil by adventitious means are only calculated to confirm it. The arts hold immediate communication with nature, and are only derived from that source. When that original impulse no longer exists, when the inspiration of genius is fled, all the attempts to recal it are no better than the tricks of galvanism* to restore the dead to life. The arts may be said to resemble Antæus* in his struggle with Hercules, who was strangled when he was raised above the ground, and only revived and recovered his strength when he touched his mother earth.

Nothing is more contrary to the fact than the supposition that in what we understand by the *fine arts*, as painting and poetry, relative perfection is only the result of repeated efforts, and that what has been once well done usually leads to something better. What is mechanical, reducible to rule, or capable of demonstration, is progressive and admits of gradual improvement: what is not mechanical or definite, but depends on genius, taste, and feeling, very soon becomes stationary, or retrograde, and loses more than it gains by transfusion. The contrary supposition is, indeed, a common error, which has grown up, like many others, from transferring an analogy of one kind to something quite distinct, without thinking of the difference in the nature of the things, or attending to the difference of the results.

For most persons, finding what wonderful advances have been
made in biblical criticism, in chemistry, in mechanics, in geometry,
astronomy, &c. *i.e.* in things depending on mere inquiry and experiment, or on absolute demonstration, have been led hastily to conclude that there was a general tendency in the efforts of the human
intellect to improve by repetition, and in all other arts and institutions to grow perfect and mature by time. We look back upon the
theological creed of our ancestors, and their discoveries in natural
philosophy with a smile of pity; science and the arts connected with it
have all had their infancy, their youth, and manhood, and seem to
have in them no principle of limitation or decay; and inquiring
no farther about the matter, we infer, in the height of our self-
congratulation, and in the intoxication of our pride, that the same
progress has been, and will continue to be made in all other things
which are the works of man. The fact, however, stares us so
plainly in the face, that one would think the smallest reflection must
suggest the truth, and overturn our sanguine theories. The greatest
poets, the ablest orators, the best painters, and the finest sculptors
that the world ever saw, appeared soon after the birth of these arts,
and lived in a state of society, which was in other respects comparatively barbarous. These arts, which depend on individual genius and
incommunicable power, have always leaped at once from infancy to
manhood, from the first rude dawn of invention to their meridian
height and dazzling lustre, and have in general declined ever. This is
the peculiar distinction and privilege of each, of science and of art; of
the one, never to attain its utmost summit of perfection, and of the
other to arrive at it almost at once. Homer, Chaucer, Spenser,
Shakspeare, Dante, and Ariosto (Milton alone was of a later age, and
not the worse for it), Raphael, Titian, Michael Angelo, Correggio,
Cervantes and Boccacio—all lived near the beginning of their
arts—perfected, and all but created them. These giant sons of genius
stand indeed upon the earth, but they tower above their fellows, and
the long line of their successors does not interpose any thing to
obstruct their view, or lessen their brightness. In strength and stature
they are unrivalled, in grace and beauty they have never been surpassed. In after-ages and more refined periods (as they are called),
great men have arisen one by one, as it were by throes and at intervals:
though in general the best of these cultivated and artificial minds
were of an inferior order, as Tasso and Pope among poets, Claude

Lorraine[1] and Vandyke among painters. But in the earliest stages of the arts, when merely the first mechanical difficulties were got over, and the language as it were acquired, they rose by clusters and in constellations, never to rise again.

* * *

Science and the mechanic arts depend not on the force with which the mind itself is endued, or with which it contemplates given things (for this is naturally much the same) but on the number of things, successively perceived by the same or different persons, and formally arranged and registered in books or memory, which admits of being varied and augmented indefinitely. The number of objects to which the understanding may be directed is endless, and the results, so far as they are positive, tangible things, may be set down and added one to another, and made use of as occasion requires, without creating any confusion, and so as to produce a perpetual accumulation of useful

[1] In speaking thus of Claude, we yield rather to common opinion than to our own. However inferior the style of his best landscapes may be, there is something in the execution that redeems all defects. In taste and grace nothing can ever go beyond them. He might be called, if not the perfect, the faultless painter. Sir Joshua Reynolds used to say, that there would be another Raphael, before there was another Claude. In Mr. Northcote's Dream of a Painter, (See his Memoirs of Sir J. Reynolds), there is an account of Claude Lorraine so full of feeling, so picturesque, so truly classical, so like Claude, that we cannot resist this opportunity of copying it out:

'Now tired with pomp and splendid shew, the glare of light and sound of warlike strains on brazen instruments, it was a relief to me when on a sudden I was surrounded by a thick cloud or mist, and my guide wafted me through the air till we alighted on a most delicious rural spot. I perceived it was the early hour of the morning, when the sun had not risen above the horizon. We were alone, except that at a little distance a young shepherd played on his flageolet as he walked before his herd, conducting them from the fold to pasture. The elevated pastoral air he played charmed me by its simplicity, and seemed to animate his obedient flock. The atmosphere was clear and perfectly calm: and now the rising sun gradually illumined the fine landscape, and began to discover to our view the distant country of immense extent. I stood a while in expectation of what might next present itself of dazzling splendour, when the only object which appeared to fill this natural, grand, and simple scene, was a rustic who entered not far from the place where we stood, who by his habiliments seemed nothing better than a peasant: he led a poor little ass, which was loaded with all the implements required by a printer in his work. After advancing a few paces, he stood still, and with an air of rapture seemed to contemplate the rising sun: he next fell on his knees, directed his eyes towards Heaven, crossed himself, and then went on with eager looks, as if to make choices of the most advantageous spot, from which to make his studies as a printer. "This," said my conductor, "is that Claude Gelee of Lorraine, who nobly disdaining the low employment, to which he was originally bred, left it with all its advantages of competence and ease to embrace his present state to poverty, in order to adorn the world with works of most accomplished excellence." '*

knowledge. What is once gained is never lost, and may be multiplied daily, because this increase of knowledge does not depend upon increasing the force of the mind, but on directing the same force to different things, all of them in their nature definite, demonstrable, existing to the mind outwardly and by signs, less as the power than as the form of truth, and in which all the difficulty lies in the first invention, not in the subsequent communication. In like manner the mechanic parts of painting for instance, such as the mode of preparing colours, the laws of perspective, &c. which may be taught by rule and method, so that the principle being once known, every one may avail himself of it, these subordinate and instrumental parts of the arts admit of uniform excellence, though from accidental cause it has happened otherwise. But it is not so in art itself, in its higher and nobler essence. 'There is no shuffling,' but 'we ourselves compelled to give in evidence even to the teeth and forehead of our faults.'* There is no room for the division of labour—for the accumulation of borrowed advantages; no artificial scale by which *to heaven we may ascend*; because here excellence does not depend on the quantity of representative knowledge, abstracted from a variety of subjects, but on the original force of capacity, and degree of attention, applied to the same given subject, natural feelings and images. To use the distinction of a technical philosophy, science depends on the discursive or *extensive*—art on the intuitive and *intensive* power of the mind.* One chemical or mathematical discovery may be added to another, because the degree and sort of faculty required to apprehend and retain them, are in both cases the same; but no one can voluntarily add the colouring of Rubens to the expression of Raphael, till he has the same eye for colour as Rubens, and for expression as Raphael—that is, the most thorough feeling of what is profound in the one, or splendid in the other—of what no rules can teach, nor words convey—and of what the mind must possess within itself, and by a kind of participation with nature, or remain for ever destitute of it. Titian and Correggio are the only painters who united to perfect colouring a degree of expression, the one in his portraits, and the other in his histories, all but equal, if not equal, to the highest. But this union of different qualities they had from nature, and not by method. In fact, we judge of science by the number of effects produced—of art by the energy which produces them. The one is knowledge—the other power.

The arts of painting and poetry are conversant with the world of thought within us, and with the world of sense without us—with what we know, and see, and feel intimately. They flow from the sacred shrine of our own breasts, and are kindled at the living lamp of nature. The pulse of the passions assuredly beat as high, the depths and soundings of the human heart were as well understood three thousand years ago, as they are at present; the face of nature and 'the human face divine'* shone as bright then as they have ever done. It is this light, reflected by true genius on art, that marks out its path before it, and sheds its glory round the Muse's feet, like that which circled Una's angel face,

> And made a sunshine in the shady place.*

Nature is the soul of art. There is a strength in the imagination which reposes entirely on nature—which nothing else can supply. There is in the old poets and painters a vigour and grasp of mind, a full possession of their subject, a confidence and firm faith, a sublime simplicity, an elevation of thought, proportioned to their depth of feeling, an increasing force and impetus, which moves, penetrates, and kindles all that comes in contact with it, which seems not theirs, but given to them. It is this reliance on the power of nature which has produced those master-pieces by the Prince of Painters,* in which expression is all in all, where one spirit—that of truth—pervades every part, brings down heaven to earth, mingles cardinals and popes with angels and apostles, and yet blends and harmonises the whole by the true touches and intense feeling of what is beautiful and grand in nature. It was the same trust in nature that inspired the genius of Chaucer, that enabled him to describe the patient sorrow of Griselda,* or the delight of that young beauty, shrouded in her bower, and listening in the morning of the year, to the singing of the nightingale, whose joy rises with the rising song, and gushes out afresh at every pause, and is borne along with the full tide of pleasure, and still increases and repeats and prolongs itself, and knows no ebb.* It is thus that Boccacio, in the divine story of the Hawk,* has represented Frederigo Alberigi steadily contemplating his favourite Falcon (the wreck and remnant of his fortune), and glad to see how fat and fair a bird she is, thinking what a dainty repast she would make for his Mistress, who had deigned to visit him in his low cell. So Isabella mourns over her pot of Basile,* and never asks for any thing but that. So Lear calls out

for his poor fool, and invokes the heavens, for they are old like him.*
So Titian impressed on the countenance of that young Neapolitan
nobleman in the Louvre,* a look that never passed away. So he painted
the picture of St. Peter Martyr,* with that cold convent-spire rising
in the distance, amidst the blue sapphire mountains and the golden
sky. So Nicolas Poussin describes some shepherds wandering out in
a morning of the spring, and coming to a tomb with this inscription,
'I also was an Arcadian!'* What have we left to console us for all this?
Why, we have Mr. Rogers's 'Pleasures of Memory,' and Mr. Campbell's
'Pleasures of Hope;' Mr. Westall's pictures, and all West's; Miss Burney's
new Novel (which is, however, some comfort), Miss Edgeworth's
Fashionable Tales, Madame de Staël's next work, whatever it may
be, and the praise of it in the Edinburgh Review, and Sir James
Macintosh's History.*

3

MR. KEAN'S SHYLOCK

MR. KEAN (of whom report had spoken highly) made his appearance at this Theatre in the character of *Shylock*. For voice, eye, action, and expression, no actor has come out for many years at all equal to him. The applause, from the first scene to the last, was general, loud, and uninterrupted. Indeed, the very first scene in which he comes on with *Bassanio* and *Anthonio*, shewed the master in his art, and at once decided the opinion of the audience. Perhaps it was the most perfect of any. Notwithstanding the complete success of Mr. KEAN in the part of *Shylock*, we question whether he will not become a greater favourite in other parts. There was a lightness and vigour in his tread, a buoyancy and elasticity of spirit, a fire and animation, which would accord better with almost any other character than with the morose, sullen, inward, inveterate, inflexible malignity of *Shylock*. The character of *Shylock* is that of a man brooding over one idea, that of its wrongs, and bent on one unalterable purpose, that of revenge. In conveying a profound impression of this feeling, or in embodying the general conception of rigid and uncontroulable self-will, equally proof against every sentiment of humanity or prejudice of opinion, we have seen actors more successful than Mr. KEAN. But in giving effect to the conflict of passions arising out of the contrast of situation, in varied vehemence of declamation, in keenness of sarcasm, in the rapidity of his transitions from one tone and feeling to another, in propriety and novelty of action, presenting a succession of striking pictures, and giving perpetually fresh shocks of delight and surprise—it would be difficult to single out a competitor. The fault of his acting was (if we may hazard the objection), an over-display of the resources of the art, which gave too much relief to the hard, impenetrable, dark groundwork of the character of *Shylock*. It would be endless to point out individual beauties, where almost every passage was received with equal and deserved applause. We thought, in one or two instances, the pauses in the voice were too long, and too great a reliance placed on the expression of the countenance, which is a language intelligible only to a part of the house. The rest of the play was, upon the whole, very respectably cast. It would be an equivocal compliment to say, of Miss SMITH,* that her acting often reminds us of Mrs. SIDDONS. RAE* played *Bassanio*; but the abrupt and harsh tones of his voice are not well adapted to the mellifluous cadences of SHAKESPEAR'S verse.

4

ON IMITATION

OBJECTS in themselves disgusting or indifferent often please in the imitation. A brick-floor, a pewter-plate, an ugly cur barking, a Dutch boor smoking or playing at skittles, the inside of a shambles, a fishmonger's or a greengrocer's stall, have been made very interesting pictures by the fidelity, truth, and spirit, with which they have been copied. One source of the pleasure thus received is undoubtedly the surprise or feeling of admiration, occasioned by the unexpected coincidence between the imitation and the object. The deception however not only pleases at first sight, or from mere novelty; but it continues to please upon farther acquaintance, and in proportion to the insight we acquire into the distinctions of nature and of art. By far the most numerous class of connoisseurs are the admirers of pictures of *still life*, which have nothing but the exactness of the imitation to recommend them. The chief reason then why imitation pleases, is, because, by exciting curiosity and inviting a comparison between the object and the representation, it opens a new field of inquiry, and leads the attention to a variety of details and distinctions not perceived before. This latter source of the pleasure derived from imitation has never been properly defined or understood.

The anatomist is delighted with a coloured plate, conveying the exact appearance of the progress of certain diseases, or of the internal parts and dissections of the human body. We have known a Jennerian Professor* as much enraptured with a delineation of the different stages of vaccination, as a florist with a bed of tulips, or an auctioneer with a collection of Indian shells. But in this case, we find that not only the imitation pleases,—the objects themselves give as much pleasure to the professional inquirer, as they would pain to the uninitiated. The learned amateur is struck with the beauty of the coats of the stomach laid bare, or contemplates with eager curiosity the transverse section of the brain, divided on the new Spurtzheim principles.* It is here then the number of the parts, their distinctions, connections, structure, uses, in short, an entire new set of ideas, which occupies the mind of the student, and overcomes the sense of pain and repugnance, which is the only feeling that the sight of a dead and mangled body presents to ordinary men. It is the same in art as in science. The painter of still life, as it is called, takes the same pleasure in the object as the spectator does in the imitation: because by habit he is led to perceive all those distinctions in nature, to which other persons never pay any attention till they are pointed out to them in the picture. The vulgar only see nature as it is reflected to them from art: the painter sees the picture in nature, before he transfers it to the canvass. He refines, he analyses, he remarks fifty things, which escape common eyes: and this affords a distinct source of reflection and amusement to him, independently of the beauty or grandeur of the objects themselves, or of their connection with other impressions besides those of sight. The charm of the Fine Arts then does not consist in any thing peculiar to imitation, even where only imitation is concerned, since *there*, where art exists in the highest perfection, namely, in the mind of the artist, the object excites the same or greater pleasure, before the imitation exists. Imitation renders an object displeasing in itself a source of pleasure, not by a repetition of the same idea, but by suggesting new ideas, by detecting new properties and endless shades of difference,—just as a close and continued contemplation of the object itself would do. Art shews us nature, divested of the medium of our prejudices. It divides and analyses objects into a thousand curious parts, which may be full of variety, beauty, and delicacy in themselves, though the object to which they belong may be disagreeable in its general appearance, or by association with other ideas. A painted marigold is inferior to a painted rose only in form and colour: it loses nothing in point of smell. Yellow hair is perfectly beautiful in a picture. To a person lying with his face close to the ground in a summer's-day, the blades of spear-grass will appear like tall forest trees, shooting up into the sky; as an insect seen through a microscope is magnified into an elephant. Art is the microscope of the mind, which sharpens the wits as the other does the sight; and converts every object into a little universe in itself.[1] Art may be said to draw aside the veil from nature. To those who are perfectly unskilled

---

[1] In a fruit or flower-piece by Vanhuysum,* the minutest details acquire a certain grace and beauty from the delicacy with which they are finished. The eye dwells with a giddy delight on the liquid drops of dew, on the gauze wings of an insect, on the hair and feathers of a bird's nest, the streaked and speckled egg-shells, the fine legs of the little travelling caterpillar. Who will suppose that the painter had not the same pleasure in detecting these nice distinctions in nature, that the critic has in tracing them in the picture?

in the practice, unimbued with the principles of art, most objects present only a confused mass. The pursuit of art is liable to be carried to a contrary excess, as where it produces a rage for the *picturesque.* You cannot go a step with a person of this class, but he stops you to point out some choice bit of landscape, and teazes you almost to death with the frequency and insignificance of his discoveries!

It is a common mistake (which may be worth noticing here), that the study of physiognomy has a tendency to make people satirical, and the knowledge of art to make them fastidious in their taste. Knowledge may indeed afford a handle to ill-nature; but it takes away the principal temptation to its exercise, by supplying the mind with better resources against *ennui.* Idiots are always mischievous; and the most superficial persons are the most disposed to find fault, because they understand the fewest things. The English are more apt than any other nation to treat foreigners with contempt, because they seldom see any thing but their own dress and manners; and it is only in petty provincial towns that you meet with persons who pride themselves on being satirical. In every country place in England there are one or two persons of this description who keep the whole neighbourhood in terror. It is not to be denied that the study of the *ideal* in art, if separated from the study of nature, may have the effect above stated, of producing dissatisfaction and contempt for every thing but itself, as all affectation must: but to the genuine artist, truth, nature, and beauty are almost different names for the same thing.

Imitation interests then by exciting a more intense perception of truth, and calling out the powers of observation and comparison: wherever this effect takes place, the interest follows of course, with or without the imitation, whether the object is real or artificial. The gardener delights in the streaks of a tulip, or 'pansy freak'd with jet;'* the mineralogist, in the varieties of certain strata, because he understands them. Knowledge is pleasure as well as power. A work of art has in this respect no advantage over a work of nature, except inasmuch as it furnishes an additional stimulus to curiosity. Again, natural objects please, in proportion as they are uncommon, by fixing the attention more steadily on their beauties or differences. The same principle of the effects of novelty in exciting the attention will account perhaps for the extraordinary discoveries and lies told by travellers, who, opening their eyes for the first time in foreign parts, are startled at every object they meet.

Why the excitement of intellectual activity pleases, is not here the question; but that it does so, is a general and acknowledged law of the human mind. We grow attached to the mathematics only from finding out their truth; and their utility chiefly consists (at present) in the contemplative pleasure they afford to the student. Lines, points, angles, squares, and circles, are not interesting in themselves; they become so by the power of mind exerted in comprehending their properties and relations. People dispute forever about Hogarth. The question has not in one respect been fairly stated. The merit of his pictures then does not so much depend on the nature of the subject, as on the knowledge displayed of it, on the number of ideas they excite, on the fund of thought and observation contained in them. They are to be looked on as works of science; they gratify our love of truth; they fill up the void of the mind: they are a series of plates of natural history, and also of that most interesting part of natural history, the history of man. The superiority of high art over the common or mechanical consists in combining truth of imitation with beauty and grandeur of subject. The historical painter is superior to the flower painter, because he combines or ought to combine human interests and passions with the same power of imitating external nature; or indeed with greater, for the greatest difficulty of imitation is the power of imitating expression. The difficulty of copying increases with our knowledge of the object; and that again with the interest we take in it. The same argument might be applied to shew that the poet and painter of imagination are superior to the mere philosopher or man of science, because they possess the powers of reason and intellect combined with nature and passion. They treat of the highest categories of the human soul, pleasure and pain.

From the foregoing train of reasoning, we may easily account for the too great tendency of art to run into pedantry and affectation. There is 'a pleasure in art which none but artists feel'* in the same degree. They see beauty where others see nothing of the sort, in wrinkles, deformity, and old age. They see it in Titian's Schoolmaster* as well as in Raphael's Galatea;* in the dark shadows of Rembrandt as well as in the splendid colours of Rubens; in an angel's or in a butterfly's wings. They see with different eyes from the multitude. But true genius, though it has new sources of pleasure opened to it, does not lose its sympathy with humanity. It combines truth of imitation with effect, the parts with the wholes, the means with the end. The mechanic artist sees only that which nobody else sees, and is conversant only with the technical language and difficulties of his art. A painter, if shewn a picture, will generally dwell upon the academic skill displayed in it, and the knowledge of the received rules of composition. A musician, if asked to play a tune, will select that which is the most difficult and the least intelligible. The poet will be struck with the harmony of versification or the elaborateness of the arrangement. The conceits in Shakespeare were his greatest delight; and improving upon this perverse method of judging, the German writers, Goethé and Schiller, look upon Werter* and the Robbers* as the worst of all their works, because they are the most popular. Some artists among ourselves have carried the same principle to a singular excess.[2] If professors themselves are liable to this kind of pedantry, connoisseurs and dilettanti are almost wholly swayed by it. They see nothing in a picture but the execution. They are proud of their knowledge, in proportion as it is a secret; for they have no sensibility, and a great deal of affectation. The worst judges of pictures in the United Kingdom are, first, picture-dealers; next, perhaps, the Directors of the British Institution;* and after them, the Members of the Royal Academy.

---

[2] We here allude particularly to Turner, the ablest landscape-painter now living, whose pictures are however too much abstractions of aerial perspective, and representations not so properly of the objects of nature as of the medium through which they are seen. They are the triumph of the knowledge of the artist, and of the power of the pencil over the barrenness of the subject. They are pictures of the elements of air, earth, and water. The artist delights to go back to the first chaos of the world, or to that state of things when the waters were separated from the dry land, and light from darkness, but as yet no living thing nor tree bearing fruit was seen upon the face of the earth. All is without form and void. Some one said of his landscapes that they were '*pictures of nothing, and very like.*'

5

ON GUSTO

GUSTO in art is power or passion defining any object.—It is not so difficult to explain this term in what relates to expression (of which it may be said to be the highest degree) as in what relates to things without expression, to the natural appearances of objects, as mere colour or form. The truth is, that there is hardly any object entirely devoid of expression, without some character of power belonging to it, some precise association with pleasure or pain; and it is in giving this truth of character from the truth of feeling, whether in the highest or the lowest degree, but always in the highest degree of which the subject is capable, that gusto consists.

There is a gusto in the colouring of Titian. Not only do his heads seem to think—his bodies seem to feel. This is what the Italians mean by the *morbidezza** of his flesh-colour. It seems sensitive and alive all over; not merely to have the look and texture of flesh, but the feeling in itself. For example, the limbs of his female figures have a luxurious softness and delicacy, which appears conscious of the pleasure of the beholder. As the objects themselves in nature would produce an impression on the sense, distinct from every other object, and having something divine in it, which the heart owns and the imagination consecrates, the objects in the picture preserve the same impression, absolute, unimpaired, stamped with all the truth of passion, the pride of the eye, and the charms of beauty. Rubens makes his flesh-colour like flowers, Albano's is like ivory,* Titian's is like flesh, and like nothing else. It is as different from that of other painters, as the skin is from a piece of white or red drapery thrown over it. The blood circulates here and there, the blue veins just appear, the rest is distinguished throughout only by that sort of tingling sensation to the eye, which the body feels within itself. This is gusto.—Vandyke's flesh-colour, though it has great truth and purity, wants gusto. It has not the internal character, the living principle in it. It is a smooth surface, not a warm, moving mass. It is painted without passion, with indifference. The hand only has been concerned. The impression slides off from the eye, and does not, like the tones of Titian's pencil, leave a sting behind it in the mind of the spectator. The eye does not acquire a taste or appetite for what it sees. In a word, gusto in painting is where the impression made on one sense excites by affinity those of another.

Michael Angelo's forms are full of gusto. They every where obtrude the sense of power upon the eye. His limbs convey an idea of muscular power, of moral grandeur, and even of intellectual dignity: they are firm, commanding, broad, and massy, capable of executing with ease the determined purposes of the will. His faces have no other expression than his figures, conscious power and capacity. They appear only to think what they shall do, and to know that they can do it. This is what is meant by saying that his style is hard and masculine. It is the reverse of Correggio's, which is effeminate. That is, the gusto of Michael Angelo consists in expressing energy of will without proportionable sensibility, Correggio's in expressing exquisite sensibility without energy of will. In Correggio's faces as well as figures we see neither bones nor muscles, but then what a soul is there, full of sweetness and of grace—pure, playful, soft, angelical! There is sentiment enough in a hand painted by Correggio to set up a school of history-painters. Whenever we look at the hands of Correggio's women or of Raphael's, we always wish to touch them.[1]

Again, Titian's landscapes have a prodigious gusto, both in the colouring and forms. We shall never forget one that we saw many years ago in the Orleans Gallery* of Acteon hunting.* It had a brown, mellow, autumnal look. The sky was of the colour of stone. The winds seemed to sing through the rustling branches of the trees, and already you might hear the twanging of bows resound through the tangled mazes of the wood. Mr. West,* we understand, has this landscape. He

---

[1] This may seem obscure. We will therefore avail ourselves of our privilege to explain as Members of Parliament do, when they let fall any thing too paradoxical, novel, or abstruse, to be immediately apprehended by the other side of the House. When the Widow Wadman looked over my Uncle Toby's map of the siege of Namur with him, and as he pointed out the approaches of his battalion in a transverse line across the plain to the gate of St. Nicholas, kept her hand constantly pressed against his, if my Uncle Toby had then 'been an artist and could paint,' (as Mr. Fox wished himself to be, that 'he might draw Bonaparte's conduct to the King of Prussia in the blackest colours') my Uncle Toby would have drawn the hand of his fair enemy in the manner we have above described. We have heard a good story of this same Bonaparte playing off a very ludicrous parody of the Widow Wadman's stratagem upon as great a Commander by sea as my Uncle Toby was by land. Now, when Sir Isaac Newton, who was sitting smoking with his mistress's hand in his, took her little finger and made use of it as a tobacco-pipe stopper, there was here a total absence of mind, or a great want of gusto.*

will know if this description of it is just. The landscape back-ground of the St. Peter Martyr is another well known instance of the power of this great painter to give a romantic interest and an appropriate character to the objects of his pencil, where every circumstance adds to the effect of the scene,—the bold trunks of the tall forest trees, the trailing ground plants, with that cold convent spire rising in the distance, amidst the blue sapphire mountains and the golden sky.

Rubens has a great deal of gusto in his Fauns and Satyrs, and in all that expresses motion, but in nothing else. Rembrandt has it in every thing; every thing in his pictures has a tangible character. If he puts a diamond in the ear of a Burgomaster's wife, it is of the first water; and his furs and stuffs are proof against a Russian winter. Raphael's gusto was only in expression; he had no idea of the character of any thing but the human form. The dryness and poverty of his stile in other respects is a phenomenon in the art. His trees are like springs of grass stuck in a book of botanical specimens. Was it that Raphael never had time to go beyond the walls of Rome? That he was always in the streets, at church, or in the bath? He was not one of the Society of Arcadians.[2]

Claude's landscapes, perfect as they are, want gusto. This is not easy to explain. They are perfect abstractions of the visible images of things; they speak the visible language of nature truly. They resemble a mirror or a microscope. They are more perfect to the eye only than any other landscapes that ever were or will be painted; they give more of nature, as cognizable by one sense alone; but they lay an equal stress on all visible impressions; they do not interpret one sense by another; they do not distinguish the character of different objects as we are taught, and can only be taught to distinguish them, by their effect on the different senses. That is, his eye wanted imagination; it did not strongly sympathise with his other faculties. He saw the atmosphere, but he did not feel it. He painted the trunk of a tree or a rock in the foreground as smooth—with as complete an abstraction of the gross, tangible impression, as any other part of the picture; his trees are perfectly beautiful, but quite immoveable. His landscapes

---

[2] Raphael not only could not paint a landscape; he could not paint people in a landscape. He could not have painted the heads or the figures or even the dresses of the St. Peter Martyr. His figures have always an *in-door* look, that is, a set, determined, voluntary, dramatic character, arising from their own passions or a watchfulness of those of others, and want that wild uncertainty of expression, which is connected with the accidents of nature and the changes of the elements. He has nothing *romantic* about him.

are unequalled imitations of nature, released from its subjection to the elements,—as if all objects were become a delightful fairy vision, and the eye had rarefied and refined away the other senses. They have a look of enchantment.

Perhaps the Greek statues want gusto for the same reason. The sense of perfect form occupies the whole mind, and hardly suffers it to dwell on any other feeling. It seems enough for them *to be*, without acting or suffering. Their forms are ideal, spiritual. Their beauty is power. 'By their beauty they are raised above the frailties of pain or passion; by their beauty they are deified.'*

The infinite quantity of dramatic invention in Shakespear takes from his gusto. The power he delights to shew is not intense, but discursive. He never insists on any thing as much as he might, except a quibble. Milton has great gusto. He repeats his blow twice; grapples with and exhausts his subject. His imagination has a double relish of its objects, an inveterate attachment to the things he describes, and to the words describing them.

> Or where Chineses drive
> With sails and wind their *cany* waggons *light.*
> * * * * * * * * * * * * *
> Wild above rule or art, *enormous* bliss.*

There is a gusto in Pope's compliments, in Dryden's satires, and Prior's tales;* and among prose-writers, Boccacio and Rabelais had the most of it. We will only mention one other work which appears to us to be full of gusto, and that is the *Beggar's Opera*.* If it is not, we are altogether mistaken in our notions on this delicate subject.

6

ON THE ELGIN MARBLES

THE Elgin Marbles* are the best answer to Sir Joshua Reynolds's Discourses.* Considered in that point of view, they are invaluable: in any other, they are not worth so much as has been said. Nothing remains of them but their style; but that is every thing, for it is the style of nature. Art is the imitation of nature: and the Elgin Marbles are in their essence and their perfection casts from nature,—from fine nature, it is true, but from real, living, moving nature: from objects in nature, answering to an idea in the artist's mind, not from an idea in the artist's mind abstracted from all objects in nature. Already these Marbles have produced a revolution in our artists' minds, and Mr. West says, in his practice: The venerable President makes an express distinction in their favour between *dignified* art and *systematic* art. Mr. Chauntry* considers simplicity and grandeur so nearly united in them, that it is almost impossible to separate them. Sir Thomas Laurence* in returning from the Elgin Marbles to his own house, where he has casts of the finest antiques, was struck with the greater degree of ease and nature in the former. Mr. Flaxman* alone holds out for the *ideal*. The whole of his evidence on this subject is, indeed, quite ideal: Mr. Payne Knight's* evidence is *learned* evidence.—It is to be hoped, however, that these Marbles with the name of Phidias* thrown into the scale of common sense, may lift the Fine Arts out of that Limbo of vanity and affectation into which they were conjured in this country about fifty years ago, and in which they have lain sprawling and fluttering, gasping for breath, wasting away, vapid and abortive ever since,—the shadow of a shade. The benefit of high examples of Art, is to prevent the mischievous effect of bad ones. A true theory of Art does not advance the student one step in practice, one hair's-breadth nearer the goal of excellence: but it takes the fetters from off his feet, and loosens the bandages from his eyes. We lay somewhat more stress on the value of the Fine Arts than Mr. Payne Knight, who considers them (we know not for what reason) as an elegant antithesis to morality. We think they are nearly related to it. All morality seems to be little more than keeping people out of mischief, as we send children to school; and the Fine Arts are in that respect a school of morality. They bribe the senses into the service of the understanding: they kill Time, the great enemy of man; they employ the mind usefully—about nothing; and by preventing *ennui*, promote the chief ends of virtue. A taste for the Fine Arts also, in periods of luxury and refinement, not ill supplies the place of religious enthusiasm. It feeds our love and admiration of the grand, the good, the beautiful. What is the respect which is felt for the names of Raphael, of Michael Angelo, of Phidias, of Homer and of Milton, but a sort of hero-worship, only with this difference, that in the one case we pay an indistinct homage to the powers of the mind, whereas the worshippers of Theseus and Hercules deified the powers and virtues of the body?

With respect to the tendency of the works here collected to promote the Fine Arts in this country, though not so sanguine as some persons, or even as the Committee of the House of Commons, we are not without our hopes.—The only possible way to improve the taste for art in a country, is by a collection of standard works of established reputation, and which are capable by the sanctity of their name of overawing the petulance of public opinion. This result can never be produced by the encouragement given to the works of contemporary artists. The public ignorance will much sooner debauch them than they will reform the want of taste in the public. But where works of the highest character and excellence are brought forward in a manner due to their merits, and rendered accessible to the public, though they may do little for the national genius, it is hard if they do not add something to the public taste. In this way also they may react upon the production of original excellence. It was in this point of view that the Gallery of the Louvre* was of the greatest importance not only to France, but to Europe. It was a means to civilize the world. There Art lifted up her head and was seated on her throne, and said, All eyes shall see me, and all knees shall bow to me. Honour was done to her and all hers. There was her treasure, and there the inventory of all she had. There she had gathered together all her pomp, and there was her shrine, and there her votaries came and worshipped as in a temple. The crown she wore was brighter than that of kings. Where the triumphs of human liberty had been, there were the triumphs of human genius. For there, in the Louvre, were the precious moments of art;—there 'stood the statue that enchants the world;'* there was the *Apollo*, the *Laocoon*, the *Dying Gladiator*, the *Head of the Antinous*, *Diana* with her *Fawn*, the *Muses* and the *Graces* in a ring, and all the glories of the antique world:—

> There was old Proteus coming from the sea,
> And wreathed Triton blew his winding horn.*

There, too, were the two *St. Jeromes*, Correggio's and Domenichino's; there was Raphael's *Transfiguration*, the St. Mark of Tintoret, Paul Veronese's *Marriage of Cana*, the *Deluge* of Nicholas Poussin, and Titian's *St. Peter Martyr*;—all these and more than these, of which the world was not worthy. The worshippers of hereditary power and native imbecility wanted at first to destroy these monuments of human genius, which give the eternal lie to their creed; they did not dare to do that, they have dispersed them, and they have done well. They were an insult to the assembled majesty of hereditary power and native imbecility, both in the genius that had produced them, and that had acquired them; and *it was fit that they should be removed.* They were an obstacle in the way, in case the great Duke should have to teach the great nation another great moral lesson by the burning of Paris, which has been a favourite object with some persons since the year 1792, and with others later; and *it was fit that they should be removed.* The French themselves did not think proper to defend what they had dearly bought with their blood, shed for their country; and *it was fit that they should be removed.* Besides these reasons, there were no others for their removal. The reason assigned in the Duke of Wellington's letter, that the works of art should be sacred to conquerors, and an heir-loom of the soil that gives them birth, is quite apocryphal. Half of the works brought from Italy had been originally brought there from Greece. If works of art are to be a sort of fixtures in every country, why are the Elgin Marbles brought here, for our Artists to strut and fret* over this acquisition to our 'glorious country?' If the French were not to retain their collection of perfect works of art, why should we be allowed to make one of still higher pretensions under pretence of carrying off only fragments and rubbish? The Earl of Elgin brought away the Theseus and the Neptune as bits of architecture, as loose pieces of stone; but no sooner do they get into the possession of our glorious country, than they are discovered to be infinitely superior to the *Apollo*, the *Venus*, and *Laocoon*, and all the rest of that class, which are found out to be no better than *modern* *antiques.* All this may be true, but it is truth with a suspicious appearance. If works of art are contemplated with peculiar interest on the spot which gave them birth, surely Athens has charms for the eyes of learning and taste as well as Rome. If there is something classical in the very air of Venice, of Antwerp, and of Rotterdam, surely there is an air at Athens which is breathed no where else.

If this reasoning would apply to such works in their perfect state, it does so still more in their approaches to decay and ruin, for then the local interest belonging to them becomes the principal impression. Lord Elgin appears not to have had the slightest authority for bringing away these statues, except a *fermaun* or permission from the Turkish Government to bring away pieces of stone from the ruins of the Parthenon, which he paid 21,000 piastres to the Governor of Athens for permission to interpret as he pleased. That it was not meant to apply to the statues, and only to fragments of the building, is also evident from this, that Lord Elgin had originally, and at the time the *fermaun* was granted, no intention, as he himself says, of bringing away the statues. Lord Aberdeen approves of bringing them away, because otherwise the French might have got them. In what we have said, we do not blame Lord Elgin for what he has done; all our feelings run the contrary way. We only blame cant and hypocrisy: we only blame those who blame others, and yet would do the very same things themselves. There does not appear to be any evidence that these statues were done by Phidias. It seems extremely probable, however, that they were done by persons under his direction, and in a style that he approved. What that style is, and what the principles of art are which are to be derived from it, we shall briefly attempt to state in another article on this interesting subject.

* * *

Who to the life an exact piece would make,
Must not from others' work a copy take;
No, not from Rubens or Vandyke;
Much less content himself to make it like
The Ideas and the Images which lie
In his own fancy, or his memory.
No; he before his sight must place
The natural and living face;

The real object must command
Each judgment of his eye and motion of his hand.*

COWLEY.

According to the account of Pliny, it does not appear certain that Phidias ever worked in marble. He mentions indeed a marble Venus at Rome, conjectured to be his; and another at Athens, without the walls, done by his scholar Alcamenes, to which Phidias was said to have put the last hand. His chief works, according to this historian, were the Olympian Jupiter, and the Minerva in the Parthenon, both in ivory: he executed other known works in brass. The words of Pliny, in speaking of Phidias, are remarkable:—'That the name of Phidias is illustrious among all the nations that have heard of the fame of the Olympian Jupiter, no one doubts; but in order that those may know that he is deservedly praised who have not even seen his works, we shall offer a few arguments, and those of his genius only: nor to this purpose shall we insist on the beauty of the Olympian Jupiter, nor on the magnitude of the Minerva at Athens, though it is twenty-six cubits in height, (about 35 feet) and is made of ivory and gold: but we shall refer to the shield, on which the battle of the Amazons is carved on the outer side; on the inside of the same is the fight of the Gods and Giants, and on the sandals that between the Lapithæ and Centaurs; so well did every part of that work display the powers of the art. Again, the Sculptures on the pedestal he called the Birth of Pandora: there are to be seen in number thirty Gods, the figure of Victory being particularly admirable: the learned also admire the figures of the serpent and the brazen sphinx, writhing under the spear. These things are mentioned, in passing, of an Artist never enough to be commended, that it may be seen that he shewed the same magnificence even in small things.'—*Natural History*, Book xxxvi.

It appears, by the above description, that Phidias did not make choice of the colossal height of this statue with a view to make size a substitute for grandeur; but in order that he might be able, among other things, to finish, fill up, and enrich every part as much as possible. Size assists grandeur in genuine art only by enabling the Artist to give a more perfect development to the parts of which the whole is composed. A miniature is inferior to a full-sized picture, not because it does not give the large and general outline, but because it does not give the smaller varieties and finer elements of nature. As a proof of this, (if the thing were not self-evident) the copy of a good portrait will always make a highly finished miniature, but the copy of a good miniature, if enlarged to the size of life, will make but a very vapid portrait. Some of our own Artists, who are fond of painting large figures, either misunderstand or misapply this principle. They make the whole figure gigantic, not that they may have room for nature, but for the motion of their brush, regarding the quantity of canvas they have to cover as an excuse for the slovenly and hasty manner in which they cover it; and thus in fact leave their pictures nothing at last but monstrous miniatures.

We should hardly have ventured to mention this figure of five and thirty feet high, which might give an inordinate expansion to the ideas of our contemporaries, but that the labour and pains bestowed upon every part of it,—the thirty Gods carved on the pedestal, the battle of the Centaurs and Lapithæ on the sandals, would at once make their magnificent projects shrink into a nutshell, or bring them within the compass of reason.—We had another inducement for extracting Pliny's account of the Minerva of Phidias, which was, to check any inclination on the part of our students to infer from the Elgin Marbles, that the perfection of ancient Grecian art consisted in the imperfect state in which its earliest remains have come down to us; or to think that fragments are better than whole works, that the trunk is more valuable without the head, and that the grandeur of the antique consists in the ruin and decay into which it has fallen through time.

The true lesson to be learned by our Students and Professors from the Elgin Marbles, is the one which the ingenious and honest Cowley has expressed in the lines prefixed to this article—To recur to nature; or as another poet has expressed it,

> To learn
> Her manner, and with rapture taste her style.*

It is evident to any one who views this collection (and it is acknowledged by our Artists themselves, in despite of all the melancholy sophistry that they have been taught or have been teaching others for half a century), that the great excellence of the figures depends on their having been copied from nature, and not from the *ideal*. The communication of art with nature is here everywhere immediate, constant, palpable. The Artist gives himself no fastidious airs of superiority over nature. He has not arrived at that stage of his progress, described at much length in Sir Joshua Reynolds's Discourses, in which having served out his apprenticeship to nature, he can set up for himself in opposition to her. According to the Greek form of drawing up the indentures in this case, we apprehend they were to last for life.—At least we can compare these Marbles to nothing but human figures petrified; they are absolute fac-similes or casts from nature, as we have already said. The details are those of nature; the masses are those of nature; the forms are from nature; the action is from nature; the whole is from nature. Let any one for instance look at the leg of the River-God, which is bent under him,—let him observe the swell and undulation of the calf, the intertexture of the muscles, the distinction and the union of all the parts, and the effect of action everywhere impressed on the external form, as if the very marble were a flexible substance, and contained the various springs of life and motion within itself; and he will acknowledge that art and nature are here the same thing. It is the same in the back of the Theseus, in the thighs and knees, and in all that remains distinguishable of these two admirable figures. It is not the same in the cast (which may be seen at Lord Elgin's) of the famous Torso of Michael Angelo, the style of which that Artist appears to have imitated too well. There every muscle has apparently the greatest prominence and force given to it of which it is capable in itself, not of which it is capable in connection with others. This fragment is an accumulation of mighty parts, without that play and reaction of each part upon the others, without that 'alternate action and repose,'* which Sir Thomas Lawrence speaks of as the characteristics of the Theseus and the Neptune, and which are as inseparable from nature, as waves from the sea. The learned however here make a distinction, and suppose that the truth of nature is in the Elgin Marbles combined with ideal forms. If by ideal forms they mean fine natural forms, we have nothing to object; but if they mean that the sculptors of the Theseus and the Neptune got the forms out of their own heads, and then tacked the truth of nature to them, we can only say, 'Let them look again, let them look again.' We consider the Elgin Marbles as a demonstration of the impossibility of separating art from nature, without a loss at every remove. The utter absence of all setness of appearance shews that they were done as studies from actual models. The several parts of the human body may be given scientifically: their modifications can only be learnt by seeing them in action; and the truth of nature is incompatible with ideal form, if the latter is meant to exclude actually existing form. The mutual action of the parts cannot be known, where the parts themselves are not seen. That the forms of these statues are not common nature, such as we see it every day, we allow: that they were not common Greek nature, we see no convincing reason to suppose. That truth of nature and ideal, or fine form, are not always or generally united, we know; but how they can ever be united in art, without being first united in nature, is to us a mystery.—Further, we are ready (for the benefit of the Fine Arts in this kingdom) to produce two casts from actual nature, which if they do not furnish practical proof of all that we have here advanced, we are willing to forfeit all that we are worth—a theory.

Finally, if the Elgin Marbles are established as authority in subjects of art, we think the following principles, which have not hitherto been generally received or acted upon, in Great Britain, will result from them:—

1. That art is the imitation of nature.
2. That the highest art is the imitation of the finest nature; that is to say, of that which conveys the strongest sense of pleasure or power.
3. That the *ideal* is selecting a particular form which expresses most forcibly the idea of given character, as of beauty, strength, activity, voluptuousness, &c. and which preserves that character with the greatest consistency throughout.
4. That the *historical* is nature in action. With regard to the face, it is expression.
5. That grandeur consists in connecting a number of parts into a whole, and not in leaving out the parts.
6. That as grandeur is the principle of connection between different parts, beauty is the principle of affinity between different forms or their gradual conversion into one another. The one harmonises, the other aggrandises our impressions of things.
7. That grace is the harmonious in what relates to position or motion.
8. That grandeur of motion is unity of motion.
9. That strength is the giving the extremes, softness the uniting them.
10. That truth is to a certain degree beauty and grandeur; for all things are connected, and all things modify one another in nature.

Simplicity is also grand and beautiful for the same reason. Elegance is ease or lightness with precision.

We shall conclude with expressing a hope, that the Elgin Marbles may not be made another national stopgap between nature and art.[1]

---

[1] In answer to some objections to what was said in a former article on the comparative propriety of removing these statues, we beg leave to put one question. It appears from the Report of the Committee, that the French Government were, in the year 1811, anxious to purchase the collection of Lord Elgin, who was then a prisoner in France. We ask then, supposing this to have been done, what would have become of it? Would not the Theseus and the Neptune have been solemnly sent back, like malefactors, 'to the place from whence they came?'—Yes, to be sure.—The Rev. Dr. Philip Hunt, in the service of Lord Elgin, declares, in his evidence before the Committee, that no objection was made nor regret expressed by the inhabitants at the removal of the Marbles. In the notes to *Childe Harold's Pilgrimage*, we find the following extract of a letter from Dr. Clarke to Lord Byron:—'When the last of the Metopes was taken from the Parthenon, and in moving it, great part of the super structure, with one of the tryglyphs, was thrown down by the workmen whom Lord Elgin employed, the Disdar, who beheld the mischief done to the building, took his pipe from his mouth, dropped a tear, and in a supplicating tone of voice, said to Lusieri, *Telos!* I was present.'*—It appears that Dr. Philip Hunt was not.

7

MRS. SIDDONS

PLAYERS should be immortal, if their own wishes or ours could make them so; but they are not. They not only die like other people, but like other people they cease to be young, and are no longer themselves, even while living. Their health, strength, beauty, voice, fails them; nor can they, without these advantages, perform the same feats or command the same applause that they did when possessed of them. It is the common lot: players are only *not* exempt from it.—Mrs. SIDDONS retired once from the stage:* why should she return to it again? She cannot retire from it twice with dignity; and yet it is to be wished that she should do all things with dignity. Any loss of reputation to her is a loss to the world. Has she not had enough of glory? The homage she has received is greater than that which is paid to Queens. The enthusiasm she excited had something idolatrous about it;—she was regarded less with admiration than with wonder, as if a being of a superior order had dropped from another sphere to awe the world with the majesty of her appearance. She raised tragedy to the skies, or brought it down from thence. It was something above nature. We can conceive of nothing grander. She embodied to our imagination the fables of mythology, of the heroic and deified mortals of elder time. She was not less than a goddess, or than a prophetess inspired by the gods. Power was seated on her brow, passion emanated from her breast as from a shrine. She was tragedy personified. She was the stateliest ornament of the public mind. She was not only the idol of the people, she not only hushed the tumultuous shouts of the pit in breathless expectation, and quenched the blaze of surrounding beauty in silent tears, but to the retired and lonely student, through long years of solitude, her face has shone as if an eye had appeared from heaven, her name has been as if a voice had opened the chambers of the human heart, or as if a trumpet had awakened the sleeping and the dead. To have seen Mrs. SIDDONS was an event in every one's life; and does she think we have forgot her? Or would she remind us of her by shewing us what *she was not*? Or is she to continue on the stage to the very last, till all her grace and all her grandeur gone leave behind them only a melancholy blank? Or is she merely to be played off as 'the baby of a girl'* for a few nights?—'Rather than so,' come, genius of Gil Blas,* thou that did'st inspire him in an evil hour to perform his promise to the Archbishop of Grenada, 'and champion us to the utterance'* of what we think on this occasion.—It is said that the Princess CHARLOTTE* has expressed a desire to see Mrs. SIDDONS in her best parts, and this, it is said, is a thing highly desirable. We do not know that the Princess has expressed any such wish, and we shall suppose that she has not, because we do not think it altogether a reasonable one. If the Princess CHARLOTTE had expressed a wish to see Mr. GARRICK, this would have been a thing highly desirable, but it would have been impossible; or if she had desired to see Mrs. SIDDONS *in her best days*, it would have been equally so; and yet without this, we do not think it desirable that she should see her at all. It is said to be desirable that a Princess should have a taste for the Fine Arts, and that this is best promoted by seeing the highest models of perfection. But it is of the first importance for Princes to acquire a taste for what is reasonable: and the second thing which it is desirable they should acquire is a deference to public opinion: and we think neither of these objects likely to be promoted in the way proposed. If it was reasonable that Mrs. SIDDONS should retire from the stage three years ago, certainly those reasons have not diminished since, nor do we think Mrs. SIDDONS would consult what is due to her powers or her fame in commencing a new career. If it is only intended that she should act a few nights in the presence of a particular person, this might be done as well in private. To all other applications she should answer—'Leave me to my repose.'*—Mrs. SIDDONS always spoke as slow as she ought: she now speaks slower than she did. 'The line too labours, and the words move slow.'* The machinery of the voice seems too ponderous for the power that wields it. There is too long a pause between each sentence, and between each word in each sentence. There is too much preparation. The stage waits for her. In the sleeping scene, she produced a different impression from what we expected. It was more laboured and less natural. In coming on formerly, her eyes were open, but the sense was shut. She was like a person bewildered and unconscious of what she did. She moved her lips involuntarily—all her gestures were involuntary and mechanical. At present she acts the part more with a view to effect. She repeats the action when she says, 'I tell you he cannot rise from his grave,'* with both hands sawing the air in the style of parliamentary oratory, the worst of all others. There was none of this weight or energy in the way she did the scene the first time we saw her, twenty years ago. She glided on and off the stage almost like an apparition. In the close of the banquet scene, Mrs. SIDDONS condescended to an imitation which we were sorry for. She said, 'Go, go,'* in the hurried familiar tone of common life, in the manner of KEAN, and without any of that sustained and graceful spirit of conciliation towards her guests, which used to characterise her mode of doing it. Lastly, if Mrs. SIDDONS has to leave the stage again, Mr. HORACE TWISS* will write another farewell address for her: if she continues on it, we shall have to criticise her performances. We do not know which of these two evils will be the greatest.

Too much praise cannot be given to Mr. KEMBLE'S performance of *Macbeth*. He was 'himself again,'* and more than himself. His action was decided, his voice audible. His tones had occasionally indeed a learned quaintness, like the colouring of POUSSIN, but the effect of the whole was fine. His action in delivering the speech 'To-morrow and to-morrow'* was particularly striking and expressive, as if he had stumbled by an accident on fate, and was baffled by the impenetrable obscurity of the future.—In that prodigious prosing paper the *Times*, which seems to be written as well as printed by a steam-engine,* Mr. KEMBLE is compared to the ruin of a magnificent temple, in which the divinity still resides. This is not the case. The temple is unimpaired: but the divinity is sometimes from home.

8

MR. KEMBLE'S KING JOHN

WE wish we had never seen Mr. KEAN. He has destroyed the KEMBLE religion; and it is the religion in which we were brought up. Never again shall we behold Mr. KEMBLE with the same pleasure that we did, nor see Mr. KEAN with the same pleasure that we have seen Mr. KEMBLE formerly. We used to admire Mr. KEMBLE's figure and manner, and had no idea that there was any want of art or nature. We feel the force and nature of Mr. KEAN's acting, but then we feel the want of Mr. KEMBLE's person. Thus an old and delightful preju- dice is destroyed, and no new enthusiasm, no second idolatry comes to take its place. Thus, by degrees, knowledge robs us of pleasure, and the cold icy hand of experience freezes up the warm current of the imagination, and crusts it over with unfeeling criticism. The know- ledge we acquire of various kinds of excellence, as successive oppor- tunities present themselves, leads us to require a combination of them which we never find realised in any individual, and all the consolation for the disappointment of our fastidious expectations is in a sort of fond and doating retrospect of the past. It is possible indeed that the force of prejudice might often kindly step in to suspend the chill- ing effects of experience, and we might be able to see an old favourite, by a voluntary forgetfulness of other things, as we saw him twenty years ago; but his friends take care to prevent this, and by provoking invidious comparisons and crying up their idol as a model of abstract perfection, force us to be ill-natured in our own defence.—We went to see Mr. KEMBLE's *King John*, and he became the part so well, in costume, look, and gesture, that if left to ourselves, we could have gone to sleep over it, and dreamt that it was fine, and 'when we waked, have cried to dream again.'* But we were told that it was really fine, as fine as GARRICK, as fine as Mrs. SIDDONS, as fine as SHAKSPEARE; so we rubbed our eyes, and kept a sharp look out, but we saw nothing but a deliberate intention on the part of Mr. KEMBLE to act the part finely. And so he did in a certain sense, but not by any means as SHAKSPEARE wrote it, nor as it might be played. He did not harrow up the feelings, he did not electrify the sense: he did not enter into the nature of the part himself, nor consequently move others with terror or pity. The introduction to the scene with *Hubert* was certainly excellent: you saw instantly, and before a syllable was uttered, partly from the change of countenance and partly from the arrangement of the scene, the purpose which had entered his mind to murder the young Prince. But the remainder of this trying scene, though the execution was elaborate—painfully elaborate, and the outline well conceived, wanted the filling up, the true and master-touches, the deep piercing heart-felt tones of nature. It was done well and skilfully, *according to the book of arithmetic*; but no more. Mr. KEMBLE when he approaches *Hubert* to sound his disposition, puts on an insidious, insinuating, fawning aspect, and so he ought; but we think it should not be, though it was, that kind of wheedling smile as if he was going to persuade him that the business he wished him to undertake was a mere jest, and his natural repugnance to it an idle prejudice that might be carried off by a certain pleasant drollery of eye and manner. Mr. KEMBLE's look, to our apprehension, was exactly as if he had just caught the eye of some person of his acquaintance in the boxes, and was trying to suppress a rising smile at the metamorphosis he had undergone since dinner. Again, he changes his voice three several times in repeating the name of *Hubert*; and the changes might be fine, but they did not vibrate on our feelings, so we cannot tell. They appeared to us like a tragic *voluntary*. Through almost the whole scene, this celebrated actor did not seem to feel the part itself as it was set down for him, but to be considering how he ought to feel it, or how he should express by rule and method what he did not feel. He was sometimes slow, and sometimes hurried: sometimes familiar and sometimes solemn: but always with an evident design and determination to be so. The varying tide of passion did not appear to burst from the source of nature in his breast, but to be drawn from a theatrical leaden cistern, and then directed through certain conduit-pipes and artificial channels to fill the audience with well regulated and harmless sympathy. We are afraid, judging from the effects of this representation, that 'man delight not us, nor woman neither:'* for we did not like Miss O'NEILL's *Constance* better nor so well as Mr. KEMBLE's *King John*. This character, more than any other of SHAKSPEARE's females, treads perhaps upon the verge of extravagance; the impatience of grief combined with the violence of her temper, borders on insanity: her imagination grows light-headed. But still the boundary between poetry and phrensy is not passed: she is neither a virago nor mad. Miss O'NEILL* gave more of the vulgar than the poetical side of the character. She generally does so of late.—Mr. CHARLES KEMBLE* in the *Bastard* laid 'the bulk, the thews, the sinews' of *Falconbridge*: would that he had had 'the spirit'* too. There was one speech which he gave well,—'Could Sir Robert make this leg?'* And suiting the action to the word, as well he might, it had a great effect upon the house.

9

CORIOLANUS

CORIOLANUS has of late been repeatedly acted here. SHAKESPEAR has in this play shewn himself well versed in history and state-affairs. *Coriolanus* is a store-house of political common-places. Any one who studies it may save himself the trouble of reading BURKE's Reflections or PAINE's Rights of Man, or the Debates in both Houses of Parliament since the French Revolution or our own. The arguments for and against aristocracy or democracy, on the privileges of the few and the claims of the many, on liberty and slavery, power and the abuse of it, peace and war, are here very ably handled, with the spirit of a poet and the acuteness of a philosopher. SHAKESPEAR himself seems to have had a leaning to the arbitrary side of the question, perhaps from some feeling of contempt for his own origin; and to have spared no occasion of baiting the rabble. What he says of them is very true: what he says of their betters is also very true, though he dwells less upon it.—The cause of the people is indeed but ill calculated as a subject for poetry: it admits of rhetoric, which goes into argument and explanation, but it presents no immediate or distinct images to the mind, 'no jutting frieze, buttress, or coigne of vantage' for poetry 'to make its pendant bed and procreant cradle in.'* The language of poetry naturally falls in with the language of power. The imagination is an exaggerating and exclusive faculty: it takes from one thing to add to another; it accumulates circumstances together to give the greatest possible effect to a favourite object. The understanding is a dividing and measuring faculty: it judges of things, not according to their immediate impression on the mind, but according to their relations to one another. The one is a monopolizing faculty, which seeks the greatest quantity of present excitement by inequality and disproportion; the other is a distributive faculty, which seeks the greatest quantity of ultimate good, by justice and proportion. The one is an aristocratical, the other a republican faculty. The principle of poetry is a very anti-levelling principle. It aims at effect, it exists by contrast. It admits of no medium. It is every thing by excess. It rises above the ordinary standard of sufferings and crimes. It presents an imposing appearance. It shews its head turretted, crowned, and crested. Its front is gilt and blood-stained. Before it, 'it carries noise, and behind it, it leaves tears.'* It has its altars and its victims, sacrifices, human sacrifices. Kings, priests, nobles, are its train-bearers; tyrants and slaves its executioners— 'Carnage is its daughter!'* Poetry is right-royal. It puts the individual for the species, the one above the infinite many, might before right. A lion hunting a flock of sheep or a herd of wild asses is a more poetical object than they; and we even take part with the lordly beast, because our vanity, or some other feeling, makes us disposed to place ourselves in the situation of the strongest party. So we feel some concern for the poor citizens of Rome when they meet together to compare their wants and grievances, till *Coriolanus* comes in, and, with blows and big words, drives this set of 'poor rats,'* this rascal scum, to their homes and beggary before him. There is nothing heroical in a multitude of miserable rogues not wishing to be starved, or complaining that they are like to be so; but when a single man comes forward to brave their cries, and to make them submit to the last indignities, from mere pride and self-will, our admiration of his prowess is immediately converted into contempt for their pusillanimity. The insolence of power is stronger than the plea of necessity. The tame submission to usurped authority, or even the natural resistance to it, has nothing to excite or flatter the imagination; it is the assumption of a right to insult or oppress others that carries an imposing air of superiority with it. We had rather be the oppressor than the oppressed. The love of power in ourselves, and the admiration of it in others, are both natural to man: the one makes him a tyrant, the other a slave. Wrong, dressed out in pride, pomp, and circumstance, has more attraction than abstract right.—*Coriolanus* complains of the fickleness of the people: yet the instant he cannot gratify his pride and obstinacy at their expense, he turns his arms against his country. If his country was not worth defending, why did he build his pride on its defence? He is a conqueror and a hero; he conquers other countries, and makes this a plea for enslaving his own; and when he is prevented from doing so, he leagues with its enemies to destroy his country. He rates the people 'as if he were a God to punish, and not a man of their infirmity.'* He scoffs at one of their tribunes for maintaining their rights and franchises: 'Mark you his absolute *shall?*'* not marking his own absolute *will* to take everything from them; his impatience of the slightest opposition to his own pretensions being in proportion to their arrogance and absurdity. If the great and powerful had the beneficence and wisdom of Gods, then all this would have been well: if with greater knowledge of what is good for the people, they had as great a care for their interest as they have for their own, if they were seated above the world, sympathising with the welfare, but not feeling the passions of men, receiving neither good nor hurt from them, but bestowing their benefits as free gifts on them, they might then rule over them like another Providence. But this is not the case. *Coriolanus* is unwilling that the Senate should shew their 'cares' for the people lest their 'cares' should be construed into 'fears,'* to the subversion of all due authority; and he is sooner disappointed in his schemes to deprive the people not only of the cares of the State, but of all power to redress themselves, than *Volumnia* is made madly to exclaim,

> Now the red pestilence strike all trades in Rome,
> And occupations perish.*

Mrs. HUNN,* we dare say, was of the same opinion the other day when she read the account of the Spa-fields meeting.* This is but natural: it is but natural for a mother to have more regard for her son than for a whole city: but then the city should be left to take some care of itself. The care of the state cannot, we here see, be safely entrusted to maternal affection, or to the domestic charities of high life. The great have private feelings of their own, to which the interests of humanity and justice must courtesy. Their interests are so far from being the same as those of the community, that they are in direct and necessary opposition to them; their power is at the expense of our weakness; their riches, of our poverty; their pride, of our degradation; their splendour, of our wretchedness; their tyranny, of our servitude. If they had the superior intelligence ascribed to them (which they have not) it would only render them so much more formidable; and from Gods would convert them into devils. The whole dramatic moral of *Coriolanus* is, that those who have little shall have less,* and that those who have much shall take all that others have left. The people are poor, therefore they ought to be starved. They are slaves, therefore they ought to be beaten. They work hard, therefore they ought to be treated like beasts of burden. They are ignorant, therefore they ought not to be allowed to feel that they want food, or clothing, or rest, that they are enslaved, oppressed, and miserable. This is the logic of the imagination and the passions; which seek to aggrandise what excites admiration and to heap contempt on misery, to raise power into tyranny, and to make tyranny absolute; to thrust down that which is low still lower, and to make wretches desperate: to exalt magistrates into kings, kings into gods, to degrade subjects to the rank of slaves, and slaves to the condition of brutes. The history of mankind is a romance, a mask, a tragedy constructed upon the principles of *poetical justice*;* it is a noble or royal hunt, in which what is sport to the few, is death to the many,* and in which the spectators halloo and encourage the strong to set upon the weak, and cry havoc in the chase, though they do not share in the spoil. We may depend upon it that what men delight to read in books, they will put in practice in reality.

Mr. KEMBLE in the part of *Coriolanus* was as great as ever. Miss O'NEILL as *Volumnia* was not so great as Mrs. SIDDONS. There is a *fleshiness*, if we may so say, about her whole manner, voice, and person, which does not suit the character of the Roman Matron. One of the most amusing things in the representation of this play is the contrast between KEMBLE and little SIMMONS.* The former seems as if he would gibbet the latter on his nose, he looks so lofty. The fidgetting, uneasy, insignificant gestures of SIMMONS are perhaps a little caricatured; and KEMBLE's supercilious airs and *nonchalance* remind one of the unaccountable abstracted air, the contracted eyebrows and suspended chin of a man who is just going to sneeze.

There have been two new farces this week: one at each house. One was saved and one was damned. One was justly damned, and the other unjustly saved. *Nota Bene*, or *the two Dr. Fungus's*, shot up and disappeared in one night, notwithstanding the inimitable acting and well oiled humour of OXBERRY in one scene, where he makes bumpkin forward love to Mrs. ORGER in a style equal to LISTON. *Love and Toothache*, though there is neither Love nor Toothache in it, is as disagreeable as the one and as foolish as the other. One farce consists of a succession of low incidents without a plot, and the other is one tedious and improbable incident without a plot. The changing of the two signs, or Nota Benes of the two Fungus's, barber and doctor, in the first, is better than any thing in the last. The only difference is, that at the one house they contrive to have their pieces cast, and get them condemned at the other. Yet this is a saying without any meaning; for in the present case they were both got up as well as they could be.—We almost despair of ever seeing another good farce. *Mr. H*—,* thou wert damned. Bright shone the morning on the play-bills that announced thy appearance, and the streets were filled with the buzz of persons asking one another if they would go to see *Mr. H*—, and answering that they would certainly; but before night the gaiety, not of the author, but of his friends and the town, was eclipsed, for thou wert damned! Hadst thou been anonymous, thou mightst have been immortal! But thou didst come to an untimely end, for thy tricks and for want of a better name to pass them off (as the old joke of Divine Right passes current under the *alias* of Legitimacy)—and since that time nothing worth naming has been offered to the stage!

10

ON ACTORS AND ACTING

PLAYERS are 'the abstracts and brief chronicles of the time;'* the motley representatives of human nature. They are the only honest hypocrites. This life is a voluntary dream; a studied madness. The height of their ambition is to be *beside themselves*. To-day kings, to-morrow beggars, it is only when they are themselves that they are nothing. Made up of mimic laughter and tears, passing from the extremes of joy or woe at the prompter's call, they wear the livery of other men's fortunes; their very thoughts are not their own. They are as it were train-bearers in the pageant of life, and hold a glass up to humanity frailer than itself. We see ourselves at secondhand in them: they shew us all that we are, all that we wish to be, and all that we dread to be. The stage is an epitome, a bettered likeness of the world, with the dull part left out; and indeed with this omission it is nearly big enough to hold all the rest. What brings the resemblance nearer, is, that as they imitate us, we in our turn imitate them. How many fine gentlemen do we owe to the stage? How many romantic lovers are mere *Romeos* in masquerade? How many soft bosoms have heaved with *Juliet's* sighs? They teach us when to laugh and when to weep, when to love and when to hate, upon principle, and with a good grace! Wherever there is a playhouse, the world will go on not amiss. The stage not only refines the manners, but it is the best teacher of morals, for it is the truest and most intelligible picture of life. It stamps the image of virtue on the mind, by first softening the rude materials, of which it is composed by a sense of pleasure. It regulates the passions by giving a loose to the imagination. It points out the selfish and depraved to our detestation; the amiable and generous to our admiration; and if it clothes the more seductive vices with the borrowed graces of wit and fancy, even those graces operate as a diversion to the coarser poison of experience and bad example, and often prevent or carry off the infection by inoculating the mind with a certain taste and elegance. To shew how little we agree with the common declamations against the immoral tendency of the stage on this score, we would hazard a conjecture, that the acting of the *Beggar's Opera* a certain number of nights every year since it was brought out has done more towards putting down the practice of highway robbery than all the gibbets that ever were erected. A person after seeing the piece is too deeply imbued with a sense of humanity, is in too good humour with himself and the rest of the world, to set about cutting throats or rifling pockets. Whatever makes a jest of vice, leaves it too much a matter of indifference for any one in his senses to rush desperately on his ruin for its sake. We suspect that just the contrary effect must be produced by the representation of *George Barnwell*,* which is too much in the style of the Ordinary's Sermon,* to have any better success. The mind, in such cases, instead of being deterred by the alarming consequences held out to it, revolts against the denunci- ation of them as an insult offered to its free-will, and, in a spirit of defiance, returns a practical answer to them, by daring the worst that can happen. The most striking lesson ever read to levity and licen- tiousness is in the last scene of the *Inconstant*,* where young *Mirabel* is preserved by the fidelity of his mistress, *Orinda*, in the disguise of a page, from the hands of assassins, into whose power he has been allured by the temptations of vice and beauty. There never was a rake who did not become in imagination a reformed man, during the representation of the last trying scenes of this admirable comedy.

If the stage is useful as a school of instruction, it is no less so as a source of amusement. It is the source of the greatest enjoyment at the time, and a never-failing fund of agreeable reflection afterwards. The merits of a new play or of a new actor are always among the first topics of polite conversation. One way in which public exhibitions contribute to refine and humanise mankind is by supplying them with ideas and subjects of conversation and interest in common. The progress of civilization is in proportion to the number of common- places current in society. For instance, if we meet with a stranger at an inn or in a stage-coach, who knows nothing but his own affairs, his shop, his customers, his farm, his pigs, his poultry, we can carry on no conversation with him on these local and personal matters: the only way is to let him have all the talk to himself. But if he has fortu- nately ever seen Mr. Liston* act, this is an immediate topic of mutual conversation; and we agree together the rest of the evening in dis- cussing the merits of that inimitable actor, with the same satisfaction as in talking over the affairs of the most intimate friend.

If the stage thus introduces us familiarly to our contemporaries, it also brings us acquainted with former times. It is an obvious revival of

past ages, manners, opinions, dresses, persons, and actions,—whether
it carries us back to the wars of York and Lancaster, or half way back
to the heroic times of Greece and Rome, in some translation from the
French—or quite back to the age of Charles II. in the scenes of
Congreve and of Etherege,* (the gay Sir George!) —happy age, when
kings and nobles led purely ornamental lives, when the utmost stretch
of a morning's study went no farther than the choice of a sword-knot,
or the adjustment of a side-curl; when the soul spoke out in all the
thoughtless eloquence of dress; and beaux and belles, enamoured of
themselves in one another's follies, fluttered like gilded butterflies,
in giddy mazes through the walks of St. James's Park! It cannot be
denied that a good company of comedians, a Theatre-Royal judi-
ciously managed, is your true Herald's College; the only Antiquarian
Society that is worth a rush. It is for this reason that there is such an
air of romance about players, and that it is pleasanter to see them,
even in their own persons, than any of the three learned professions.
We feel more respect for John Kemble, in a plain coat, than for the
Lord Chancellor on the Woolsack. He is surrounded, to our eyes,
with a greater number of recollections: he is a more reverend piece of
formality; a more complicated tissue of costume. We do not know
whether to look upon this accomplished actor as *Pierre** or *King John*
or *Coriolanus* or *Cato* or *Leontes* or the *Stranger.** But we see in him
a stately hieroglyphic of humanity; a living monument of departed
greatness; a sombre comment on the rise and fall of kings. We look
after him till he is out of sight, as we listen to a story of one of Ossian's
heroes, to 'a tale of other times!'*

It has been considered as the misfortune of great talents for the
stage, that they leave no record behind them except that of vague
rumour, and that the genius of a great actor perishes with him,
'leaving the world no copy.'* This is a misfortune, or at least an
unpleasant circumstance, to actors; but it is, perhaps, an advantage to
the stage. It leaves an opening to originality. The stage is always
beginning anew—the candidates for theatrical reputation are always
setting out afresh, unincumbered by the affectation of the faults or
excellences of their predecessors. In this respect, we should imagine
that the average quantity of dramatic talent remains more nearly the
same than that of any other walk of art. In no other instance do the
complaints of the degeneracy of the moderns seem so unfounded as
in this; and Colley Cibber's account of the regular decline of the

stage,* from the time of Shakespear to that of Charles II., and from
the time of Charles II. to the beginning of George II. appears quite
ridiculous. The stage is a place where genius is sure to come upon its
legs in a generation or two at farthest. In the other arts (as painting
and poetry), it has been contended that what has been well done
already, by giving rise to endless vapid imitations, is an obstacle to
what might be done well hereafter: that the models or *chef-d'œuvres* of
art, where they are accumulated, choke up the path to excellence; and
that the works of genius, where they can be rendered permanent and
handed down from age to age, not only prevent, but render superfluous
future productions of the same kind. We have not, neither do we
want, two Shakespears, two Miltons, two Raphaels, any more than we
require two suns in the same sphere. Even Miss O'Neill stands a little
in the way of our recollections of Mrs. Siddons. But Mr. Kean is an
excellent substitute for the memory of Garrick, whom we never saw.
When an author dies, it is no matter, for his works remain. When
a great actor dies, there is a void produced in society, a gap which
requires to be filled up. Who does not go to see Kean? Who, if Garrick
were alive, would go to see him? At least, one or the other must have
quitted the stage!—We have seen what a ferment has been excited
among our living artists by the exhibition of the works of the old
Masters at the British Gallery.* What would the actors say to it, if by
any spell or power of necromancy all the celebrated actors for the
last hundred years could be made to appear again on the boards of
Covent-Garden and Drury-Lane for the last time in all their most
brilliant parts? What a rich treat for the town, what a feast for the
critics, to go and see Betterton and Booth and Wilks and Sandford
and Nokes and Leigh and Penkethman and Bullock and Estcourt
and Dogget and Mrs. Barry and Mrs. Montfort and Mrs. Oldfield and
Mrs. Bracegirdle and Mrs. Cibber and Cibber himself, the prince of
coxcombs, and Macklin and Quin and Peg Woffington and Mrs. Clive
and Mrs. Pritchard and Mrs. Abington and Weston and Shuter* and
Garrick, and all the rest of those, who 'gladdened life, and whose
deaths eclipsed the gaiety of nations!'* We should certainly be there.
We should buy a ticket for the season. We should enjoy our hundred
days* again. We should not miss a single night. We would not for
a great deal be absent from Betterton's *Hamlet* or his *Brutus*, or from
Booth's *Cato* (as it was first acted to the contending applause of
Whigs and Tories). We should be in the first row when Mrs. Barry

(who was kept by Lord Rochester, and with whom Otway was in love)
played *Monimia* or *Belvidera*;* and we suppose we should go to see
Mrs. Bracegirdle (with whom all the world was in love) in all her
parts. We should then know exactly whether Penkethman's manner
of picking a chicken, and Bullock's mode of devouring asparagus
answered to the ingenious account of them in the *Tatler*,* and
whether Dogget was equal to Dowton*—Whether Mrs. Montfort or
Mrs. Abington was the finest lady, whether Wilks* or Cibber was the
best *Sir Harry Wildair**—Whether Macklin was really 'the Jew that
Shakespear drew,'* and whether Garrick was really so great an actor
as the world have made him out! Many people have a strong desire
to pry into the secrets of futurity: for our own parts, we should be
satisfied if we had the power to recal the dead, and live the past over
again, as often as we pleased!* We have no curiosity about things or
persons that we never heard of. Mr. Coleridge professes in his Lay
Sermon* to have discovered a new faculty, by which he can divine the
future. This is lucky for himself and his friends, who seem to have lost
all recollection of the past.

Colley Cobber, in his *Apology*, gives the following lively description
of Mrs. Montfort, one of the actresses mentioned above, and whom
we should desire to have seen:—

'What found most employment for her whole various excellence
at once, was the part of *Melantha* in *Marriage a-la-Mode. Melantha* is
as finished an impertinent as ever fluttered in a drawing-room, and
seems to contain the most complete system of female foppery, that
could possibly be crowded into the tortured form of a fine lady.
Her language, dress, motion, manners, soul and body, are in a continual hurry to be something more than is necessary or commendable.
And though I doubt it will be a vain labour to offer you a just likeness
of Mrs. Montfort's action, yet the fantastick impression is still so
strong in my memory, that I cannot help saying something, though
fantastically, about it. The first ridiculous airs that break from her are
upon a gallant never seen before, who delivers her a letter from her
father, recommending him to her good graces, as an honourable lover.
Here, now, one would think she might naturally shew a little of the
sex's decent reserve, though never so slightly covered! No, Sir;
not a tittle of it: modesty is the virtue of a poor-soul'd country
gentlewoman; she is too much a court lady, to be under so vulgar
a confusion; she reads the letter, therefore, with a careless, dropping

lip, and an erected brow, humming it hastily over, as if she were impatient to outgo her father's commands, by making a complete conquest of him at once: and that the letter might not embarrass her attack, crack! she crumbles it at once into her palm, and pours upon him her whole artillery of airs, eyes, and motion; down goes her dainty, diving body to the ground, as if she were sinking under the conscious load of her own attractions; then launches into a flood of fine language and compliment, still playing her chest forward in fifty falls and risings, like a swan upon waving water; and to complete her impertinence, she is so rapidly fond of her own wit, that she will not give her lover leave to praise it: Silent assenting bows and vain endeavours to speak, are all the share of the conversation he is admitted to, which at last he is relieved from, by her engagement to half a score visits, which she *swims* from him to make, with a promise to return in a twinkling.' —*The Life of Mr. Colley Cibber*, p. 138.

The whole of Colley Cibber's work is very amusing to a dramatic amateur. It gives an interesting account of the progress of the stage, which in his time appears to have been in a state *militant*. Two actors, *Kynaston* and *Montfort*, were run through the body in disputes with gentlemen, with impunity; and the Master of the Revels arrested any of the two companies who was refractory to the Managers, at his pleasure. *Dogget* was brought up in this manner from Norwich, by two constables; but *Dogget* being a Whig, and a surly fellow, got a *Habeas Corpus*, and the Master of the Revels was driven from the field.

A London engagement is generally considered by actors as the *ne plus ultra* of their ambition, as 'a consummation devoutly to be wished,'* as the great prize in the lottery of their professional life. But this appears to us, who are not in the secret, to be rather the prose termination of their adventurous career: it is the provincial commencement that is the poetical and truly enviable part of it. After that, they have comparatively little to hope or fear. 'The wine of life is drunk, and but the lees remain.'* In London, they become gentlemen, and the King's servants: but it is the romantic mixture of the hero and the vagabond that constitutes the essence of the player's life. It is the transition from their real to their assumed characters, from the contempt of the world to the applause of the multitude, that gives its zest to the latter, and raises them as much above common humanity at night, as in the day-time they are depressed below it. 'Hurried from fierce extremes, by contrast made more fierce'*—it is rags and a flock-bed which give their splendour to a plume of feathers and a throne. We should suppose, that if the most admired actor on the London stage could be brought to confession on this point, he would acknowledge that all the applause he had received from 'brilliant and overflowing audiences' was nothing to the light-headed intoxication of unlooked-for success in a barn. In town, actors are criticised: in country-places, they are wondered at, or hooted at: it is of little consequence which, so that the interval is not too long between. For ourselves, we own that the description of the strolling player in *Gil Blas*,* soaking his dry crusts in the well by the road-side, presents to us a perfect picture of human felicity.

11

MACBETH

The poet's eye in a fine frenzy rolling
Doth glance from heaven to earth, from earth to heaven;
And as imagination bodies forth
The forms of things unknown, the poet's pen
Turns them to shape, and gives to airy nothing
A local habitation and a name.*

MACBETH and *Lear*, *Othello* and *Hamlet*, are usually reckoned Shakespear's four principal tragedies. *Lear* stands first for the profound intensity of the passion; *Macbeth* for the wildness of the imagination and the rapidity of the action;* *Othello* for the progressive interest and powerful alternations of feeling; *Hamlet* for the refined development of thought and sentiment. If the force of genius shewn in each of these works is astonishing, their variety is not less so. They are like different creations of the same mind, not one of which has the slightest reference to the rest. This distinctness and originality is indeed the necessary consequence of truth and nature. Shakespear's genius alone appeared to possess the resources of nature. He is 'your only *tragedy-maker*.'* His plays have the force of things upon the mind. What he represents is brought home to the bosom as a part of our experience, implanted in the memory as if we had known the places, persons, and things of which he treats. MACBETH is like a record of a preternatural and tragical event. It has the rugged severity of an old chronicle with all that the imagination of the poet can engraft upon traditional belief. The castle of Macbeth, round which 'the air smells wooingly,'* and where 'the temple-haunting martlet builds,'* has a real subsistence in the mind; the Weïrd Sisters meet us in person on 'the blasted heath;'* the 'air-drawn dagger'* moves slowly before our eyes; the 'gracious Duncan,'* the 'blood-boultered Banquo'* stand before us; all that passed through the mind of Macbeth passes, without the loss of a tittle, through our's. All that could actually take place, and all that is only possible to be conceived, what was said and what was done, the workings of passion, the spells of magic, are brought before us with the same absolute truth and vividness.—Shakespear

excelled in the openings of his plays: that of Macbeth is the most
striking of any. The wildness of the scenery, the sudden shifting of
the situations and characters, the bustle, the expectations excited,
are equally extraordinary. From the first entrance of the Witches and
the description of them when they meet Macbeth,

> ————What are these
> So wither'd and so wild in their attire,
> That look not like the inhabitants of th' earth
> And yet are on't?*

the mind is prepared for all that follows.

This tragedy is alike distinguished for the lofty imagination it displays, and for the tumultuous vehemence of the action; and the one is
made the moving principle of the other. The overwhelming pressure
of preternatural agency urges on the tide of human passion with
redoubled force. Macbeth himself appears driven along by the violence of his fate like a vessel drifting before a storm; he reels to and
fro like a drunken man; he staggers under the weight of his own purposes and the suggestions of others; he stands at bay with his situation; and from the superstitious awe and breathless suspense into
which the communications of the Weïrd Sisters throw him, is hurried
on with daring impatience to verify their predictions, and with impious
and bloody hand to tear aside the veil which hides the uncertainty of
the future. He is not equal to the struggle with fate and conscience.
He now 'bends up each corporal instrument to the terrible feat;'* at
other times his heart misgives him, and he is cowed and abashed by
his success. 'The deed, no less than the attempt, confounds him.'*
His mind is assailed by the stings of remorse, and full of 'preternatural solicitings.'* His speeches and soliloquies are dark riddles on
human life, baffling solution, and entangling him in their labyrinths.
In thought he is absent and perplexed, sudden and desperate in act,
from a distrust of his own resolution. His energy springs from the
anxiety and agitation of his mind. His blindly rushing forward on
the objects of his ambition and revenge, or his recoiling from them,
equally betrays the harassed state of his feelings.—This part of his
character is admirably set off by being brought in connection with
that of Lady Macbeth, whose obdurate strength of will and masculine firmness give her the ascendancy over her husband's faultering
virtue. She at once seizes on the opportunity that offers for the

accomplishment of all their wished-for greatness, and never flinches from her object till all is over. The magnitude of her resolution almost covers the magnitude of her guilt. She is a great bad woman, whom we hate, but whom we fear more than we hate. She does not excite our loathing and abhorrence like Regan and Gonerill. She is only wicked to gain a great end; and is perhaps more distinguished by her commanding presence of mind and inexorable self-will, which do not suffer her to be diverted from a bad purpose, when once formed, by weak and womanly regrets, than by the hardness of her heart or want of natural affections. The impression which her lofty determination of character makes on the mind of Macbeth is well described where he exclaims,

> ———Bring forth men children only;
> For thy undaunted mettle should compose
> Nothing but males!*

Nor do the pains she is at to 'screw his courage to the sticking-place',* the reproach to him, not to be 'lost so poorly in himself,'* the assurance that 'a little water clears them of this deed,'* shew any thing but her greater consistency in depravity. Her strong-nerved ambition furnishes ribs of steel to 'the sides of his intent;'* and she is herself wound up to the execution of her baneful project with the same unshrinking fortitude in crime, that in other circumstances she would probably have shewn patience in suffering. The deliberate sacrifice of all other considerations to the gaining 'for their future days and nights sole sovereign sway and masterdom,'* by the murder of Duncan, is gorgeously expressed in her invocation on hearing of 'his fatal entrance under her battlements:'*——

> ———Come all you spirits
> That tend on mortal thoughts, unsex me here:
> And fill me, from the crown to th' toe, top-full
> Of direst cruelty; make thick my blood,
> Stop up the access and passage to remorse,
> That no compunctious visitings of nature
> Shake my fell purpose, nor keep peace between
> The effect and it. Come to my woman's breasts,
> And take my milk for gall, you murthering ministers,
> Wherever in your sightless substances
> You wait on nature's mischief. Come, thick night!

> And pall thee in the dunnest smoke of hell,
> That my keen knife see not the wound it makes,
> Nor heav'n peep through the blanket of the dark,
> To cry, hold, hold!—*

When she first hears that 'Duncan comes there to sleep' she is so overcome by the news, which is beyond her utmost expectations, that she answers the messenger, 'Thou'rt mad to say it:'* and on receiving her husband's account of the predictions of the Witches, conscious of his instability of purpose, and that her presence is necessary to goad him on to the consummation of his promised greatness, she exclaims—

> ————Hie thee hither,
> That I may pour my spirits in thine ear,
> And chastise with the valour of my tongue
> All that impedes thee from the golden round,
> Which fate and metaphysical aid doth seem
> To have thee crowned withal.*

This swelling exultation and keen spirit of triumph, this uncontroulable eagerness of anticipation, which seems to dilate her form and take possession of all her faculties, this solid, substantial flesh and blood display of passion, exhibit a striking contrast to the cold, abstracted, gratuitous, servile malignity of the Witches, who are equally instrumental in urging Macbeth to his fate for the mere love of mischief, and from a disinterested delight in deformity and cruelty. They are hags of mischief, obscene panders to iniquity, malicious from their impotence of enjoyment, enamoured of destruction, because they are themselves unreal, abortive, half-existences, and who become sublime from their exemption from all human sympathies and contempt for all human affairs, as Lady Macbeth does by the force of passion! Her fault seems to have been an excess of that strong principle of self-interest and family aggrandisement, not amenable to the common feelings of compassion and justice, which is so marked a feature in barbarous nations and times. A passing reflection of this kind, on the resemblance of the sleeping king to her father, alone prevents her from slaying Duncan with her own hand.

In speaking of the character of Lady Macbeth, we ought not to pass over Mrs. Siddons's manner of acting that part. We can conceive of nothing grander. It was something above nature. It seemed almost as if a being of a superior order had dropped from a higher sphere to awe the world with the majesty of her appearance. Power was seated on her brow, passion emanated from her breast as from a shrine; she was tragedy personified. In coming on in the sleeping-scene, her eyes were open, but their sense was shut. She was like a person bewildered and unconscious of what she did. Her lips moved involuntarily—all her gestures were involuntary and mechanical. She glided on and off the stage like an apparition. To have seen her in that character was an event in every one's life, not to be forgotten.

The dramatic beauty of the character of Duncan, which excites the respect and pity even of his murderers, has been often pointed out. It forms a picture of itself. An instance of the author's power of giving a striking effect to a common reflection, by the manner of introducing it, occurs in a speech of Duncan, complaining of his having been deceived in his opinion of the Thane of Cawdor, at the very moment that he is expressing the most unbounded confidence in the loyalty and services of Macbeth.

> There is no art
> To find the mind's construction in the face:
> He was a gentleman, on whom I built
> An absolute trust.
> O worthiest cousin, (*addressing himself to Macbeth*)
> The sin of my ingratitude e'en now
> Was great upon me,* &c.

Another passage to shew that Shakespear lost sight of nothing that could in any way give relief or heightening to his subject, is the conversation which takes place between Banquo and Fleance immediately before the murder-scene of Duncan.

Banquo. How goes the night, boy?

Fleance. The moon is down: I have not heard the clock

Banquo. And she goes down at twelve.

Fleance. I take't, 'tis later, Sir.

Banquo. Hold, take my sword. There's husbandry in heav'n,
Their candles are all out.—
A heavy summons lies like lead upon me,
And yet I would not sleep: Merciful Powers,
Restrain in me the cursed thoughts that nature
Gives way to in repose.*

In like manner, a fine idea is given of the gloomy coming on of evening, just as Banquo is going to be assassinated.

> Light thickens and the crow
> Makes wing to the rooky wood.
> * * * * * * * * * * *
> Now spurs the lated traveller apace
> To gain the timely inn.*

MACBETH (generally speaking) is done upon a stronger and more systematic principle of contrast than any other of Shakespear's plays. It moves upon the verge of an abyss, and is a constant struggle between life and death. The action is desperate and the reaction is dreadful. It is a huddling together of fierce extremes, a war of opposite natures which of them shall destroy the other. There is nothing but what has a violent end or violent beginnings. The lights and shades are laid on with a determined hand; the transitions from triumph to despair, from the height of terror to the repose of death, are sudden and startling; every passion brings in its fellow-contrary, and the thoughts pitch and jostle against each other as in the dark. The whole play is an unruly chaos of strange and forbidden things, where the ground rocks under our feet. Shakespear's genius here took its full swing, and trod upon the farthest bounds of nature and passion. This circumstance will account for the abruptness and violent antitheses of the style, the throes and labour which run through the expression, and from defects will turn them into beauties. 'So fair and foul a day I have not seen,'* &c. 'Such welcome and unwelcome news together.'* 'Men's lives are like the flowers in their caps, dying or ere they sicken.'* 'Look like the innocent flower, but be the serpent under it.'* The scene before the castle-gate follows the appearance of the Witches on the heath, and is followed by a midnight murder. Duncan is cut off betimes by treason leagued with witchcraft, and Macduff is ripped untimely from his mother's womb to avenge his death. Macbeth, after the death of Banquo, wishes for his presence in extravagant terms, 'To him and all we thirst,' and when his ghost appears, cries out, 'Avaunt and quit my sight,'* and being gone, he is 'himself again.'* Macbeth resolves to get rid of Macduff, that 'he may sleep in spite of thunder;'* and cheers his wife on the doubtful intelligence of Banquo's taking-off with the encouragement—'Then be thou jocund: ere the bat has flown his cloistered flight; ere to black

Hecate's summons the shard-born beetle has rung night's yawning peal, there shall be done—a deed of dreadful note.'* In Lady Macbeth's speech 'Had he not resembled my father as he slept, I had done 't,'* there is murder and filial piety together, and in urging him to fulfil his vengeance against the defenceless king, her thoughts spare the blood neither of infants nor old age. The description of the Witches is full of the same contradictory principle; they 'rejoice when good kings bleed,'* they are neither of the earth nor the air, but both; 'they should be women, but their beards forbid it;'* they take all the pains possible to lead Macbeth on to the height of his ambition, only to betray him in deeper consequence,* and after shewing him all the pomp of their art, discover their malignant delight in his disappointed hopes, by that bitter taunt, 'Why stands Macbeth thus amazedly?'* We might multiply such instances every where.

The leading features in the character of Macbeth are striking enough, and they form what may be thought at first only a bold, rude, Gothic outline. By comparing it with other characters of the same author we shall perceive the absolute truth and identity which is observed in the midst of the giddy whirl and rapid career of events. Macbeth in Shakespear no more loses his identity of character in the fluctuations of fortune or the storm of passion, than Macbeth in himself would have lost the identity of his person. Thus he is as distinct a being from Richard III. as it is possible to imagine, though these two characters in common hands, and indeed in the hands of any other poet, would have been a repetition of the same general idea, more or less exaggerated. For both are tyrants, usurpers, murderers, both aspiring and ambitious, both courageous, cruel, treacherous. But Richard is cruel from nature and constitution. Macbeth becomes so from accidental circumstances. Richard is from his birth deformed in body and mind, and naturally incapable of good. Macbeth is full of 'the milk of human kindness,'* is frank, sociable, generous. He is tempted to the commission of guilt by golden opportunities, by the instigations of his wife, and by prophetic warnings. Fate and metaphysical aid conspire against his virtue and his loyalty. Richard on the contrary needs no prompter, but wades through a series of crimes to the height of his ambition from the ungovernable violence of his temper and a reckless love of mischief. He is never gay but in the prospect or in the success of his villainies: Macbeth is full of horror at the thoughts of the murder of Duncan, which he is with difficulty

prevailed on to commit, and of remorse after its perpetration. Richard
has no mixture of common humanity in his composition, no regard to
kindred or posterity, he owns no fellowship with others, he is 'himself
alone.'* Macbeth is not destitute of feelings of sympathy, is accessible
to pity, is even made in some measure the dupe of his uxoriousness,
ranks the loss of friends, of the cordial love of his followers, and of his
good name, among the causes which have made him weary of life, and
regrets that he has ever seized the crown by unjust means, since he
cannot transmit it to his posterity—

> For Banquo's issue have I 'fil'd my mind—
> For them the gracious Duncan have I murther'd,
> To make them kings, the seed of Banquo kings.*

In the agitation of his thoughts, he envies those whom he has sent
to peace. 'Duncan is in his grave; after life's fitful fever he sleeps
well.'*—It is true, he becomes more callous as he plunges deeper
in guilt, 'direness is thus rendered familiar to his slaughterous
thoughts,'* and he in the end anticipates his wife in the boldness and
bloodiness of his enterprises, while she for want of the same stimulus
of action, is 'troubled with thick-coming fancies that rob her of her
rest,'* goes mad and dies. Macbeth endeavours to escape from reflection on his crimes by repelling their consequences, and banishes
remorse for the past by the meditation of future mischief. This is
not the principle of Richard's cruelty, which resembles the wanton
malice of a fiend as much as the frailty of human passion. Macbeth is
goaded on to acts of violence and retaliation by necessity; to Richard,
blood is a pastime.—There are other decisive differences inherent in
the two characters. Richard may be regarded as a man of the world,
a plotting, hardened knave, wholly regardless of every thing but
his own ends, and the means to secure them—Not so Macbeth. The
superstitions of the age, the rude state of society, the local scenery and
customs, all give a wildness and imaginary grandeur to his character.
From the strangeness of the events that surround him, he is full of
amazement and fear; and stands in doubt between the world of reality
and the world of fancy. He sees sights not shewn to mortal eye, and
hears unearthly music. All is tumult and disorder within and without
his mind; his purposes recoil upon himself, are broken and disjointed;
he is the double thrall of his passions and his evil destiny. Richard is
not a character either of imagination or pathos, but of pure self-will.

There is no conflict of opposite feelings in his breast. The apparitions which he sees only haunt him in his sleep; nor does he live like Macbeth in a waking dream. Macbeth has considerable energy and manliness of character; but then he is 'subject to all the skyey influences.'* He is sure of nothing but the present moment. Richard in the busy turbulence of his projects never loses his self-possession, and makes use of every circumstance that happens as an instrument of his long-reaching designs. In his last extremity we can only regard him as a wild beast taken in the toils: we never entirely lose our concern for Macbeth; and he calls back all our sympathy by that fine close of thoughtful melancholy—

> My way of life is fallen into the sear,
> The yellow leaf; and that which should accompany old age,
> As honour, troops of friends, I must not look to have;
> But in their stead, curses not loud but deep,
> Mouth-honour, breath, which the poor heart
> Would fain deny and dare not.*

We can conceive a common actor to play Richard tolerably well; we can conceive no one to play Macbeth properly, or to look like a man that had encountered the Weïrd Sisters. All the actors that we have ever seen, appear as if they had encountered them on the boards of Covent-garden or Drury-lane, but not on the heath at Fores, and as if they did not believe what they had seen. The Witches of MACBETH indeed are ridiculous on the modern stage, and we doubt if the furies of Æschylus would be more respected. The progress of manners and knowledge has an influence on the stage, and will in time perhaps destroy both tragedy and comedy. Filch's picking pockets, in the *Beggars' Opera*, is not so good a jest as it used to be: by the force of the police and of philosophy, Lillo's murders* and the ghosts in Shakespear will become obsolete. At last there will be nothing left, good nor bad, to be desired or dreaded, on the theatre or in real life. A question has been started with respect to the originality of Shakespear's Witches, which has been well answered by Mr. Lamb in his notes to the 'Specimens of Early Dramatic Poetry.'—

'Though some resemblance may be traced between the charms in MACBETH, and the incantations in this play, (the Witch of Middleton*) which is supposed to have preceded it, this coincidence will not detract much from the originality of Shakespear. His Witches are distinguished from the Witches of Middleton by essential differences. These are creatures to whom man or woman plotting some dire mischief might resort for occasional consultation. Those originate deeds of blood, and begin bad impulses to men. From the moment that their eyes first meet with Macbeth's, he is spell-bound. That meeting sways his destiny. He can never break the fascination. These Witches can hurt the body; those have power over the soul.—Hecate in Middleton has a son, a low buffoon: the hags of Shakespear have neither child of their own, nor seem to be descended from any parent. They are foul anomalies, of whom we know not whence they are sprung, nor whether they have beginning or ending. As they are without human passions, so they seem to be without human relations. They come with thunder and lightning, and vanish to airy music. This is all we know of them.—Except Hecate, they have no names, which heightens their mysteriousness. The names, and some of the properties which Middleton has given to his hags, excite smiles. The Weïrd Sisters are serious things. Their presence cannot co-exist with mirth. But, in a lesser degree, the Witches of Middleton are fine creations. Their power too is, in some measure, over the mind. They raise jars, jealousies, strifes, *like a thick scurf o'er life.'*

THIS is that Hamlet the Dane, whom we read of in our youth, and whom we seem almost to remember in our after-years; he who made that famous soliloquy on life, who gave the advice to the players, who thought 'this goodly frame, the earth, a steril promontory, and this brave o'er-hanging firmament, the air, this majestical roof fretted with golden fire, a foul and pestilent congregation of vapours;'* whom 'man delighted not, nor woman neither;'* he who talked with the grave-diggers, and moralised on Yorick's skull; the school-fellow of Rosencraus and Guildenstern at Wittenberg; the friend of Horatio; the lover of Ophelia; he that was mad and sent to England; the slow avenger of his father's death; who lived at the court of Horwendillus five hundred years before we were born, but all whose thoughts we seem to know as well as we do our own, because we have read them in Shakespear.

Hamlet is a name: his speeches and sayings but the idle coinage of the poet's brain. What then, are they not real? They are as real as our own thoughts. Their reality is in the reader's mind. It is *we* who are Hamlet. This play has a prophetic truth, which is above that of history. Whoever has become thoughtful and melancholy through his own mishaps or those of others; whoever has borne about with him the clouded brow of reflection, and thought himself 'too much i' th' sun;'* whoever has seen the golden lamp of day dimmed by envious mists rising in his own breast, and could find in the world before him only a dull blank with nothing left remarkable in it; whoever has known 'the pangs of despised love, the insolence of office, or the spurns which patient merit of the unworthy takes;'* he who has felt his mind sink within him, and sadness cling to his heart like a malady, who has had his hopes blighted and his youth staggered by the appar-itions of strange things; who cannot be well at ease, while he sees evil hovering near him like a spectre; whose powers of action have been eaten up by thought, he to whom the universe seems infinite, and himself nothing; whose bitterness of soul makes him careless of con-sequences, and who goes to a play as his best resource to shove off, to a second remove, the evils of life by a mock-representation of them—this is the true Hamlet.

We have been so used to this tragedy that we hardly know how to criticise it any more than we should know how to describe our own faces. But we must make such observations as we can. It is the one of Shakespear's plays that we think of oftenest, because it abounds most in striking reflections on human life, and because the distresses of Hamlet are transferred, by the turn of his mind, to the general account of humanity. Whatever happens to him, we apply to ourselves, because he applies it so himself as a means of general reasoning. He is a great moraliser; and what makes him worth attending to is, that he moralises on his own feelings and experience. He is not a common-place pedant. If *Lear* shews the greatest depth of passion, HAMLET is the most remarkable for the ingenuity, originality, and unstudied developement of character. Shakespear had more magnanimity than any other poet, and he has shewn more of it in this play than in any other. There is no attempt to force an interest: every thing is left for time and circumstances to unfold. The attention is excited without effort, the incidents succeed each other as matters of course, the characters think and speak and act just as they might do, if left entirely to themselves. There is no set purpose, no straining at a point. The observations are suggested by the passing scene—the gusts of passion come and go like sounds of music borne on the wind. The whole play is an exact transcript of what might be supposed to have taken place at the court of Denmark, at the remote period of time fixed upon, before the modern refinements in morals and manners were heard of. It would have been interesting enough to have been admitted as a by-stander in such a scene, at such a time, to have heard and seen something of what was going on. But here we are more than spectators. We have not only 'the outward pageants and the signs of grief;'* but 'we have that within which passes shew.'* We read the thoughts of the heart, we catch the passions living as they rise. Other dramatic writers give us very fine versions and paraphrases of nature: but Shakespear, together with his own comments, gives us the original text, that we may judge for ourselves. This is a very great advantage.

The character of Hamlet* is itself a pure effusion of genius. It is not a character marked by strength of will or even of passion, but by refinement of thought and sentiment. Hamlet is as little of the hero as a man can well be: but he is a young and princely novice, full of high enthusiasm and quick sensibility—the sport of circumstances, questioning with fortune and refining on his own feelings, and forced from the natural bias of his disposition by the strangeness of his situation. He seems incapable of deliberate action, and is only hurried into extremities on the spur of the occasion, when he has no time to reflect, as in the scene where he kills Polonius, and again, where he alters the letters which Rosencraus and Guildenstern are taking with them to England, purporting his death. At other times, when he is most bound to act, he remains puzzled, undecided, and sceptical, dallies with his purposes, till the occasion is lost, and always finds some pretence to relapse into indolence and thoughtfulness again. For this reason he refuses to kill the King when he is at his prayers, and by a refinement in malice, which is in truth only an excuse for his own want of resolution, defers his revenge to some more fatal opportunity, when he shall be engaged in some act 'that has no relish of salvation in it.'*

> He kneels and prays,
> And now I'll do't, and so he goes to heaven,
> And so am I reveng'd: *that would be scann'd.*
> He kill'd my father, and for that,
> I, his sole son, send him to heaven.
> Why this is reward, not revenge.
> Up sword and know thou a more horrid time,
> When he is drunk, asleep, or in a rage.*

He is the prince of philosophical speculators, and because he cannot have his revenge perfect, according to the most refined idea his wish can form, he misses it altogether. So he scruples to trust the suggestions of the Ghost, contrives the scene of the play to have surer proof of his uncle's guilt, and then rests satisfied with this confirmation of his suspicions, and the success of his experiment, instead of acting upon it. Yet he is sensible of his own weakness, taxes himself with it, and tries to reason himself out of it.

> How all occasions do inform against me,
> And spur my dull revenge! What is a man,
> If his chief good and market of his time
> Be but to sleep and feed? A beast; no more.
> Sure he that made us with such large discourse,
> Looking before and after, gave us not
> That capability and god-like reason
> To rust in us unus'd: now whether it be
> Bestial oblivion, or some craven scruple

Of thinking too precisely on th' event,—
A thought which quarter'd, hath but one part wisdom,
And ever three parts coward;—I do not know
Why yet I live to say, this thing's to do;
Sith I have cause, and will, and strength, and means
To do it. Examples gross as earth excite me:
Witness this army of such mass and charge,
Led by a delicate and tender prince,
Whose spirit with divine ambition puff'd,
Makes mouths at the invisible event,
Exposing what is mortal and unsure
To all that fortune, death, and danger dare,
Even for an egg-shell. 'Tis not to be great,
Never to stir without great argument;
But greatly to find quarrel in a straw,
When honour's at the stake. How stand I then,
That have a father kill'd, a mother stain'd,
Excitements of my reason and my blood,
And let all sleep, while to my shame I see
The imminent death of twenty thousand men,
That for a fantasy and trick of fame,
Go to their graves like beds, fight for a plot
Whereon the numbers cannot try the cause,
Which is not tomb enough and continent
To hide the slain?—O, from this time forth,
My thoughts be bloody or be nothing worth.*

Still he does nothing; and this very speculation on his own infirmity only affords him another occasion for indulging it. It is not for any want of attachment to his father or abhorrence of his murder that Hamlet is thus dilatory, but it is more to his taste to indulge his imagination in reflecting upon the enormity of the crime and refining on his schemes of vengeance, than to put them into immediate practice. His ruling passion is to think, not to act: and any vague pretence that flatters this propensity instantly diverts him from his previous purposes.

The moral perfection of this character has been called in question, we think, by those who did not understand it. It is more interesting than according to rules: amiable, though not faultless. The ethical delineations of 'that noble and liberal casuist'* (as Shakespear has been well called) do not exhibit the drab-coloured quakerism of morality. His plays are not copied either from The Whole Duty of Man,* or from The Academy of Compliments!* We confess, we are a little shocked at the want of refinement in those who are shocked at the want of refinement in Hamlet. The want of punctilious exactness in his behaviour either partakes of the 'license of the time,' or else belongs to the very excess of intellectual refinement in the character, which makes the common rules of life, as well as his own purposes, sit loose upon him. He may be said to be amenable only to the tribunal of his own thoughts, and is too much taken up with the airy world of contemplation to lay as much stress as he ought on the practical consequences of things. His habitual principles of action are unhinged and out of joint with the time. His conduct to Ophelia is quite natural in his circumstances. It is that of assumed severity only. It is the effect of disappointed hope, of bitter regrets, of affection suspended, not obliterated, by the distractions of the scene around him! Amidst the natural and preternatural horrors of his situation, he might be excused in delicacy from carrying on a regular courtship. When 'his father's spirit was in arms,'* it was not a time for the son to make love in. He could neither marry Ophelia, nor wound her mind by explaining the cause of his alienation, which he durst hardly trust himself to think of. It would have taken him years to have come to a direct explanation on the point. In the harassed state of his mind, he could not have done otherwise than he did. His conduct does not contradict what he says when he sees her funeral,

> I loved Ophelia: forty thousand brothers
> Could not with all their quantity of love
> Make up my sum.*

Nothing can be more affecting or beautiful than the Queen's apostrophe to Ophelia on throwing flowers into the grave.

> ————Sweets to the sweet, farewell.
> I hop'd thou should'st have been my Hamlet's wife:
> I thought thy bride-bed to have deck'd, sweet maid,
> And not have strew'd thy grave.*

Shakespear was thoroughly a master of the mixed motives of human character, and he here shews us the Queen, who was so criminal in some respects, not without sensibility and affection in other relations of life.—Ophelia is a character almost too exquisitely touching to be dwelt upon. Oh rose of May, oh flower too soon faded!* Her love, her madness, her death, are described with the truest touches of tenderness and pathos. It is a character which nobody but Shakespear could have drawn in the way that he has done, and to the conception of which there is not even the smallest approach, except in some of the old romantic ballads. Her brother, Laertes, is a character we do not like so well: he is too hot and choleric, and somewhat rodomontade. Polonius is a perfect character in its kind; nor is there any foundation for the objections which have been made to the consistency of this part. It is said that he acts very foolishly and talks very sensibly. There is no inconsistency in that. Again, that he talks wisely at one time and foolishly at another; that his advice to Laertes is very sensible, and his advice to the King and Queen on the subject of Hamlet's madness very ridiculous. But he gives the one as a father, and is sincere in it; he gives the other as a mere courtier, a busy-body, and is accordingly officious, garrulous, and impertinent. In short, Shakespear has been accused of inconsistency in this and other characters, only because he has kept up the distinction which there is in nature, between the understandings and the moral habits of men, between the absurdity of their ideas and the absurdity of their motives. Polonius is not a fool, but he makes himself so. His folly, whether in his actions or speeches, comes under the head of impropriety of intention.

We do not like to see our author's plays acted, and least of all, HAMLET. There is no play that suffers so much in being transferred to the stage. Hamlet himself seems hardly capable of being acted. Mr. Kemble unavoidably fails in this character from a want of ease and variety. The character of Hamlet is made up of undulating lines; it has the yielding flexibility of 'a wave o' th' sea.'* Mr. Kemble plays it like a man in armour, with a determined inveteracy of purpose, in one undeviating straight line, which is as remote from the natural grace and refined susceptibility of the character, as the sharp angles and abrupt starts which Mr. Kean introduces into the part. Mr. Kean's Hamlet is as much too splenetic and rash as Mr. Kemble's is too deliberate and formal. His manner is too strong and pointed. He throws a severity, approaching to virulence, into the common observations and answers. There is nothing of this in Hamlet. He is, as it were, wrapped up in his reflections, and only *thinks aloud*. There should therefore be no attempt to impress what he says upon others by a studied exaggeration of emphasis or manner; no *talking at* his hearers. There should be as much of the gentleman and scholar as possible infused into the part, and as little of the actor. A pensive air of sadness should sit reluctantly upon his brow, but no appearance of fixed and sullen gloom. He is full of weakness and melancholy, but there is no harshness in his nature. He is the most amiable of misanthropes.

13

CHARACTER OF MR. BURKE

IT is not without reluctance that we speak of the vices and infirmities of such a mind as Burke's: But the poison of high example has by far the widest range of destruction; and, for the sake of public honour and individual integrity, we think it right to say, that however it may be defended upon other grounds, the political career of that eminent individual has no title to the praise of consistency. Mr Burke, the opponent of the American war—and Mr Burke, the opponent of the French Revolution, are not the same person, but opposite persons—not opposite persons only, but deadly enemies. In the latter period, he abandoned not only all his practical conclusions, but all the principles on which they were founded. He proscribed all his former sentiments, denounced all his former friends, rejected and reviled all the maxims to which he had formerly appealed as incontestable. In the American war he constantly spoke of the rights of the people as inherent, and inalienable: After the French Revolution, he began by treating them with the chicanery of a sophist, and ended by raving at them with the fury of a maniac. In the former case, he held out the duty of resistance to oppression, as the palladium, and only ultimate resource, of natural liberty; in the latter, he scouted, prejudged, vilified and nicknamed, all resistance in the abstract, as a foul and unnatural union of rebellion and sacrilege. In the one case, to answer the purposes of faction, he made it out, that the people are always in the right; in the other, to answer different ends, he made it out that they are always in the wrong—lunatics in the hands of their royal keepers, patients in the sick-wards of an hospital, or felons in the condemned cells of a prison. In the one, he considered that there was a constant tendency on the part of the prerogative to encroach on the rights of the people, which ought always to be the object of the most watchful jealousy, and of resistance, when necessary: In the other, he pretended to regard it as the sole occupation and ruling passion of those in power, to watch over the liberties and happiness of their subjects. The burthen of all his speeches on the American war was conciliation, concession, timely reform, as the only practicable or desirable alternative of rebellion: The object of all his writings on the French

Revolution was, to deprecate and explode all concession and all reform, as encouraging rebellion, and an irretrievable step to revolution and anarchy. In the one, he insulted kings personally, as among the lowest and worst of mankind; in the other, he held them up to the imagination of his readers as sacred abstractions. In the one case, he was a partisan of the people, to court popularity; in the other, to gain the favour of the Court, he became the apologist of all courtly abuses. In the one case, he took part with those who were actually rebels against his Sovereign; in the other, he denounced, as rebels and traitors, all those of his own countrymen who did not yield sympathetic allegiance to a foreign Sovereign, whom we had always been in the habit of treating as an arbitrary tyrant.

Judging from plain facts and principles, then, it is difficult to conceive more ample proofs of inconsistency. But try it by the more vulgar and palpable test of comparison. Even Mr Fox's enemies, we think, allow *him* the praise of consistency. *He* asserted the rights of the people in the American war, and continued to assert them in the French Revolution. He remained visibly in his place; and spoke, throughout, the same principles in the same language. When Mr Burke abjured these principles, he left this associate; nor did it ever enter into the mind of a human being to impute the defection to any change in Mr Fox's sentiments—any desertion by him of the maxims by which his public life had been guided. Take another illustration, from an opposite quarter. Nobody will accuse the principles of his present Majesty, or the general measures of his reign, of inconsistency. If they had no other merit, they have at least that of having been all along actuated by one uniform and constant spirit: Yet Mr Burke at one time vehemently opposed, and afterwards most intemperately extolled them; and it was for his recanting his opposition, not for his persevering in it, that he received his pension.* He does not himself mention his flaming speeches in the American war, as among the public services which had entitled him to this remuneration.

The truth is, that Burke was a man of fine fancy and subtle reflection; but not of sound and practical judgment—nor of high or rigid principles.—As to his understanding, he certainly was not a great philosopher; for his works of mere abstract reasoning are shallow and inefficient:—Nor a man of sense and business; for, both in counsel and in conduct, he alarmed his friends as much at least as his opponents:—But he was a keen and accomplished pamphleteer—an ingenious political essayist. He applied the habit of reflection, which he had borrowed from his metaphysical studies, but which was not competent to the discovery of any elementary truth in that department, with great felicity and success, to the mixed mass of human affairs. He knew more of the political machine than a recluse philosopher; and he speculated more profoundly on its principles and general results than a mere politician. He saw a number of fine distinctions and changeable aspects of things, the good mixed with the ill, the ill mixed with the good; and with a sceptical indifference, in which the exercise of his own ingenuity was always the governing principle, suggested various topics to qualify or assist the judgment of others. But for this very reason he was little calculated to become a leader or a partisan in any important practical measure: For the habit of his mind would lead him to find out a reason for or against any thing: And it is not on speculative refinements, (which belong to *every* side of a question), but on a just estimate of the aggregate mass and extended combinations of objections and advantages, that we ought to decide and act. Burke had the power, almost without limit, of throwing true or false weights into the scales of political casuistry, but not firmness of mind—or, shall we say, honesty enough—to hold the balance. When he took a side, his vanity or his spleen more frequently gave the casting vote than his judgment; and the fieriness of his zeal was in exact proportion to the levity of his understanding, and the want of conscious sincerity.

He was fitted by nature and habit for the studies and labours of the closet; and was generally mischievous when he came out;—because the very subtlety of his reasoning, which, left to itself, would have counteracted its own activity, or found its level in the common sense of mankind, became a dangerous engine in the hands of power, which is always eager to make use of the most plausible pretexts to cover the most fatal designs. That which, if applied as a general observation on human affairs, is a valuable truth suggested to the mind, may, when forced into the interested defence of a particular measure or system, become the grossest and basest sophistry. Facts or consequences never stood in the way of this speculative politician. He fitted them to his preconceived theories, instead of conforming his theories to them. They were the playthings of his style, the sport of his fancy. They were the straws of which his imagination made a blaze, and were consumed, like straws, in the blaze they had served to kindle. The fine things he said about Liberty and Humanity, in his speech on the

Begum's affairs,* told equally well, whether Warren Hastings was a tyrant or not: Nor did he care one jot who caused the famine he described, so that he described it in a way to attract admiration.* On the same principle, he represents the French priests and nobles under the old regime as excellent moral people, very charitable, and very religious, in the teeth of notorious facts,*—to answer to the handsome things he has to say in favour of priesthood and nobility in general; and, with similar views, he falsifies the records of our English Revolution, and puts an interpretation on the word *abdication*,* of which a schoolboy would be ashamed. He constructed his whole theory of government, in short, not on rational, but on picturesque and fanciful principles; as if the King's crown were a painted gewgaw, to be looked at on gala-days; titles an empty sound to please the ear; and the whole order of society a theatrical procession. His lamentation over the age of chivalry,* and his projected crusade to restore it, is about as wise as if any one, from reading the Beggar's Opera, should take to picking of pockets; or, from admiring the landscapes of Salvator Rosa,* should wish to convert the abodes of civilized life into the haunts of wild beasts and banditti. On this principle of false refinement, there is no abuse, nor system of abuses, that does not admit of an easy and triumphant defence; for there is something which a merely speculative inquirer may always find out, good as well as bad, in every possible system, the best or the worst; and if we can once get rid of the restraints of common sense and honesty, we may easily prove, by plausible words, that liberty and slavery, peace and war, plenty and famine, are matters of perfect indifference. This is the school of politics, of which Mr Burke was at the head; and it is perhaps to his example, in this respect, that we owe the prevailing tone of many of those newspaper paragraphs, which Mr Coleridge thinks so invaluable an accession to our political philosophy.*

Burke's literary talents, were, after all, his chief excellence. His style has all the familiarity of conversation, and all the research of the most elaborate composition. He says what he wants to say, by any means, nearer or more remote, within his reach. He makes use of the most common or scientific terms, of the longest or shortest sentences, of the plainest and most downright, or of the most figurative modes of speech. He gives for the most part loose reins to his imagination, and follows it as far as the language will carry him. As long as the one or the other has any resources in store to make the reader feel and see the thing as he has conceived it,—in its nicest shade of difference, in its utmost degree of force and splendour,—he never disdains, and never fails to employ them. Yet, in the extremes of his mixed style there is not much affectation, and but little either of pedantry or of coarseness. He everywhere gives the image he wishes to give, in its true and appropriate colouring: and it is the very crowd and variety of these images that have given to his language its peculiar tone of animation, and even of passion. It is his impatience to transfer his conceptions entire, living, in all their rapidity, strength, and glancing variety—to the minds of others, that constantly pushes him to the verge of extravagance, and yet supports him there in dignified security—

> Never so sure our rapture to create,
> As when he treads the brink of all we hate.*

He is, with the exception of Jeremy Taylor,* the most poetical of prose writers, and at the same time his prose never degenerates into the mere glitter or tinkling of poetry; for he always aims at overpowering rather than at pleasing; and consequently sacrifices beauty and grandeur to force and vividness. He has invariably a task to perform, a positive purpose to execute, an effect to produce. His only object is therefore to strike hard, and in the right place; if he misses his mark, he repeats his blow; and does not care how ungraceful the action, or how clumsy the instrument, provided it brings down his antagonist.

14

WHAT IS THE PEOPLE?

—AND who are you that ask the question? One of the people. And yet you would be something! Then you would not have the People nothing. For what is the People? Millions of men, like you, with hearts beating in their bosoms, with thoughts stirring in their minds, with the blood circulating in their veins, with wants and appetites, with passions and anxious cares, and busy purposes and affections for others and a respect for themselves, and a desire of happiness, and a right to freedom and a will to be free. And yet you would tear out this mighty heart of a nation to lay it bare and bleeding at the foot of despotism: you would slay the mind of a country to fill up the dreary aching void with the old, obscene, drivelling prejudices of superstition and tyranny: you would tread out the eye of Liberty (the light of nations) like 'a vile jelly,'* that mankind may be led about darkling to its endless drudgery, like the Hebrew Sampson (shorn of his strength and blind) by his insulting taskmasters: you would make the throne every thing, and the people nothing, to be yourself less than nothing, a very slave, a reptile, a creeping cringing sycophant, a court favorite, a pander to Legitimacy*—that detestable fiction, which would make you and me and all mankind its slaves or victims; which would, of right and with all the sanctions of religion and morality, sacrifice the lives of millions to the least of its caprices; which subjects the rights, the happiness and liberty of nations to the will of some of the lowest of the species; which rears its bloated hideous form to brave the will of a whole people; that claims mankind as its property, and allows human nature to exist only upon sufferance; that haunts the understanding like a frightful spectre, and oppresses the very air with a weight that is not to be borne; that like a witch's spell covers the earth with a dim and envious mist, and makes us turn our eyes from the light of heaven which we have no right to look at without its leave; robs us of 'the unbought grace of life,'* the pure delight and conscious pride in works of art or nature; leaves us no thought or feeling that we dare call our own; makes genius its lacquey, and virtue its easy prey; sports with human happiness, and mocks at human misery; suspends the breath of liberty, and almost of life; exenterates us of our affections, blinds our understandings, debases our imaginations, converts the very hope of emancipation from its yoke into sacrilege, binds the successive countless generations of men together in its chains like strings of felons or galley-slaves, lest they should 'resemble the flies of a summer,'* considers any remission of its absolute claims as a gracious boon, an act of royal clemency and favour, and confounds all sense of justice, reason, truth, liberty, humanity, in one low servile deathlike dread of power without limit and without remorse!* Such is the old doctrine of Divine Right, new-vamped up under the style and title of Legitimacy. 'Fine word, Legitimate!'* We wonder where our English politicians picked it up. Is it an echo from the tomb of the martyred monarch, Charles the First? Or was it the last word which his son, James the Second, left behind him in his flight, and bequeathed with his *abdication*, to his legitimate successors? It is not written in our annals in the years 1688, in 1715, or 1745. It was not sterling then, which was only fifteen years before his present Majesty's accession to the throne. Has it become so since? Is the Revolution of 1688 at length acknowledged to be a blot in the family escutcheon of the Prince of Orange or the Elector of Hanover? Is the choice of the people, which raised them to the throne, found to be the only flaw in their title to the succession; the weight of royal gratitude growing more uneasy with the distance of the obligation? Is the alloy of liberty, mixed up with it, thought to debase that *fine carrat*, which should compose the regal diadem? Are the fire-new specimens of the principle of the Right-Liners, and of Sir Robert Filmer's* patriarchal scheme, to be met with in the *Courier*, the *Day*, the *Sun*, and some time back, in *The Times*, handed about to be admired in the highest circle, like the new gold coinage of sovereigns and half-sovereigns? We do not know. It may seem to be *Latter Lammas*ature with this doctrine at this time of day; but better late than never. By taking root in the soil of France, from which it was expelled (not quite so long as from our own) it may in time stretch out its *feelers* and strong suckers to this country; and present an altogether curious and novel aspect, by ingrafting the principles of the House of Stuart on the illustrious stock of the House of Brunswick.

Miratur novos fructus, et non sua poma.*

What then is the people? We will answer, first, by saying what it is not; and this we cannot do better than in the words of a certain author,* whose testimony on this subject is not to be despised. That eyeless drudge of despotism,* who at one moment asks 'Where is the mad man that maintains the doctrine of divine right?' and the next affirms that 'Louis XVIII. has the same right to the throne of France, independently of his merits or conduct, that Mr. Coke of Norfolk has to his estate at Holkham'*— has given us a tolerable clue to what we have to expect from that mild paternal sway to which he would so kindly make us and the rest of the world over in hopeless perpetuity. In a violent philippic against the author of the Political Register, he thus inadvertently expresses himself. 'Mr. Cobbett had been sentenced to two years imprisonment for a libel, and during the time that he was in Newgate, it was discovered that he had been in treaty with Government to avoid the sentence passed upon him; and that he had proposed to certain of the agents of Ministers, that if they would let him off, they might make what future use they pleased of him; *he would entirely betray the cause of the people*; he would either write or not write, or *write against them*, as he had once done before, just as Ministers thought proper. To this, however, it was replied, that "Cobbett had written on too many sides already *to be worth a groat for the service of Government*;" and he accordingly suffered his confinement!'*—We here then see plainly enough what it is that, in the opinion of this very competent judge, alone renders any writer 'worth a groat for the service of government,' *viz.*—that he shall be able and willing entirely to betray the cause of the people. It follows from this principle (by which he seems to estimate the value of his lucubrations in the service of government—we do not know whether the government judge of them in the same way) that the cause of the people and the cause of the government, who are represented as thus anxious to suborn their creatures to write against the people, are not the same, but the reverse of one another. This slip of the pen in our professional retainer of legitimacy, though a libel on our own government is, notwithstanding, a general philosophic truth (the only one he ever hit upon) and an axiom in political mechanics, which we shall make the text of the following commentary.—What are the interests of the people? Not the interests of those who would betray them. Who is to judge of those interests? Not those who would suborn others to betray them.

That Government is instituted for the benefit of the governed, there can be little doubt; but the interests of the government (when once it

becomes absolute and independent of the people) are directly at variance with those of the governed. The interests of the one are common
and equal rights: of the other, exclusive and invidious privileges. The
essence of the first is to be shared alike by all, and to benefit the community in proportion as they are spread: the essence of the last is to
be destroyed by communication, and to subsist only—in wrong of the
people. Rights and privileges are a contradiction in terms: for if one
has more than his right, others must have less. They are the deadly
nightshade of the common-wealth, near which no wholesome plant
can thrive; the ivy clinging round the trunk of the British oak, blight-
ing its verdure, drying up its sap, and oppressing its stately growth.
The insufficient checks and balances opposed to the overbearing influence of hereditary rank and power in our own constitution, and in
every government which retains the least trace of freedom, are so many
illustrations of this principle, if it needed any. The tendency in arbitrary power to encroach upon the liberties and comforts of the people,
and to convert the public good into a stalking-horse to its own pride
and avarice, has never (that we know) been denied by any one but
'the professional gentleman,'* who writes in the *Day and New Times*. The
great and powerful, in order to be what they aspire to be, and what this
gentleman would have them, perfectly independent of the will of the
people, ought also to be perfectly independent of the assistance of
the people. To be formally invested with the attributes of Gods upon
earth, they ought first to be raised above its petty wants and appetites:
they ought to give proofs of the beneficence and wisdom of *Gods*,
before they can be trusted with the power. When we find them seated
above the world, sympathising with the welfare, but not feeling the
passions of men, receiving neither good nor hurt, neither tilth nor
tythe from them, but bestowing their benefits as free gifts on all, they
may then be expected, but not till then, to rule over us like another
Providence. We may make them a present of all the taxes they do not
apply to their own use: they are perfectly welcome to all the power, to
the possession of which they are perfectly indifferent, and to the abuse
of which they can have no possible temptation. But Legitimate
Governments (flatter them as we will) are not another Heathen mythology. They are neither so cheap nor so splendid as the Delphin edition
of Ovid's Metamorphoses.* They are indeed 'Gods to punish,' but
in other respects 'men of our infirmity.'* They do not feed on ambrosia
or drink nectar; but live on the common fruits of the earth, of which

they get the largest share, and the best. The wine they drink is made of grapes: the blood they shed is that of their subjects: the laws they make are not against themselves: the taxes they vote, they afterwards devour. They have the same wants that we have: and having the power, very naturally help themselves first, out of the common stock, without thinking that others are to come after them. With the same natural necessities, they have a thousand artificial ones besides; and with a thousand times the means to gratify them, they are still voracious, importunate, unsatisfied. Our state-paupers have their hands in every man's dish, and fare sumptuously every day. They live in palaces, and loll in coaches. In spite of Mr. Malthus,* their studs of horses consume the produce of our fields, their dog-kennels receive the food which would maintain the children of the poor. They cost us so much a year in dress and furniture, so much in stars and garters, blue ribbons, and grand crosses, so much in dinners, breakfasts, and suppers, and so much in suppers, breakfasts, and dinners.[1] These Heroes of the Income tax, Worthies of the civil list, Saints of the court-calendar, *(compagnons du lys,**) have their naturals and non-naturals,* like the rest of the world, but at a dearer rate. They are real *bona fide* personages, and do not live upon air. You will find it easier to keep them a week than a month; and at the end of that time, waking from the sweet dream of legitimacy, you may say with Caliban, 'Why, what a fool was I to take this drunken monster for a God!'*——In fact, the case on the part of the people is so far self-evident. There is but a limited earth and a limited fertility to supply the demands both of government and people; and what the one gains, in the division of the spoil, beyond its average proportion, the other must needs go without. Do you suppose that our gentlemen placemen, and pensioners, would suffer so many wretches to be perishing in our streets and highways, if they could relieve their extreme misery without parting with any of their own superfluities?——If the government take a fourth of the produce of the poor man's labour, they will be rich, and he will be in want. If they can contrive to take one half of it by legal means, or by a stretch of arbitrary power, they will be just twice as rich, twice as insolent and tyrannical, and he will be twice as poor, twice as miserable and oppressed, in a mathematical ratio to the end of the chapter, that is, till the one can extort and the other can endure no more.——It is the same

---

[1] See the description of Gargantua in Rabelais.*

with respect to power. The will and passions of the great are not exerted in regulating the seasons, or rolling the planets round their orbits for our good, without fee or reward, but in controling the will and passions of others, in making the follies and vices of mankind subservient to their own, and marring—

> Because men suffer it, their toy, the world.*

This is self-evident, like the former. Their will cannot be paramount, while any one in the community, or the whole community together, has the power to oppose it. A king cannot attain absolute power, while the people remain perfectly free; yet what king would not attain absolute power? While any trace of liberty is left among a people, ambitious princes will never be easy, never at peace, never of sound mind; nor will they ever rest or leave one stone unturned, till they have succeeded in destroying the very name of liberty, or making it into a bye word, and in rooting out the germs of every popular right and liberal principle from a soil once sacred to liberty. It is not enough that they have secured the whole power of the state in their hands, that they carry every measure they please without the chance of an effectual opposition to it: but a word uttered against it is torture to their ears, a thought that questions their wanton exercise of the royal prerogative rankles in their breasts like poison. Till all distinctions of right and wrong, liberty and slavery, happiness and misery, are looked upon as matters of indifference, or as saucy, insolent pretensions, are sunk and merged in their idle caprice and pampered self-will, they will still feel themselves 'cribbed, confined, and cabin'd in:'* but if they can once more set up the doctrine of Legitimacy, 'the right divine of kings to govern wrong,'* and set mankind at defiance with impunity, they will then be 'broad and casing as the general air, whole as the rock.'* This is the point from which they set out, and to which by the grace of God and the help of man they may return again. Liberty is short, and fleeting, a transient grace that lights upon the earth by stealth and at long intervals—

> —Like the lightning's form
> Evanishing amid the storm;
>   Or like the Borealis race
> That shift ere you can point their place;
> Or like the snow, falls in the river,
> A moment white, then melts for ever!*

But power is eternal; it is 'enthroned in the hearts of kings.'* If you want the proofs, look at history, look at geography, look abroad; but do not look at home!

* * *

The power of an arbitrary king or an aspiring minister does not increase with the liberty of the subject, but must be circumscribed by it. It is aggrandized by perpetual systematic, insidious, or violent encroachments on popular freedom and natural rights, as the sea gains upon the land by swallowing it up. What then can we expect from the mild paternal sway* of absolute power, and its sleek minions? What the world has always received at its hands, an abuse of power as vexatious, cowardly, and unrelenting, as the power itself was unprincipled, preposterous, and unjust. They who get wealth and power from the people, who drive them like cattle to slaughter or to market, 'and levy cruel wars, wasting the earth;'* they who wallow in luxury while the people are 'steeped in poverty to the very lips,'* and bowed to the earth with unremitted labour, can have but little sympathy with those whose loss of liberty and property is their gain. What is it that the wealth of thousands is composed of? The tears, the sweat, and blood of millions. What is it that constitutes the glory of the sovereigns of the earth? To have millions of men their slaves. Wherever the government does not emanate (as in our own excellent constitution) from the people, the principle of the government, *the esprit de corps*, the point of honour, in all those connected with it, and raised by it to privileges above the law and above humanity, will be hatred of the people. Kings who would be thought to reign in contempt of the people, will shew their contempt of them in every act of their lives. Parliaments, not chosen by the people, will only be instruments of kings, who do not reign in the hearts of their people, 'to betray the cause of the people.'* Ministers, not responsible to the people, will squeeze the last shilling out of them. *Charity begins at home*, is a maxim as true of governments as of individuals. When the English parliament insisted on its right of taxing the Americans without their consent, it was not from an apprehension that the Americans would by being left to themselves lay such heavy duties on their own produce and manufactures, as would afflict the generosity of the mother-country, and put the mild paternal sentiments of Lord North to the blush. If any future king of England should keep a wistful eye on the map of that country, it would rather be to hang it up as a trophy of legitimacy, and to 'punish the last successful example of a democratic rebellion,'* than from any yearnings of fatherly goodwill to the American people, or from finding his 'large heart' and capacity for good government, 'confined in too narrow room'* in the United Kingdoms of Great Britain, Ireland, and Hanover. If Ferdinand refuses the South American patriots leave to plant the olive, or the vine throughout that vast continent, it is his pride, not his humanity that feeds his royal resolution.[2]

In 1781, the Controller-General of France, under Louis XVI. Monsieur Joli de Fleuri, defined the people of France to be *un peuple serf, corveable et baillable, a merci et misericorde.** When Louis XVIII. as the Count de Lille, protested against his brother's accepting the constitution of 1792 (he has since become an accepter of constitutions himself, if not an observer of them) as compromising the rights and privileges of the noblesse and clergy as well as of the crown, he was right in considering the Bastille or 'king's castle'* with the picturesque episode of the Man in the Iron Mask, the fifteen thousand *lettres de cachet*,* issued in the mild reign of Louis XV., *corvees*,* tythes, game-laws, holy water, the right of pillaging, imprisoning, massacring, persecuting, harassing, insulting, and ingeniously tormenting the minds and bodies of the whole French people at every moment of their lives, on every possible pretence, and without any check or control but their own mild paternal sentiments towards them, as among the *menus plaisirs*,* the chief points of etiquette, the immemorial privileges, and favourite amusements of kings, priests, and nobles, from the beginning to the end of time, without which the bare title of king, priest, or noble, with nothing to do, would not be worth a farthing!

The breasts of kings and courtiers then are not the only safe depository of the interests of the people. But they know best what is for their good! Yes—to prevent it! The people may indeed feel their grievance, but their betters, it is said, must apply the remedy—which

---

[2] The Government of Ovando, a Spanish grandee and knight of Alcantara, who had been sent over to Mexico soon after its conquest, exceeded in treachery, cruelty, wanton bloodshed, and deliberate extortion, that of all those who had preceded him; and the complaints became so loud that Queen Isabel on her death-bed requested that he might be recalled; but Ferdinand found that Ovando had sent home *much gold*, and he retained him in his situation.—*See Capt. Burney's History of the Buccaneers.**

they take good care never to do! If the people want judgment in their own affairs (which is not certain, for they only meddle with their own affairs when they are forcibly brought home to them in a way which they can hardly misunderstand) this is at any rate better than the want of sincerity, which would constantly and systematically lead their superiors to betray those interests, from their having other ends of their own to serve. It is better to trust to ignorance than malice—to run the risk of some times miscalculating the odds than to play against loaded dice. The people would in this way stand as little chance in defending their purses or their persons against Mr. C—— or Lord C———,* as an honest country gentleman would have had in play-ing at put or hazard with Count Fathom or Jonathan Wild.* A certain degree of folly, or rashness, or indecision, or even violence in attain-ing an object, is surely less to be dreaded than a malignant, deliberate, mercenary intention in others to deprive us of it. If the people must have attorneys, and the advice of counsel, let them have attorneys and counsel of their own chusing, not those who are employed by special retainer against them, or who regularly hire others *to betray their cause*.

> ————————O silly sheep,
> Come ye to seek the lamb here of the wolf?*

This then is the cause of the people, the good of the people, judged of by common feeling and public opinion. Mr. Burke contemptuously defines the people to be 'any faction that at the time can get the power of the sword into its hands.'* No: that may be a description of the government, but it is not the people. The people is the hand, heart, and head of the whole community acting to one purpose, and with a mutual and thorough consent. The hand of the people so employed to execute what the heart feels, and the head thinks, must be employed more beneficially for the cause of the people, than in executing any measures which the cold hearts, and contriving heads of any faction, with distinct privileges and interests, may dictate to betray their cause. The will of the people necessarily tends to the general good as its end; and it must attain that end, and can only attain it, in propor-tion as it is guided—First, by popular feeling, as arising out of the immediate wants and wishes of the great mass of the people,—secondly, by public opinion as arising out of the impartial reason and enlightened intellect of the community. What is it that determines the opinion of any number of persons in things they actually feel in their practical and home results? Their common interest. What is it that determines their opinion in things of general inquiry, beyond their immediate experience or interest? Abstract reason. In matters of feeling and common sense, of which each individual is the best judge, the majority are in the right; in things requiring a greater strength of mind to comprehend them, the greatest power of understanding will prevail, if it has but fair play. These two, taken together, as the test of the practical measures or general principles of government, must be right, cannot be wrong. It is an absurdity to suppose that there can be any better criterion of national grievances, or the proper remedies for them, than the aggregate amount of the actual, dear-bought experience, the honest feelings, and heart-felt wishes of a whole people, informed and directed by the greatest power of understanding in the community, unbiassed by any sinister motive. Any other standard of public good or ill must, in proportion as it deviates from this, be vitiated in principle, and fatal in its effects. *Vox populi vox dei*,* is the rule of all good government: for in that voice truly collected and freely expressed (not when it is made the servile echo of a corrupt court, or a designing minister) we have all the sincerity and all the wisdom of the community. If we could suppose society to be transformed into one great animal (like Hobbes's Leviathan*) each member of which had an intimate connection with the head or government, so that every want or intention of every individual in it could be made known and have its due weight, the state would have the same consciousness of its own wants and feelings, and the same interest in providing for them, as an individual has with respect to his own welfare. Can any one doubt that such a state of society in which the greatest knowledge of its interests was thus combined with the greatest sympathy with its wants, would realise the idea of a perfect commonwealth? But such a government would be the precise idea of a truly popular or *representative* government. The opposite extreme is the purely hereditary and despotic form of government, where the people are an inert, torpid mass, without the power, scarcely with the will to make its wants or wishes known: and where the feelings of those who are at the head of the state, centre in their own exclusive interests, pride, passions, prejudices; and all their thoughts are employed in defeating the happiness and undermining the liberties of a country.

It is not denied that the people are best acquainted with their own wants, and most attached to their own interests. But then a question is started, as if the persons asking it were at a great loss for the answer,—Where are we to find the intellect of the people? Why, all the intellect that ever was is theirs. The public opinion expresses not only the collective sense of the whole people, but of all ages and nations, of all those minds that have devoted themselves to the love of truth and the good of mankind, who have bequeathed their instructions, their hopes, and their example to posterity, who have thought, spoke, written, acted, and suffered in the name and on the behalf of our common nature. All the greatest poets, sages, heroes, are ours originally, and by right. But surely Lord Bacon* was a great man? Yes; but not because he was a lord. There is nothing of hereditary growth but pride and prejudice. That 'fine word legitimate' never produced any thing but bastard philosophy and patriotism! Even Burke was one of the people, and would have remained with the people to the last, if there had been no court-side for him to go over to. The King gave him his pension, not his understanding or his eloquence. It would have been better for him and for mankind if he had kept to his principles, and gone without his pension. It is thus that the tide of power constantly setting in against the people, swallows up natural genius and acquired knowledge in the vortex of corruption, and then they reproach us with our want of leaders of weight and intellect, to stem the torrent. All that has ever been done for society, has, however, been done for it by this intellect, before it was cheapened to be a cat's-paw of divine right. All discoveries and all improvements in arts, in science, in legislation, in civilization, in every thing dear and valuable to the heart of man, have been made by this intellect—all the triumphs of human genius over the rudest barbarism, the darkest ignorance, the grossest and most inhuman superstition, the most unmitigated and remorseless tyranny, have been gained for themselves by the people. Great kings, great law-givers, great founders, and great reformers of religion have almost all arisen from among the people. What have hereditary monarchs, or regular governments, or established priesthoods ever done for the people? Did the Pope and cardinals first set on foot the reformation? Did the Jesuits attempt to abolish the Inquisition? For what one measure of civil or religious liberty did our own Bench of bishops ever put themselves forward? What judge ever proposed a reform in the laws? Have not the House of Commons, with all their 'tried wisdom,'* voted for every measure of ministers for the last twenty-five years, except the income-tax?* It is the press that has done every thing for the people, and even for governments. 'If they had not ploughed with our heifer, they would not have found out our riddle.'*—And it has done this by slow degrees, by repeated, incessant, and incredible struggles with the oldest, most inveterate, powerful, and active enemies of the freedom of the press and of the people, who wish, in spite of the nature of things and of society, to retain the idle and mischievous privileges they possess as the relics of barbarous and feudal times, who have an exclusive interest as a separate *cast* in the continuance of all existing abuses, and who plead a permanent *vested right* in the prevention of the progress of reason, liberty, and civilization. Yet they tax us with our want of intellect; and *we* ask them in return for their court-list of great names in arts or philosophy, for the coats of arms of their heroic vanquishers of error and intolerance, for their devout benefactors and royal martyrs of humanity. We will take four names familiar to the reader, Franklin, Howard, Clarkson, and Bentham,* and ask them to match them with any four names out of the Red Book, or Collins's Peerage. What are the claims of the people—the obvious, undoubted rights of common justice and humanity, forcibly withheld from them by pride, bigotry, and selfishness, demanded for them, age after age, year after year, by the wisdom and virtue of the enlightened and disinterested part of mankind, and only grudgingly yielded up, with indecent, disgusting excuses, and sickening delays, when the burning shame of their refusal can be no longer concealed by fear of favour from the whole world. What did it not cost to abolish the Slave Trade? How long will the Catholic Claims be withheld by our state-jugglers?* How long, and for what purpose? We may appeal, in behalf of the people, from the interested verdict of the worst and weakest men now living, to the disinterested reason of the best and wisest men among the living and the dead. We appeal from the corruption of courts, the hypocrisy of zealots, and the dotage of hereditary imbecility to the innate love of liberty in the human breast, and to the growing intellect of the world. We appeal to the pen, and they answer us with the point of the bayonet; and, at one time, when that had failed, they were for recommending the dagger.[3] They quote Burke, but rely on the Attorney-General.—They hold Universal Suffrage to be the most dreadful of all things, and a Standing Army the best representatives

---

[3] See Coleridge's *Friend*, No. 15.*

of the people abroad and at home. They think Church and King mobs good things, for the same reason that they are alarmed at a meeting to petition for a reform of parliament. They consider the cry of No Popery a sound, excellent, and constitutional cry, but the cry of a starving population for food strange and unnatural. They exalt the war-whoop of the Stock-Exchange into the voice of undissembled patriotism, while they set down the cry for peace as the work of the Jacobins, the ventriloquism of the secret enemies of their country. The writers on the popular side of the question are factious, design-ing demagogues, who delude the people to make tools of them: but the government-writers, who echo every calumny, and justify every encroachment on the people, are profound philosophers and very honest men. Thus when Mr. John Gifford, the Editor of the Anti-Jacobin, (not Mr. William Gifford, who at present holds the same office under government, as the Editor of the Quarterly Review), denounced Mr. Coleridge as a person, who had 'left his wife destitute and his children fatherless,' and proceeded to add—'*Ex hoc disce* his friends Lamb and Southey'*—we are to suppose that he was influ-enced in this gratuitous statement purely by his love for his king and country. Loyalty, patriotism, and religion are regarded as the natural virtues and plain, unerring instincts of the common people: the mix-ture of ignorance or prejudice is never objected to in these: it is only their love of liberty or hatred of oppression that are discovered, by the same liberal-minded junto, to be proofs of a base and vulgar dis-position. The Bourbons are set over the immense majority of the French people against their will, because a talent for governing does not go with numbers. This argument was not thought of when Buonaparte tried to shew his talent for governing the people of the continent against their will, though he had quite as much talent as the Bourbons. Mr. Canning rejoiced that the first successful resistance to Buonaparte was made in Russia, a country of barbarians and slaves. The heroic struggles of 'the universal Spanish nation'* in the cause of freedom and independence, have ended in the destruction of the Cortes and the restoration of the Inquisition; but without making the Duke of Wellington look thoughtful:—not a single renegado poet has vented his indignation in a single ode, elegy, or sonnet;* nor does Mr. Southey 'make him a willow cabin at its gate, write loyal cantos of contemned love, and sing them loud even in the dead of the night!'* He indeed assures us in the Quarterly Review that the Inquisition was restored by the voice of the Spanish people. He also asks, in the same place, 'whether the voice of God was heard in the voice of the people at Jerusalem, when they cried, "Crucify him, crucify him?"' We do not know; but we suppose, he would hardly go to the chief Priests and Pharisees to find it. This great historian, politician, and logician breaks out into a rhapsody against the old maxim, *vox populi vox Dei*, in the midst of an article of 55 pages, written expressly to prove that the last war was 'the most popular, *because* the most just and necessary war that ever was carried on.'* He shrewdly asks, 'Has the *vox populi* been the *vox Dei* in France for the last twenty-five years?'* But, at least, according to his own shewing, it has been so in this country for all that period. We, however, do not think so. The voice of the country has been for war, because the voice of the king was for it, which was echoed by Parliament, both Lords and Commons, by clergy and gentry, and by the populace, till, as Mr. Southey himself states in the same connected chain of reasoning, the cry for war became *so* popular, that all those who did not join in it (of which number the poet-laureate himself was one) were 'persecuted, insulted, and injured in their persons, fame, and fortune.'* This is the true way of accounting for the fact, but it unfortunately knocks the poet's inference on the head. Mr. Locke has observed* that there are not so many wrong opinions in the world, as we are apt to believe, because most people take their opinions on trust from others. Neither are the opinions of the people their own, when they have been bribed or bullied into them by a mob of lords and gentlemen, following in full cry at the heels of the court. The *vox populi* is the *vox Dei* only when it springs from the individual, unbiassed feelings and unfettered, independent opinion of the people. Mr. Southey does not understand the terms of this good old adage, now that he is so furious against it: we fear, he understood them no better when he was as loudly in favour of it.

All the objections indeed to the voice of the people being the best rule for government to attend to, arise from the stops and impediments to the expression of that voice, to the attempts to stifle or to give it a false bias, and to cut off its free and open communication with the head and heart of the people,—by the government itself. The sincere expression of the feelings of the people must be true; the full and free development of the public opinion must lead to truth, to the gradual discovery and diffusion of knowledge in this as in all other departments of human inquiry. It is the interest of governments in general to keep the people in a state of vassalage as long as they can—to prevent the expression of their sentiments, and the exercise and improvement of their understandings by all the means in their power. They have a patent, and a monopoly, which they do not like to have looked into or to share with others. The argument for keeping the people in a state of lasting wardship, or for treating them as lunatics, incapable of self-government, wears a very suspicious aspect as it comes from those who are trustees to the estate, or keepers of insane asylums. The long minority of the people would at this rate never expire, while those who had an interest, had also the power to prevent them from arriving at years of discretion: their government-keepers have nothing to do but to drive the people mad by ill-treatment, and to keep them so by worse, in order to retain the pretence for applying the gag, the strait waistcoat, and the whip as long as they please. It is like the dispute between Mr. Epps, the ham-shop keeper in the Strand, and his journeyman, whom he would restrict from setting up for himself.* Shall we never serve out our apprenticeship to liberty? Must our indentures to slavery bind us for life? It is well, it is perfectly well. You teach us nothing, and you will not let us learn. You deny us education, like Orlando's eldest brother, and then 'stying us,'* in the den of legitimacy, you refuse to let us take the management of our own affairs into our own hands, or to seek our fortunes in the world ourselves. You found a right to treat us with indignity on the plea of your own neglect and injustice. You abuse a trust in order to make it perpetual. You profit of our ignorance and of your own wrong. You degrade and then enslave us; and by enslaving, you degrade us more, to make us more and more incapable of ever escaping from your selfish, sordid yoke. There is no end of this.—It is the fear of the progress of knowledge and a *Reading Public** that has produced all the fuss and bustle and cant about Bell and Lancaster's plans,* Bible and Missionary and Auxiliary and Cheap Tract Societies, and that, when it was impossible to prevent our reading something, made the Church and State so anxious to provide us with that sort of food for our stomachs, which they thought best. The Bible is an excellent book; and when it becomes the Statesman's Manual, in its precepts of charity—not of beggarly alms-giving, but of peace on earth and good will to man, the people may read nothing else. It reveals the glories of the world to come, and records the preternatural dispensations of providence to mankind two thousand years ago. But it does not describe the present state of Europe or give an account of the measures of the last or of the next reign, which yet it is important the people of England should look to. We cannot learn from Moses and the Prophets what Mr. Vansittart and the Jews are about in 'Change-alley.* Those who prescribe us the study of the miracles and prophecies, themselves laugh to scorn the promised deliverance of Joanna Southcott and the Millennium.* Yet they would have us learn patience and resignation from the miraculous interpositions of Providence recorded in the Scriptures. '*When the sky falls*—the proverb is somewhat musty.'* The worst compliment ever paid to the Bible was the recommendation of it as a political palliative by the Lay Preachers of the day.

To put this question in a clearer light, we might ask, What is the public? and examine what would be the result of depriving the people of the use of their understandings in other matters as well as government, to put them into the go-cart of prescriptive prejudice and hereditary pretension. Take the stage as an example. Suppose Mr. Kean should have a son, a little crook-kneed, raven-voiced, disagreeable, mischievous, stupid urchin, with the faults of his father's acting exaggerated tenfold, and none of his fine qualities,—what if Mr. Kean should take it into his head to get out letters-patent to empower him and his heirs for ever, with this hopeful commencement, to play all the chief parts in tragedy by the grace of God and the favour of the Prince Regent! What a precious race of tragedy kings and heroes we should have! They would not even play the villain with a good grace. The theatres would soon be deserted, and the race of the Keans would 'hold a barren sceptre' over empty houses, to be 'wrenched from them by an unlineal hand!'* But no! For it would be necessary to uphold theatrical order, the cause of the Legitimate drama, and so to levy a tax on all those who staid away from the theatre or to drag them into it by force. Every one seeing the bayonet at the door would be compelled to applaud the hoarse tones and lengthened pauses of the illustrious house of Kean, the newspaper critics would grow wanton in their praise, and all those would be held as rancorous enemies of their country, and of the prosperity of the stage, who did not join in the praises of the best of actors. What a falling off would there be from the present system of universal suffrage, and open competition among the candidates, the frequency of rows in the pit, the noise in the gallery, the whispers in the boxes, and the lashing in the newspapers the next day!

In fact, the argument drawn from the supposed incapacity of the people against a representative government comes with the worst grace in the world from the patrons and admirers of hereditary government. Surely, if government were a thing requiring the utmost stretch of genius, wisdom, and virtue to carry it on, the office of king would never even have been dreamt of as hereditary, any more than that of poet, painter, or philosopher. It is easy here 'for the Son to tread in the Sire's steady steps.'* It requires nothing but the will to do it. Extraordinary talents are not once looked for. Nay, a person, who would never have risen by natural abilities to the situation of church-warden or parish beadle, succeeds by unquestionable right to the possession of a throne, and wields the energies of an empire, or decides the fate of the world with the smallest possible share of human understanding. The line of distinction which separates the regal purple from the slabbering-bib is sometimes fine indeed; as we see in the case of the two Ferdinands.* Any one above the rank of an ideot is supposed capable of exercising the highest functions of royal state. Yet these are the persons who talk of the people as a swinish multitude,* and taunt them with their want of refinement and philosophy.

* * *

It is the cause, it is the cause, my soul.*

The great problem of political science is not of so profoundly metaphysical or highly poetical a cast as Mr. Burke represents it. It is simply a question on the one part, with how little expense of liberty and property the government, 'that complex constable,'* as it has been quaintly called, can keep the peace, and on the other part, for how great a sacrifice of both, the splendour of the throne and the safety of the state can be made a pretext. Kings and their ministers generally strive to get their hands in our pockets, and their feet on our necks; the people and their representatives will be wise enough, if they can only contrive to prevent them; but this, it must be confessed, they do not always succeed in. For a people to be free, it is sufficient that they will to be free.* But the love of liberty is less strong than the love of power, and is guided by a less sure instinct in attaining its object. Milton only spoke the sentiments of the English people of his day, (sentiments too which they had acted upon) in strong language when he said, in answer to a foreign pedant,—'*Liceat, queso, populo qui servitulis jugum in cervicibus grave sentit, tam sapienti esse, tam docto,* *tamque nobili, ut sciat quid faciendum sit, etiamsi neque exteros neque grammaticos sciscitatum mittat.'** (Defensio pro populo Anglicano, cap. I.) Happily, the whole of the passage is not applicable to their descendants in the present day; but at all times, a people may be allowed to know when they are oppressed, enslaved, and miserable, to feel their wrongs and to demand a remedy—from the superior knowledge and humanity of ministers, who if they cannot cure the state-malady, ought in decency, like other doctors, to resign their authority over the patient. The people are not subject to fanciful wants, speculative longings, or hypochondriacal complaints. Their disorders are real, their complaints substantial and well-founded. Their grumblings are in general seditions of the belly. They do not cry out till they are hurt. They do not stand upon nice questions or trouble themselves with Mr. Burke's Sublime and Beautiful:* but when they find the money conjured clean out of their pockets, and the Constitution suspended over their heads, they think it time to look about them. For example, poor Evans, that amateur of music and politics* (strange combination of tastes) thought it hard, no doubt, to be sent to prison and deprived of his flute by a state-warrant, because there was no ground for doing it by law; and Mr. Hiley Addington,* being himself a flute-player, thought so too: though, in spite of this romantic sympathy, the minister prevailed over the musician, and Mr. Evans has, we believe, never got back his flute nor out of his arcade.* For an act of injustice, by the new system, if complained of 'forsooth,'* becomes justifiable by the very resistance to it: if not complained of, nobody knows any thing about it, and so it goes equally unredressed in either way. Or to take another obvious instance and sign of the times; a tenant or small farmer who has been distrained upon and sent to gaol or to the workhouse, probably thinks, and with some appearance of reason, that he was better off before this change of circumstances; and Mr. Cobbett in his twopenny registers, proves to him so clearly that this change for the worse, is owing to the war and taxes which have driven him out of his house and home, that Mr. Cobbett himself has been forced to quit the country* to argue the question, whether two and two make four, with Mr. Vansittart, upon safer ground to himself, and more equal ground to the Chancellor of the Exchequer. Such questions as these are, one would think, within the verge of common sense and reason. For any thing we could ever find, the people have as much common sense and sound judgment as any other class of the community. Their folly is second-hand, derived from their being the dupes of the passions, interests, and prejudices of their superiors. When they judge for themselves, they in general judge right. At any rate, the way to improve their judgment in their own concerns (and if they do not judge for themselves, they will infallibly be cheated both of liberty and property, by those who kindly insist on relieving them of that trouble) is not to deny them the use and exercise of their judgment altogether.—Nothing can be pleasanter than one of the impositions thus attempted to be put upon the people, by persuading them that economy is no part of a wise government. The people must be pretty competent judges of the cheapness of a government. But it is pretended by our high-flying sinecurists and pensioners, that this is a low and vulgar view of the subject, taken up by interested knaves, like Paine and Cobbett, to delude, and in the end make their market of the people. With all the writers and orators who compose the band of gentlemen pensioners and their patrons, politics is entirely a thing of sentiment and imagination. To speak of the expenses of government as if it were a little paltry huckstering calculation of profit and loss, quite shocks their lofty, liberal, and disinterested notions. They have no patience with the people if they are not ready to sacrifice their all for the public good! This is something like a little recruiting cavalry-lieutenant we once met with, who, sorely annoyed at being so often dunned for the arrears of board and lodging by the people where he took up his quarters, exclaimed with the true broad Irish accent and emphasis—'*Vulgar ideas! These wretches always expect one to pay for what one has of them!*' Our modest lieutenant thought that while he was employed on his Majesty's service, he had a right to pick the pockets of his subjects, and that if they complained of being robbed of what was their own, they were blackguards and *no gentlemen*! Mr. Canning hit upon nothing so good as this, in his luminous defence of his Lisbon Job!*

But allow the people to be as gross and ignorant as you please, as base and stupid as you can make them or keep them, 'duller than the fat weed that roots itself at ease on Lethe's wharf,'*—Is nothing ever to rouse them? Grant that they are slow of apprehension,—that they do not see till they feel. Is that a reason that they are not to feel then, neither? Would you blindfold them with the double bandages of bigotry, or quench their understandings with 'the dim suffusion,' 'the drop serene' of Legitimacy, that 'they may roll in vain and find no dawn'* of liberty, no ray of hope? Because they do not see tyranny till it is mountain-high, 'making Ossa like a wart,'* are they not to feel its weight when it is heaped upon them, or to throw it off with giant strength, and a convulsive effort? If they do not see the evil till it has grown enormous, palpable, and undeniable, is that a reason why others should then deny that it exists, or why it should not be removed? They do not snuff arbitrary power a century off: they are not shocked at it on the other side of the globe, or of the channel: are they not therefore to see it, could it in time be supposed to stalk over their heads, to trample and grind them to the earth? If in their uncertainty how to deal with it, they sometimes strike random blows, if their despair makes them dangerous, why do not they who from their elevated situation see so much farther and deeper into the principles and consequences of things—in their boasted wisdom, prevent the causes of complaint in the people before they accumulate to a terrific height, and burst upon the heads of their oppressors? The higher classes who would disqualify the people from taking the cure of their disorders into their own hands, might do this very effectually, by preventing the first symptoms of their disorders. They would do well, instead of abusing the blunders and brutishness of the multitude, to shew their superior penetration and zeal in detecting the first approaches of mischief, in withstanding every encroachment on the comforts and rights of the people, in guarding every bulwark against the influence and machinations of arbitrary power, as a precious, inviolable, sacred trust. Instead of this, they are the first to be lulled into security— a security 'as gross as ignorance made drunk'*—the last to believe the consequences, because they are the last to feel them. Instead of this, the patience of the lower classes in submitting to privations and insults is only surpassed by the callousness of their betters in witnessing them. The one never set about the redress of grievances or the reform of abuses till they are no longer to be borne, the others will not hear of it even then. It is for this reason among others that the *Vox populi* is the *Vox Dei*, that it is the agonizing cry of human nature raised, and only raised, against intolerable oppression and the utmost extremity of human suffering. The people do not rise up till they are trod down. They do not turn upon their tormentors till they are goaded to madness. They do not complain till the thumbscrews have been applied, and have been strained to the last turn. Nothing can ever wean the affections or confidence of a people from a government (to which habit, prejudice, natural pride, perhaps old benefits and joint struggles for liberty have attached them) but an excessive degree of irritation and disgust, occasioned either by a sudden and violent stretch of power contrary to the spirit and forms of the established government, or by a blind and wilful adherence to old abuses and established forms, when the changes in the state of manners and opinion have rendered them as odious as they are ridiculous. The Revolutions of Switzerland, the Low Countries, and of America are examples of the former, the French Revolution of the latter; our own Revolution of 1688 was a mixture of the two. As a general rule, it might be laid down, that for every instance of national resistance to tyranny there ought to have been many more, and that all those which have been attempted ought to have succeeded. In the case of Wat Tyler, for instance, which has been so naturally dramatised by the Poet-Laureate, the rebellion was crushed, and the ring-leaders hanged by the treachery of the government, but the grievances of which they had complained, were removed a few years after, and the rights they had claimed granted to the people, from the necessary progress of civilization and knowledge. Did not Mr. Southey know, when he applied for an injunction against Wat Tyler,* that the feudal system had been abolished long ago?—Again, as nothing rouses the people to resistance but extreme and aggravated injustice, so nothing can make them persevere in it, or push their efforts to a successful and triumphant issue, but the most open and unequivocal determination to brave their cries and insult their misery. They have no principle of union in themselves, and nothing brings or holds them together but the strong pressure of want, the stern hand of necessity—'a necessity that is not chosen, but chuses,—a necessity paramount to deliberation, that admits of no discussion and demands no evidence, that can alone, (according to Mr. Burke's theory) justify a resort to anarchy,'* and that alone ever did or can produce it. In fine, there are but two things in the world, might and right. Whenever one of these is overcome, it is by the other. The triumphs of the people, or the stand which they at any time make against arbitrary sway, are the triumphs of reason and justice over the insolence of individual power and authority, which, unless as it is restrained, curbed and corrected by popular feeling, or public opinion, can be guided only by its own drunken, besotted, mad pride, selfishness and caprice, and must be productive of all the mischief, which it can wantonly or deliberately commit with impunity.

The people are not apt, like a fine lady, to affect the vapours of discontent; nor to volunteer a rebellion for the theatrical eclat of the thing. But the least plausible excuse, one kind word, one squeeze of the hand, one hollow profession of good will subdues the soft heart of rebellion, (which is 'too foolish fond and pitiful'* to be a match for the callous hypocrisy opposed to it) dissolves and melts the whole fabric of popular innovation like butter in the sun. Wat Tyler is a case in point again. The instant the effeminate king and his unprincipled courtiers gave them fair words, they dispersed, relying in their infatuation on the word of the king as binding, on the oath of his officers as sincere; and no sooner were they dispersed than they cut off their leaders heads, and poor John Ball's* along with them, in spite of all his texts of scripture. The story is to be seen in all the shop-windows, *written in very choice blank verse.** That the people are rash in trusting to the promises of their friends, is true; they are more rash in believing their enemies. If they are led to expect too much in theory, they are satisfied with too little in reality. Their anger is sometimes fatal while it lasts, but it is not roused very soon, nor does it last very long. Of all dynasties anarchy is the shortest lived. They are violent in their revenge, no doubt; but it is because justice has been long denied them, and they have to pay off a very long score at a very short notice. What Caesar says of himself, might be applied well enough to the people, that they 'did never wrong but with just cause.'* The errors of the people are the crimes of governments. They apply sharp remedies to lingering diseases, and when they get sudden power in their hands, frighten their enemies, and wound themselves with it. They rely on brute force and the fury of despair, in proportion to the treachery which surrounds them, and to the degradation, the want of general information and mutual co-operation, in which they have been kept, on purpose to prevent them from ever acting in concert, with wisdom, energy, confidence and calmness, for the public good. The American revolution produced no horrors, because its enemies could not succeed in sowing the seeds of terror, hatred, mutual treachery and universal dismay in the hearts of the people. The French revolution under the auspices of Mr. Burke and other friends of social order, was tolerably prolific of these horrors. But that should not be charged as the fault of the Revolution or of the people. Timely reforms are the best preventives of violent revolutions. If Governments are determined that the people shall have no redress, no remedies for their acknowledged grievances, but violent and desperate ones, they may thank themselves for the obvious consequences. Despotism must always have the most to fear from the reaction of popular fury, where it has been guilty of the greatest abuses of power, and where it has shewn the greatest tenaciousness of those abuses, putting an end to all prospect of amicable arrangements, and provoking the utmost vengeance of its oppressed and insulted victims. This tenaciousness of power is the chief obstacle to improvement, and the cause of the revulsions which follow the attempts at it. In America, a free government was easy of accomplishment, because it was not necessary, in building up, to pull down; there were no nuisances to abate. The thing is plain. Reform in old governments is just like the new improvements in the front of Carlton House, that would go on fast enough but for the vile, old, dark, dirty, crooked streets which cannot be removed without giving the inhabitants notice to quit.* Mr. Burke in regretting these old institutions as the result of the wisdom of ages, and not the remains of Gothic ignorance and barbarism, played the part of Crockery in the farce of Exit by Mistake* who sheds tears of affection over the loss of the old windows and buttresses of the houses that no longer jut out to meet one another, and stop up the way.

There is one other consideration which may induce hereditary sovereigns to allow some weight to the arguments in favour of popular feeling and public opinion. They are the only security which they themselves possess individually for the continuance of their splendour and power. Absolute monarchs have nothing to fear from the people, but they have every thing to fear from their slaves and one another. Where power is lifted beyond the reach of the law or of public opinion, there is no principle to oppose it, and he who can obtain possession of the throne (by whatever means) is always the rightful possessor of it, till he is supplanted by a more fortunate or artful successor, and so on in a perpetual round of treasons, conspiracies, murders, usurpations, regicides, and rebellions, with which the people have nothing to do, but as passive, unconcerned spectators. Where the son succeeds to the father's throne by assassination, without being amenable to public justice, he is liable to be cut off himself by the same means, and with the same impunity. The only thing that can give stability or confidence to power, is that very will of the people, and public censure exercised upon public acts, of which legitimate sovereigns are so disproportionately apprehensive. For one regicide committed by the people, there have been thousands committed by Kings themselves. A constitutional King of England reigns in greater security than the Persian Sophi, or the Great Mogul; and the Emperor of Turkey, or the Autocrat of all the Russias, has much more to fear from a cup of coffee or the bowstring, than the Prince Regent from the speeches and writings of all the Revolutionists in Europe. By removing the barrier of public opinion which interferes with their own lawless acts, despotic kings lay themselves open to the hand of the assassin, and while they reign in contempt of the will, the voice, the heart and mind of a whole people, hold their crowns and every moment of their lives at the mercy of the meanest of their slaves.

15

ON COURT-INFLUENCE

> To be honest as this world goes, is to be one man picked out of
> ten thousand.*

IT is not interest alone, but prejudice or fashion that sways the
generality of mankind. Opinion governs opinion. It is not merely
what we can get by a certain line of conduct that we have to consider,
but what others will think of it. The possession of money is but one
mode of recommending ourselves to the good opinion of the world,
of securing distinction and respect. Except as a bribe to popularity,
money is of very limited value. Avarice is (oftener than we might at
first suspect) only vanity in disguise. We should not want fine clothes
or fine houses, an equipage or livery servants, but for what others will
think of us for having or wanting them. The chief and most expensive
commodity that money is laid out in purchasing, is respect. Money,
like other things, is worth no more than it will fetch. It is a passport
into society: but if other things will answer the same purpose; as
beauty, birth, wit, learning, desert in art or arms, dress, behaviour, the
want of money is not felt as a very severe privation. If a man, who,
from whatever pretensions, is received into good company, behaves
with propriety and converses rationally, it is not inquired after he is
gone, nor once thought of while he is present, whether he is rich or
poor. In the mixed intercourse of private society every one finds his
level, in proportion as he can contribute to its amusement or information. It is even more so in the general intercourse of the world, where
a poet and a man of genius (if extrinsic circumstances make any difference) is as much courted and run after for being a common plough-
man, as for being a peer of the realm. Burns, had he been living,
would have started fair with Lord Byron in the race of popularity, and
would not have lost it.

The temptation to men in public life to swerve from the path of
duty less frequently arises from a sordid regard to their private interests than from an undue deference to popular applause. A want of
political principle is, in nine cases out of ten, a want of firmness of
mind to differ with those around us, and to stand the brunt of their
avowed hostility or secret calumnies.

But still the world and its dread laugh prevails!*

An honest man is one whose sense of right and wrong is stronger than his anxiety that others should think or speak well of him. A man in the same sense forfeits his character for political integrity, whose love of truth truckles to his false shame and cringing complaisance, and who tampers with his own convictions, that he may stand well with the world. A man who sells his opinion merely to gain by his profligacy, is not a man without public principle, but common honesty. He ranks in the same class with a highwayman or a pickpocket.—It is true, interest and opinion are in general linked together; but opinion flies before, and interest comes limping after. As a woman first loses her virtue through her heart, so the yielding patriot generally sacrifices his character to his love of reputation.

It is usually supposed by those who make no distinction between the highest point of integrity and the lowest mercenariness, that Mr. Burke changed his principles to gain a pension; and that this was the main-spring of his subsequent conduct. We do not think so; though this may have been one motive, and a strong one to a needy and extravagant man. But the pension which he received was something more than a mere grant of money—it was a mark of royal favour, it was a tax upon public opinion. If any thing were wanting to fix his veering loyalty, it was the circumstance of the King's having his *Reflections on the French Revolution* bound in Morocco (not an unsuitable binding) and giving it to all his particular friends, saying, 'It was a book which every gentleman ought to read!'* This praise would go as far with a vain man as a pension with a needy one; and we may be sure, that if there were any lurking seeds of a leaning to the popular side remaining in the author's breast, he would after this lose no time in rooting them out of the soil, that his works might reflect the perfect image of his royal master's mind, and have no plebeian stains left to sully it. Kings are great critics: they are the fountain of honour; the judges of merit. After such an authority had pronounced it 'a book which every gentleman ought to read,' what gentleman could refuse to read, or dare to differ with it? With what a feeling a Privy Counsellor would open the leaves of a book, which the King had had richly bound, and presented with his own hand! How Lords of the Bed-chamber would wonder at the profound arguments! How Peeresses in their own right must simper over the beautiful similes! How the

Judges must puzzle over it! How the Bishops would bless themselves at the number of fine things; and our great classical scholars, Doctors Parr and Burney, set down for the first time in their lives to learn English, to write themselves into a Bishopric! Burke had long laboured hard to attain a doubtful pre-eminence. He had worked his way into public notice by talents which were thought specious rather than solid, and by sentiments which were obnoxious to some, suspected by others. His connections and his views were ambiguous. He professedly espoused the cause of the people, and found it as hard to defend himself against popular jealousy as ministerial resentment. He saw Court-lacqueys put over his head; and country Squires elbowing him on one side. He was neither understood by friends nor enemies. He was opposed, thwarted, cross-questioned, and obliged to present 'a certificate of merit'* (as he himself says) at every stage of his progress through life. But the King's having pronounced that 'his book was one which every gentleman ought to read,' floated him at once out of the flats and shallows in which his voyage of popularity had been bound, into the full tide of court-favour; settled all doubts; smoothed all difficulties; rubbed off old scores; made the crooked strait, and the rough plain;—what was obscure, became profound;—what was extravagant, lofty; every sentiment was liberality, every expression elegance; and from that time to this, Burke has been the oracle of every dull venal pretender to taste or wisdom. Those who had never heard of or despised him before, now joined in his praise. He became a fashion; he passed into a proverb; he was an idol in the eyes of his readers, as much as he could ever, in the days of his youthful vanity, have been in his own; he was dazzled with his own popularity; and all this was owing to the king. No wonder he was delighted with the change, infatuated with it, infuriated! It was better to him than four thousand pounds a year for his own life, and fifteen hundred a year to his widow during the joint-lives of four other persons. It was what all his life he had been aiming at.—'Thou hast it now, king, Cawdor, Glamis, all!'* It was what the nurses had prophecied of him, and what the school-boy had dreamt; and that which is first, is also last in our thoughts. It was this that tickled his vanity more than his pension: it was this that raised his gratitude, that melted his obdurate pride, that opened the sluices of his heart to the poison of corruption, that exorcised the low, mechanic, vulgar, morose, sour principles of liberty clean out of him, left his mind 'swept and

garnished,'* parched and dry, fevered with revenge, bloated with adulation; and made him as shameless and abandoned in sacrificing every
feeling of attachment or obligation to the people, as he had before been
bold and prodigal in heaping insult and contumely upon the throne.
He denounced his former principles, in the true spirit of an apostate,
with a fury equal to the petulant and dogmatical tone in which he had
asserted them; and then proceeded to abuse all those who doubted the
honesty or wisdom of this change of opinion. He, in short, looked
upon every man as his enemy who did not think 'his book fit for
a gentleman to read;' and would willingly have committed every such
presumptuous sceptic to the flames for not bowing down in servile
adoration before this idol of his vanity and reputation. Hence the frantic philippics in his latter revolutionary speeches and writings, and the
alteration from a severe and stately style of eloquence and reasoning in
his earlier compositions to the most laboured paradoxes and wildest
declamation. We do not mean to say that his latest works did not display the greatest genius. His native talents blazed out, undisguised and
unconfined in them. *Indignatio facit versus.** Burke's best Muse was his
vanity or spleen. He felt quite at home in giving vent to his personal
spite and venal malice. He pleaded his own cause and the cause of the
passions better, and with more eloquence, than he ever pleaded the
cause of truth or justice. He felt the one rankling in his heart with all
their heat and fury, he only conceived the other with his understanding coldly and circuitously.—The Letters of William Burke give one,
however, a low idea of Burke's honesty, even in a pecuniary point of
view. (See Barry's Life.) He constantly tells Barry, as a source of consolation to his friend, and a compliment to his brother, 'that though
his party had not hitherto been successful, or had not considered him
as they ought, matters were not so bad with him but that he could still
afford to be honest, and not desert the cause.'* This is very suspicious.
This querulous tone of disappointment, and cockering up of his
boasted integrity, must have come from Burke himself; who would
hardly have expressed such a view of the subject, if it had not been
frequently in his thoughts; or if he had not made out a previous debtor
and creditor account between preferment and honesty, as one of the
regular principles of his political creed.

The same narrow view of the subject, drawn from a supposition
that money, or interest in the grossest sense, is the only inducement
to a dereliction of principle or sinister conduct, has been applied to

shew the sincerity of the present Laureate in his change of opinions; for it was said that the paltry salary of 100*l.* a year was not a sufficient temptation to any man of common sense, and who had other means of gaining an ample livelihood honourably, to give up his principles and his party, unless he did so conscientiously. That is not the real alternative of the case. It is not the hundred pounds salary, it is the honour (some may think it disgrace) conferred along with it, that enhances the prize. 'And with it words of so sweet breath composed, as made the gift more rare.'[1]* It is the introduction to Carlton-House, the smile, the squeeze by the hand that awaits him there, 'escap'd from Pyrrho's maze, and Epicurus' sty.'* The being presented at Court is worth more than a hundred pounds a year. A person with a hundred thousand pounds a year can only be presented at Court, and would consider it the greatest mortification to be shut out. It is the highest honour in the land; and Mr. Southey, by accepting his place and discarding his principles, receives that highest honour as a matter of course, in addition to his salary and his butt of sack. He is ushered into the Royal presence as by a magic charm, the palace-gates fly open at the sight of his laurel-crown, and he stands in the midst of 'Britain's warriors, her statesmen, and her fair,'* as if suddenly dropped from the clouds. Is this nothing to a vain man? Is it nothing to the author of *Wat Tyler* and *Joan of Arc* to have those errors of his youth veiled in the honours of his riper years? To fill the poetic throne of Dryden, of Shadwell, of Cibber, and of Pye? To receive distinctions which Spenser, Shakspeare, and Milton never received, and to chaunt to the unaverted ear of Sovereignty strains such as they never sung? To be seen on each returning birth-day joining the bright throng, the lengthened procession, gay, gilt, painted, coronetted, garlanded, that as it pass to and fro to St. James's, all London, in sunshine or in shower, pours out to gaze at? We tremble for the consequences, should any thing happen to disturb the Laureate in his dream of perfect felicity. Racine died broken-hearted, because Louis XIV. frowned upon him as he passed; and yet Racine was as great a poet and as pious a man as Mr. Southey.

To move in the highest circles, to be in favour at Courts, to be familiar with Princes, is then an object of ambition, which may be

---

[1] We hope Mr. Southey has not found the truth of the latter part of the passage. 'Rich gifts wax poor, when givers prove unkind.'*

supposed to fascinate a less romantic mind than Mr. Southey's, setting the lucrativeness of his conversion out of the question. Many persons have paid dear for this proud elevation with bankrupt health and beggared fortunes. How many are ready to do so still! Mr. Southey only paid for it *with his opinion*; and some people think it as much as his opinion was worth. Are we to suppose Mr. Southey's vanity of so sordid a kind, that it must be bribed by his avarice? Might not the Poet Laureate be supposed to catch at a title or a blue ribbon, without a round salary attached to it?

Why do country gentlemen wish to get into Parliament, but to be seen there? Why do grown merchants and rich nabobs wish to sit there, like so many overgrown school-boys? Look at the hundreds of thousands of pounds squandered in contested elections? It is not interest but opinion that provokes the combatants. Do you suppose that these persons expect to repay themselves by making a market of their constituents, and selling their votes to the best bidder? No: but they wish to be thought to have the greatest influence, the greatest number of friends and adherents in their county; and they will pay any price for it. We put into the lottery, indeed, in hopes of what we can get, but in the lottery of life honour is the great prize. It is the opinion of the people for which the candidate at an election contends; and on the same principle he will barter the opinion of the people, their rights and liberty, and his own independence and character, not for gold, but for the friendship of a court-favourite. Not that gold has not its weight too, for the great and powerful have that also to bestow:—it is true, that

> ——In their Livery
> Walk Crowns and Crownets, Realms and Islands,
> As Plates drop from their Pockets.*

But opinion is a still more insinuating and universal menstruum for dissolving honesty. *That sweet smile that hangs on princes' favours** is more effectual than even the favours themselves!

* * *

We are all of us more or less the slaves of opinion. There is no one, however mean or insignificant, whose approbation is altogether indifferent to us; whose flattery does not please, whose contempt does not mortify us. There is an atmosphere of this sort always about us, from which we can no more withdraw ourselves than from the air we breathe. But the air of a Court is the concentrated essence of the opinion of the world. The atmosphere there is mephitic. It is subtle poison, the least exhalation of which taints the vitals of its victims. It is made up of servile adulation, of sneering compliments, of broken promises, of smiling professions, of stifled opinions, of hollow thanks, of folly and lies—

> Soul-killing lies, and truths that work small good.*

It is infected with the breath of flatterers, and the thoughts of Kings! Let us see how its influence descends:—from the King to the people, to his Ministers first, from the Ministers to both Houses of Parliament, from Lords to Ladies, from the Clergy to the Laity, from the high to the low, from the rich to the poor, and 'pierces through the body of the city, country, court'*—it is beauty, birth, wit, learning, riches, numbers; it is fear and favour; it has all the splendour that can seduce, all the power that can intimidate, all the interest that can corrupt, on its side; so that the opinion of the King is the opinion of the nation; and if that opinion is not a wise one, hangs like a millstone round its neck, oppresses it like a night-mare, weighs upon it like lead, makes truth a lie, right wrong, turns liberty into slavery, peace into war, plenty to famine, turns the heads of a whole people, and bows their bodies to the earth. 'Whosoever shall stumble against this stone, it shall bruise him: but whomsoever it falls upon, it shall grind him to powder.'* Who is there in his senses that can withstand this torrent of opinion setting in upon him from the throne, and absorbing by degrees every thing in its vortex—undermining every principle of independence, confounding every distinction of the understanding, and obliterating every trace of liberty? To argue against it, is like arguing against the motion of the world with which we are carried along: its influence is as powerful and as imperceptible. To question it, is folly; to resist it, madness. To differ with the opinion of a whole nation, seems as presumptuous as it is unwise: and yet the very circumstance which makes it so uniform, is that which makes it worth nothing. Authority is more absolute than reason. Truth curtesies to power. No arguments could persuade ten millions of men in one country to be all of one mind, and thirty millions in another country to be of just the contrary; but the word of a King does it! We do not like to differ from the company we are in. How much more difficult is

it to brave the opinion of the world! No man likes to be frowned out
of society. No man likes to be without sympathy. He must be a proud
man indeed who can do without it; and proud men do not like to be
made a mark for 'scorn to point his slow and moving finger at.'* No
man likes to be thought the enemy of his king and country, without
just cause. No man likes to be called a fool or a knave, merely because
he is not a fool and a knave. It is not desirable to have to answer arguments backed with informations filed *ex officio*; it is not amusing to
become a bye-word with the mob. A nickname is *the hardest stone that
the devil can throw at a man*.* It will knock down any man's resolution.
It will stagger his opinion. It will tame his pride. Fasten it upon any
man, and he will try to shake it off, at any rate, though he should part
with honour and honesty along with it. To be shut out from public
praise or private friendship, to be lampooned in newspapers or Anti-
Jacobin reviews, to be looked blank upon in company, is not 'a consummation devoutly to be wished.'* The unfavourable opinion of
others gives you a bad opinion of yourself or them: and neither of
these conduces to persevering, high-minded integrity. To wish to
serve mankind, we should think well of them. To be able to serve
them, they should think well of us. To keep well with the public, is not
more necessary to a man's private interest than to his general utility.
It is a hopeless task to be always striving against the stream: it is
a thankless one to be in a state of perpetual litigation with the community. The situation of a strange dog in a country town, barked at
and worried by all the curs in the village, is about as enviable as that
of a person who affects singularity in politics. What is a man to do
who gets himself into this predicament, in an age when patriotism is
a misnomer in language, and public principle a solecism in fact? If he
cannot bring the world round to his opinion, he must as a forlorn
hope go over to theirs, and be content to be knave—or nothing.

Such is the force of opinion, that we would undertake to drive
a first Minister from his place and out of the country, by merely being
allowed to hire a number of dirty boys to hoot him along the streets
from his own house to the treasury and from the treasury back again.
How would a certain distinguished character,* remarkable for uniting
the *suaviter in modo* with the *fortiter in re*, and who, with an invariable
consistency in his political principles, carries the easiness of his temper to a degree of apparent *nonchalance*, bear to have a starling in his
neighbourhood taught to repeat nothing but Walcheren,* or to ring

the changes in his ears upon the names of Castles, Oliver, and
Reynolds?* Can we wonder then at the feats which such Ministers
have performed with the Attorney-General* at their backs, and
the country at their heels, in full cry against every one who was not
a creature of the Ministers,—for whose morals they could not
vouch as government-spies, or whose talents they did not reward
as government-critics?—Mr. Coleridge, in his Literary Biography,*
lately published, complains with pathetic bitterness of the wanton
and wilful slanders formerly circulated with so much zeal in the Anti-
Jacobin Review against himself, Mr. Southey, and his other poetical
friends, merely for a difference of political opinion; and he signifi-
cantly assigns these slanders as the reason why himself and his friends
remained so long adverse to the party who were the authors of them!
We will venture to go a little further, and say that they were not only
the reason of their long estrangement from the Court-party, but of
their final reconciliation to it. They had time to balance and reflect,
and to take a choice of evils—they deliberated between the loss of
principle and of character, and they were undone. They thought it
better to be the accomplices of venality and corruption than the mark
for them to shoot their arrows at: they took shelter from the abuse by
joining in the cry. Mr. Southey says that he has not changed his principles, but that circumstances have changed, and that he has grown
wiser from the events of five-and-twenty years. How is it that his
present friend and associate in the Quarterly Review,* who was
formerly a contributor to the Beauties of the Anti-Jacobin, has not
changed too? The world has gone round in his time too, but he
remains firm to his first principles. He worships the sun wherever he
sees it. Court-favour, 'the cynosure of longing eyes,'* sheds a more
steady influence on its votaries than vague popularity. The confined,
artificial air of a Court has a wonderful effect in stopping that progress of the mind with the march of events, of which Mr. Southey boasts,
and prematurely fixes the volatility of genius in a *caput mortuum* of
prejudice and servility, in those who are admitted within the magic
circle! The Anti-Jacobin poet and orator, Mr. Canning, has not become
a renegado to the opinions of the Court: the Jacobin poet and prose-
writer, Mr. Southey, has become a renegado to his own.—In an article
in the Quarterly Review (some months back) there was an argument
to shew that the late war against France was all along the undoubted
result of popular opinion, 'because from the first party-spirit ran so

high upon this subject, that any one who expressed an opinion against it did so at the hazard of his reputation, fortune, or even life.'* The author of this singular argument, we believe, was one of those, who did not at the critical period here alluded to approve of it, and who has since become a convert to its justice and humanity. His own statement may account for his change of opinion. What a pity for a man to hazard his life and fortune in a cause by maintaining an opinion, and to lose his character afterwards by relinquishing it. The present Poet-laureate has missed indeed the crown of martyrdom, and has gained a crown of laurel in its stead!

The same consistent writers, and friends of civil and religious liberty, who are delighted with the restoration of the Bourbons, of the Pope, and the Inquisition, have lately made an attempt to run down the Dissenters in this country;* and in this they are right. They dwell with fondness on 'the single-heartedness of the Spanish nation,'* who are slaves and bigots to a man, and scoff at the Presbyterians and Independents of this country, who ousted Popery and slavery at the Revolution, and who had a main hand in placing and continuing the present family on the throne—as but half-Englishmen, and as equally disaffected to Church and State. There is some ground for this antipathy of our political changelings to a respectable, useful, and conscientious body of men: and we will here, in discharge of an old debt,* say what this ground is. If it were only meant that the Dissenters are but half Englishmen, because they are not professed slaves—that they are disaffected to the Constitution in Church and State, because they are not prepared to go all the lengths of despotism and intolerance under a Protestant hierarchy and Constitutional King, which they resisted 'at the peril of their characters, their fortunes, and their lives,'* under a persecuting priesthood and an hereditary Pretender, this would be well: but there is more in it than this. Our sciolists would persuade us that the different sects are hot-beds of sedition, because they are nurseries of public spirit, and independence, and sincerity of opinion in all other respects. They are so necessarily, and by the supposition. They are Dissenters from the Established Church: they submit voluntarily to certain privations, they incur a certain portion of obloquy and ill-will, for the sake of what they believe to be the truth: they are not time-servers on the face of the evidence, and that is sufficient to expose them to the instinctive hatred and ready ribaldry of those who think venality the first of virtues, and prostitution of principle the best sacrifice a man can make to the Graces or his Country. The Dissenter does not change his sentiments with the seasons: he does not suit his conscience to his convenience. This is enough to condemn him for a pestilent fellow. He will not give up his principles because they are unfashionable, therefore he is not to be trusted. He speaks his mind bluntly and honestly, therefore he is a secret disturber of the peace, a dark conspirator against the State. On the contrary, the different sects in this country are, or have been, the steadiest supporters of its liberties and laws: they are checks and barriers against the insidious or avowed encroachments of arbitrary power, as effectual and indispensable as any others in the Constitution: they are depositaries of a principle as sacred and somewhat rarer than a devotion to Court-influence—we mean the love of truth. It is hard for any one to be an honest politician who is not born and bred a Dissenter. Nothing else can sufficiently inure and steel a man against the prevailing prejudices of the world, but that habit of mind which arises from non-conformity to its decisions in matters of religion. There is a natural alliance between the love of civil and religious liberty, as much as between Church and State. Protestantism was the first school of political liberty in Europe: Presbyterianism has been one great support of it in England. The sectary in religion is taught to appeal to his own bosom for the truth and sincerity of his opinions, and to arm himself with stern indifference to what others think of them. This will no doubt often produce a certain hardness of manner and cold repulsiveness of feeling in trifling matters, but it is the only sound discipline of truth, or inflexible honesty in politics as well as in religion. The same principle of independent inquiry and unbiassed conviction which makes him reject all undue interference between his Maker and his conscience, will give a character of uprightness and disregard of personal consequences to his conduct and sentiments in what concerns the most important relations between man and man. He neither subscribes to the dogmas of priests nor truckles to the mandates of Ministers. He has a rigid sense of duty which renders him superior to the caprice, the prejudices, and the injustice of the world; and the same habitual consciousness of rectitude of purpose, which leads him to rely for his self-respect on the testimony of his own heart, enables him to disregard the groundless malice and rash judgements of his opponents. It is in vain for him to pay his court to the world, to fawn upon power; he labours under certain insurmountable

disabilities for becoming a candidate for its favour: he dares to contradict its opinion and to condemn its usages in the most important
article of all. The world will always look cold and askance upon him;
and therefore he may defy it with less fear of its censures. The
Presbyterian is said to be sour: he is not therefore over-complaisant—

> Or if severe in thought,
> The love he bears to virtue is in fault.*

Dissenters are the safest partizans, and the steadiest friends. Indeed
they are almost the only people who have an idea of an abstract attachment to a cause or to individuals, from a sense of fidelity, independently of prosperous or adverse circumstances, and in spite of
opposition.* No patriotism, no public spirit, not reared in that
inclement sky and harsh soil, in 'the *hortus siccus* of dissent,'* will
generally last: it will either bend in the storm or droop in the sunshine. *Non ex quovis ligno fit Mercurius.** You cannot engraft a medlar
on a crab-apple. A thorough-bred Dissenter will never make an
accomplished Courtier. The antithesis of a Presbyterian Divine of the
old school is a Poet-laureate of the new. We have known instances of
both; and give it decidedly in favour of old-fashioned honesty over
new-fangled policy.

We have known instances of both. The one we would willingly forget;
the others we hope never to forget, nor can we ever. A Poet-laureate is
an excrescence even in a Court; he is doubly nugatory as a Courtier
and a Poet; he is a refinement upon insipidity, and a superfluous piece
of supererogation. But a Dissenting Minister is a character not so
easily to be dispensed with, and whose place cannot well be supplied.
It is the fault of sectarianism that it tends to scepticism; and so relaxes
the springs of moral courage and patience into levity and indifference.
The prospect of future rewards and punishments is a useful set-off
against the immediate distribution of places and pensions; the antici-
pations of faith call off our attention from the grosser illusions of sense.
It is a pity that this character has worn itself out; that that pulse of
thought and feeling has ceased almost to beat in the heart of a nation,
who, if not remarkable for sincerity and plain downright well-
meaning, are remarkable for nothing. But we have known some such,*
in happier days; who had been brought up and lived from youth to
age in the one constant belief of God and of his Christ, and who
thought all other things as dross compared with the glory hereafter to

be revealed. Their youthful hopes and vanity had been mortified in them, even in their boyish days, by the neglect and supercilious regards of the world; and they turned to look into their own minds for something else to build their hopes and confidence upon. They were true Priests. They set up an image in their own minds, it was truth: they worshipped an idol there, it was justice. They looked on man as their brother, and only bowed the knee to the Highest. Separate from the world, they walked humbly with their God, and lived in thought with those who had borne testimony of a good conscience, with the spirits of just men in all ages. They saw Moses when he slew the Egyptian, and the Prophets who overturned the brazen images; and those who were stoned and sawn asunder. They were with Daniel in the lions' den, and with the three children who passed through the fiery furnace, Meshech, Shadrach, and Abednego; they did not crucify Christ twice over, or deny him in their hearts, with St. Peter; the Book of Martyrs* was open to them; they read the story of William Tell, of John Huss and Jerome of Prague, and the old one-eyed Zisca; they had Neale's History of the Puritans* by heart, and Calamy's Account of the Two Thousand Ejected Ministers,* and gave it to their children to read, with the pictures of the polemical Baxter, the silver-tongued Bates, the mild-looking Calamy, and old honest Howe;* they believed in Lardner's Credibility of the Gospel History:* they were deep-read in the works of the *Fratres Poloni*,* Pripscovius, Crellius, Cracovius, who sought out truth in texts of Scripture, and grew blind over Hebrew points; their aspiration after liberty was a sigh uttered from the towers, 'time-rent,'* of the Holy Inquisition; and their zeal for religious toleration was kindled at the fires of Smithfield. Their sympathy was not with the oppressors, but the oppressed. They cherished in their thoughts—and wished to transmit to their posterity—those rights and privileges for asserting which their ancestors had bled on scaffolds, or had pined in dungeons, or in foreign climes. Their creed too was 'Glory to God, peace on earth, good will to man.'* This creed, since profaned and rendered vile, they kept fast through good report and evil report. This belief they had, that looks at something out of itself, fixed as the stars, deep as the firmament, that makes of its own heart an altar to truth, a place of worship for what is right, at which it does reverence with praise and prayer like a holy thing, apart and content: that feels that the greatest being in the universe is always near it, and that all things work together for the good of his creatures, under his guiding hand. This covenant they kept, as the stars keep their courses: this principle they stuck by, for want of knowing better, as it sticks by them to the last. It grew with their grouth, it does not wither in their decay. It lives when the almond-tree flourishes, and is not bowed down with the tottering knees. It glimmers with the last feeble eyesight, smiles in the faded cheek like infancy, and lights a path before them to the grave.—This is better than the life of a whirligig Court poet.

Happy are they, who live in the dream of their own existence, and see all things by the light of their own minds; who walk by faith and hope, not by knowledge; to whom the guiding-star of their youth still shines from afar, and into whom the spirit of the world has not entered! They have not been 'hurt by the archers,'* nor has the iron entered their souls. They live in the midst of arrows and of death, unconscious of harm. The evil thing comes not nigh them. The shafts of ridicule pass unheeded by, and malice loses its sting. The example of vice does not rankle in their breasts, like the poisoned shirt of Nessus.* Evil impressions fall off from them, like drops of water. The yoke of life is to them light and supportable. The world has no hold on them. They are in it, not of it; and a dream and a glory is ever about them.*

16

ON FASHION

Born of nothing, begot of nothing.*

> His garment neither was of silk nor say,
> But painted plumes in goodly order dight,
> Like as the sun-burnt Indians do array
> Their tawny bodies in their proudest plight:
> As those same plumes, so seem'd he vain and light,
> That by his gait might easily appear;
> For still he far'd as dancing in delight,
> And in his hands a windy fan did bear,
> That in the idle air he mov'd still here and there.*

FASHION is an odd jumble of contradictions, of sympathies and antipathies. It exists only by its being participated among a certain number of persons, and its essence is destroyed by being communicated to a greater number. It is a continual struggle between 'the great vulgar and small,'* to get the start of or keep up with each other in the race of appearances, by an adoption on the part of the one of such external and fantastic symbols as strike the attention and excite the envy or admiration of the beholder, which are no sooner made known and exposed to public view for this purpose, than they are successfully copied by the multitude, the slavish herd of imitators, who do not wish to be behind-hand with their betters in outward show and pretensions, and which then sink, without any farther notice, into disrepute and contempt. Thus fashion lives only in a perpetual round of giddy innovation and restless vanity. To be old fashioned is the greatest crime a coat or a hat can be guilty of. To look like nobody else is a sufficiently mortifying reflection; to be in danger of being mistaken for one of the rabble is worse. Fashion constantly begins and ends in the two things it abhors most, singularity and vulgarity. It is the perpetual setting up and disowning a certain standard of taste, elegance, and refinement, which has no other foundation or authority than that it is the prevailing distinction of the moment, which was yesterday ridiculous from its being new, and tomorrow will be odious from its being common. It is one of the most slight and insignificant of all things. It cannot be lasting, for it depends on the constant change and shifting of its own harlequin disguises; it cannot be sterling, for, if it were, it could not depend on the breath of caprice; it must be superficial, to produce its immediate effect on the gaping crowd; and frivolous, to admit of its being assumed at pleasure by the numbers of those who affect, by being in the fashion, to be distinguished from the rest of the world. It is not any thing in itself, nor the sign of any thing but the folly and vanity of those who rely upon it as their greatest pride and ornament. It takes the firmest hold of the most flimsy and narrow minds, of those whose emptiness conceives of nothing excellent but what is thought so by others, and whose self-conceit makes them willing to confine the opinion of all excellence to themselves and those like them. That which is true or beautiful in itself, is not the less so for standing alone. That which is good for any thing, is the better for being more widely diffused. But fashion is the abortive issue of vain ostentation and exclusive egotism: it is haughty, trifling, affected, servile, despotic, mean, and ambitious, precise and fantastical, all in a breath—tied to no rule, and bound to conform to every whim of the minute. 'The fashion of an hour old mocks the wearer.'* It is a sublimated essence of levity, caprice, vanity, extravagance, idleness, and selfishness. It thinks of nothing but not being contaminated by vulgar use, and winds and doubles like a hare, and betakes itself to the most paltry shifts to avoid being overtaken by the common hunt that are always in full chase after it. It contrives to keep up its fastidious pretensions, not by the difficulty of the attainment, but by the rapidity and evanescent nature of the changes. It is a sort of conventional badge, or understood passport into select circles, which must still be varying (like the water-mark in bank-notes) not to be counterfeited by those without the pale of fashionable society; for to make the test of admission to all the privileges of that refined and volatile atmosphere depend on any real merit or extraordinary accomplishment, would exclude too many of the pert, the dull, the ignorant, too many shallow, upstart, and self-admiring pretenders, to enable the few that passed muster to keep one another in any tolerable countenance. If it were the fashion, for instance, to be distinguished for virtue, it would be difficult to set or follow the example; but then this would confine the pretension to a small number, (not the most fashionable part of the community,) and would carry a very singular air with it. Or if excellence in any art or science were made the standard of fashion, this would also effectually prevent vulgar imitation, but then it would

equally prevent fashionable impertinence. There would be an obscure
circle of *virtù** as well as virtue, drawn within the established circle of
fashion, a little province of a mighty empire;—the example of honesty would spread slowly, and learning would still have to boast
a respectable minority. But of what use would such uncourtly and
out-of-the-way accomplishments be to the great and noble, the rich
and the fair, without any of the *eclat*, the noise and nonsense which
belong to that which is followed and admired by all the world alike?
The real and solid will never do for the current coin, the common
wear and tear of foppery and fashion. It must be the meretricious, the
showy, the outwardly fine, and intrinsically worthless—that which
lies within the reach of the most indolent affectation, that which can
be put on or off at the suggestion of the most wilful caprice, and for
which, through all its fluctuations, no mortal reason can be given, but
that it is the newest absurdity in vogue! The shape of a head-dress,
whether flat or piled (curl on curl) several stories high by the help of
pins and pomatum,* the size of a pair of paste buckles, the quantity
of gold-lace on an embroidered waistcoat, the mode of taking a pinch
of snuff or of pulling out a pocket handkerchief, the lisping and
affected pronunciation of certain words, the saying *Me'm* for *Madam*,
Lord Foppington's* *Tam* and *'Paun honour*, with a regular set of visiting phrases and insipid sentiments ready sorted for the day, were what
formerly distinguished the mob of fine gentlemen and ladies from the
mob of their inferiors. These marks and appendages of gentility had
their day, and were then discarded for others equally peremptory and
unequivocal. But in all this chopping and changing, it is generally one
folly that drives out another; one trifle that by its specific levity
acquires a momentary and surprising ascendancy over the last. There
is no striking deformity of appearance or behaviour that has not been
made 'the sign of an inward and invisible grace.'* Accidental imperfections are laid hold of to hide real defects. Paint, patches, and powder, were at one time synonymous with health, cleanliness, and
beauty. Obscenity, irreligion, small oaths, tippling, gaming, effemin-
acy in the one sex and Amazon airs in the other, any thing is the fashion, while it lasts. In the reign of Charles II. the profession and
practice of every species of extravagance and debauchery were looked
upon as the indispensable marks of an accomplished cavalier. Since
that period the court has reformed, and has had rather a rustic air.
Our belles formerly overloaded themselves with dress: of late years,

they have affected to go almost naked,—'and are, when unadorned, adorned the most.'* The women having left off stays, the men have taken to wear them, if we are to believe the authentic Memoirs of the Fudge Family.* The Niobe head* is at present buried in the *poke* bonnet,* and the French milliners and *marchands des modes** have proved themselves an overmatch for the Greek sculptors, in matters of taste and costume.

A very striking change has, however, taken place in dress of late years, and some progress has been made in taste and elegance, from the very circumstance, that, as fashion has extended its empire in that direction, it has lost its power. While fashion in dress included what was costly, it was confined to the wealthier classes: even this was an encroachment on the privileges of rank and birth, which for a long time were the only things that commanded or pretended to command respect, and we find Shakespear complaining that 'the city madam bears the cost of princes on unworthy shoulders;'* but, when the appearing in the top of the mode no longer depended on the power of purchasing certain expensive articles of dress, or on the right of wearing them, the rest was so obvious and easy, that any one who chose might cut as coxcombical a figure as the best. It became a matter of mere affectation on the one side, and gradually ceased to be made a matter of aristocratic assumption on the other. 'In the grand carnival of this our age,'* among other changes this is not the least remarkable, that the monstrous pretensions to distinction in dress have dwindled away by tacit consent, and the simplest and most graceful have been in the same request with all classes. In this respect, as well as some others, 'the age is grown so picked, the peasant's toe comes so near the courtier's heel, it galls his kibe;'* a lord is hardly to be distinguished in the street from an attorney's clerk; and a plume of feathers is no longer mistaken for the highest distinction in the land! The ideas of natural equality and the Manchester steam-engines together have, like a double battery, levelled the high towers and artificial structures of fashion in dress, and a white muslin gown is now the common costume of the mistress and the maid, instead of their wearing, as heretofore, rich silks and satins or coarse linsey-wolsey. It would be ridiculous (on a similar principle) for the courtier to take the wall* of the citizen, without having a sword by his side to maintain his right of precedence; and, from the stricter notions that have prevailed of a man's personal merit and identity, a cane dangling from his arm is the greatest extension of his figure that can be allowed to the modern *petit-maitre*.*

What shews the worthlessness of mere fashion is, to see how easily this vain and boasted distinction is assumed, when the restraints of decency or circumstances are once removed, by the most uninformed and commonest of the people. I know an undertaker that is the greatest prig in the streets of London, and an Aldermanbury haberdasher, that has the most military strut of any lounger in Bond Street or St James's. We may, at any time, raise a regiment of fops from the same number of fools, who have vanity enough to be intoxicated with the smartness of their appearance, and not sense enough to be ashamed of themselves. Every one remembers the story in Peregrine Pickle,* of the strolling gipsy that he picked up in spite, had well scoured, and introduced her into genteel company, where she met with great applause, till she got into a passion by seeing a fine lady cheat at cards, rapt out a volley of oaths, and let nature get the better of art. Dress is the great secret of address. Clothes and confidence will set any body up in the trade of modish accomplishment. Look at the two classes of well-dressed females whom we see at the play-house, in the boxes. Both are equally dressed in the height of the fashion, both are *rouged*, and wear their neck and arms bare,—both have the same conscious, haughty, theatrical air;—the same toss of the head, the same stoop in the shoulders, with all the grace that arises from a perfect freedom from embarrassment, and all the fascination that arises from a systematic disdain of formal prudery,—the same pretence and jargon of fashionable conversation,—the same mimicry of tones and phrases,—the same 'lisping, and ambling, and painting, and nicknaming of Heaven's creatures;'*—the same every thing but real propriety of behaviour, and real refinement of sentiment. In all the externals, they are as like as the reflection in the looking-glass. The only difference between the woman of fashion and the woman of pleasure is, that the one *is* what the other only *seems to be*; and yet, the victims of dissipation who thus rival and almost outshine women of the first quality in all the blaze, and pride, and glitter of shew and fashion, are, in general, no better than a set of raw, uneducated, inexperienced country girls, or awkward coarse-fisted servant maids, who require no other apprenticeship or qualification to be on a level with persons of the highest distinction in society, in all the brilliancy and elegance of outward appearance, than that they have forfeited its common privileges, and every title to respect in reality. The truth is, that real virtue, beauty, or understanding, are the same, whether 'in a high or low degree;'* and the airs and graces pretended superiority over these which the highest classes give themselves, from mere frivolous and external accomplishments, are easily imitated, with provoking success, by the lowest,—whenever they *dare*.

The two nearest things in the world are gentility and vulgarity—

And thin partitions do their bounds divide.*

Where there is much affectation of the one, we may be always sure of meeting with a double share of the other. Those who are conscious to themselves of any real superiority or refinement, are not particularly jealous of the adventitious marks of it. Miss Burney's novels all turn upon this slender distinction. It is the only thing that can be said against them. It is hard to say which she has made out to be the worst; low people always aping gentility, or people in high life always avoiding vulgarity. Mr Smith and the Brangtons* were everlastingly trying to do as their fashionable acquaintances did, and these again were always endeavouring *not* to do and say what Mr Smith and the Brangtons did or said. What an instructive game at cross purposes! 'Kings are naturally lovers of low company,'* according to the observation of Mr Burke; because their rank cannot be called into question by it, and they can only hope to find, in the opposite extreme of natural and artificial inequality, any thing to confirm them in the belief, that their personal pretensions at all answer to the ostensible superiority to which they are raised. By associating only with the worst and weakest, they persuade themselves that they are the best and wisest of mankind.

17

MINOR THEATRES

THIS is a subject on which we shall treat, with satisfaction to ourselves, and, we hope, to the edification of the reader. Indeed, we are not a little vain of the article we propose to write on this occasion; and we feel the pen in our hands flutter its feathered down with more than its usual specific levity, at the thought of the idle, careless career before it. No Theatre-Royal* oppresses the imagination, and entombs it in a mausoleum of massy pride; no manager's pompous pretensions choak up the lively current of our blood: no long-announced performance, big with expectation, comes to nothing, and yet compels us gravely to record its failure, and compose its epitaph. We have here 'ample scope and verge enough;'* we pick and chuse as we will, light where we please, and stay no longer than we have a mind—saying 'this I like, that I loath, as one picks pears:'*—hover over the Surry theatre;* or snatch a grace beyond the reach of art* from the Miss Dennetts at the Adelphi;* or take a peep (like the Devil upon Two Sticks*) at Mr. Booth at the Cobourg*—and one peep is sufficient:—Or stretch our legs and strain our fancies (as a pure voluntary exercise of dramatic faith and charity) as far as Mr. Rae and the East London,* where Mrs. Gould (late Miss Burrell), makes fine work with Don Giovanni and the Furies!* We are not, in this case, to be 'constrained by mastery.'*—Escaped from under the more immediate inspection of the Lord Chamberlain's eye, fastidious objections, formal method, regular details, strict moral censure, cannot be expected at our hands: our 'speculative and officed instruments'* may be well laid aside for a time. At sight of the purlieus of taste, and suburbs of the drama, criticism 'clappeth his wings, and straitway he is gone!'* In short, we feel it as our bounden duty to strike a truce with gravity, and give a furlough to fancy; and, in entering on this part of our subject, to let our thoughts wander over it, sport and trifle with it at pleasure, like the butter-fly of whom Spenser largely and loftily sings in his Muiopotmos.—

> There he arriving, round about doth fly
> From bed to bed, from one to other border,
> And takes survey, with curious busy eye,

Of every flower and herb there set in order;
Now this, now that he tasteth tenderly,
Yet none of them he rudely doth disorder,
Nor with his feet their silken leaves deface,
But pastures on the pleasures of each place.

What more felicity can fall to creature
Than to enjoy Delight with Liberty,
And to be lord of all the works of Nature,
To reign in th' air from earth to highest sky:
To feed on flowers, and weeds of glorious feature,
To take whatever thing doth please the eye?
Who rests not pleased with such happiness,
Well worthy he to taste of wretchedness!*

If we could but once realise this idea of a butterfly-critic, extracting
sweets from flowers, and turning gall to honey, we might well hope to
soar above the Grubstreet race, and confound, by the novelty of our
appearance, and the gaiety of our flight, the idle conjectures of ignorant or malicious pretenders in entomology!—

Besides, having once got out of the vortex of prejudice and fashion,
that surrounds our large Winter Theatres, what is there to hinder us
(or what shall) from dropping down from the verge of the metropolis
into the haunts of the provincial drama;—from taking coach to Bath
or Brighton, or visiting the Land's-End, or giving an account of
Botany-bay theatricals, or the establishment of a new theatre at
Venezuela? One reason that makes the Minor Theatres interesting is,
that they are the connecting link, that lets us down, by an easy transition, from the highest pomp and proudest display of the Thespian
art, to its first rudiments and helpless infancy.—With conscious
happy retrospect, they lead the eye back, along the *vista* of the imagination, to the village barn, or travelling booth, or old-fashioned town-
hall, or more genteel assembly-room, in which Momus first unmasked
to us his fairy revels, and introduced us, for the first time in our lives,
to that strange anomaly in existence, that fanciful reality, that gay
waking dream, *a company of strolling players!* Sit still, draw close
together, hold in your breath—not a word, not a whisper—the laugh
is ready to start away, 'like greyhound on the slip,'* the big tear of
wonder and expectation is ready to steal down 'the full eyes and fair
cheeks of childhood,'* almost before the time. Only another moment,
and amidst blazing tapers, and the dancing sounds of music, and light

throbbing hearts, and eager looks, the curtain rises, and the picture of the world appears before us in all its glory and in all its freshness. Life throws its gaudy shadow across the stage; Hope shakes his many-coloured wings, 'embalmed with odours;'* Joy claps his hands, and laughs in a hundred happy faces. Oh childish fancy, what a mighty empire is thine; what endless creations thou buildest out of nothing; what 'a wide O'* indeed, thou chusest to act thy thoughts, and unrivalled feats upon! Thou art better than the gilt trophy that decks the funeral pall of kings; thou art brighter than the costly mace that precedes them on their coronation-day! Thy fearfullest visions are enviable happiness; thy wildest fictions are the solidest truths. Thou art the only reality. All other possessions mock our idle grasp: but thou performest by promising; thy smile is fruition; thy blandishments are all that we can fairly call our own; thou art the balm of life, the heaven of childhood, the poet's idol, and the player's pride! The world is but thy painting; and the stage is thine enchanted mirror.—When it first displays its shining surface to our view, how glad, how surprised are we! We have no thought of any deception in the scene, no wish but to realise it ourselves with inconsiderate haste and fond impatience. We say to the air-drawn gorgeous phantom, 'Come, let me clutch thee!'* A new sense comes upon us, the scales fall off our eyes, and the scenes of life start out in endless quick succession crowded with men and women-actors, such as we see before us—comparable to 'those gay creatures of the element, that live in the rainbow, and play i' th' plighted clouds!'* Happy are we who look on and admire; and happy, we think, must they be who are so looked at and admired; and sometimes we begin to feel uneasy till we can ourselves mingle in the gay, busy, talking, fluttering, powdered, painted, perfumed, peruked, quaintly-accoutred throng of coxcombs and coquettes,—of tragedy heroes or heroines,—in good earnest; or turn stage-players and represent them in jest, with all the impertinent and consequential airs of the originals!

It is no insignificant epoch in one's life the first time that odd-looking thing, a play-bill, is left at our door in a little market town in the country (say W——m in S——shire*). The Manager, somewhat fatter and more erect, 'as Manager beseems,' than the rest of his Company, with more of the man of business, and not less of the cox-comb, in his strut and manner, knocks at the door with the end of a walking cane (a badge of office!) and a bundle of papers under his arm; presents one of them printed in large capitals, with a respectful bow and a familiar shrug; hopes to give satisfaction in the town; hints at the liberal encouragement they received at W——ch,* the last place they stopped at; had every possible facility afforded by the Magistrates; supped one evening with the Rev. Mr. J——s,* a dissenting clergyman, and really a very well-informed, agreeable, sensible man, full of anecdote—no illiberal prejudices against the profession:—then talks of the strength of his company, with a careless mention of his own favourite line—his benefit fixed for an early day, but would do himself the honour to leave farther particulars at a future opportunity—speaks of the stage as an elegant amusement, that most agreeably enlivened a spare evening or two in the week, and, under proper management (to which he himself paid the most assiduous attention) might be made of the greatest assistance to the cause of virtue and humanity—had seen Mr. Garrick act the last night but one before his retiring from the stage—had himself had offers from the London boards, and indeed could not say he had given up all thoughts of one day surprising them—as it was, had no reason to repine—Mrs. F—— tolerably advanced in life—his eldest son a prodigious turn for the higher walks of tragedy—had said perhaps too much of himself—had given universal satisfaction—hoped that the young gentleman and lady, at least, would attend on the following evening, when the West-Indian* would be performed at the market-hall, with the farce of No Song No Supper*—and so having played his part, withdraws in the full persuasion of having made a favourable impression, and of meeting with every encouragement the place affords! Thus he passes from house to house, and goes through the routine of topic after topic, with that sort of modest assurance, which is indispensable in the manager of a country theatre. This fellow, who floats over the troubles of life as the froth above the idle wave, with all his little expedients and disappointments, with pawned paste-buckles, mortgaged scenery, empty exchequer, and rebellious orchestra, is not of all men the most miserable:—he is little less happy than a king, though not much better off than a beggar. He has little to think of, much to do, more to say; and is accompanied, in his incessant daily round of trifling occupations, with a never-failing sense of authority and self-importance, the one thing needful (above all others) to the heart of man. This however is their man of business in the company; he is a sort of fixture in their little state; like Nebuchadnezzar's image,* but half of earth and half of finer metal: he is not 'of imagination all compact:'* he is not, like the rest of his aspiring crew, a feeder upon air, a drinker of applause, tricked out in vanity and in nothing else; he is not quite mad, nor quite happy. The whining Romeo, who goes supperless to bed, and on his pallet of straw dreams of a crown of laurel, of waving handkerchiefs, of bright eyes, and billet-doux breathing boundless love: the ranting Richard, whose infuriate execrations are drowned in the shouts of the all-ruling pit; he who, without a coat to his back, or a groat in his purse, snatches at Cato's robe, and binds the diadem of Cæsar on his brow;—these are the men that Fancy has chosen for herself, and placed above the reach of fortune, and almost of fate. They take no thought for the morrow. What is it to them what they shall eat, or what they shall drink, or how they shall be clothed? 'Their mind to them a kingdom is.'*—It is not a poor ten shillings a week, their share in the profits of the theatre, with which they have to pay for bed, board, and lodging, that bounds their wealth. They share (and not unequally) in all the wealth, the pomp, and pleasures of the world. They wield sceptres, conquer kingdoms, court princesses, are clothed in purple, and fare sumptuously every night. They taste, in imagination, 'of all earth's bliss, both living and loving:'* whatever has been most the admiration or most the envy of mankind, they, for a moment, in their own eyes, and in the eyes of others, become. The poet fancies others to be this or that; the player fancies himself to be all that the poet but describes. A little rouge makes him the lover, a plume of feathers a hero, a brazen crown an emperor. Where will you buy rank, office, supreme delights so cheap as at his shop of fancy? Is it nothing to dream whenever we please, and *seem* whatever we desire? Is real greatness, is real prosperity, more than what it seems? Where shall we find, or where shall the votary of the stage find, Fortunatus's Wishing Cap,* but in the wardrobe which we laugh at; or borrow the philosopher's stone but from the *property-man* of the theatre? He has discovered the true Elixir of Life, which is freedom from care: he quaffs the pure *aurum potabile*,* which is popular applause. He who is smit with the love of this *ideal* existence, cannot be weaned from it. Hoot him from the stage, and he will stay to sweep the lobbies or shift the scenes. Offer him twice the salary to go into a counting-house, or stand behind a counter, and he will return to poverty, steeped in contempt, but eked out with fancy, at the end of a week. Make a laughing-stock of an actress, lower her salary, tell her she is too tall, awkward, stupid, and ugly; try to get rid of her all you can—she will remain, only to hear herself courted, to listen to the echo of her borrowed name, to live but one short minute in the lap of vanity and tinsel shew. Will you give a man an additional ten shillings a week, and ask him to resign the fancied wealth of the world, which he 'by his so potent art'* can conjure up, and glad his eyes, and fill his heart with it? When a little change of dress, and the muttering a few talismanic words, make all the difference between the vagabond and the hero, what signifies the interval so easily passed? Would you not yourself consent to be alternately a beggar and a king, but that you have not the secret skill to be so? The player has that 'happy alchemy of mind:'*—why then would you reduce him to an equality with yourself?—The moral of this reasoning is known and felt, though it may be gainsayed. Wherever the players come, they send a welcome before them, and leave an air in the place behind them.[1] They shed a light upon the day, that does not very soon pass off. See how they glitter along the street, wandering, not where business but the bent of pleasure takes them, like mealy-coated butterflies, or insects flitting in the sun. They seem another, happier, idler race of mortals, prolonging the carelessness of childhood to old age, floating down the stream of life, or wafted by the wanton breeze to their final place of rest. We remember one (we must make the reader acquainted with him) who once overtook us* loitering by 'Severn's sedgy side,'* on a fine May morning, with a score of play-bills streaming from his pockets, for the use of the neighbouring villages, and a music-score in his hand, which he sung blithe and clear, advancing with light step and a loud voice! With a sprightly *bon jour*, he passed on, carolling to the echo of the babbling stream, brisk as a bird, gay as a mote, swift as an arrow from a twanging bow, heart-whole, and with shining face that shot back the sun's broad rays!—What is become of this favourite of mirth and song? Has care touched him? Has death tripped up his heels? Has an indigestion imprisoned him, and all his gaiety, in a living dungeon? Or is he himself lost and buried amidst the rubbish of one of our larger, or else of one of our Minor Theatres?

>   ——Alas! how changed from him,
> That life of pleasure, and that soul of whim!*

[1] So the old song joyously celebrates their arrival:
'The beggars are coming to town,
Some in rags, and some in jags, and some in velvet gowns.'*

But as this was no doubt the height of his ambition, why should we wish to debar him of it?

This brings us back, after our intended digression, to the subject from whence we set out,—the smaller theatres of the metropolis; which we visited lately, in hopes to find in them a romantic contrast to the presumptuous and exclusive pretensions of the legitimate drama, and to revive some of the associations of our youth above described.—The first attempt we made was at the Cobourg, and we were completely baulked. Judge of our disappointment. This was not owing, we protest, to any fault or perversity of our own; to the crust and scales of formality which had grown over us; to the panoply of criticism in which we go armed, and which made us inaccessible to 'pleasure's finest point;'* or to the *cheveux-de-fris** of objections, which cut us off from all cordial participation in what was going forward on the stage. No such thing. We went not only willing, but determined to be pleased. We had laid aside the pedantry of rules, the petulance of sarcasm, and had hoped to open once more, by stealth, the source of sacred tears, of bubbling laughter, and concealed sighs. We were not formidable. On the contrary, we were 'made of penetrable stuff.'* Stooping from our pride of place, we were ready to be equally delighted with a clown in a pantomime, or a lord-mayor in a tragedy. We were all attention, simplicity, and enthusiasm. But we saw neither attention, simplicity, nor enthusiasm in any body else; and our whole scheme of voluntary delusion and social enjoyment was cut up by the roots. The play was indifferent, but that was nothing. The acting was bad, but that was nothing. The audience were low, but that was nothing. It was the heartless indifference and hearty contempt, shown by the performers for their parts, and by the audience for the players and the play, that disgusted us with all of them. Instead of the rude, naked, undisguised expression of curiosity and wonder, of overflowing vanity and unbridled egotism, there was nothing but an exhibition of the most petulant cockneyism and vulgar slang. All our former notions and theories were turned topsy-turvy. The genius of St. George's Fields prevailed, and you felt yourself in a bridewell, or a brothel, amidst Jew-boys, pickpockets, prostitutes, and mountebanks, instead of being in the precincts of Mount Parnassus, or in the company of the Muses. The object was not to admire or to excel, but to vilify and degrade every thing. The audience did not hiss the actors (that would have implied a serious feeling of disapprobation, and something like a disappointed wish to be pleased) but they laughed, hooted at, nick-named, pelted them with oranges and witticisms, to show their unruly contempt for them and their art; while the performers, to be even with the audience, evidently slurred their parts, as if ashamed to be thought to take any interest in them, laughed in one another's faces, and in that of their friends in the pit, and most effectually marred the process of theatrical illusion, by turning the whole into a most unprincipled burlesque. We cannot help thinking that some part of this indecency and licentiousness is to be traced to the diminutive size of these theatres, and to the close contact into which these unmannerly censors come with the objects of their ignorant and unfeeling scorn. Familiarity breeds contempt. By too narrow an inspection, you take away that fine, hazy medium of abstraction, by which (in moderation) a play is best set off: you are, as it were, admitted behind the scenes; 'see the puppets dallying;'* shake hands, across the orchestra, with an actor whom you know, or take one you do not like by the beard, with equal impropriety:—you distinguish the paint, the individual fea-tures, the texture of the dresses, the patch-work and machinery by which the whole is made up; and this in some measure destroys the effect, distracts attention, suspends the interest, and makes you dis-posed to quarrel with the actors as impostors, and 'not the men you took them for.'*—You here see Mr. Booth, in Brutus, with every motion of his face *articulated*, with his under-jaws grinding out sen-tences, and his upper-lip twitching at words and syllables, as if a nee-dle and thread had been passed through each corner of it, and the *gude wife* still continued sewing at her work:—you perceive the contortion and barrenness of his expression (in which there is only one variety of bent brows, and close pent-up mouth for all occasions) the parsimony of his figure is exposed, and the refuse tones of his voice fall with undiminished vulgarity on the pained ear:—you have Mr. Higman as Prior Aymer in Ivanhoe, who used to play the Gipsey so well at Covent-garden in Guy Mannering, and who certainly is an admirable bass singer:—you have Mr. Stanley,* from the Theatre-Royal, Bath, and whom we thought an interesting actor there (such as poor Wilson might have been who trod the same boards, and with whom our readers will remember that Miss Lydia Melford, in Humphrey Clinker, fell in love):—you have Mr. Barrymore, that old and deserv-ing favourite with the public in the best days of Mrs. Siddons and of John Kemble, superintending, we believe, the whole, from a little oval window in a stage-box, like Mr. Bentham eying the hopeful circle of delinquents in his Panopticon:*—and, to sum up all in one word, you have here Mr. H. Kemble,* whose hereditary gravity is put to the last test, by the yells and grins of the remorseless rabble!—

'My soul turn from them!'—'Turn we to survey,'* where the Miss Dennetts, at the Adelphi Theatre, (which should once more from them be called the *Sans Pareil*) weave the airy, the harmonious, liquid dance. Of each of them it might be said, and we believe has been said*—

> Her lovely Venus at a birth
> With two Sister Graces more
> To ivy-crowned Bacchus bore.*

Such figures, no doubt, gave rise to the fables of ancient mythology, and might be worshipped. They revive the ideas of classic grace, life, and joy. They do not seem like taught dancers, Columbines, and figurantes* on an artificial stage; but come bounding forward like nymphs in vales of Arcady, or, like Italian shepherdesses, join in a lovely group of easy gracefulness, while 'vernal airs attune the trembling leaves'* to their soft motions. If they were nothing in themselves, they would be complete in one another. Each owes a double grace, youth, and beauty, to her reflection in the other two. It is the principle of proportion or harmony personified. To deny their merit or criticise their style, is to be blind and dead to the felicities of art and nature. Not to feel the force of their united charms, (united, yet divided, different and yet the same) is not to see the beauty of 'four red roses on a stalk,'*—or of the mingled hues of the rainbow, or of the halcyon's breast, reflected in the stream,—or 'the witchery of the soft blue sky,'* or grace in the waving of the branch of a tree, or tenderness in the bending of a flower, or liveliness in the motion of a wave of the sea. We shall not try to defend them against the dancing-school critics; there is another school, different from that of the *pied a plomb* and *pirouette* cant, the school of taste and nature. In this school, the Miss Dennetts are (to say the least) delicious novices. Theirs is the only performance on the stage (we include the Opera) that gives the uninitiated spectator an idea, that dancing can be an emanation of instinctive gaiety, or express the language of sentiment. We might shew them to the Count Stendhal, who speaks so feelingly* of the beauties of a dance by Italian peasant girls, as our three English Graces; and we might add, as a farther proof of national liberality and public taste, that they had been discarded from one of our larger, to take refuge in one of our petty theatres, on a disagreement about a pound a week in their joint salaries. Yet we suppose if these young ladies were to marry, and not volunteer to put ten thousand pounds in the pockets of some liberally disposed manager, we should hear a very pitiful story of their ingratitude to their patrons and the public. It is the way of the world. There is a Mr. Reeve* at this theatre (the Adelphi in the Strand) of whom report had spoken highly in his particular department as a mimic, and in whom we were considerably disappointed. He is not so good as Matthews,* who, after all, is by no means a *fac-simile* of those he pretends to represent. We knew most of Mr. Reeve's likenesses, and that is the utmost we can say in their praise; for we thought them very bad ones. They were very slight, and yet contrived to be very disagreeable. Farren was the most amusing, from a certain oddity of voice and manner in the ingenious and eccentric original. Harley* again was not at all the thing. There was something of the external dress and deportment, but none of the spirit, the frothy essence. He made him out a great burly swaggering ruffian, instead of being what he is—a pleasant, fidgetty person, pert as a jack-daw, light as a grasshopper. In short, from having seen Mr. Reeve, no one would wish to see Mr. Harley, though there is no one who has seen him but wishes to see him again; and, though mimicry has the privilege of turning into ridicule the loftier pretensions of tragic heroes, we believe it always endeavours to set off the livelier peculiarities of comic ones in the most agreeable light. Mr. Kean was bad enough. It might have been coarse and repulsive enough, and yet like; but it wanted point and energy, and this was inexcusable. We have heard much of ludicrous and admirable imitations of Mr. Kean's acting. But the only person who ever caricatures Mr. Kean well, or from whose exaggerations he has any thing to fear, is himself.—There are several other actors at the Adelphi who are, and must continue to be, nameless. There are also some better known to the town, as Mr. Wilkinson, Mrs. Alsop, &c. This lady has lost none of her exuberant and piquant vivacity by her change of situation. She also looks much the same: and as you see her near, this circumstance is by no means to her advantage. The truth is, that there are not good actors or agreeable actresses enough in town to make one really good company (by which we mean a company able to get up any one really good play throughout) and of course there are not a sufficient number (unless by a miracle) to divide into eight or ten different establishments.

Of the Haymarket and Lyceum,* which come more properly under the head of *Summer Theatres*, it is not at present 'our hint to speak;'* but we may shortly take a peep into the Surrey and East London Theatres,[2] and enlarge upon them as we see cause. Of the latter it is sufficient to observe, that Mr. Rae is the principal tragic actor there, and Mr. Peter Moore* the chief manager. After this, is it to be wondered at that Covent-garden is almost deserted, and that Mr. Elliston* cannot yet afford to give up the practice of puffing at the bottom of his play-bills!—

The larger, as well as the smaller, theatres have been closed during the greater part of the last month. There has been one new piece, the *Antiquary*,* brought out at Covent-garden, since our last report. It is founded, as our readers will suppose, on the admirable novel of that name, by the author of Waverley, but it is only a slight sketch of the story and characters, and not, we think, equal to the former popular melo-drames taken from the same prolific source. The characters in general were not very intelligibly brought out, nor very strikingly cast. Liston made but an indifferent Mr. Jonathan Oldbuck. He was dressed in a snuff-coloured coat and plain bob-wig, and that was all. It was quaint and dry, and accordingly inefficient, and quite unlike his admirable portrait of Dominie Sampson,* which is one of the finest pieces of acting on the stage, both for humour and feeling, invention and expression. The little odd ways and antiquarian whims and crotchets of Mr. Oldbuck, even were they as well managed in the drama as they are exquisitely hit off in the novel, would hardly tell in Liston's hands. Emery* made an impressive Edie Ochiltree; but he was somewhat too powerful a preacher, and too sturdy a beggar. Mr. Abbott personated the haughty, petulant Captain MacIntire to a great nicety of resemblance. Mr. Duruset as young Lovell 'warbled'* in a manner that Jacques would not have found fault with. Miss Stephens* sang one or two airs very sweetly, and was complimented at the end very rapturously and unexpectedly by the *ungallant* Mr. Oldbuck. The scene on the sea-shore, where she is in danger of

---

[2] The story of the Heart of Mid Lothian was, we understand, got up at the Surrey Theatre last year by Mr. Dibdin,* in a most creditable style. A Miss Taylor, we hear, made an inimitable Jenny Deans, Miss Copeland was surprising as Madge Wildfire, Mrs. Dibdin, as Queen Caroline, was also said to be a complete piece of royal wax-work, and Dumbydikes was done to the life. Would we had seen them so done; but we can answer for these things positively on no authority but our own. If they make as good a thing of Ivanhoe, they will do more than the author has done.

being overtaken by the tide, with her father and old Edie, had an admirable effect, as far as the imitation of the rolling of the waves of the sea on a London stage could produce admiration. The part of old Elspith of Craigie Burn Wood, was strikingly performed by Mrs. Fawcett, who, indeed, acts whatever she undertakes well; and the scene with Lord Glenallan, in which she unfolds to him the dreadful story of his life, was given at much length and with considerable effect. But what can come up to the sublime, heart-breaking pathos, the terrific painting of the original work? The story of this unhappy feudal lord is the most harrowing in all these novels (rich as they are in the materials of nature and passion): and the description of the old woman, who had been a principal subordinate instrument in the tragedy, is done with a more masterly and withering hand than any other. Her death-like appearance, her strange existence, like one hovering between this world and the next, or like a speaking corpse; her fixed attitude, her complete forgetfulness of every thing but the one subject that loads her thoughts, her preternatural self-possession on that, her prophetic and awful denunciations, her clay-cold and shrivelled body, consumed and kept alive by a wasting fire within, are all given with a subtlety, a truth, a boldness and originality of conception, that were never, perhaps, surpassed. But the author does not want our praise; nor can we withhold from him our admiration.

Mr. Kean, the week before we saw him in Coriolanus, played Othello; and as we would always prefer bearing testimony to his genius, to recording his comparative failures, we will here express our opinion of his performance of this character in the words of a contemporary journal,* a short time back:—

Mr. Kean's Othello is, we suppose, the finest piece of acting in the world. It is impossible either to describe or praise it adequately. We have never seen any actor so wrought upon, so 'perplexed in the extreme.' The energy of passion, as it expresses itself in action, is not the most terrific part: it is the agony of his soul, shewing itself in looks and tones of voice. In one part, where he listens in dumb despair to the fiend-like insinuations of Iago, he presented the very face, the marble aspect of Dante's Count Ugolino. On his fixed eye-lids, 'horror sat plumed.' In another part, where a gleam of hope or of tenderness returns to subdue the tumult of his passions, his voice broke in faltering accents from his overcharged breast. His lips might be said less to utter words, than to distil drops of blood, gushing from his heart. An instance of this was in his pronunciation of the line, 'of one that loved not wisely but too well.' The whole of this last speech was indeed given with exquisite force and beauty. We only object to the virulence with which he delivers the last line, and with which he stabs himself—a virulence which Othello would neither feel against himself at the moment, nor against the 'turbaned Turk' (whom he had slain) at such a distance of time. His exclamation on seeing his wife, 'I cannot think but Desdemona's honest,' was 'the glorious triumph of exceeding love;' a thought flashing conviction on his mind, and irradiating his countenance with joy, like sudden sunshine. In fact, almost every scene or sentence in this extraordinary exhibition is a masterpiece of natural passion. The convulsed motion of the hands, and the involuntary swellings of the veins in the forehead in some of the most painful situations, should not only suggest topics of critical panegyric, but might furnish studies to the painter or anatomist.

18

ON THE PLEASURE OF PAINTING

'THERE is a pleasure in painting which none but painters know.'* In writing, you have to contend with the world: in painting, you have only to carry on a friendly strife with nature. You sit down to your task, and are happy. From the moment that you take up the pencil, and look nature in the face, you are at peace with your own heart. No angry passions rise to disturb the silent progress of the work,—to shake the hand, or dim the brow: no irritable humours are set afloat: you have no absurd opinions to combat—no point to strain—no adversary to crush—no fool to annoy; you are actuated by fear or favour of no man. There is 'no juggling here,'* no sophistry, no intrigue, no tampering with the evidence, no attempt to make black white, or white black: but you resign yourself into the hands of a greater power,—that of Nature,—with the simplicity of a child, and the devotion of an enthusiast—'study with joy her manner, and with rapture taste her style.'* The mind is calm, and full at the same time. The hand and eye are equally employed. In tracing the commonest object—a plant or the stump of a tree—you learn something every moment. You perceive unexpected differences, and discover likenesses where you looked for no such thing. You try to set down what you see, find out your error, and correct it. You need not play tricks, or purposely mistake: with all your pains, you are still far short of the mark. Patience grows out of the endless pursuit, and turns it into a luxury. A streak in a flower, a wrinkle in a leaf, a tinge in a cloud, a stain in an old wall or ruin grey, are seized with avidity, as the *spolia opima** of this sort of mental warfare, and furnish out labour for another half-day. The hours pass away untold, without chagrin, and without *ennui*; nor would you ever wish to pass them otherwise. Innocence is joined with industry, pleasure with business; and the mind is satisfied, though it is not engaged in thinking, or doing, any mischief.[1]

---

[1] There is a passage in Werter* which contains a very pleasing illustration of this doctrine, and is as follows:—

'About a league from the town is a place called Walheim. It is very agreeably situated on the side of a hill: from one of the paths which leads out of the village, you have a view of the whole country; and there is a good old woman who sells wine, coffee, and tea

I have not much pleasure in writing these Essays, or in reading them afterwards; though I own I now and then meet with a phrase that I like, or a thought that strikes me as a true one. But after I begin them, I am only anxious to get to the end of them, which I am not sure I shall do, for I seldom see my way a page, or even a sentence, before-hand; and when I have, as by a miracle, escaped, I trouble myself little more about them. I sometimes have to write them twice over: then it is necessary to read the *proof,* to prevent mistakes by the printer; so that by the time they appear in a tangible shape, and one can con them over with a conscious, sidelong glance to the public approbation, they have lost their gloss and relish, and become 'more tedious than a twice-told tale.'* For a person to read his own works over with any great delight, he ought first to forget that he ever wrote them. Familiarity naturally breeds contempt. It is, in fact, like poring fondly over a piece of blank paper:—from repetition, the words convey no distinct meaning to the mind, are mere idle sounds, except that our vanity claims an interest and property in them. I have more satisfac-tion in my own thoughts than in dictating them to others: words are necessary to explain the impression of certain things upon me to the reader, but they rather weaken, and draw a veil over, than strengthen it to myself. Although I might say with the poet, 'My mind to me a kingdom is,'* yet I have little ambition 'to set a throne or chair of state in the understandings of other men.'* The ideas we cherish most, exist best in a kind of shadowy abstraction—

Pure in the last recesses of the mind;*

there:—but better than all this, are two lime trees before the church, which spread their branches over a little green, surrounded by barns and cottages. I have seen few places more retired and peaceful. I send for a chair and table from the old woman's, and there I drink my coffee and read Homer. It was by accident that I discovered this place one fine afternoon: all was perfect stillness; every body was in the fields, except a little boy about four years old, who was sitting on the ground, and holding, between his knees, a child of about six months; he pressed it to his bosom with his little arms, which made a sort of great chair for it; and, notwithstanding the vivacity which sparkled in his eyes, he sat perfectly still. Quite delighted with the scene, I sat down on a plough opposite, and had great pleasure in drawing this little picture of brotherly tenderness. I added a bit of the hedge, the barn-door, and some broken cart-wheels, without any order, just as they hap-pened to lie;—and, in about an hour, I found I had made a drawing of great expression, and very correct design, without having put in any thing of my own. This confirmed me in the resolution I had made before, only to copy nature for the future. Nature is inexhaust-ible, and alone forms the greatest masters. * * * * Say what you will of rules, they alter the true features, and the natural expression.'

and derive neither force nor interest from being exposed to public view. They are old familiar acquaintance, and any change in them, arising from the adventitious ornaments of style or dress, is little to their advantage. After I have once written on a subject, it goes out of my mind: my feelings about it have been melted down into words, and *them* I forget. I have, as it were, discharged my memory of its old habitual reckoning, and rubbed out the score of real sentiment. For the future, it exists only for the sake of others.—But I cannot say, from my own experience, that the same process takes place in transferring our ideas to canvas. They gain more than they lose in the mechanical transformation. One is never tired of painting, because you have to set down, not what you knew already, but what you have just discovered. In the former case, you translate feelings into words; in the latter, names into things. There is a continual creation out of nothing going on. With every stroke of the brush, a new field of inquiry is laid open. New difficulties arise, and new triumphs are prepared over them. By comparing the imitation with the original, you see what you have done, and how much you have still to do. The test of the senses is severer than that of fancy, and an over-match even for the delusions of our self-love. One part of a picture shames another, and you determine to paint up to yourself, if you cannot come up to nature. Every object becomes lustrous from the light thrown back upon it by the mirror of art: and by the aid of the pencil we may be said to touch and handle the objects of sight. The air-drawn visions, that hover on the verge of existence, have a bodily presence given them on the canvas: the form of beauty is changed into a substance: the dream and the glory of the universe is made 'palpable to feeling as to sight.'*—And see! a rainbow starts from the canvas, with all its humid train of glory, as if it were drawn from its cloudy arch in heaven. The spangled landscape glitters with drops of dew after the shower. The 'fleecy fools'* show their coats in the gleams of the setting sun. The shepherds pipe their farewell notes in the fresh evening air. And is this bright vision made from a dead dull blank, like a bubble reflecting the mighty fabric of the universe? Who would think this miracle of Rubens's pencil possible to be performed? Who, having seen it, would not spend his life to do the like? See how the rich fallows, the bare stubble-field, the scanty harvest-home, drag in Rembrandt's landscapes! How often have I looked at them and nature, and tried to do the same, till the very 'light thickened,'* and there was an earthiness in the feeling of the air! There is no end of the refinements of art and nature in this respect. One may look at the misty glimmering horizon till the eye dazzles and the imagination is lost, in hopes to transfer the whole interminable expanse at one blow upon the canvas. Wilson said,* he used to try to paint the effect of the motes dancing in the setting sun. At another time, a friend, coming into his painting-room, when he was sitting on the ground in a melancholy posture, observed that his picture looked like a landscape after a shower of rain. He started up with great delight, and said, 'That is the effect I intended to produce, but thought I had failed.' Wilson was neglected; and, by degrees, neglected his art to apply himself to brandy. His hand became unsteady, so that it was only by repeated attempts that he could produce the effect he aimed at; and when he had done a little to a picture, he would say to any acquaintance, who chanced to drop in, 'I have painted enough for one day: come, let us go somewhere.' It was not so that Claude left his pictures, or his studies on the banks of the Tiber, to go in search of other enjoyments,—or ceased to gaze upon the glittering sunny vales and distant hills!* While his eye drank-in the clear sparkling hues and lovely forms of nature, his hand stamped them on the lucid canvas to last there for ever.—One of the most delightful parts of my life was one fine summer, when I used to walk out of an evening to catch the last light of the sun, gemming the green slopes or russet lawns, and gilding tower or tree, while the blue sky gradually turning to purple and gold, or skirted with dusky grey, hung its broad marble pavement over all—as we see it in the great master of Italian landscape. But to come to a more particular explanation of the subject.

The first head I ever tried to paint* was an old woman, with the upper part of the face shaded by her bonnet,—and I certainly laboured it with great perseverance. It took me numberless sittings to do it. I have it by me still, and sometimes look at it with surprise, to think how much pains were thrown away to little purpose—yet not altogether in vain, if it taught me to see good in every thing,* and to know that there is nothing vulgar in nature seen with the eye of science or of true art. Refinement creates beauty everywhere; it is the grossness of the spectator that discovers nothing but grossness in the object. Be this as it may, I spared no pains to do my best. If art was long, I thought that life was so too* at that moment. I got in the general effect the first day; and pleased and surprised enough I was at my success. The rest was a work of time—of weeks, and months (if need were) of patient toil and careful finishing. I had seen an old head by Rembrandt at Burleigh-house, and if I could produce a head at all like Rembrandt in a year—in my life-time—it would be glory and felicity, and wealth and fame enough for me! The head I had seen at Burleigh was an exact and wonderful fac-simile of nature, and I resolved to make mine (as nearly as I could), an exact fac-simile of nature. I did not then, nor do I now believe, with Sir Joshua, that the perfection of art consists in giving general appearances without individual details,* but in giving general appearances with individual details. Otherwise, I had done my work the first day. But I saw something more in nature than general effect, and thought it worth my while to give it in the picture. There was a gorgeous effect of light and shade: but there was a delicacy as well as depth in the *chiaro scuro*, which I was bound to follow into all its dim, and scarce perceptible variety of tone and shadow. Then I had to make the transition from a strong light to as dark a shade, preserving the masses, but gradually softening off the intermediate parts. It was so in nature: the difficulty was to make it so in the copy. I tried, and failed again and again; I strove harder, and succeeded as I thought. The wrinkles in Rembrandt were not hard lines; but broken and irregular. I saw the same appearance in nature, and strained every nerve to give it. If I could hit off this edgy appearance, and insert the reflected light in the furrows of old age in half a morning, I did not think I had lost a day. Beneath the shrivelled yellow parchment look of the skin, there was, here and there, a streak of the blood-colour tinging the face: this I made a point of conveying, and did not cease to compare what I saw with what I did, with jealous lynx-eyed watchfulness, till I succeeded to the best of my ability and judgment. How many revisions were there! How many attempts to catch an expression which I had seen the day before! How often did we try to get the old position, and wait for the return of the same light! There was a puckering up of the lips, a cautious introversion of the eye under the shadow of the bonnet, indicative of the feebleness and suspicion of old age, which at last we managed, after many trials, and some quarrels, to a tolerable nicety! The picture was never finished, and I might have gone on with it to the present hour.[2] I used

---

[2] It is at present covered with a thick slough of oil and varnish, (the perishable vehicle of the English school,) like an envelope of gold-beaters' skin, so as to be hardly visible.

to set it on the ground when my day's work was done, and saw revealed to me, with swimming eyes, the birth of new hopes, and of a new world of objects. The painter thus learns to look at nature with different eyes. He before saw her 'as in a glass darkly, but now face to face.'* He understands the texture and meaning of the visible universe, and 'sees into the life of things,'* not by the help of mechanical instruments, but of the improved exercise of his faculties, and an intimate sympathy with nature. The meanest thing is not lost upon him, for he looks at it with an eye to itself, not merely to his own vanity or interest, or the opinion of the world. Even where there is neither beauty nor use—if that ever were—still there is truth, and a sufficient source of gratification in the indulgence of curiosity and activity of mind. The humblest painter is a true scholar; and the best of scholars—the scholar of nature. For myself, speaking for the real comfort and satisfaction of the thing, I had rather have been Jan Steen or Gerard Dow,* than the greatest casuist or philologer that ever lived. The painter does not view things in cloud or 'mist, the common gloss of theologians,'* but applies the same standard of truth and disinterested spirit of inquiry, that influence his daily practice, to other subjects. He perceives form, he distinguishes character. He reads men and books with an intuitive eye. He is a critic as well as a connoisseur. The conclusions he draws are clear and convincing, because they are taken from the things themselves. He is not a fanatic, a dupe, or a slave; for the habit of seeing for himself, also disposes him to judge for himself. The most sensible men I know (taken as a class), are painters; that is, they are the most lively observers of what passes in the world about them; and the closest observers of what passes in their own minds. From their profession they in general mix more with the world than authors, and if they have not the same fund of acquired knowledge, are obliged to rely more on individual sagacity. I might mention the names of Opie, Fuseli, Northcote, as persons distinguished for striking description and acquaintance with the subtle traits of character.[3] Painters in ordinary society, or in obscure situations where their value is not known, and they are treated with

---

[3] Men in business, who are answerable with their fortunes for their opinions, and are therefore accustomed to ascertain pretty accurately the grounds on which they act, before they commit themselves on the event, are often men of remarkably quick and sound judgments. Artists, in like manner, must know tolerably well what they are about, before they can bring the result of their observations to the test of ocular demonstration.

neglect and indifference, have sometimes a forward self-sufficiency of manner: but this is not so much their fault as that of others. Perhaps their want of regular education may also be in fault, in such cases. Richardson, who is very tenacious of the respect in which the profession ought to be held, tells a story of Michael Angelo, that, after a quarrel between him and Pope Julius II. 'upon account of a slight which he conceived the pontiff had put upon him, Michael Angelo was introduced by a bishop, who, thinking to serve the artist by it, made it an argument that the Pope should be reconciled to him, because men of his profession were commonly ignorant, and of no consequence otherwise: his holiness, enraged at the bishop, struck him with his staff, and told him it was he that was the blockhead, and affronted the man himself would not offend; the prelate was driven out of the chamber, and Michael Angelo had the Pope's benediction accompanied with presents. This bishop had fallen into the vulgar error, and was rebuked accordingly.'*

Besides the exercise of the mind, painting exercises the body. It is a mechanical as well as a liberal art. To do any thing,—to dig a hole in the ground, to plant a cabbage, to hit a mark, to move a shuttle, to work a pattern,—in a word, to attempt to produce any effect, and to *succeed*, has something in it that gratifies the love of power, and carries off the restless activity of the mind of man. Indolence is a delightful but distressing state: we must be doing something to be happy. Action is no less necessary than thought to the instinctive tendencies of the human frame; and painting combines them both incessantly.[4] The hand furnishes a practical test of the correctness of the eye; and the eye, thus admonished, imposes fresh tasks of skill and industry upon the hand. Every stroke tells, as the verifying of a new truth, and every new observation, the instant it is made, passes into an act and emanation of the will. Every step is nearer what we wish, and yet there is always more to do. In spite of the facility, the fluttering grace, the evanescent hues, that play round the pencil of Rubens and Vandyke, however I may admire, I do not *envy* them this power so much as the slow, patient, laborious execution of Correggio, Leonardo da Vinci, and Andrea del Sarto,—where every touch seems conscious of its charge, emulous of truth, and where the painful artist has so distinctly wrought,

---

[4] The famous Schiller used to say, that he found the great happiness of life, after all, to consist in the discharge of some mechanical duty.*

That you might almost say his picture thought!*

In the one case, the colours seem breathed on the canvas as by magic, the work and the wonder of a moment: in the other, they seem inlaid into the body of the work, and as if it took the artist years of unremitting labour, and of delightful never-ending progress to perfection.[5] Who would wish ever to come to the close of such works,—not to dwell on them, to return to them, to be wedded to them to the last? Rubens, with his florid, rapid style, complained that when he had just learned his art, he should be forced to die: Leonardo, in the slow advances of his, had lived long enough!

Painting is not, like writing, what is properly understood by a sedentary employment. It requires, not indeed a strong, but a continued and steady exertion of muscular power. The precision and delicacy of the manual operation, makes up for the want of vehemence—as to balance himself for any time, in the same position, the rope-dancer must strain every nerve. Painting for a whole morning gives one as excellent an appetite for one's dinner, as old Abraham Tucker acquired for his by riding over Banstead Downs. It is related of Sir Joshua Reynolds, that 'he took no other exercise than what he used in his painting-room'*—the writer means, in walking backwards and forwards to look at his picture; but the act of painting itself, of laying on the colours in the proper place, and proper quantity, was a much harder exercise than this alternate receding from and returning to the picture. This last would be rather a relaxation and relief than an effort. It is not to be wondered at that an artist like Sir Joshua, who delighted so much in the sensual and practical part of his art, should have found himself at a considerable loss when the decay of his sight precluded him, for the last year or two of his life, from the following up of his profession—'the source,' according to his own remark, 'of thirty years' uninterrupted enjoyment and prosperity to him.'* It is only those who never think at all, or else who have accustomed themselves to brood incessantly on abstract ideas, that never feel *ennui*!

To give one instance more, and go on with this rambling discourse.— One of my first attempts was a picture of my father,* who was then in a green old age, with strong-marked features, and scarred with the

---

[5] The rich *impasting* of Titian and Giorgione combines something of the advantages of both these styles, the felicity of the one with the carefulness of the other, and is perhaps to be preferred to either.

smallpox. I drew it with a broad light crossing the face, looking down, with spectacles on, reading. The book was Shaftesbury's Characteristics, in a fine old binding, with Gribelin's etchings.* My father would as lieve it had been any other book; but for him to read was to be content, was 'riches fineless.'* The sketch promised well; and I set to work to finish it, determined to spare no time nor pains. My father was willing to sit as long as I pleased; for there is a natural desire in the mind of man to sit for one's picture, to be the object of continued attention, to have one's likeness multiplied; and besides his satisfaction in the picture, he had some pride in the artist, though he would rather I should have written a sermon than painted like Rembrandt or like Raphael. Those winter-days, with the gleams of sunshine coming through the chapel-windows, and cheered by the notes of the robin red-breast in our garden,—(that 'ever in the haunch of winter sings'*)—as my afternoon's work drew to a close,—were among the happiest of my life. When I gave the effect I intended to any part of the picture for which I had prepared my colours—when I imitated the roughness of the skin by a lucky stroke of the pencil—when I hit the clear pearly tone of a vein—when I gave the ruddy complexion of health, the blood circulating under the broad shadows of one side of the face, I thought my fortune made; or rather it was already more than made, in my fancying that I might one day be able to say with Correggio, '*I also am a painter!*'* It was an idle thought, a boy's conceit;* but it did not make me less happy at the time. I used regularly to set my work in the chair to look at it through the long evenings; and many a time did I return to take leave of it before I could go to bed at night. I remember sending it with a throbbing heart to the Exhibition,* and seeing it hung up there by the side of one of the Honourable Mr. Skeffington* (now Sir George). There was nothing in common between them, but that they were the portraits of two very good-natured men. I think, but am not sure, that I finished this portrait (or another afterwards), on the same day that the news of the battle of Austerlitz* came; I walked out in the afternoon, and, as I returned, saw the evening star set over a poor man's cottage* with other thoughts and feelings than I shall ever have again! Oh! for the revolution of the great Platonic year,* that those times might come over again! I could sleep out the three hundred and sixty-five thousand intervening years very contentedly!—The picture is left: the table, the chair, the window where I learned to read Livy, the chapel* where my father preached, remain where they were; but he himself is gone to rest, full of years, of faith, of hope, and charity!—......

The painter not only takes a delight in nature,—he has a new and exquisite source of pleasure opened to him in the study and contemplation of works of art—

> Whate'er Lorraine light touch'd with soft'ning hue,
> Or savage Rosa dash'd, or learned Poussin drew.*

He turns aside to view a country-gentleman's seat with eager looks, thinking it may contain some of the rich products of art. There is an air round Lord Radnor's Park,* for there hang the two Claudes, the Morning and Evening of the Roman empire—round Wilton-house, for there is Vandyke's picture of the Pembroke family—round Blenheim, for there is his picture of the Duke of Buckingham's children, and the most magnificent collection of Rubenses in the world—at Knowsley, for there is Rembrandt's Hand-writing on the Wall—and at Burleigh, for there are some of Guido's angelic heads. The young artist makes a pilgrimage to each of these places, eyes them wistfully at a distance, 'embowered deep in tufted trees,'* and feels an interest in them, of which the owner is scarce conscious: he enters the well-swept walks and echoing archways, passes the threshold, is led through wainscotted rooms, is shown the furniture, the rich hangings, the tapestry, the massy services of plate,—and, at last, is ushered into the room, where his treasure is, the idol of his vows—some speaking face or bright landscape! It is stamped on his brain, and lives there thence forward, a tally for nature, and a test of art. He furnishes out the chambers of the mind from the spoils of time, picks and chooses which shall have the best places, nearest his heart. He goes away richer than he came, richer than the possessor; and thinks that he may one day return, when he, perhaps, shall have done something like them, or even from failure shall have learned to admire truth and genius more.

My first initiation in the mysteries of the art was at the Orleans Gallery:* it was there I formed my taste, such as it is; so that I am irreclaimably of the old school in painting. I was staggered when I saw the works there collected, and looked at them with wondering and with longing eyes. A mist passed away from my sight: the scales fell off.* A new sense came upon me, a new heaven and a new earth stood before me. I saw the soul speaking in the face—'hands that the rod of empire had swayed'* in mighty ages past—'a forked mountain or blue promontory,'

> ————with trees upon't
> That nod unto the world, and mock our eyes with air.*

Old Time had unlocked his treasures, and Fame stood portress at the door. We had all heard of the names of Titian, Raphaël, Guido, Domenichino, the Caracci—but to see them face to face, to be in the same room with their deathless productions, was like breaking some mighty spell,—was almost an effect of necromancy! From that time I lived in a world of pictures. Battles, sieges, speeches in parliament, seemed mere idle noise and fury, 'signifying nothing,'* compared with those mighty works and dreaded names, that spoke to me in the eternal silence of thought. This was the more remarkable, as it was but a short time before that I was not only totally ignorant of, but insensible to the beauties of art. As an instance, I remember that one afternoon I was reading the Provoked Husband,* with the highest relish, with a green woody landscape of Ruysdael, or Hobbima, just before me, at which I looked off the book, now and then, and wondered what there could be in that sort of work to satisfy or delight the mind—at the same time, asking myself, as a possible question, whether I should ever feel an interest in it like what I took in reading Vanbrugh and Cibber?—

I had made some progress in painting when I went to the Louvre* to study, and I never did any thing afterwards. I never shall forget conning over the catalogue, which a friend lent me* just before I set out. The pictures, the names of the painters, seemed to relish in the mouth. There was one of Titian's Mistress* at her toilette. Even the colours with which the painter had adorned her hair were not more golden, more amiable to sight, than those which played round and tantalised my fancy ere I saw the picture.—There were two portraits by the same hand—'A young Nobleman with a glove,'*—another, 'A companion to it:'—I read the description over and over with fond expectancy, and filled up the imaginary outline with all I could conceive of grace, and dignity, and an antique *gusto*—all but equal to the original. There was the Transfiguration too. With what awe I saw it in my mind's eye, and was overshadowed with the spirit of the artist! When I say that I was not disappointed with these works afterwards, I pay the highest compliment I can pay to their transcendant merits.

Indeed, it was from seeing other works of the same great masters that I had formed a vague, but no disparaging idea of these.—The first day I got there, I was kept for some time in the French exhibition-room, and thought I should not be able to get a sight of the old masters. I just caught a peep at them through the door, (vile hinderance!) like looking out of purgatory into Paradise,—from Poussin's noble mellow-looking landscapes to where Rubens hung out his gaudy banner, and down the glimmering vista to the rich jewels of Titian and the Italian school. At last, by much importunity, I was admitted, and lost not an instant in making use of my new privilege.—It was *un beau jour** to me. I marched delighted through a quarter of a mile of the proudest efforts of the mind of man, a whole creation of genius, a universe of art! I ran the gauntlet of all the schools from the bottom to the top; and in the end got admitted into the inner room, where they had been repairing some of their greatest works. Here the Transfiguration, the St. Peter Martyr, and the St. Jerome of Domenichino stood on the floor, as if they had bent their knees, like camels stooping, to unlade their riches to the spectator. On one side, on an easel, stood Hippolito de Medici* (a portrait by Titian,) with a boar-spear in his hand, looking through those he saw, till you turned away from the keen glance: and thrown together in heaps were landscapes of the same hand, green pastoral hills and vales, and shepherds piping to their mild mistresses underneath the flowering shade. Reader, 'if thou hast not seen the Louvre, thou art damned!'* for thou hast not seen the choicest remains of the works of art; or thou hast not seen all these together, with their mutually reflected glories. I say nothing of the statues; for I know but little of sculpture, and never liked any till I saw the Elgin marbles.—Here, for four months together, I strolled and studied, and daily heard the warning sound—'*Quatres heures passées, il faut fermer, citoyens*' (ah! why did they ever change their style?) muttered in coarse provincial French; and brought away with me some loose draughts and fragments, which I have been forced to part with,* like drops of life-blood, for 'hard money.'* How often, thou tenantless mansion of godlike magnificence—how often has my heart since gone a pilgrimage to thee!

It has been made a question, whether the artist, or the mere man of taste and natural sensibility, receives most pleasure from the contemplation of works of art? And I think this question might be answered by another, as a sort of *experimentum crucis*,* namely, whether any one out of that 'number numberless'* of mere gentlemen and amateurs, who visited Paris at the period here spoken of, felt as much interest, as much pride or pleasure, in this display of the most striking monuments of art, as the humblest student would? The first entrance into the Louvre of the former would be only one of the events of his journey—not an event in his life, remembered ever after with thankfulness and regret. He would explore it with the same unmeaning curiosity and idle wonder, as he would the regalia in the Tower, or the Botanic Garden in the Thuilleries, but not with the fond enthusiasm of an artist. How should he? His is 'casual fruition, joyless, unendeared:'* but the painter is wedded to his art, the mistress, queen, and idol of his soul. He has embarked his all in it, fame, time, fortune, peace of mind, his hopes in youth, his consolation in age: and shall he not feel a more intense interest in whatever relates to it than the mere indolent trifler? Natural sensibility alone, without the entire application of the mind to that one object, will not enable the possessor to sympathise with all the degrees of beauty and power in the conceptions of a Titian, or a Correggio; but it is he only who does this, who follows them into all their force and matchless grace, that does or can feel their full value. Knowledge is pleasure as well as power. No one but the artist who has studied nature, and contended with the difficulties of art, can be aware of the beauties, or become intoxicated with a passion for painting. No one who has not limited his prospects and wishes to the pursuit of art, can feel the same exultation in its brightest ornaments and loftiest triumphs, which an artist does. Where the treasure is, there the heart is also. It is now seventeen years since I was studying in the Louvre, (and I have long since given up all thoughts of the art as a profession,) but long after I returned, and even still, I sometimes dream, of being there again,—of asking for the old pictures,—and not finding them, or finding them changed or faded from what they were, I cry myself awake! What gentleman-amateur ever does this at such a distance of time,—that is, ever received pleasure, or took interest enough in them, to produce so lasting an impression?

But it is said, that if a person had the same natural taste, and the same acquired knowledge as an artist, without the petty interests and technical notions, he would derive a purer pleasure from seeing a fine portrait, a fine landscape, and so on. This, however, is not so much begging the question, as asking an impossibility: he cannot have the same insight into the end, without having studied the means; nor the same love of art, without the same habitual and exclusive devotion to it. Painters are, no doubt, often actuated by jealousy, partiality, and a sordid attention to that only which they find useful to themselves in painting. W——* has been seen poring over the texture of a Dutch cabinet-picture, so that he could not see the picture itself.—But this is the perversion and pedantry of the profession, and not its true or genuine spirit. If W—— had never looked at any thing but megilps and handling, he never would have put the soul of life and manners into his pictures, as he has done. Another objection is, that the instrumental parts of the art, the means, the first rudiments, paints, oils, and brushes, are painful and disgusting; and that the consciousness of the difficulty and anxiety with which perfection has been attained, must take away from the pleasure of the finest performance. This, however, is only an additional proof of the greater pleasure derived by the artist from his profession; for these things which are said to interfere with and destroy the common interest in works of art, do not disturb him; he never once thinks of them, he is absorbed in the pursuit of a higher object, he is intent not on the means but the end, he is taken up, not with the difficulties, but with the triumph over them. As in the case of the anatomist, who overlooks many things in the eagerness of his search after abstract truth, or the alchemist, who, while he is raking into his soot and furnaces, lives in a golden dream, a lesser gives way to a greater object.—But it is pretended that the painter may be supposed to submit to the unpleasant part of the process only for the sake of the fame or profit in view. So far is this from being a true state of the question, that I will venture to say, in the instance of a friend of mine* who has lately succeeded in an important undertaking in his art, that not all the fame he has acquired, not all the money he has received from thousands of admiring spectators, not all the newspaper puffs,—not even the praise of the Edinburgh Review,* nor Mrs. Siddons's having pronounced his Head of Christ sublime,*—not all these things, put together, ever gave him at any time the same genuine, undoubted satisfaction, as any one half-hour employed in the ardent and propitious pursuit of his art—in finishing to his heart's content a foot, a hand, or even a piece of drapery. What is the state of mind of an artist while he is at work? He is then in the act of realising the highest idea he can form of beauty or grandeur: he conceives, he embodies that which he understands and loves best: that is, he is in full and perfect possession of that which is to him the source of the highest happiness and intellectual excitement which he can enjoy.

In short, as a conclusion to this argument, I will mention a circumstance which fell under my knowledge the other day. A friend had bought a print of Titian's Mistress, the same to which I have alluded above. He was anxious to show it me on this account. I told him it was a spirited engraving, but it had not the look of the original. I believe he thought this fastidious, till I offered to show him a rough sketch of it, which I had by me. Having seen this, he said, he perceived exactly what I meant, and could not bear to look at the print afterwards. He had good sense enough to see the difference in the individual instance; but a person better acquainted with Titian's manner, and with art in general, that is, of a more cultivated and refined taste, would know that it was a bad print, without having any immediate model to compare it with. He would perceive with a glance of the eye, with a sort of instinctive feeling, that it was hard, and without that bland, expansive, and nameless expression which always distinguished Titian's most famous works. Any one who is familiar with a head in a picture, can never reconcile himself to a print from it: but to the ignorant they are both the same. To a vulgar eye, there is no difference between a Guido and a daub, between a penny-print, or the vilest scrawl, and the most finished performance. In other words, all that excellence which lies between these two extremes,—all at least that marks the excess above mediocrity,—all that constitutes true beauty, harmony, refinement, grandeur, is lost upon the common observer. But it is from this point, that the delight, the glowing raptures of the true adept commence. An uninformed spectator may like an ordinary drawing better than the ablest connoisseur; but for that very reason he cannot like the highest specimens of art so well. The refinements, not only of execution, but of truth and nature, are inaccessible to unpractised eyes. The exquisite gradations in a sky of Claude's are not perceived by such persons, and consequently the harmony cannot be felt. Where there is no conscious apprehension, there can be no conscious pleasure. Wonder at the first sight of works of art, may be the effect of ignorance and novelty: but real admiration, and permanent delight in them, are the growth of taste and knowledge. 'I would not wish to have your eyes,' said a good-natured man to a critic, who was finding fault with a picture, in which the other saw no blemish. Why so? The idea which prevented the one from admiring this inferior production, was a higher idea of truth and beauty, which was ever present with him, and a continual source of pleasing and lofty contemplations. It may be different in a taste for outward luxuries, and the privations of mere sense; but the idea of perfection, which acts as an intellectual foil, is always an addition, a support, and a proud consolation!

Richardson, in his Essays,* which ought to be better known, has left some striking examples of the felicity and infelicity of artists, both as it relates to their external fortune, and to the practice of their art. In speaking of *the knowledge of hands*, he exclaims—

When one is considering a picture, or a drawing, one, at the same time, thinks this was done by him[6] who had many extraordinary endowments of body and mind, but was withal very capricious; who was honoured in life and death, expiring in the arms of one of the greatest princes of that age, Francis I. King of France, who loved him as a friend. Another is of him[7] who lived a long and happy life, beloved of Charles V. emperor; and many others of the first princes of Europe. When one has another in hand, we think this was done by one[8] who so excelled in three arts, as that any of them in that degree had rendered him worthy of immortality; and one moreover, that durst contend with his sovereign (one of the haughtiest popes that ever was) upon a slight offered to him, and extricated himself with honour. Another is the work of him[9] who, without any one exterior advantage but mere strength of genius, had the most sublime imaginations, and executed them accordingly, yet lived and died obscurely. Another we shall consider as the work of him[10] who restored painting when it had almost sunk; of him, whom art made honourable, but who neglecting and despising greatness with a sort of cynical pride, was treated suitably to the figure he gave himself, not his intrinsic worth; which, not having philosophy enough to bear it, broke his heart. Another is done by one[11] who, (on the contrary) was a fine gentleman, and lived in great magnificence, and was much honoured by his own and foreign princes; who was a courtier, a statesman, and a painter: and so much all these, that when he acted in either character, *that* seemed to be his business, and the others his diversion. I say, when one thus reflects, besides the pleasure arising from the beauties and excellences of the work, the fine ideas it gives us of natural things, the noble way of thinking it may suggest to us, an additional pleasure results from the above considerations. But oh! the pleasure, when a connoisseur and lover of art, has before him a picture or drawing, of which he can say, this is the hand, these are the thoughts of him[12] who was

---

[6] Leonardo da Vinci.   [7] Titian.   [8] Michael Angelo.   [9] Correggio.
[10] Annibal Caracci.   [11] Rubens.   [12] Rafaelle.

one of the politest, best-natured gentlemen that ever was; and beloved, and assisted by the greatest wits, and the greatest men then in Rome: of him who lived in great fame, honour, and magnificence, and died extremely lamented; and missed a Cardinal's hat, only by dying a few months too soon; but was particularly esteemed and favoured by two popes, the only ones who filled the chair of St. Peter in his time, and as great men as ever sat there since that apostle, if at least he ever did: one, in short, who could have been a Leonardo, a Michael Angelo, a Titian, a Correggio, a Parmegiano, an Annibal, a Rubens, or any other when he pleased, but none of them could ever have been a Rafaelle.

The same writer speaks feelingly of the change in the style of different artists from their change of fortune; and as the circumstances are little known, I will quote the passage relating to two of them.

Guido Reni, from a prince-like affluence of fortune (the just reward of his angelic works) fell to a condition, like that of a hired servant to one who supplied him with money for what he did at a fixed rate; and that by his being bewitched with a passion for gaming, whereby he lost vast sums of money; and even, what he got in this, his state of servitude by day, he commonly lost at night: nor could he ever be cured of this cursed madness. Those of his works, therefore, which he did in this unhappy part of his life, may easily be conceived to be in a different style to what he did before, which in some things, that is, in the airs of his heads (in the gracious kind) had a delicacy in them peculiar to himself, and almost more than human. But I must not multiply instances. Parmegiano is one that alone takes in all the several kinds of variation, and all the degrees of goodness, from the lowest of the indifferent, up to the sublime. I can produce evident proofs of this in so easy a gradation, that one cannot deny but that he that did this, might do that, and very probably did so; and thus one may ascend and descend, like the angels on Jacob's ladder, whose foot was upon the earth, but its top reached to heaven.

And this great man had his unlucky circumstance: he became mad after the philosopher's stone, and did but very little in painting or drawing afterwards. Judge what that was, and whether there was not an alteration of style from what he had done, before this devil possessed him. His creditors endeavoured to exorcise him, and did him some good; for he set himself to work again in his own way: but if a drawing I have of a Lucretia be that he made for his last picture, as it probably is (Vasari says, that was the subject of it) it is an evident proof of his decay: it is good indeed, but it wants much of the delicacy which is commonly seen in his works; and so I always thought before I knew or imagined it to be done in this his ebb of genius.

We have had two artists of our own country, whose fate has been as singular as it was hard. Gandy* was a portrait-painter in the beginning of the last century, whose heads were said to have come near to Rembrandt's, and he was the undoubted prototype of Sir Joshua Reynolds's style. Yet his name has scarcely been heard of; and his reputation, like his works, never extended beyond his own county. What did he think of himself, and of a fame so bounded! Did he ever dream he was indeed an artist? Or how did this feeling in him differ from the vulgar conceit of the lowest pretender? The best known of his works is a portrait of an alderman of Exeter, in some public building in that city.*

Poor Dan. Stringer!* Forty years ago he had the finest hand, and the clearest eye of any artist of his time, and produced heads and drawings that would not have disgraced a brighter period in the art. But he fell a martyr (like Burns) to the society of country-gentlemen, and then of those whom they would consider as more his equals. I saw him many years ago, when he treated the masterly sketches he had by him (one in particular of the group of citizens in Shakspeare 'swallowing the tailor's news*),' as 'bastards of his genius, not his children;'* and seemed to have given up all thoughts of his art. Whether he is since dead, I cannot say: the world do not so much as know that he ever lived!

PEOPLE have about as substantial an idea of Cobbett as they have of Cribb.* His blows are as hard, and he himself is as impenetrable. One has no notion of him as making use of a fine pen, but a great mutton-fist; his style stuns his readers, and he 'fillips the ear of the public with a three-man beetle.'* He is too much for any single newspaper antagonist; 'lays waste'* a city orator or Member of Parliament, and bears hard upon the government itself. He is a kind of *fourth estate** in the politics of the country. He is not only unquestionably the most powerful political writer of the present day, but one of the best writers in the language. He speaks and thinks plain, broad, downright English. He might be said to have the clearness of Swift, the naturalness of Defoe, and the picturesque satirical description of Mandeville; if all such comparisons were not impertinent. A really great and original writer is like nobody but himself. In one sense, Sterne was not a wit, nor Shakespear a poet. It is easy to describe second-rate talents, because they fall into a class and enlist under a standard: but first-rate powers defy calculation or comparison, and can be defined only by themselves. They are *sui generis*, and make the class to which they belong. I have tried half a dozen times to describe Burke's style without ever succeeding;—its severe extravagance; its literal boldness; its matter-of-fact hyperboles; its running away with a subject, and from it at the same time—but there is no making it out, for there is no example of the same thing any where else. We have no common measure to refer to; and his qualities contradict even themselves.

Cobbett is not so difficult. He has been compared to Paine; and so far it is true there are no two writers who come more into juxta-position from the nature of their subjects, from the internal resources on which they draw, and from the popular effect of their writings and their adaptation (though that is a bad word in the present case) to the capacity of every reader. But still if we turn to a volume of Paine's (his Common Sense or Rights of Man) we are struck (not to say somewhat refreshed) by the difference. Paine is a much more sententious writer than Cobbett. You cannot open a page in any of his best and earlier works without meeting with some maxim, some antithetical and memorable saying, which is a sort of starting-place for the argument, and the goal to which it returns. There is not a single *bon-mot*, a single sentence in Cobbett that has ever been quoted again. If any thing is ever quoted from him, it is an epithet of abuse or a nickname. He is an excellent hand at invention in that way, and has 'damnable iteration in him.'* What could be better than his pestering Erskine year after year with his second title of Baron Clackmannan?* He is rather too fond of *the Sons and Daughters of Corruption*. Paine affected to reduce things to first principles, to announce self-evident truths. Cobbett troubles himself about little but the details and local circumstances. The first appeared to have made up his mind beforehand to certain opinions, and to try to find the most compendious and pointed expressions for them: his successor appears to have no clue, no fixed or leading principles, nor ever to have thought on a question till he sits down to write about it; but then there seems no end of his matters of fact and raw materials, which are brought out in all their strength and sharpness from not having been squared or frittered down or vamped up to suit a theory—he goes on with his descriptions and illustrations as if he would never come to a stop; they have all the force of novelty with all the familiarity of old acquaintance; his knowledge grows out of the subject, and his style is that of a man who has an absolute intuition of what he is talking about, and never thinks of any thing else. He deals in premises and speaks to evidence—the coming to a conclusion and summing up (which was Paine's *forte*) lies in a smaller compass. The one could not compose an elementary treatise on politics to become a manual for the popular reader; nor could the other in all probability have kept up a weekly journal for the same number of years with the same spirit, interest, and untired perseverance. Paine's writings are a sort of introduction to political arithmetic on a new plan: Cobbett keeps a day-book and makes an entry at full of all the occurrences and troublesome questions that start up throughout the year. Cobbett with vast industry, vast information, and the utmost power of making what he says intelligible, never seems to get at the beginning or come to the end of any question: Paine in a few short sentences seems by his peremptory manner 'to clear it from all controversy, past, present, and to come.'* Paine takes a bird's-eye view of things. Cobbett sticks close to them, inspects the component parts, and keeps fast hold of the smallest advantages they afford him. Or if I might here be indulged in a pastoral allusion, Paine tries to

enclose his ideas in a fold for security and repose; Cobbett lets *his*
pour out upon the plain like a flock of sheep to feed and batten.
Cobbett is a pleasanter writer for those to read who do not agree with
him; for he is less dogmatical, goes more into the common grounds of
fact and argument to which all appeal, is more desultory and various,
and appears less to be driving at a previous conclusion than urged on
by the force of present conviction. He is therefore tolerated by all
parties, though he has made himself by turns obnoxious to all; and
even those he abuses read him. The Reformers read him when he was
a Tory, and the Tories read him now that he is a Reformer. He must,
I think, however, be *caviare* to the Whigs.[1]*

If he is less metaphysical and poetical than his celebrated prototype,
he is more picturesque and dramatic. His episodes, which are numerous as they are pertinent, are striking, interesting, full of life and
naïveté, minute, double measure running over, but never tedious—*nunquam sufflaminandus erat.** He is one of those writers who
can never tire us, not even of himself; and the reason is, he is always
'full of matter.'* He never runs to lees, never gives us the vapid leav-
ings of himself, is never 'weary, stale, and unprofitable,'* but always
setting out afresh on his journey, clearing away some old nuisance,
and turning up new mould. His egotism is delightful, for there is
no affectation in it. He does not talk of himself for lack of something
to write about, but because some circumstance that has happened to
himself is the best possible illustration of the subject, and he is not
the man to shrink from giving the best possible illustration of the
subject from a squeamish delicacy. He likes both himself and his subject too well. He does not put himself before it, and say—'admire me
first'—but places us in the same situation with himself, and makes us
see all that he does. There is no blindman's-buff, no conscious hints,
no awkward ventriloquism, no testimonies of applause, no abstract,
senseless self-complacency, no smuggled admiration of his own person by proxy: it is all plain and above-board. He writes himself plain
William Cobbett, strips himself quite as naked as any body would
wish—in a word, his egotism is full of individuality, and has room for
very little vanity in it. We feel delighted, rub our hands, and draw our
chair to the fire, when we come to a passage of this sort: we know it

---

[1] The late Lord Thurlow used to say that Cobbett was the only writer that deserved
the name of a political reasoner.*

will be something new and good, manly and simple, not the same insipid story of self over again. We sit down at table with the writer, but it is to a course of rich viands, flesh, fish, and wild-fowl, and not to a nominal entertainment, like that given by the Barmecide* in the Arabian Nights, who put off his visitors with calling for a number of exquisite things that never appeared, and with the honour of his company. Mr. Cobbett is not a *make-believe* writer. His worst enemy cannot say that of him. Still less is he a vulgar one. He must be a puny, common-place critic indeed, who thinks him so. How fine were the graphical descriptions he sent us from America: what a transatlantic flavour, what a native *gusto*, what a fine *sauce piquante* of contempt they were seasoned with! If he had sat down to look at himself in the glass, instead of looking about him like Adam in Paradise, he would not have got up these articles in so capital a style. What a noble account of his first breakfast after his arrival in America!* It might serve for a month. There is no scene on the stage more amusing. How well he paints the gold and scarlet plumage of the American birds, only to lament more pathetically the want of the wild wood-notes of his native land! The groves of the Ohio that had just fallen beneath the axe's stroke 'live in his description,' and the turnips that he transplanted from Botley 'look green'* in prose! How well at another time he describes the poor sheep that had got the tick and had tumbled down in the agonies of death! It is a portrait in the manner of Bewick,* with the strength, the simplicity, and feeling of that great naturalist. What havoc he makes, when he pleases, of the curls of Dr. Parr's wig* and of the Whig consistency of Mr. ——!* His Grammar* too is as entertaining as a story-book. He is too hard upon the style of others, and not enough (sometimes) on his own.

As a political partisan, no one can stand against him. With his brandished club, like Giant Despair in the Pilgrim's Progress, he knocks out their brains; and not only no individual, but no corrupt system could hold out against his powerful and repeated attacks, but with the same weapon, swung round like a flail, that he levels his antagonists, he lays his friends low, and puts his own party *hors de combat*. This is a bad propensity, and a worse principle in political tactics, though a common one. If his blows were straight forward and steadily directed to the same object, no unpopular Minister could live before him; instead of which he lays about right and left, impartially and remorselessly, makes a clear stage, has all the ring to himself, and then runs out of it, just when he should stand his ground. He throws his head into his adversary's stomach, and takes away from him all inclination for the fight, hits fair or foul, strikes at every thing, and as you come up to his aid or stand ready to pursue his advantage, trips up your heels or lays you sprawling, and pummels you when down as much to his heart's content as ever the Yanguesian carriers* belaboured Rosinante with their pack-staves. '*He has the back-trick simply the best of any man in Illyria.*'* He pays off both scores of old friendship and new-acquired enmity in a breath, in one perpetual volley, one raking fire of 'arrowy sleet'* shot from his pen. However his own reputation or the cause may suffer in consequence, he cares not one pin about that, so that he disables all who oppose, or who pretend to help him. In fact, he cannot bear success of any kind, not even of his own views or party; and if any principle were likely to become popular, would turn round against it to shew his power in shouldering it on one side. In short, wherever power is, there is he against it: he naturally butts at all obstacles, as unicorns are attracted to oak-trees, and feels his own strength only by resistance to the opinions and wishes of the rest of the world. To sail with the stream, to agree with the company, is not his humour. If he could bring about a Reform in Parliament, the odds are that he would instantly fall foul of and try to mar his own handy-work; and he quarrels with his own creatures as soon as he has written them into a little vogue—and a prison. I do not think this is vanity or fickleness so much as a pugnacious disposition, that must have an antagonist power to contend with, and only finds itself at ease in systematic opposition. If it were not for this, the high towers and rotten places of the world would fall before the battering-ram of his hard-headed reasoning: but if he once found them tottering, he would apply his strength to prop them up, and disappoint the expectations of his followers. He cannot agree to any thing established, nor to set up any thing else in its stead. While it is established, he presses hard against it, because it presses upon him, at least in imagination. Let it crumble under his grasp, and the motive to resistance is gone. He then requires some other grievance to set his face against. His principle is repulsion, his nature contradiction: he is made up of mere antipathies, an Ishmaelite* indeed without a fellow. He is always playing at *hunt-the-slipper* in politics. He turns round upon whoever is next him. The way to wean him from any opinion, and make him conceive an intolerable hatred against it, would be to place somebody near him who was perpetually dinning it in his ears. When he is in England, he does nothing but abuse the Boroughmongers,* and laugh at the whole system: when he is in America, he grows impatient of freedom and a republic. If he had staid there a little longer, he would have become a loyal and a loving subject of his Majesty King George IV. He lampooned the French Revolution when it was hailed as the dawn of liberty by millions: by the time it was brought into almost universal ill-odour by some means or other (partly no doubt by himself) he had turned, with one or two or three others, staunch Buonapartist. He is always of the militant, not of the triumphant party: so far he bears a gallant shew of magnanimity; but his gallantry is hardly of the right stamp. It wants principle: for though he is not servile or mercenary, he is the victim of self-will. He must pull down and pull in pieces: it is not in his disposition to do otherwise. It is a pity; for with his great talents he might do great things, if he would go right forward to any useful object, make thorough-stitch work of any question, or join hand and heart with any principle. He changes his opinions as he does his friends, and much on the same account. He has no comfort in fixed principles: as soon as any thing is settled in his own mind, he quarrels with it. He has no satisfaction but in the chase after truth, runs a question down, worries and kills it, then quits it like vermin, and starts some new game, to lead him a new dance, and give him a fresh breathing through bog and brake, with the rabble yelping at his heels and the leaders perpetually at fault. This he calls sport-royal. He thinks it as good as cudgel-playing or single-stick,* or any thing else that has life in it. He likes the cut and thrust, the falls, bruises, and dry blows of an argument: as to any good or useful results that may come of the amicable settling of it, any one is welcome to them for him. The amusement is over, when the matter is once fairly decided.

There is another point of view in which this may be put. I might say that Mr. Cobbett is a very honest man with a total want of principle, and I might explain this paradox thus. I mean that he is, I think, in downright earnest in what he says, in the part he takes at the time; but in taking that part, he is led entirely by headstrong obstinacy, caprice, novelty, pique or personal motive of some sort, and not by a stedfast regard for truth or habitual anxiety for what is right uppermost in his mind. He is not a feed, time-serving, shuffling advocate (no man could write as he does who did not believe himself sincere)—but his understanding is the dupe and slave of his momentary, violent, and irritable humours. He does not adopt an opinion 'deliberately or for money;'* yet his conscience is at the mercy of the first provocation he receives, of the first whim he takes in his head; he sees things through the medium of heat and passion, not with reference to any general principles, and his whole system of thinking is deranged by the first object that strikes his fancy or sours his temper.—One cause of this phenomenon is perhaps his want of a regular education. He is a self-taught man, and has the faults as well as excellences of that class of persons in their most striking and glaring excess. It must be acknowledged that the Editor of the Political Register (the *two-penny trash*,* as it was called, till a bill passed the House* to raise the price to sixpence) is not 'the gentleman and scholar:'* though he has qualities that, with a little better management, would be worth (to the public) both those titles. For want of knowing what has been discovered before him, he has not certain general landmarks to refer to, or a general standard of thought to apply to individual cases. He relies on his own acuteness and the immediate evidence, without being acquainted with the comparative anatomy or philosophical structure of opinion. He does not view things on a large scale or at the horizon (dim and airy enough perhaps)—but as they affect himself, close, palpable, tangible. Whatever he finds out, is his own, and he only knows what he finds out. He is in the constant hurry and fever of gestation: his brain teems incessantly with some fresh project. Every new light is the birth of a new system, the dawn of a new world to him. He is continually outstripping and overreaching himself. The last opinion is the only true one. He is wiser to-day than he was yesterday. Why should he not be wiser to-morrow than he was to-day?—Men of a learned education are not so sharp-witted as clever men without it: but they know the balance of the human intellect better; if they are more stupid, they are more steady; and are less liable to be led astray by their own sagacity and the overweening petulance of hard-earned and late-acquired wisdom. They do not fall in love with every meretricious extravagance at first sight, or mistake an old battered hypothesis for a vestal, because they are new to the ways of this old world. They do not seize upon it as a prize, but are safe from gross imposition by being as wise and no wiser than those who went before them.

Paine said on some occasion*—'What I have written, I have written'—as rendering any farther declaration of his principles unnecessary. Not so Mr. Cobbett. What he has written is no rule to him what he is to write. He learns something every day, and every week he takes the field to maintain the opinions of the last six days against friend or foe. I doubt whether this outrageous inconsistency, this headstrong fickleness, this understood want of all rule and method, does not enable him to go on with the spirit, vigour, and variety that he does. He is not pledged to repeat himself. Every new Register is a kind of new Prospectus. He blesses himself from all ties and shackles on his understanding; he has no mortgages on his brain; his notions are free and unincumbered. If he was put in trammels, he might become a vile hack like so many more. But he gives himself 'ample scope and verge enough.'* He takes both sides of a question, and maintains one as sturdily as the other. If nobody else can argue against him, he is a very good match for himself. He writes better in favour of Reform than any body else; he used to write better against it. Wherever he is, there is the tug of war, the weight of the argument, the strength of abuse. He is not like a man in danger of being *bed-rid* in his faculties—he tosses and tumbles about his unwieldy bulk,* and when he is tired of lying on one side, relieves himself by turning on the other. His shifting his point of view from time to time not merely adds variety and greater compass to his topics (so that the Political Register is an armoury and magazine for all the materials and weapons of political warfare) but it gives a greater zest and liveliness to his manner of treating them. Mr. Cobbett takes nothing for granted as what he has proved before; he does not write a book of reference. We see his ideas in their first concoction, fermenting and overflowing with the ebullitions of a lively conception. We look on at the actual process, and are put in immediate possession of the grounds and materials on which he forms his sanguine, unsettled conclusions. He does not give us samples of reasoning, but the whole solid mass, refuse and all.

> ——He pours out all as plain
> As downright Shippen or as old Montaigne.*

This is one cause of the clearness and force of his writings. An argument does not stop to stagnate and muddle in his brain, but passes at once to his paper. His ideas are served up, like pancakes, hot and hot.* Fresh theories give him fresh courage. He is like a young and lusty bridegroom that divorces a favourite speculation every morning, and marries a new one every night. He is not wedded to his notions, not he. He has not one Mrs. Cobbett among all his opinions. He makes the most of the last thought that has come in his way, seizes fast hold of it, rumples it about in all directions with rough strong hands, has his wicked will of it, takes a surfeit, and throws it away.—Our author's changing his opinions for new ones is not so wonderful: what is more remarkable is his facility in forgetting his old ones. He does not pretend to consistency (like Mr. Coleridge); he frankly disavows all connexion with himself. He feels no personal responsibility in this way, and cuts a friend or principle with the same decided indifference that Antipholis of Ephesus cuts Ægeon of Syracuse.* It is a hollow thing. The only time he ever grew romantic was in bringing over the relics of Mr. Thomas Paine* with him from America to go a progress with them through the disaffected districts. Scarce had he landed in Liverpool when he left the bones of a great man to shift for themselves; and no sooner did he arrive in London than he made a speech to disclaim all participation in the political and theological sentiments of his late idol, and to place the whole stock of his admiration and enthusiasm towards him to the account of his financial speculations, and of his having predicted the fate of paper-money. If he had erected a little gold statue to him, it might have proved the sincerity of this assertion: but to make a martyr and a patron-saint of a man, and to dig up 'his canonised bones'* in order to expose them as objects of devotion to the rabble's gaze, asks something that has more life and spirit in it, more mind and vivifying soul, than has to do with any calculation of pounds, shillings, and pence! The fact is, he *ratted* from his own project. He found the thing not so ripe as he had expected. His heart failed him: his enthusiasm fled, and he made his retractation. His admiration is short-lived: his contempt only is rooted, and his resentment lasting.—The above was only one instance of his building too much on practical *data*. He has an ill habit of prophesying, and goes on, though still deceived. The art of prophesying does not suit Mr. Cobbett's style. He has a knack of fixing names and times and places. According to him, the Reformed Parliament was to meet in March, 1818—it did not, and we heard no more of the matter. When his predictions fail, he takes no farther notice of them, but applies himself to new ones—like the country-people who turn to see what weather there is in the almanac for the next week, though it has been out in its reckoning every day of the last.

Mr. Cobbett is great in attack, not in defence: he cannot fight an up-hill battle. He will not bear the least punishing. If any one turns upon him (which few people like to do) he immediately turns tail. Like an overgrown school-boy, he is so used to have it all his own way, that he cannot submit to any thing like competition or a struggle for the mastery; he must lay on all the blows, and take none. He is bullying and cowardly; a Big Ben in politics,* who will fall upon others and crush them by his weight, but is not prepared for resistance, and is soon staggered by a few smart blows. Whenever he has been set upon, he has slunk out of the controversy. The Edinburgh Review* made (what is called) a dead set at him some years ago, to which he only retorted by an eulogy on the superior neatness of an English kitchen-garden to a Scotch one. I remember going one day into a bookseller's shop in Fleet-street to ask for the Review; and on my expressing my opinion to a young Scotchman, who stood behind the counter, that Mr. Cobbett might hit as hard in his reply, the North Briton said with some alarm—'But you don't think, Sir, Mr. Cobbett will be able to injure the Scottish nation?' I said I could not speak to that point, but I thought he was very well able to defend himself. He however did not, but has borne a grudge to the Edinburgh Review ever since, which he hates worse than the Quarterly. I cannot say I do.[2]

---

[2] Mr. Cobbett speaks almost as well as he writes. The only time I ever saw him* he seemed to me a very pleasant man—easy of access, affable, clear-headed, simple and mild in his manner, deliberate and unruffled in his speech, though some of his expressions were not very qualified. His figure is tall and portly. He has a good sensible face—rather full, with little grey eyes, a hard, square forehead, a ruddy complexion, with hair grey or powdered; and had on a scarlet broad-cloth waistcoat with the flaps of the pockets hanging down, as was the custom for gentlemen-farmers in the last century, or as we see it in the pictures of Members of Parliament in the reign of George I. I certainly did not think less favourably of him for seeing him.

20

THE INDIAN JUGGLERS

COMING forward and seating himself on the ground in his white dress and tightened turban, the chief of the Indian Jugglers* begins with tossing up two brass balls, which is what any of us could do, and concludes with keeping up four at the same time, which is what none of us could do to save our lives, nor if we were to take our whole lives to do it in. Is it then a trifling power we see at work, or is it not something next to miraculous? It is the utmost stretch of human ingenuity, which nothing but the bending the faculties of body and mind to it from the tenderest infancy with incessant, ever-anxious application up to manhood can accomplish or make even a slight approach to. Man, thou art a wonderful animal, and thy ways past finding out!* Thou canst do strange things, but thou turnest them to little account!—To conceive of this effort of extraordinary dexterity distracts the imagination and makes admiration breathless. Yet it costs nothing to the performer, any more than if it were a mere mechanical deception with which he had nothing to do but to watch and laugh at the astonishment of the spectators. A single error of a hair's-breadth, of the smallest conceivable portion of time, would be fatal: the precision of the movements must be like a mathematical truth, their rapidity is like lightning. To catch four balls in succession in less than a second of time, and deliver them back so as to return with seeming consciousness to the hand again, to make them revolve round him at certain intervals, like the planets in their spheres, to make them chase one another like sparkles of fire, or shoot up like flowers or meteors, to throw them behind his back and twine them round his neck like ribbons or like serpents, to do what appears an impossibility, and to do it with all the ease, the grace, the carelessness imaginable, to laugh at, to play with the glittering mockeries, to follow them with his eye as if he could fascinate them with its lambent fire or as if he had only to see that they kept time with the music on the stage—there is something in all this which he who does not admire may be quite sure he never really admired any thing in the whole course of his life. It is skill surmounting difficulty, and beauty triumphing over skill. It seems as if the difficulty once mastered naturally resolved itself into ease and grace, and as if to be overcome at all, it must be overcome without an effort. The smallest awkwardness or want of pliancy or self-possession would stop the whole process. It is the work of witchcraft, and yet sport for children. Some of the other feats are quite as curious and wonderful, such as the balancing the artificial tree and shooting a bird from each branch through a quill; though none of them have the elegance or facility of the keeping up of the brass balls. You are in pain for the result and glad when the experiment is over; they are not accompanied with the same unmixed, unchecked delight as the former; and I would not give much to be merely astonished without being pleased at the same time. As to the swallowing of the sword, the police ought to interfere to prevent it. When I saw the Indian Juggler do the same things before, his feet were bare, and he had large rings on the toes, which kept turning round all the time of the performance, as if they moved of themselves.—The hearing a speech in Parliament, drawled or stammered out by the Honourable Member or the Noble Lord, the ringing the changes on their common-places, which any one could repeat after them as well as they, stirs me not a jot, shakes not my good opinion of myself: but the seeing the Indian Jugglers does. It makes me ashamed of myself. I ask what there is that I can do as well as this? Nothing. What have I been doing all my life? Have I been idle, or have I nothing to shew for all my labour and pains? Or have I passed my time in pouring words like water into empty sieves, rolling a stone up a hill* and then down again, trying to prove an argument in the teeth of facts, and looking for causes in the dark, and not finding them? Is there no one thing in which I can challenge competition, that I can bring as an instance of exact perfection, in which others cannot find a flaw? The utmost I can pretend to is to write a description of what this fellow can do. I can write a book: so can many others who have not even learned to spell. What abortions are these Essays! What errors, what ill-pieced transitions, what crooked reasons, what lame conclusions! How little is made out, and that little how ill! Yet they are the best I can do. I endeavour to recollect all I have ever observed or thought upon a subject, and to express it as nearly as I can. Instead of writing on four subjects at a time, it is as much as I can manage to keep the thread of one discourse clear and unentangled. I have also time on my hands to correct my opinions, and polish my periods: but the one I cannot, and the other I will not do. I am fond of arguing: yet with a good deal of pains and practice it is often as much as I can do to beat my man; though he may be a very indifferent hand. A common fencer would disarm his adversary in the twinkling of an eye, unless he were a professor like himself. A stroke of wit will sometimes produce this effect, but there is no such power or superiority in sense or reasoning. There is no complete mastery of execution to be shewn there: and you hardly know the professor from the impudent pretender or the mere clown.[1]

I have always had this feeling of the inefficacy and slow progress of intellectual compared to mechanical excellence, and it has always made me somewhat dissatisfied. It is a great many years since I saw Richer, the famous rope-dancer, perform at Sadler's Wells. He was matchless in his art, and added to his extraordinary skill exquisite ease, and unaffected, natural grace. I was at that time employed in copying a half-length picture of Sir Joshua Reynolds's;* and it put me out of conceit with it. How ill this part was made out in the drawing! How heavy, how slovenly this other was painted! I could not help saying to myself, 'If the rope-dancer had performed his task in this manner, leaving so many gaps and botches in his work, he would have broke his neck long ago; I should never have seen that vigorous elasticity of nerve and precision of movement!'—Is it then so easy an undertaking (comparatively) to dance on a tight-rope? Let any one, who thinks so, get up and try. There is the thing. It is that which at first we cannot do at all, which in the end is done to such perfection. To account for this in some degree, I might observe that mechanical dexterity is confined to doing some one particular thing, which you can repeat as often as you please, in which you know whether you succeed or fail, and where the point of perfection consists in succeeding in a given undertaking.—In mechanical efforts, you improve by perpetual practice, and you do so infallibly, because the object to be attained is not a matter of taste or fancy or opinion, but of actual

---

[1] The celebrated Peter Pindar (Dr. Wolcot) first discovered and brought out the talents of the late Mr. Opie, the painter. He was a poor Cornish boy, and was out at work in the fields, when the poet went in search of him. 'Well, my lad, can you go and bring me your very best picture?' The other flew like lightning, and soon came back with what he considered as his master-piece. The stranger looked at it, and the young artist, after waiting for some time without his giving any opinion, at length exclaimed eagerly, 'Well, what do you think of it?'—'Think of it?' said Wolcot, 'why, I think you ought to be ashamed of it—that you who might do so well, do no better!' The same answer would have applied to this artist's latest performances, that had been suggested by one of his earliest efforts.

experiment, in which you must either do the thing or not do it. If a man is put to aim at a mark with a bow and arrow, he must hit it or miss it, that's certain. He cannot deceive himself, and go on shooting wide or falling short, and still fancy that he is making progress. The distinction between right and wrong, between true and false, is here palpable; and he must either correct his aim or persevere in his error with his eyes open, for which there is neither excuse nor temptation. If a man is learning to dance on a rope, if he does not mind what he is about, he will break his neck. After that, it will be in vain for him to argue that he did not make a false step. His situation is not like that of Goldsmith's pedagogue.—

> In argument they own'd his wondrous skill,
> And e'en though vanquish'd, he could argue still.*

Danger is a good teacher, and makes apt scholars. So are disgrace, defeat, exposure to immediate scorn and laughter. There is no opportunity in such cases for self-delusion, no idling time away, no being off your guard (or you must take the consequences)—neither is there any room for humour or caprice or prejudice. If the Indian Juggler were to play tricks in throwing up the three case-knives, which keep their positions like the leaves of a crocus in the air, he would cut his fingers. I can make a very bad antithesis without cutting my fingers. The tact of style is more ambiguous than that of double-edged instruments. If the Juggler were told that by flinging himself under the wheels of the Jaggernaut,* when the idol issues forth on a gaudy day, he would immediately be transported into Paradise, he might believe it, and nobody could disprove it. So the Brahmins may say what they please on that subject, may build up dogmas and mysteries without end, and not be detected: but their ingenious countryman cannot persuade the frequenters of the Olympic Theatre that he performs a number of astonishing feats without actually giving proofs of what he says.—There is then in this sort of manual dexterity, first a gradual aptitude acquired to a given exertion of muscular power, from constant repetition, and in the next place, an exact knowledge how much is still wanting and necessary to be supplied. The obvious test is to increase the effort or nicety of the operation, and still to find it come true. The muscles ply instinctively to the dictates of habit. Certain movements and impressions of the hand and eye, having been repeated together an infinite number of times, are unconsciously but unavoidably cemented into closer and closer union; the limbs require little more than to be put in motion for them to follow a regular track with ease and certainty; so that the mere intention of the will acts mathematically like touching the spring of a machine, and you come with Locksley in Ivanhoe, in shooting at a mark, 'to allow for the wind.'*

Farther, what is meant by perfection in mechanical exercises is the performing certain feats to a uniform nicety, that is, in fact, undertaking no more than you can perform. You task yourself, the limit you fix is optional, and no more than human industry and skill can attain to: but you have no abstract, independent standard of difficulty or excellence (other than the extent of your own powers). Thus he who can keep up four brass balls does this *to perfection*; but he cannot keep up five at the same instant, and would fail every time he attempted it. That is, the mechanical performer undertakes to emulate himself, not to equal another.[2] But the artist undertakes to imitate another, or to do what nature has done, and this it appears is more difficult, *viz.* to copy what she has set before us in the face of nature or 'human face divine,'* entire and without a blemish, than to keep up four brass balls at the same instant, for the one is done by the power of human skill and industry, and the other never was nor will be. Upon the whole, therefore, I have more respect for Reynolds, than I have for Richer; for, happen how it will, there have been more people in the world who could dance on a rope like the one than who could paint like Sir Joshua. The latter was but a bungler in his profession to the other, it is true; but then he had a harder task-master to obey, whose will was more wayward and obscure, and whose instructions it was more difficult to practise. You can put a child apprentice to a tumbler or rope-dancer with a comfortable prospect of success, if they are but sound of wind and limb: but you cannot do the same thing in painting. The odds are a million to one. You may make indeed as many H——s and H——s,* as you put into that sort of machine, but not one Reynolds amongst them all, with his grace, his grandeur, his blandness of *gusto*, 'in tones and gestures hit,'* unless you could make the man over again. To snatch this grace* beyond the reach of art is then the height of art—where fine art begins, and where mechanical skill ends. The soft suffusion of the

---

[2] If two persons play against each other at any game, one of them necessarily fails.

soul, the speechless breathing eloquence, the looks 'commercing with the skies,'* the ever-shifting forms of an eternal principle, that which is seen but for a moment, but dwells in the heart always, and is only seized as it passes by strong and secret sympathy, must be taught by nature and genius, not by rules or study. It is suggested by feeling, not by laborious microscopic inspection: in seeking for it without, we lose the harmonious clue to it within: and in aiming to grasp the substance, we let the very spirit of art evaporate. In a word, the objects of fine art are not the objects of sight but as these last are the objects of taste and imagination, that is, as they appeal to the sense of beauty, of pleasure, and of power in the human breast, and are explained by that finer sense, and revealed in their inner structure to the eye in return. Nature is also a language. Objects, like words, have a meaning; and the true artist is the interpreter of this language, which he can only do by knowing its application to a thousand other objects in a thousand other situations. Thus the eye is too blind a guide of itself to distinguish between the warm or cold tone of a deep blue sky, but another sense acts as a monitor to it, and does not err. The colour of the leaves in autumn would be nothing without the feeling that accompanies it; but it is that feeling that stamps them on the canvas, faded, seared, blighted, shrinking from the winter's flaw,* and makes the sight as true as touch*—

> And visions, as poetic eyes avow,
> Cling to each leaf and hang on every bough.*

The more ethereal, evanescent, more refined and sublime part of art is the seeing nature through the medium of sentiment and passion, as each object is a symbol of the affections and a link in the chain of our endless being. But the unravelling this mysterious web of thought and feeling is alone in the Muse's gift, namely, in the power of that trembling sensibility which is awake to every change and every modification of its ever-varying impressions, that

> Thrills in each nerve, and lives along the line.*

This power is indifferently called genius, imagination, feeling, taste; but the manner in which it acts upon the mind can neither be defined by abstract rules, as is the case in science, nor verified by continual unvarying experiments, as is the case in mechanical performances. The mechanical excellence of the Dutch painters in colouring and handling is that which comes the nearest in fine art to the perfection of certain manual exhibitions of skill. The truth of the effect and the facility with which it is produced are equally admirable. Up to a certain point, every thing is faultless. The hand and eye have done their part. There is only a want of taste and genius. It is after we enter upon that enchanted ground that the human mind begins to droop and flag as in a strange road, or in a thick mist, benighted and making little way with many attempts and many failures, and that the best of us only escape with half a triumph. The undefined and the imaginary are the regions that we must pass like Satan, difficult and doubtful, 'half flying, half on foot.'* The object in sense is a positive thing, and execution comes with practice.

Cleverness is a certain *knack* or aptitude at doing certain things, which depend more on a particular adroitness and off-hand readiness than on force or perseverance, such as making puns, making epigrams, making extempore verses, mimicking the company, mimicking a style, &c. Cleverness is either liveliness and smartness, or something answering to *sleight of hand*, like letting a glass fall sideways off a table, or else a trick, like knowing the secret spring of a watch. Accomplishments are certain external graces, which are to be learnt from others, and which are easily displayed to the admiration of the beholder, *viz.* dancing, riding, fencing, music, and so on. These ornamental acquirements are only proper to those who are at ease in mind and fortune. I know an individual* who if he had been born to an estate of five thousand a year, would have been the most accomplished gentleman of the age. He would have been the delight and envy of the circle in which he moved—would have graced by his manners the liberality flowing from the openness of his heart, would have laughed with the women, have argued with the men, have said good things and written agreeable ones, have taken a hand at piquet or the lead at the harpsichord, and have set and sung his own verses—*nugæ canoræ**—with tenderness and spirit; a Rochester without the vice, a modern Surrey! As it is, all these capabilities of excellence stand in his way. He is too versatile for a professional man, not dull enough for a political drudge, too gay to be happy, too thoughtless to be rich. He wants the enthusiasm of the poet, the severity of the prose-writer, and the application of the man of business.—Talent is the capacity of doing any thing that depends on application and industry, such as writing a criticism, making a speech, studying the law. Talent differs from genius, as voluntary differs from involuntary power. Ingenuity is genius in trifles, greatness is genius in undertakings of much pith and moment. A clever or ingenious man is one who can do any thing well, whether it is worth doing or not: a great man is one who can do that which when done is of the highest importance. Themistocles* said he could not play on the flute, but that he could make of a small city a great one. This gives one a pretty good idea of the distinction in question.

Greatness is great power, producing great effects. It is not enough that a man has great power in himself, he must shew it to all the world in a way that cannot be hid or gainsaid. He must fill up a certain idea in the public mind. I have no other notion of greatness than this two-fold definition, great results springing from great inherent energy. The great in visible objects has relation to that which extends over space: the great in mental ones has to do with space and time. No man is truly great, who is great only in his life-time. The test of greatness is the page of history. Nothing can be said to be great that has a dis-tinct limit, or that borders on something evidently greater than itself. Besides, what is short-lived and pampered into mere notoriety, is of a gross and vulgar quality in itself. A Lord Mayor is hardly a great man. A city orator or patriot of the day only shew, by reaching the height of their wishes, the distance they are at from any true ambi-tion. Popularity is neither fame nor greatness. A king (as such) is not a great man. He has great power, but it is not his own. He merely wields the lever of the state, which a child, an idiot, or a madman can do. It is the office, not the man we gaze at. Any one else in the same situation would be just as much an object of abject curiosity. We laugh at the country girl who having seen a king expressed her disappoint-ment by saying, 'Why, he is only a man!' Yet, knowing this, we run to see a king as if he was something more than a man.—To display the greatest powers, unless they are applied to great purposes, makes nothing for the character of greatness. To throw a barley-corn through the eye of a needle, to multiply nine figures by nine in the memory, argues infinite dexterity of body and capacity of mind, but nothing comes of either. There is a surprising power at work, but the effects are not proportionate, or such as take hold of the imagination. To impress the idea of power on others, they must be made in some way to feel it. It must be communicated to their understandings in the shape of an increase of knowledge, or it must subdue and overawe them by subjecting their wills. Admiration to be solid and lasting must be founded on proofs from which we have no means of escaping; it is neither a slight nor a voluntary gift. A mathematician who solves a profound problem, a poet who creates an image of beauty in the mind that was not there before, imparts knowledge and power to others, in which his greatness and his fame consists, and on which it reposes. Jedediah Buxton* will be forgotten; but Napier's bones* will live. Lawgivers, philosophers, founders of religion, conquerors and heroes, inventors and great geniuses in arts and sciences, are great men, for they are great public benefactors, or formidable scourges to mankind. Among ourselves, Shakespear, Newton, Bacon, Milton, Cromwell, were great men, for they shewed great power by acts and thoughts, which have not yet been consigned to oblivion. They must needs be men of lofty stature, whose shadows lengthen out to remote posterity. A great farce-writer may be a great man; for Moliere was but a great farce-writer. In my mind, the author of Don Quixote was a great man. So have there been many others. A great chess-player is not a great man, for he leaves the world as he found it. No act terminating in itself constitutes greatness. This will apply to all displays of power or trials of skill, which are confined to the momentary, individual effort, and construct no permanent image or trophy of themselves without them. Is not an actor then a great man, because 'he dies and leaves the world no copy?'* I must make an exception for Mrs. Siddons, or else give up my definition of greatness for her sake. A man at the top of his profession is not therefore a great man. He is great in his way, but that is all, unless he shews the marks of a great moving intellect, so that we trace the master-mind, and can sympathise with the springs that urge him on. The rest is but a craft or *mystery*. John Hunter* was a great man—*that* any one might see without the smallest skill in surgery. His style and manner shewed the man. He would set about cutting up the carcase of a whale with the same greatness of *gusto* that Michael Angelo would have hewn a block of marble. Lord Nelson was a great naval commander; but for myself, I have not much opinion of a sea-faring life. Sir Humphry Davy* is a great chemist, but I am not sure that he is a great man. I am not a bit the wiser for any of his discoveries, nor I never met with any one that was. But it is in the nature of greatness to propagate an idea of itself, as wave impels wave, circle without circle. It is a contradiction in terms for a coxcomb to be a great man. A really great man has always an idea of something greater than himself. I have observed that certain sectaries and polemical writers have no higher compliment to pay their most shining lights than to say that 'Such a one was a considerable man in his day.' Some new elucidation of a text sets aside the authority of the old interpretation, and a 'great scholar's memory out-lives him half a century,'* at the utmost. A rich man is not a great man, except to his dependants and his steward. A lord is a great man in the idea we have of his ancestry, and probably of himself, if we know nothing of him but his title. I have heard a story of two bishops, one of whom said (speaking of St. Peter's at Rome) that when he first entered it, he was rather awe-struck, but that as he walked up it, his mind seemed to swell and dilate with it, and at last to fill the whole building—the other said that as he saw more of it, he appeared to himself to grow less and less every step he took, and in the end to dwindle into nothing. This was in some respects a striking picture of a great and little mind—for greatness sympathises with greatness, and littleness shrinks into itself. The one might have become a Wolsey;* the other was only fit to become a Mendicant Friar—or there might have been court-reasons for making him a bishop. The French have to me a character of littleness in all about them; but they have produced three great men that belong to every country, Moliere, Rabelais, and Montaigne.

To return from this digression, and conclude the Essay. A singular instance of manual dexterity was shewn in the person of the late John Cavanagh,* whom I have several times seen. His death was celebrated at the time in an article in the Examiner* newspaper, (Feb. 7, 1819) written apparently between jest and earnest: but as it is *pat* to our purpose, and falls in with my own way of considering such subjects, I shall here take leave to quote it.

'Died at his house in Burbage-street, St. Giles's, John Cavanagh, the famous hand fives-player. When a person dies, who does any one thing better than any one else in the world, which so many others are trying to do well, it leaves a gap in society. It is not likely that any one will now see the game of fives played in its perfection for many years to come—for Cavanagh is dead, and has not left his peer behind him. It may be said that there are things of more importance than striking a ball against a wall—there are things indeed that make more noise and do as little good, such as making war and peace, making speeches and answering them, making verses and blotting them; making money and throwing it away. But the game of fives is what no one despises who has ever played at it. It is the finest exercise for the body, and the best relaxation for the mind. The Roman poet said that 'Care mounted behind the horseman and stuck to his skirts.'* But this remark would not have applied to the fives-player. He who takes to playing at fives is twice young. He feels neither the past nor future 'in the instant.'* Debts, taxes, 'domestic treason, foreign levy, nothing can touch him further.'* He has no other wish, no other thought, from the moment the game begins, but that of striking the ball, of placing it, of *making* it! This Cavanagh was sure to do. Whenever he touched the ball, there was an end of the chase. His eye was certain, his hand fatal, his presence of mind complete. He could do what he pleased, and he always knew exactly what to do. He saw the whole game, and played it; took instant advantage of his adversary's weakness, and recovered balls, as if by a miracle and from sudden thought, that every one gave for lost. He had equal power and skill, quickness, and judgment. He could either outwit his antagonist by finesse, or beat him by main strength. Sometimes, when he seemed preparing to send the ball with the full swing of his arm, he would by a slight turn of his wrist drop it within an inch of the line. In general, the ball came from his hand, as if from a racket, in a straight horizontal line; so that it was in vain to attempt to overtake or stop it. As it was said of a great orator that he never was at a loss for a word, and for the properest word, so Cavanagh always could tell the degree of force necessary to be given to a ball, and the precise direction in which it should be sent. He did his work with the greatest ease; never took more pains than was necessary; and while others were fagging themselves to death, was as cool and collected as if he had just entered the court. His style of play was as remarkable as his power of execution. He had no affectation, no trifling. He did not throw away the game to show off an attitude, or try an experiment. He was a fine, sensible, manly player, who did what he could, but that was more than any one else could even affect to do. His blows were not undecided and ineffectual—lumbering like Mr. Wordsworth's epic poetry, nor wavering like Mr. Coleridge's lyric prose, nor short of the mark like Mr. Brougham's speeches, nor wide of it like Mr. Canning's wit, nor foul like the *Quarterly*, not *let* balls like the *Edinburgh Review*. Cobbett and Junius* together would have made a Cavanagh. He was the best *up-hill* player in the world; even when his adversary was fourteen, he would play on the same or better, and as he never flung away the game through carelessness and conceit, he never gave it up through laziness or want of heart. The only peculiarity of his play was that he never *volleyed*, but let the balls hop; but if they rose an inch from the ground, he never missed having them. There was not only nobody equal, but nobody second to him. It is supposed that he could give any other player half the game, or beat them with his left hand. His service was tremendous. He once played Woodward and Meredith together (two of the best players in England) in the Fives-court, St. Martin's-street, and made seven and twenty aces following by services alone—a thing unheard of. He another time played Peru, who was considered a first-rate fives-player, a match of the best out of five games, and in the three first games, which of course decided the match, Peru got only one ace. Cavanagh was an Irishman by birth, and a house-painter by profession. He had once laid aside his working-dress, and walked up, in his smartest clothes, to the Rosemary Branch* to have an afternoon's pleasure. A person accosted him, and asked him if he would have a game. So they agreed to play for half a crown a game, and a bottle of cider. The first game began—it was seven, eight, ten, thirteen, fourteen, all. Cavanagh won it. The next was the same. They played on, and each game was hardly contested. 'There,' said the unconscious fives-player, 'there was a stroke that Cavanagh could not take: I never played better in my life, and yet I can't win a game. I don't know how it is.' However, they played on, Cavanagh winning every game, and the by-standers drinking the cider and laughing all the time. In the twelfth game, when Cavanagh was only four, and the stranger thirteen, a person came in, and said, 'What! are you here, Cavanagh?' The words were no sooner pronounced than the astonished player let the ball drop from his hand, and saying, 'What! have I been breaking my heart all this time to beat Cavanagh?' refused to make another effort. 'And yet, I give you my word,' said Cavanagh, telling the story with some triumph, 'I played all the while with my clenched fist.'—He used frequently to play matches at Copenhagen-house* for wagers and dinners. The wall against which they play is the same that supports the kitchen-chimney, and when the wall resounded louder than usual, the cooks exclaimed, 'Those are the Irishman's balls,' and the joints trembled on the spit!—Goldsmith consoled himself* that there were places where he too was admired: and Cavanagh was the admiration of all the fives-courts, where he ever played. Mr. Powell,* when he played matches in the Court in St. Martin's-street, used to fill his gallery at half-a-crown a head, with amateurs and admirers of talent in whatever department it is shown. He could not have shown himself in any ground in England, but he would have been immediately surrounded with inquisitive gazers, trying to find out in what part of his frame his unrivalled skill lay, as politicians wonder to see the balance of Europe suspended in Lord Castlereagh's face, and admire the trophies of the British Navy lurking under Mr. Croker's hanging brow. Now Cavanagh was as good-looking a man as the Noble Lord, and much better looking than the Right Hon. Secretary. He had a clear, open countenance, and did not look sideways or down, like Mr. Murray the bookseller.* He was a young fellow of sense, humour, and courage. He once had a quarrel with a waterman at Hungerford-stairs, and they say, served him out in great style. In a word, there are hundreds at this day, who cannot mention his name without admiration, as the best fives-player that perhaps ever lived (the greatest excellence of which they have any notion)—and the noisy shout of the ring happily stood him in stead of the unheard voice of posterity!—The only person who seems to have excelled as much in another way as Cavanagh did in his, was the late John Davies,* the racket-player. It was remarked of him that he did not seem to follow the ball, but the ball seemed to follow him. Give him a foot of wall, and he was sure to make the ball. The four best racket-players of that day were Jack Spines, Jem. Harding, Armitage, and Church.* Davies could give any one of these two hands a time, that is, half the game, and each of these, at their best, could give the best player now in London the same odds. Such are the gradations in all exertions of human skill and art. He once played four capital players together, and beat them. He was also a first-rate tennis-player, and an excellent fives-player. In the Fleet or King's Bench,* he would have stood against Powell, who was reckoned the best open-ground player of his time. This last-mentioned player is at present the keeper of the Fives-court, and we might recommend to him for a motto over his door—'Who enters here, forgets himself, his country, and his friends.'* And the best of it is, that by the calculation of the odds, none of the three are worth remembering!—Cavanagh died from the bursting of a blood-vessel, which prevented him from playing for the last two or three years. This, he was often heard to say, he thought hard upon him. He was fast recovering, however, when he was suddenly carried off, to the regret of all who knew him. As

Mr. Peel made it a qualification of the present Speaker, Mr. Manners Sutton,* that he was an excellent moral character, so Jack Cavanagh was a zealous Catholic, and could not be persuaded to eat meat on a Friday, the day on which he died. We have paid this willing tribute to his memory.

> Let no rude hand deface it,
> And his forlorn '*Hic Jacet*.'*

21

ON A LANDSCAPE OF NICOLAS POUSSIN

ORION, the subject of this landscape,* was the classical Nimrod, and is called by Homer, 'a hunter of shadows, himself a shade.'* He was the son of Neptune, and having lost an eye* in some affray between the Gods and men, was told that if he would go to meet the rising sun, he would recover his sight. He is represented setting out on his journey, with men on his shoulders to guide him; a bow in his hand, and Diana in the clouds greeting him. He stalks along, a giant upon earth, and reels and falters in his gait, as if just awaked out of sleep, or uncertain of his way, so that you see his blindness, though his back is turned. Mists rise around him, and veil the sides of the green forests; earth is dank and fresh with dews, 'the grey dawn and the Pleiades before him dance,'* and in the distance are seen the blue hills and sullen ocean. Nothing was ever more finely conceived or done. It breathes the spirit of the morning; its moisture, its repose, its obscurity, waiting the miracle of light to kindle it into smiles: the whole is, like the principal figure in it, 'a forerunner of the dawn.'* The same atmosphere tinges and imbues every object, the same dull light 'shadowy sets off'* the face of nature: one feeling of vastness, of strangeness, and of primeval forms pervades the painter's canvas, and we are thrown back upon the first integrity of things. This great and learned man might be said to see nature through the glass of time: he alone has a right to be considered as the painter of classical antiquity. Sir Joshua has* done him justice in this respect. He could give to the scenery of his heroic fables that unimpaired look of original nature, full, solid, large, luxuriant, teeming with life and power; or deck it with all the pomp of art, with temples and towers, and mythologic groves. His pictures 'denote a foregone conclusion.'* He moulds nature to his purposes, works out her images according to the standard of his thoughts, embodies high fictions; and, the first conception being given, the rest seem to grow out of, and be assimilated to it, by the invariable process of a studious imagination. Like his own Orion, he overlooks the surrounding scene, appears to 'take up the isles as a very little thing, and to lay the earth in a balance.'* With a laborious and mighty grasp, he put nature into the mould of the ideal and antique; and was among painters (more than any body else) what Milton was among poets. There is in both something of the same pedantry, the same stiffness, the same elevation, the same grandeur, the same mixture of art and nature, the same richness of borrowed materials, the same unity of character. Neither the poet nor the painter lowered the subjects they treated, but filled up the outline in the fancy, and added strength and reality to it; and thus, not only satisfied, but surpassed the expectations of the spectator and the reader. This is held for the triumph and the perfection of works of art. To give us nature, such as we see it, is well and deserving of praise; to give us nature, such as we have never seen, but have often wished to see it, is better, and deserving of higher praise. He who can show the world in its first naked glory, with the hues of fancy spread over it, or in its high and palmy state,* with the gravity of history stamped on the proud monuments of vanished empire,—who, by his 'so potent art,'* can recal time past, transport us to distant places, and join the regions of imagination (a new conquest) to those of reality,—who shows us not only what nature is, but what she has been, and is capable of,—he who does this, and does it with simplicity, with truth, and grandeur, is lord of nature and her powers; and his mind is universal, and his art the master-art!

There is nothing in this 'more than natural,'* if criticism could be persuaded to think so. The historic painter does not neglect or contravene nature, but follows her more closely up into her fantastic heights, or hidden recesses. He demonstrates what she would be in conceivable circumstances, and under implied conditions. He 'gives to airy nothing a local habitation,' not 'a name.'* At his touch, words start up into images, thoughts become things. He clothes a dream, a phantom with form and colour, and the wholesome attributes of reality. *His* art is a second nature, not a different one. There are those, indeed, who think that not to copy nature, is the rule for attaining perfection. Because they cannot paint the objects which they have seen, they fancy themselves qualified to paint the ideas which they have not seen. But it is possible to fail in this latter and more difficult style of imitation, as well as in the former humbler one. The detection, indeed, is not so easy, because the objects are not so nigh at hand to compare, and therefore there is more room, both for false pretension, and for self-deceit. They take an epic motto, or subject, and think that the spirit is implied as a thing of course. They paint inferior portraits,

maudlin lifeless faces, without ordinary expression, or one look, feature, or particle of nature in them, and think that this is to rise to the
truth of history. They vulgarise and degrade whatever is interesting
or sacred to the mind, and think that they thus add to the dignity of
their profession. They represent a face that looks as if no thought or
feeling of any kind had ever passed through it; and would have you
believe that this is the very sublime of expression, such as it would
appear in heroes, or demi-gods of old, when rapture or agony was
raised to its height. They show you a landscape that looks as if the sun
never shone upon it, and tell you that it is not modern—that so earth
looked when Titan first kissed it with his rays. This is not the true
ideal. It is not to fill the moulds of the imagination, but to deface and
injure them: it is not to come up to, but to fall short of the poorest
conception in the public mind. Such pictures should not be hung in
the same room with that of

> Blind Orion hungry for the morn.[1]*

   Poussin was of all painters, the most poetical. He was the painter of
ideas. No one ever told a story half so well, nor so well knew what was
capable of being told by the pencil. He seized on, and struck off with
grace and precision, just that point of view which would be likely to
catch the reader's fancy. There is a significance, a consciousness in
whatever he does (sometimes a vice, but oftener a virtue) beyond any
other painter. His Giants sitting on the tops of craggy mountains, as

---

   [1] Every thing tends to show the manner in which a great artist is formed. If any one
could claim an exemption from the careful imitation of individual objects, it was Nicolas
Poussin. He studied the Antique, but he also studied nature. 'I have often admired,' says
Vignuel de Marville, who knew him at a late period of his life, 'the love he had for his art.
Old as he was, I frequently saw him among the ruins of ancient Rome, out in the
Campagna, or along the banks of the Tyber, sketching a scene that had pleased him; and
I often met him with his handkerchief full of stones, moss, or flowers, which he carried
home, that he might copy them exactly from nature. One day I asked him how he had
attained to such a degree of perfection, as to have gained so high a rank among the great
painters of Italy? He answered, I HAVE NEGLECTED NOTHING.'—*See his Life lately
published*.* It appears from this account that he had not fallen into a recent error, that
Nature puts the man of genius out. As a contrast to the foregoing description, I might
mention, that I remember an old gentleman once asking Mr. West in the British Gallery,
if he had ever been at Athens? To which the President made answer, No; nor did he feel
any great desire to go; for that he thought he had as good an idea of the place from the
Catalogue, as he could get by living there for any number of years. What would he have
said, if any one had told him, they could get as good an idea of the subject of one of his
great works from reading the Catalogue of it, as from seeing the picture itself! Yet the
answer was characteristic of the genius of the painter.

huge themselves, and playing idly on their Pan's-pipes, seem to have been seated there these three thousand years, and to know the beginning and the end of their own story. An infant Bacchus, or Jupiter, is big with his future destiny. Even inanimate and dumb things speak a language of their own. His snakes, the messengers of fate, are inspired with human intellect. His trees grow and expand their leaves in the air, glad of the rain, proud of the sun, awake to the winds of Heaven. In his Plague of Athens,* the very buildings seem stiff with horror. His picture of the Deluge* is, perhaps, the finest historical landscape in the world. You see a waste of waters, wide, interminable: the sun is labouring, wan and weary, up the sky; the clouds, dull and leaden, lie like a load upon the eye, and heaven and earth seem commingling into one confused mass! His human figures are sometimes 'o'er-informed'* with this kind of feeling. Their actions have too much gesticulation, and the set expression of the features borders too much on the mechanical and caricatured style. In this respect, they form a contrast to Raphael's, whose figures never appear to be sitting for their pictures, or to be conscious of a spectator, or to have come from the painter's hand. In Nicolas Poussin, on the contrary, every thing seems to have a mutual understanding with the artist: 'the very stones prate of their whereabout:'* each object has its part and place assigned, and is in a sort of compact with the rest of the picture. It is this conscious keeping, and, as it were, *internal* design, that gives their peculiar character to the works of this artist. There was a picture of Aurora* in the British Gallery a year or two ago. It was a suffusion of golden light. The Goddess wore her saffron-coloured robes, and appeared just risen from the gloomy bed of old Tithonus. Her very steeds, milk-white, were tinged with the yellow dawn. It was a personification of the morning.—Poussin succeeded better in classic than in sacred subjects. The latter are comparatively heavy, forced, full of violent contrasts of colour, of red, blue, and black, and without the true prophetic inspiration of the characters. But in his Pagan allegories and fables he was quite at home. The native gravity and native levity of the Frenchman were combined with Italian scenery and an antique gusto, and gave even to his colouring an air of learned indifference. He wants, in one respect, grace, form, expression; but he has every where sense and meaning, perfect costume and propriety. His personages always belong to the class and time represented, and are strictly versed in the business in hand. His grotesque compositions in particular, his Nymphs and Fauns, are superior (at least, as far as style is concerned) even to Rubens's. They are taken more immediately out of fabulous history. Rubens's Satyrs and Bacchantes have a more jovial and voluptuous aspect, are more drunk with pleasure, more full of animal spirits and riotous impulses, they laugh and bound along—

Leaping like wanton kids in pleasant spring;*

but those of Poussin have more of the intellectual part of the character, and seem vicious on reflection, and of set purpose. Rubens's are noble specimens of a class; Poussin's are allegorical abstractions of the same class, with bodies less pampered, but with minds more secretly depraved. The Bacchanalian groups of the Flemish painter were, however, his master-pieces in composition. Witness those prodigies of colour, character, and expression, at Blenheim. In the more chaste and refined delineation of classic fable, Poussin was without a rival. Rubens, who was a match for him in the wild and picturesque, could not pretend to vie with the elegance and purity of thought, in his picture of Apollo giving a poet a cup of water to drink; nor with the gracefulness of design in the figure of a nymph squeezing the juice of a bunch of grapes from her fingers (a rosy wine-press) which falls into the mouth of a chubby infant below. But, above all, who shall celebrate, in terms of fit praise, his picture of the shepherds* in the Vale of Tempe going out in a fine morning of the spring, and coming to a tomb with this inscription:—ET EGO IN ARCADIA VIXI!* The eager curiosity of some, the expression of others who start back with fear and surprise, the clear breeze playing with the branches of the shadowing trees, 'the valleys low, where the mild zephyrs use,'* the distant, uninterrupted, sunny prospect speak (and for ever will speak on) of ages past to ages yet to come![2]

Pictures are a set of chosen images, a stream of pleasant thoughts passing through the mind. It is a luxury to have the walls of our rooms hung round with them, and no less so to have such a gallery in the mind, to con over the relics of ancient art bound up 'within the book and volume of the brain, unmixed (if it were possible) with baser matter!'* A life passed among pictures, in the study and the love of

[2] Poussin has repeated this subject more than once, and appears to have revelled in its witcheries. I have before alluded to it, and may again. It is hard that we should not be allowed to dwell as often as we please on what delights us, when things that are disagreeable recur so often against our will.

art, is a happy, noiseless dream: or rather, it is to dream and to be awake at the same time; for it has all 'the sober certainty of waking bliss,'* with the romantic voluptuousness of a visionary and abstracted being. They are the bright consummate essences of things, and 'he who knows of these delights to taste and interpose them oft, is not unwise!'*—The Orion, which I have here taken occasion to descant upon, is one of a collection of excellent pictures, as this collection is itself one of a series from the old masters, which have for some years back embrowned the walls of the British Gallery, and enriched the public eye. What hues, (those of nature mellowed by time) breathe around, as we enter! What forms are there, woven into the memory! What looks, which only the answering looks of the spectator can express! What intellectual stores have been yearly poured forth from the shrine of ancient art! The works are various, but the names the same—heaps of Rembrandts frowning from the darkened walls, Rubens's glad gorgeous groups, Titian's more rich and rare, Claude's always exquisite, sometimes beyond compare, Guido's endless cloying sweetness, the learning of Poussin and the Caracci, and Raphael's princely magnificence, crowning all. We read certain letters and syllables in the catalogue, and at the well-known magic sound, a miracle of skill and beauty starts to view. One would think that one year's prodigal display of such perfection would exhaust the labours of one man's life; but the next year, and the next to that, we find another harvest reaped and gathered in to the great garner of art, by the same immortal hands—

> Old GENIUS the porter of them was;
> He letteth in, he letteth out to wend.*—

Their works seem endless as their reputation—to be many as they are complete—to multiply with the desire of the mind to see more and more of them; as if there were a living power in the breath of Fame, and in the very names of the great heirs of glory 'there were propagation too!'* It is something to have a collection of this sort to look forward to once a year; to have one last, lingering look yet to come. Pictures are scattered like stray gifts* through the world, and while they remain, earth has yet a little gilding left, not quite rubbed out, dishonoured and defaced. There are plenty of standard works still to be found in this country, in the collections at Blenheim, at Burleigh,* and in those belonging to Mr. Angerstein, Lord Grosvenor, the

Marquis of Stafford and others, to keep up this treat to the lovers of art for many years: and it is the more desirable to reserve a privileged sanctuary of this sort, where the eye may doat, and the heart take its fill of such pictures as Poussin's Orion, since the Louvre is stripped* of its triumphant spoils, and since he, who collected it, and wore it as a rich jewel in his Iron Crown, the hunter of greatness and of glory, is himself a shade!*—

22

THE FIGHT

——The *fight*, the *fight*'s the thing,
Wherein I'll catch the conscience of the king.*

WHERE there's a will, there's a way.—I said so to myself, as I walked down Chancery-lane, about half-past six o'clock on Monday the 10th of December, to inquire at Jack Randall's* where the fight the next day was to be;* and I found 'the proverb' nothing 'musty'* in the present instance. I was determined to see this fight, come what would, and see it I did, in great style. It was my *first fight*, yet it more than answered my expectations. Ladies! it is to you I dedicate this description; nor let it seem out of character for the fair to notice the exploits of the brave. Courage and modesty are the old English virtues; and may they never look cold and askance on one another! Think, ye fairest of the fair, loveliest of the lovely kind, ye practisers of soft enchantment, how many more ye kill with poisoned baits than ever fell in the ring; and listen with subdued air and without shuddering, to a tale tragic only in appearance, and sacred to the FANCY!*

I was going down Chancery-lane, thinking to ask at Jack Randall's where the fight was to be, when looking through the glass-door of the *Hole in the Wall*, I heard a gentleman asking the same question *at* Mrs. Randall, as the author of Waverley would express it. Now Mrs. Randall stood answering the gentleman's question, with the authenticity of the lady of the Champion of the Light Weights. Thinks I, I'll wait till this person comes out, and learn from him how it is. For to say a truth, I was not fond of going into this house of call for heroes and philosophers, ever since the owner of it (for Jack is no gentleman) threatened once upon a time to kick me out of doors for wanting a mutton-chop at his hospitable board, when the conqueror in thirteen battles was more full of *blue ruin** than of good manners. I was the more mortified at this repulse, inasmuch as I had heard Mr. James Simpkins, hosier in the Strand, one day when the character of the *Hole in the Wall* was brought in question, observe—'The house is a very good house, and the company quite genteel: I have been there myself!' Remembering this unkind treatment of mine host, to which mine hostess was also a party, and not wishing to put

her in unquiet thoughts at a time jubilant like the present, I waited at
the door, when, who should issue forth but my friend Jo. Toms,* and
turning suddenly up Chancery-lane with that quick jerk and impatient stride which distinguishes a lover of the FANCY, I said, 'I'll be
hanged if that fellow is not going to the fight, and is on his way to get
me to go with him.' So it proved in effect, and we agreed to adjourn
to my lodgings to discuss measures with that cordiality which makes
old friends like new, and new friends like old, on great occasions. We
are cold to others only when we are dull in ourselves, and have neither
thoughts nor feelings to impart to them. Give a man a topic in his
head, a throb of pleasure in his heart, and he will be glad to share it
with the first person he meets. Toms and I, though we seldom meet,
were an *alter idem** on this memorable occasion, and had not an idea
that we did not candidly impart; and 'so carelessly did we fleet the
time,'* that I wish no better, when there is another fight, than to have
him for a companion on my journey down, and to return with my
friend Jack Pigott,* talking of what was to happen or of what did happen, with a noble subject always at hand, and liberty to digress to
others whenever they offered. Indeed, on my repeating the lines from
Spenser in an involuntary fit of enthusiasm,

> What more felicity can fall to creature,
> Than to enjoy delight with liberty?*

my last-named ingenious friend stopped me by saying that this,
translated into the vulgate, meant '*Going to see a fight.*'

Jo. Toms and I could not settle about the method of going down.
He said there was a caravan, he understood, to start from Tom
Belcher's* at two, which would go there *right out* and back again the
next day. Now I never travel all night, and said I should get a cast to
Newbury by one of the mails. Jo. swore the thing was impossible, and
I could only answer that I had made up my mind to it. In short, he
seemed to me to waver, said he only came to see if I was going, had
letters to write, a cause coming on the day after, and faintly said at
parting (for I was bent on setting out that moment)—'Well, we meet
at Philippi!'* I made the best of my way to Piccadilly. The mail coach
stand was bare. 'They are all gone,' said I—'this is always the way with
me—in the instant I lose the future—if I had not stayed to pour out
that last cup of tea, I should have been just in time'—and cursing my
folly and ill-luck together, without inquiring at the coach-office whether

the mails were gone or not, I walked on in despite, and to punish my own dilatoriness and want of determination. At any rate, I would not turn back: I might get to Hounslow, or perhaps farther, to be on my road the next morning. I passed Hyde Park Corner (my Rubicon), and trusted to fortune. Suddenly I heard the clattering of a Brentford stage, and the fight rushed full upon my fancy. I argued (not unwisely) that even a Brentford coachman was better company than my own thoughts (such as they were just then), and at his invitation mounted the box with him. I immediately stated my case to him—namely, my quarrel with myself for missing the Bath or Bristol mail, and my determination to get on in consequence as well as I could, without any disparagement or insulting comparison between longer or shorter stages. It is a maxim with me that stage-coaches, and consequently stage-coachmen, are respectable in proportion to the distance they have to travel: so I said nothing on that subject to my Brentford friend. Any incipient tendency to an abstract proposition, or (as he might have construed it) to a personal reflection of this kind, was however nipped in the bud; for I had no sooner declared indignantly that I had missed the mails, than he flatly denied that they were gone along, and lo! at the instant three of them drove by in rapid, provoking, orderly succession, as if they would devour the ground before them. Here again I seemed in the contradictory situation of the man in Dryden who exclaims,

I follow Fate, which does too hard pursue!*

If I had stopped to inquire at the White Horse Cellar, which would not have taken me a minute, I should now have been driving down the road in all the dignified unconcern and *ideal* perfection of mechanical conveyance. The Bath mail I had set my mind upon, and I had missed it, as I missed every thing else, by my own absurdity, in putting the will for the deed, and aiming at ends without employing means. 'Sir,' said he of the Brentford, 'the Bath mail will be up presently, my brother-in-law drives it, and I will engage to stop him if there is a place empty.' I almost doubted my good genius; but, sure enough, up it drove like lightning, and stopped directly at the call of the Brentford Jehu.* I would not have believed this possible, but the brother-in-law of a mail-coach driver is himself no mean man. I was transferred without loss of time from the top of one coach to that of the other, desired the guard to pay my fare to the Brentford coachman for me as I had no change, was accommodated with a great coat, put up my umbrella to keep off a drizzling mist, and we began to cut through the air like an arrow. The mile-stones disappeared one after another, the rain kept off; Tom Turtle,* the trainer, sat before me on the coach-box, with whom I exchanged civilities as a gentleman going to the fight; the passion that had transported me an hour before was subdued to pensive regret and conjectural musing on the next day's battle; I was promised a place inside at Reading, and upon the whole, I thought myself a lucky fellow. Such is the force of imagination! On the outside of any other coach on the 10th of December with a Scotch mist drizzling through the cloudy moonlight air, I should have been cold, comfortless, impatient, and, no doubt, wet through; but seated on the Royal mail, I felt warm and comfortable, the air did me good, the ride did me good, I was pleased with the progress we had made, and confident that all would go well through the journey. When I got inside at Reading, I found Turtle and a stout valetudinarian, whose costume bespoke him one of the FANCY, and who had risen from a three months' sick bed to get into the mail to see the fight. They were intimate, and we fell into a lively discourse. My friend the trainer was confined in his topics to fighting dogs and men, to bears and badgers; beyond this he was 'quite chap-fallen,'* had not a word to throw at a dog,* or indeed very wisely fell asleep, when any other game was started. The whole art of training (I, however, learnt from him,) consists in two things, exercise and abstinence, abstinence and exercise, repeated alternately and without end. A yolk of an egg with a spoonful of rum in it is the first thing in a morning, and then a walk of six miles till breakfast. This meal consists of a plentiful supply of tea and toast and beef-steaks. Then another six or seven miles till dinner-time, and another supply of solid beef or mutton with a pint of porter, and perhaps, at the utmost, a couple of glasses of sherry. Martin* trains on water, but this increases his infirmity on another very dangerous side. The Gas-man takes now and then a chirping glass (under the rose) to console him, during a six weeks probation, for the absence of Mrs. Hickman—an agreeable woman, with (I understand) a pretty fortune of two hundred pounds. How matter presses on me! What stubborn things are facts! How inexhaustible is nature and art! 'It is well,' as I once heard Mr. Richmond* observe, 'to see a variety.' He was speaking of cock-fighting as an edifying spectacle. I cannot deny but that one learns more of what *is* (I do not say of what *ought to be*) in this desultory mode of practical study, than

from reading the same book twice over, even though it should be
a moral treatise. Where was I? I was sitting at dinner with the candidate for the honours of the ring, 'where good digestion waits on appetite, and health on both.'* Then follows an hour of social chat and
native glee;* and afterwards, to another breathing over heathy hill or
dale. Back to supper, and then to bed, and up by six again—Our hero

> Follows so the ever-running sun,
> With profitable *ardour*—*

to the day that brings him victory or defeat in the green fairy circle.
Is not this life more sweet than mine?* I was going to say; but I will
not libel any life by comparing it to mine, which is (at the date of these
presents) bitter as coloquintida* and the dregs of aconitum!

The invalid in the Bath mail soared a pitch above the trainer, and
did not sleep so sound, because he had 'more figures and more fantasies.'* We talked the hours away merrily. He had faith in surgery,* for
he had had three ribs set right, that had been broken in a *turn-up* at
Belcher's, but thought physicians old women, for they had no antidote in their catalogue for brandy. An indigestion is an excellent
common-place for two people that never met before. By way of
ingratiating myself, I told him the story of my doctor, who, on my
earnestly representing to him that I thought his regimen had done me
harm, assured me that the whole pharmacopeia contained nothing
comparable to the prescription he had given me; and, as a proof of its
undoubted efficacy, said, that 'he had had one gentleman with my
complaint under his hands for the last fifteen years.' This anecdote
made my companion shake the rough sides of his three great coats
with boisterous laughter; and Turtle, starting out of his sleep, swore
he knew how the fight would go, for he had had a dream about it. Sure
enough the rascal told us how the three first rounds went off, but 'his
dream,' like others, 'denoted a foregone conclusion.'* He knew his
men. The moon now rose in silver state, and I ventured, with some
hesitation, to point out this object of placid beauty, with the blue
serene beyond, to the man of science, to which his ear he 'seriously
inclined,'* the more as it gave promise *d'un beau jour*ic* for the morrow,
and shewed the ring undrenched by envious showers,* arrayed in
sunny smiles. Just then, all going on well, I thought on my friend
Toms, whom I had left behind, and said innocently, 'There was
a blockhead of a fellow I left in town, who said there was no possibility

of getting down by the mail, and talked of going by a caravan from Belcher's at two in the morning, after he had written some letters.' 'Why,' said he of the lapells, 'I should not wonder if that was the very person we saw running about like mad from one coach-door to another, and asking if any one had seen a friend of his, a gentleman going to the fight, whom he had missed stupidly enough by staying to write a note.' 'Pray Sir,' said my fellow-traveller, 'had he a plaid-cloak on?'—'Why, no,' said I, 'not at the time I left him, but he very well might afterwards, for he offered to lend me one.' The plaid-cloak and the letter decided the thing. Joe, sure enough, was in the Bristol mail, which preceded us by about fifty yards. This was droll enough. We had now but a few miles to our place of destination, and the first thing I did on alighting at Newbury, both coaches stopping at the same time, was to call out, 'Pray, is there a gentleman in that mail of the name of Toms?' 'No,' said Joe, borrowing something of the vein of Gilpin,* 'for I have just got out.' 'Well!' says he, 'this is lucky; but you don't know how vexed I was to miss you; for,' added he, lowering his voice, 'do you know when I left you I went to Belcher's to ask about the caravan, and Mrs. Belcher said very obligingly, she couldn't tell about that, but there were two gentlemen who had taken places by the mail and were gone on in a landau, and she could frank us. It's a pity I didn't meet with you; we could then have got down for nothing. But *mum's the word*.' It's the devil for any one to tell me a secret, for it is sure to come out in print. I do not care so much to gratify a friend, but the public ear is too great a temptation to me.

Our present business was to get beds and a supper at an inn; but this was no easy task. The public-houses were full, and where you saw a light at a private house, and people poking their heads out of the casement to see what was going on, they instantly put them in and shut the window, the moment you seemed advancing with a suspicious overture for accommodation. Our guard and coachman thundered away at the outer gate of the Crown for some time without effect—such was the greater noise within;—and when the doors were unbarred, and we got admittance, we found a party assembled in the kitchen round a good hospitable fire, some sleeping, others drinking, others talking on politics and on the fight. A tall English yeoman (something like Matthews* in the face, and quite as great a wag)—

A lusty man to ben an abbot able,—*

was making such a prodigious noise about rent and taxes, and the price of corn now and formerly, that he had prevented us from being heard at the gate. The first thing I heard him say was to a shuffling fellow who wanted to be off a bet for a shilling glass of brandy and water—'Confound it, man, don't be *insipid*!' Thinks I, that is a good phrase. It was a good omen. He kept it up so all night, nor flinched with the approach of morning. He was a fine fellow, with sense, wit, and spirit, a hearty body and a joyous mind, free-spoken, frank, convivial—one of that home English breed that went with Harry the Fifth to the siege of Harfleur—'standing like greyhounds* on the slips,' &c. We ordered tea and eggs (beds were soon found to be out of the question) and this fellow's conversation was *sauce piquante*. It did one's heart good to see him brandish his oaken towel* and to hear him talk. He made mince-meat of a drunken, stupid, red-faced, quarrelsome, *frowsy* farmer, whose nose 'he moralized into a thousand similes,'* making it out a firebrand like Bardolph's.* 'I'll tell you what, my friend,' says he, 'the landlady has only to keep you here to save fire and candle. If one was to touch your nose, it would go off like a piece of charcoal.' At this the other only grinned like an idiot, the sole variety in his purple face being his little peering grey eyes and yellow teeth; called for another glass, swore he would not stand it; and after many attempts to provoke his humorous antagonist to single combat, which the other turned off (after working him up to a ludicrous pitch of choler) with great adroitness, he fell quietly asleep with a glass of liquor in his hand, which he could not lift to his head. His laughing persecutor made a speech over him, and turning to the opposite side of the room, where they were all sleeping in the midst of this 'loud and furious fun,'* said, 'There's a scene, by G—d, for Hogarth to paint. I think he and Shakspeare were our two best men at copying life!' This confirmed me in my good opinion of him. Hogarth, Shakspeare, and Nature, were just enough for him (indeed for any man) to know. I said, 'You read Cobbett, don't you? At least,' says I, 'you talk just as well as he writes.' He seemed to doubt this. But I said, 'We have an hour to spare: if you'll get pen, ink and paper, and keep on talking, I'll write down what you say; and if it doesn't make a capital Political Register, I'll forfeit my head. You have kept me alive tonight, however. I don't know what I should have done without you.' He did not dislike this view of the thing, nor my asking if he was not about the size of Jem Belcher; and told me soon afterwards, in the confidence of friendship, that 'the circumstance which had given him nearly the greatest concern in his life, was Cribb's beating Jem* after he had lost his eye by racket playing.'—The morning dawns; that dim but yet clear light appears, which weighs like solid bars of metal on the sleepless eyelids; the guests drop down from their chambers one by one—but it was too late to think of going to bed now (the clock was on the stroke of seven), we had nothing for it but to find a barber's (the pole that glittered in the morning sun lighted us to his shop), and then a nine miles march to Hungerford. The day was fine, the sky was blue, the mists were retiring from the marshy ground, the path was tolerably dry, the sitting-up all night had not done us much harm—at least the cause was good; we talked of this and that with amicable difference, roving and sipping of many subjects, but still invariably we returned to the fight. At length, a mile to the left of Hungerford, on a gentle eminence, we saw the ring surrounded by covered carts, gigs, and carriages, of which hundreds had passed us on the road; Toms gave a youthful shout, and we hastened down a narrow lane to the scene of action.

Reader! have you ever seen a fight? If not, you have a pleasure to come, at least if it is a fight like that between the Gas-man and Bill Neate. The crowd was very great when we arrived on the spot; open carriages were coming up, with streamers flying and music playing, and the country-people were pouring in over hedge and ditch in all directions, to see their hero beat or be beaten. The odds were still on Gas, but only about five to four. Gully,* had been down to try Neate, and had backed him considerably, which was a damper to the sanguine confidence of the adverse party. About two hundred thousand pounds were pending. The Gas says, he has lost 3,000*l.* which were promised him by different gentlemen if he had won. He had presumed too much on himself, which had made others presume on him. This spirited and formidable young fellow seems to have taken for his motto the old maxim, that 'there are three things necessary to success in life—*Impudence! Impudence! Impudence!*'* It is so in matters of opinion, but not in the *Fancy,* which is the most practical of all things, though even here confidence is half the battle, but only half. Our friend had vapoured and swaggered too much, as if he wanted to grin and bully his adversary out of the fight. 'Alas! the Bristol man was not so tamed!'*—'This is *the grave-digger*' (would Tom Hickman exclaim in the moments of intoxication from gin and success, shewing his tremendous right hand), 'this will send many of them to their long homes; I haven't done with them yet!' Why should he—though he had licked four of the best men within the hour, yet why should he threaten to inflict dishonourable chastisement on my old master Richmond, a veteran going off the stage, and who has borne his sable honours meekly? Magnanimity, my dear Tom, and bravery, should be inseparable. Or why should he go up to his antagonist, the first time he ever saw him at the Fives Court,* and measuring him from head to foot with a glance of contempt, as Achilles surveyed Hector,* say to him—'What, are you Bill Neate? I'll knock more blood out of that great carcase of thine, this day fortnight, than you ever knock'd out of a bullock's!' It was not manly, 'twas not fighter-like. If he was sure of the victory (as he was not), the less said about it the better. Modesty should accompany the *Fancy* as its shadow. The best men were always the best behaved. Jem Belcher, the Game Chicken* (before whom the Gas-man could not have lived) were civil, silent men. So is Cribb, so is Tom Belcher, the most elegant of sparrers, and not a man for every one to take by the nose. I enlarged on this topic in the mail (while Turtle was asleep), and said very wisely (as I thought) that impertinence was a part of no profession. A boxer was bound to beat his man, but not to thrust his fist, either actually or by implication, in every one's face. Even a highwayman, in the way of trade, may blow out your brains, but if he uses foul language at the same time, I should say he was no gentleman. A boxer, I would infer, need not be a blackguard or a coxcomb, more than another. Perhaps I press this point too much on a fallen man—Mr. Thomas Hickman has by this time learnt that first of all lessons, 'That man was made to mourn.'* He has lost nothing by the late fight but his presumption; and that every man may do as well without! By an over-display of this quality, however, the public had been prejudiced against him, and the *knowing-ones* were taken in. Few but those who had bet on him wished Gas to win. With my own prepossessions on the subject, the result of the 11th of December appeared to me as fine a piece of poetical justice as I had ever witnessed. The difference of weight between the two combatants (14 stone to 12) was nothing to the sporting men. Great, heavy, clumsy, long-armed Bill Neate kicked the beam in the scale of the Gas-man's vanity. The amateurs were frightened at his big words, and thought they would make up for the difference of six feet and five feet nine. Truly, the FANCY are not men of imagination. They judge of what has been, and cannot conceive of any thing that is to be. The Gas-man had won hitherto; therefore he must beat a man half as big again as himself—and that to a certainty. Besides, there are as many feuds, factions, prejudices, pedantic notions in the FANCY as in the state or in the schools. Mr. Gully is almost the only cool, sensible man among them, who exercises an unbiassed discretion, and is not a slave to his passions in these matters. But enough of reflections, and to our tale. The day, as I have said, was fine for a December morning. The grass was wet and the ground miry, and ploughed up with multitudinous feet, except that, within the ring itself, there was a spot of virgin-green closed in and unprofaned by vulgar tread, that shone with dazzling brightness in the mid-day sun. For it was now noon, and we had an hour to wait. This is the trying time. It is then the heart sickens, as you think what the two champions are about, and how short a time will determine their fate. After the first blow is struck, there is no opportunity for nervous apprehensions; you are swallowed up in the immediate interest of the scene—but

> Between the acting of a dreadful thing
> And the first motion, all the interim is
> Like a phantasma, or a hideous dream.*

I found it so as I felt the sun's rays clinging to my back, and saw the white wintry clouds sink below the verge of the horizon. 'So, I thought, my fairest hopes* have faded from my sight!—so will the Gas-man's glory, or that of his adversary, vanish in an hour.' The *swells** were parading in their white box-coats, the outer ring was cleared with some bruises on the heads and shins of the rustic assembly (for the *cockneys* had been distanced by the sixty-six miles); the time drew near, I had got a good stand; a bustle, a buzz, ran through the crowd, and, from the opposite side entered Neate, between his second and bottle-holder. He rolled along, swathed in his loose great coat, his knock-knees bending under his huge bulk; and, with a modest cheerful air, threw his hat into the ring. He then just looked round, and began quietly to undress; when from the other side there was a similar rush and an opening made, and the Gas-man came forward with a conscious air of anticipated triumph, too much like the cock-of-the-walk. He strutted about more than became a hero, sucked oranges with a supercilious air, and threw away the skin with a toss of his head, and went up and looked at Neate, which was an act of supererogation. The only sensible thing he did was, as he strode away from the modern Ajax, to fling out his arms, as if he wanted to try whether they would do their work that day. By this time they had stripped, and presented a strong contrast in appearance. If Neate was like Ajax, 'with Atlantean shoulders, fit to bear'* the pugilistic reputation of all Bristol, Hickman might be compared to Diomed, light, vigorous, elastic, and his back glistened in the sun, as he moved about, like a panther's hide. There was now a dead pause—attention was awe-struck. Who at that moment, big with a great event, did not draw his breath short—did not feel his heart throb? All was ready. They tossed up for the sun, and the Gas-man won. They were led up to the *scratch**—shook hands, and went at it.

In the first round every one thought it was all over. After making play a short time, the Gas-man flew at his adversary like a tiger, struck five blows in as many seconds, three first, and then following him as he staggered back, two more, right and left, and down he fell, a mighty ruin. There was a shout, and I said, 'There is no standing this.' Neate seemed like a lifeless lump of flesh and bone, round which the Gas-man's blows played with the rapidity of electricity or lightning, and you imagined he would only be lifted up to be knocked down again. It was as if Hickman held a sword or a fire in that right-hand of his, and directed it against an unarmed body. They met again, and Neate seemed, not cowed, but particularly cautious. I saw his teeth clenched together and his brows knit close against the sun. He held out both his arms at full length straight before him, like two sledge-hammers, and raised his left an inch or two higher. The Gas-man could not get over this guard—they struck mutually and fell, but without advantage on either side. It was the same in the next round; but the balance of power was thus restored—the fate of the battle was suspended. No one could tell how it would end. This was the only moment in which opinion was divided; for, in the next, the Gas-man aiming a mortal blow at his adversary's neck, with his right hand, and failing from the length he had to reach, the other returned it with his left at full swing, planted a tremendous blow on his cheek-bone and eyebrow, and made a red ruin of that side of his face. The Gas-man went down, and there was another shout—a roar of triumph as the waves of fortune rolled tumultuously from side to side. This was a settler. Hickman got up, and 'grinned horrible a ghastly smile,'* yet he was evidently dashed in his opinion of himself; it was the first time he had ever been so punished; all one side of his face was perfect scarlet, and his right eye was closed in dingy blackness, as he advanced to the fight, less confident, but still determined. After one or two rounds, not receiving another such remembrancer, he rallied and went at it with his former impetuosity. But in vain. His strength had been weakened,—his blows could not tell at such a distance,—he was obliged to fling himself at his adversary, and could not strike from his feet; and almost as regularly as he flew at him with his right-hand, Neate warded the blow, or drew back out of its reach, and felled him with the return of his left. There was little cautious sparring—no half-hits—no tapping and trifling, none of the *petit-maitreship* of the art—they were almost all knock-down blows:—the fight was a good stand-up fight. The wonder was the half-minute-time. If there had been a minute or more allowed between each round, it would have been intelligible how they should by degrees recover strength and resolution; but to see two men smashed to the ground, smeared with gore, stunned, senseless, the breath beaten out of their bodies; and then, before you recover from the shock, to see them rise up with new strength and courage, stand ready to inflict or receive mortal offence, and rush upon each other 'like two clouds over the Caspian'*—this is the most astonishing thing of all:—this is the high and heroic state of man! From this time forward the event became more certain every round; and about the twelfth it seemed as if it must have been over. Hickman generally stood with his back to me; but in the scuffle, he had changed positions, and Neate just then made a tremendous lunge at him, and hit him full in the face. It was doubtful whether he would fall backwards or forwards; he hung suspended for a second or two, and then fell back, throwing his hands in the air, and with his face lifted up to the sky. I never saw any thing more terrific than his aspect just before he fell. All traces of life, of natural expression, were gone from him. His face was like a human skull, a death's head, spouting blood. The eyes were filled with blood, the nose streamed with blood, the mouth gaped blood. He was not like an actual man, but like a preternatural, spectral appearance, or like one of the figures in Dante's *Inferno*. Yet he fought on after this for several rounds, still striking the first desperate blow, and Neate standing on the defensive, and using the same cautious guard to the last, as if he had still all his work to do; and it was not till the Gas-man was so stunned in the seventeenth or eighteenth round, that his senses forsook him, and he could not come to time, that the battle was declared over.[1] Ye who despise the Fancy, do something to shew as much *pluck*, or as much self-possession as this, before you assume a superiority which you have never given a single proof of by any one action in the whole course of your lives!—When the Gas-man came to himself, the first words he uttered were, 'Where am I? What is the matter?' 'Nothing is the matter, Tom,—you have lost the battle, but you are the bravest man alive.' And Jackson* whispered to him, 'I am collecting a purse for you, Tom.'—Vain sounds, and unheard at that moment! Neate instantly went up and shook him cordially by the hand, and seeing some old acquaintance, began to flourish with his fists, calling out, 'Ah! you always said I couldn't fight—What do you think now?' But all in good humour, and without any appearance of arrogance; only it was evident Bill Neate was pleased that he had won the fight. When it was over, I asked Cribb if he did not think it was a good one? He said, '*Pretty well!*' The carrier-pigeons now mounted into the air, and one of them flew with the news of her husband's victory to the bosom of Mrs. Neate. Alas, for Mrs. Hickman!—

Mais au revoir, as Sir Fopling Flutter says.* I went down with Toms; I returned with Jack Pigott, whom I met on the ground. Toms is a rattle-brain; Pigott is a sentimentalist. Now, under favour, I am a sentimentalist too—therefore I say nothing, but that the interest of the excursion did not flag as I came back. Pigott and I marched along the causeway leading from Hungerford to Newbury, now observing the effect of a brilliant sun on the tawny meads or moss-coloured cottages, now exulting in the fight, now digressing to some topic of general and elegant literature. My friend was dressed in character for the occasion, or like one of the FANCY; that is, with a double portion of great coats, clogs, and overhauls: and just as we had agreed with a couple of country-lads to carry his superfluous wearing-apparel to the next town, we were overtaken by a return post-chaise, into which I got, Pigott preferring a seat on the bar. There were two strangers already in the chaise, and on their observing they supposed I had been to the fight, I said I had, and concluded they had done the same. They

---

[1] Scroggins* said of the Gas-man, that he thought he was a man of that courage, that if his hands were cut off, he would still fight on with the stumps—like that of Widrington,—

————In doleful dumps,
Who, when his legs were smitten off,
Still fought upon his stumps.*

appeared, however, a little shy and sore on the subject; and it was not till after several hints dropped, and questions put, that it turned out that they had missed it. One of these friends had undertaken to drive the other there in his gig: they had set out, to make sure work, the day before at three in the afternoon. The owner of the one-horse vehicle scorned to ask his way, and drove right on to Bagshot, instead of turning off at Hounslow: there they stopped all night, and set off the next day across the country to Reading, from whence they took coach, and got down within a mile or two of Hungerford, just half an hour after the fight was over. This might be safely set down as one of the miseries of human life. We parted with these two gentlemen who had been to see the fight, but had returned as they went, at Wolhampton, where we were promised beds (an irresistible temptation, for Pigott had passed the preceding night at Hungerford as we had done at Newbury), and we turned into an old bow-windowed parlour with a carpet and a snug fire; and after devouring a quantity of tea, toast, and eggs, sat down to consider, during an hour of philosophic leisure, what we should have for supper. In the midst of an Epicurean deliberation between a roasted fowl and mutton-chops with mashed potatoes, we were interrupted by an inroad of Goths and Vandals— *O procul este profani**—not real flash-men, but interlopers, noisy pretenders, butchers from Tothill-fields, brokers from Whitechapel, who called immediately for pipes and tobacco, hoping it would not be disagreeable to the gentlemen, and began to insist that it was *a cross.** Pigott withdrew from the smoke and noise into another room, and left me to dispute the point with them for a couple of hours *sans intermission* by the dial.* The next morning we rose refreshed; and on observing that Jack had a pocket volume in his hand, in which he read in the intervals of our discourse, I inquired what it was, and learned to my particular satisfaction that it was a volume of the New Eloise.* Ladies, after this, will you contend that a love for the FANCY is incompatible with the cultivation of sentiment?—We jogged on as before, my friend setting me up in a genteel drab great coat and green silk handkerchief (which I must say became me exceedingly), and after stretching our legs for a few miles, and seeing Jack Randall, Ned Turner,* and Scroggins, pass on the top of one of the Bath coaches, we engaged with the driver of the second to take us to London for the usual fee. I got inside, and found three other passengers. One of them was an old gentleman with an aquiline nose, powdered hair, and a pigtail, and who looked as if he had played many a rubber at the Bath rooms. I said to myself, he is very like Mr. Windham;* I wish he would enter into conversation, that I might hear what fine observations would come from those finely-turned features. However, nothing passed, till, stopping to dine at Reading, some inquiry was made by the company about the fight, and I gave (as the reader may believe) an eloquent and animated description of it. When we got into the coach again, the old gentleman, after a graceful exordium, said, he had, when a boy, been to a fight between the famous Broughton and George Stevenson,* who was called the *Fighting Coachman*, in the year 1770, with the late Mr. Windham. This beginning flattered the spirit of prophecy within me, and he riveted my attention. He went on—'George Stevenson was coachman to a friend of my father's. He was an old man when I saw him some years afterwards. He took hold of his own arm and said, "there was muscle here once, but now it is no more than this young gentleman's." He added, "well, no matter; I have been here long, I am willing to go hence, and hope I have done no more harm than another man." Once,' said my unknown companion, 'I asked him if he had ever beat Broughton? He said Yes; that he had fought with him three times, and the last time he fairly beat him, though the world did not allow it. "I'll tell you how it was, master. When the seconds lifted us up in the last round, we were so exhausted that neither of us could stand, and we fell upon one another, and as Master Broughton fell uppermost, the mob gave it in his favour, and he was said to have won the battle. But," says he, "the fact was, that as his second (John Cuthbert) lifted him up, he said to him, 'I'll fight no more, I've had enough;' which," says Stevenson, "you know gave me the victory. And to prove to you that this was the case, when John Cuthbert was on his death-bed, and they asked him if there was any thing on his mind which he wished to confess, he answered, 'Yes, that there was one thing he wished to set right, for that certainly Master Stevenson won that last fight with Master Broughton; for he whispered him as he lifted him up in the last round of all, that he had had enough.'"' 'This,' said the Bath gentleman, 'was a bit of human nature;' and I have written this account of the fight on purpose that it might not be lost to the world. He also stated as a proof of the candour of mind in this class of men, that Stevenson acknowledged that Broughton could have beat him in his best day; but that he (Broughton) was getting old in their last rencounter. When we stopped in Piccadilly,

I wanted to ask the gentleman some questions about the late Mr. Windham, but had not courage. I got out, resigned my coat and green silk handkerchief to Pigott (loth to part with these ornaments of life), and walked home in high spirits.

P. S. Toms called upon me the next day, to ask me if I did not think the fight was a complete thing? I said I thought it was. I hope he will relish my account of it.

23

ON FAMILIAR STYLE

IT is not easy to write a familiar style. Many people mistake a familiar for a vulgar style, and suppose that to write without affectation is to write at random. On the contrary, there is nothing that requires more precision, and, if I may so say, purity of expression, than the style I am speaking of. It utterly rejects not only all unmeaning pomp, but all low, cant phrases, and loose, unconnected, *slipshod* allusions. It is not to take the first word that offers, but the best word in common use; it is not to throw words together in any combinations we please, but to follow and avail ourselves of the true idiom of the language. To write a genuine familiar or truly English style, is to write as any one would speak in common conversation, who had a thorough command and choice of words, or who could discourse with ease, force, and perspicuity, setting aside all pedantic and oratorical flourishes. Or to give another illustration, to write naturally is the same thing in regard to common conversation, as to read naturally is in regard to common speech. It does not follow that it is an easy thing to give the true accent and inflection to the words you utter, because you do not attempt to rise above the level of ordinary life and colloquial speaking. You do not assume indeed the solemnity of the pulpit, or the tone of stage-declamation: neither are you at liberty to gabble on at a venture, without emphasis or discretion, or to resort to vulgar dialect or clownish pronunciation. You must steer a middle course. You are tied down to a given and appropriate articulation, which is determined by the habitual associations between sense and sound, and which you can only hit by entering into the author's meaning, as you must find the proper words and style to express yourself by fixing your thoughts on the subject you have to write about. Any one may mouth out a passage with a theatrical cadence, or get upon stilts to tell his thoughts: but to write or speak with propriety and simplicity is a more difficult task. Thus it is easy to affect a pompous style, to use a word twice as big as the thing you want to express: it is not so easy to pitch upon the very word that exactly fits it. Out of eight or ten words equally common, equally intelligible, with nearly equal pretensions, it is a matter of some nicety and discrimination to pick out the very one, the preferableness of which is scarcely perceptible, but decisive. The reason why I object to Dr. Johnson's style is, that there is no discrimination, no selection, no variety in it. He uses none but 'tall, opaque words,'* taken from the 'first row of the rubric:'*—words with the greatest number of syllables, or Latin phrases with merely English terminations. If a fine style depended on this sort of arbitrary pretension, it would be fair to judge of an author's elegance by the measurement of his words, and the substitution of foreign circumlocutions (with no precise associations) for the mother-tongue.[1] How simple is it to be dignified without ease, to be pompous without meaning! Surely, it is but a mechanical rule for avoiding what is low to be always pedantic and affected. It is clear you cannot use a vulgar English word, if you never use a common English word at all. A fine tact is shewn in adhering to those which are perfectly common, and yet never falling into any expressions which are debased by disgusting circumstances, or which owe their signification and point to technical or professional allusions. A truly natural or familiar style can never be quaint or vulgar, for this reason, that it is of universal force and applicability, and that quaintness and vulgarity arise out of the immediate connection of certain words with coarse and disagreeable, or with confined ideas. The last form what we understand by *cant* or *slang* phrases.—To give an example of what is not very clear in the general statement. I should say that the phrase *To cut with a knife*, or *To cut a piece of*, is perfectly free from vulgarity, because it is perfectly common: but to *cut an acquaintance* is not quite unexceptionable, because it is not perfectly common or intelligible, and has hardly yet escaped out of the limits of slang phraseology. I should hardly therefore use the word in this sense without putting it in italics as a license of expression, to be received *cum grano salis*.* All provincial or byephrases come under the same mark of reprobation—all such as the writer transfers to the page from his fire-side or a particular *coterie*, or that he invents for his own sole use and convenience. I conceive that words are like money, not the worse for being common, but that it is the stamp of custom alone that gives them circulation or value. I am fastidious in this respect, and would almost as soon coin the

---

[1] I have heard of such a thing as an author, who makes it a rule never to admit a monosyllable into his vapid verse. Yet the charm and sweetness of Marlow's lines depended often on their being made up almost entirely of monosyllables.

currency of the realm as counterfeit the King's English. I never invented or gave a new and unauthorised meaning to any word but one single one (the term *impersonal* applied to feelings*) and that was in an abstruse metaphysical discussion to express a very difficult distinction. I have been (I know) loudly accused* of revelling in vulgarisms and broken English. I cannot speak to that point: but so far I plead guilty to the determined use of acknowledged idioms and common elliptical expressions. I am not sure that the critics in question know the one from the other, that is, can distinguish any medium between formal pedantry and the most barbarous solecism. As an author, I endeavour to employ plain words and popular modes of construction, as were I a chapman and dealer, I should common weights and measures.

The proper force of words lies not in the words themselves, but in their application. A word may be a fine-sounding word, of an unusual length, and very imposing from its learning and novelty, and yet in the connection in which it is introduced, may be quite pointless and irrelevant. It is not pomp or pretension, but the adaptation of the expression to the idea that clenches a writer's meaning:—as it is not the size or glossiness of the materials, but their being fitted each to its place, that gives strength to the arch; or as the pegs and nails are as necessary to the support of the building as the larger timbers, and more so than the mere shewy, unsubstantial ornaments. I hate any thing that occupies more space than it is worth. I hate to see a load of band-boxes go along the street, and I hate to see a parcel of big words without any thing in them. A person who does not deliberately dispose of all his thoughts alike in cumbrous draperies and flimsy disguises, may strike out twenty varieties of familiar every-day language, each coming somewhat nearer to the feeling he wants to convey, and at last not hit upon that particular and only one, which may be said to be identical with the exact impression in his mind. This would seem to shew that Mr. Cobbett is hardly right in saying that the first word that occurs is always the best.* It may be a very good one; and yet a better may present itself on reflection or from time to time. It should be suggested naturally, however, and spontaneously, from a fresh and lively conception of the subject. We seldom succeed by trying at improvement, or by merely substituting one word for another that we are not satisfied with, as we cannot recollect the name of a place or person by merely plaguing ourselves about it. We wander farther from the point by persisting in a wrong scent; but it starts up accidentally in the memory when we least expected it, by touching some link in the chain of previous association.

There are those who hoard up and make a cautious display of nothing but rich and rare phraseology;—ancient medals, obscure coins, and Spanish pieces of eight. They are very curious to inspect; but I myself would neither offer nor take them in the course of exchange. A sprinkling of archaisms is not amiss; but a tissue of obsolete expressions is more fit *for keep than wear*. I do not say I would not use any phrase that had been brought into fashion before the middle or the end of the last century; but I should be shy of using any that had not been employed by any approved author during the whole of that time. Words, like clothes, get old-fashioned, or mean and ridiculous, when they have been for some time laid aside. Mr. Lamb is the only imitator of old English style I can read with pleasure; and he is so thoroughly imbued with the spirit of his authors, that the idea of imitation is almost done away. There is an inward unction, a marrowy vein both in the thought and feeling, an intuition, deep and lively, of his subject, that carries off any quaintness or awkwardness arising from an antiquated style and dress. The matter is completely his own, though the manner is assumed. Perhaps his ideas are altogether so marked and individual, as to require their point and pungency to be neutralised by the affectation of a singular but traditional form of conveyance. Tricked out in the prevailing costume, they would probably seem more startling and out of the way. The old English authors, Burton, Fuller, Coryate, Sir Thomas Brown, are a kind of mediators between us and the more eccentric and whimsical modern, reconciling us to his peculiarities. I do not however know how far this is the case or not, till he condescends to write like one of us. I must confess that what I like best of his papers under the signature of Elia* (still I do not presume, amidst such excellence, to decide what is most excellent) is the account of *Mrs. Battle's Opinions on Whist*,* which is also the most free from obsolete allusions and turns of expression—

A well of native English undefiled.*

To those acquainted with his admired prototypes, these Essays of the ingenious and highly gifted author have the same sort of charm and relish, that Erasmus's Colloquies* or a fine piece of modern Latin have to the classical scholar. Certainly, I do not know any borrowed pencil that has more power or felicity of execution than the one of which I have here been speaking.

It is as easy to write a gaudy style without ideas, as it is to spread a pallet of shewy colours, or to smear in a flaunting transparency. 'What do you read?'—'Words, words, words.'—'What is the matter?'*—'*Nothing*,' it might be answered. The florid style is the reverse of the familiar. The last is employed as an unvarnished medium to convey ideas; the first is resorted to as a spangled veil to conceal the want of them. When there is nothing to be set down but words, it costs little to have them fine. Look through the dictionary, and cull out a *florilegium*,* rival the *tulippomania*.* *Rouge* high enough, and never mind the natural complexion. The vulgar, who are not in the secret, will admire the look of preternatural health and vigour; and the fashionable, who regard only appearances, will be delighted with the imposition. Keep to your sounding generalities, your tinkling phrases, and all will be well. Swell out an unmeaning truism to a perfect tympany of style. A thought, a distinction is the rock on which all this brittle cargo of verbiage splits at once. Such writers have merely *verbal* imaginations, that retain nothing but words. Or their puny thoughts have dragon-wings, all green and gold. They soar far above the vulgar failing of the *Sermo humi obrepens**—their most ordinary speech is never short of an hyperbole, splendid, imposing, vague, incomprehensible, magniloquent, a cento of sounding common-places. If some of us, whose 'ambition is more lowly,'* pry a little too narrowly into nooks and corners to pick up a number of 'unconsidered trifles,'* they never once direct their eyes or lift their hands to seize on any but the most gorgeous, tarnished, thread-bare patch-work set of phrases, the left-off finery of poetic extravagance, transmitted down through successive generations of barren pretenders. If they criticise actors and actresses, a huddled phantasmagoria of feathers, spangles, floods of light, and oceans of sound float before their morbid sense, which they paint in the style of Ancient Pistol. Not a glimpse can you get of the merits or defects of the performers: they are hidden in a profusion of barbarous epithets and wilful rhodomontade. Our hypercritics are not thinking of these little fantoccini beings—

That strut and fret their hour upon the stage*—

but of tall phantoms of words, abstractions, *genera* and *species*, sweeping clauses, periods that unite the Poles, forced alliterations, astounding antitheses—

And on their pens *Fustian* sits plumed.*

If they describe kings and queens, it is an Eastern pageant. The Coronation at either House is nothing to it. We get at four repeated images—a curtain, a throne, a sceptre, and a foot-stool. These are with them the wardrobe of a lofty imagination; and they turn their servile strains to servile uses. Do we read a description of pictures? It is not a reflection of tones and hues which 'nature's own sweet and cunning hand laid on,'* but piles of precious stones, rubies, pearls, emeralds, Golconda's mines, and all the blazonry of art. Such persons are in fact besotted with words, and their brains are turned with the glittering, but empty and sterile phantoms of things. Personifications, capital letters, seas of sunbeams, visions of glory, shining inscriptions, the figures of a transparency, Britannia with her shield, or Hope leaning on an anchor, make up their stock in trade. They may be considered as *hieroglyphical* writers. Images stand out in their minds isolated and important merely in themselves, without any ground-work of feeling—there is no context in their imaginations. Words affect them in the same way, by the mere sound, that is, by their possible, not by their actual application to the subject in hand. They are fascinated by first appearances, and have no sense of consequences. Nothing more is meant by them than meets the ear: they understand or feel nothing more than meets their eye. The web and texture of the universe, and of the heart of man, is a mystery to them: they have no faculty that strikes a chord in unison with it. They cannot get beyond the daubings of fancy, the varnish of sentiment. Objects are not linked to feelings, words to things, but images revolve in splendid mockery, words represent themselves in their strange rhapsodies. The categories of such a mind are pride and ignorance—pride in outside show, to which they sacrifice every thing, and ignorance of the true worth and hidden structure both of words and things. With a sovereign contempt for what is familiar and natural, they are the slaves of vulgar affectation—of a routine of high-flown phrases. Scorning to imitate realities, they are unable to invent any thing, to strike out one original idea. They are not copyists of nature, it is true: but they are the poorest of all plagiarists, the plagiarists of words. All is far-fetched, dear-bought, artificial, oriental in subject and allusion: all is mechanical, conventional, vapid, formal, pedantic in style and execution. They startle and confound the understanding of the reader, by the remoteness and obscurity of their illustrations: they soothe the ear by the monotony of the same everlasting round of circuitous metaphors. They are the *mock-school* in poetry and prose. They flounder about between fustian in expression, and bathos in sentiment. They tantalise the fancy, but never reach the head nor touch the heart. Their Temple of Fame is like a shadowy structure raised by Dulness to Vanity, or like Cowper's description of the Empress of Russia's palace of ice, 'as worthless as in shew 'twas glittering'—

It smiled, and it was cold!*

24

ON THE SPIRIT OF MONARCHY

Strip it of its externals, and what is it but *a jest?*

Charade on the word MAJESTY.

As for politics, I think poets are *Tories* by nature, supposing them
to be by nature poets. The love of an individual person or family,
that has worn a crown for many successions, is an inclination
greatly adapted to the fanciful tribe. On the other hand,
mathematicians, abstract reasoners, of no manner of attachment
to persons, at least to the visible part of them, but prodigiously
devoted to the ideas of virtue, liberty, and so forth, are generally
Whigs. It happens agreeably enough to this maxim, that the
Whigs are friends to that wise, plodding, unpoetical people, the
Dutch.*—*Shenstone's Letters*, 1746.

THE Spirit of Monarchy then is nothing but the craving in the
human mind after the Sensible and the One. It is not so much a matter of state-necessity or policy, as a natural infirmity, a disease, a false
appetite in the popular feeling, which must be gratified. Man is an
individual animal with narrow faculties, but infinite desires, which he
is anxious to concentrate in some one object within the grasp of his
imagination, and where, if he cannot be all that he wishes himself, he
may at least contemplate his own pride, vanity, and passions, displayed in their most extravagant dimensions in a being no bigger and
no better than himself. Each individual would (were it in his power)
be a king, a God: but as he cannot, the next best thing is to see this
reflex image of his self-love, the darling passion of his breast, realized,
embodied out of himself in the first object he can lay his hands on for
the purpose. The slave admires the tyrant, because the last *is*, what
the first *would be*. He surveys himself all over in the glass of royalty.
The swelling, bloated self-importance of the one is the very counter-
part and ultimate goal of the abject servility of the other. But both
hate mankind for the same reason, because a respect for humanity is
a diversion to their inordinate self-love, and the idea of the general
good is a check to the gross intemperance of passion. The worthlessness of the object does not diminish but irritate the propensity to
admire. It serves to pamper our imagination equally, and does not

provoke our envy. All we want is to aggrandize our own vain-glory at second-hand; and the less of real superiority or excellence there is in the person we fix upon as our proxy in this dramatic exhibition, the more easily can we change places with him, and fancy ourselves as good as he. Nay, the descent favours the rise; and we heap our tribute of applause the higher, in proportion as it is a free gift. An idol is not the worse for being of coarse materials: a king should be a common-place man. Otherwise, he is superior in his own nature, and not dependent on our bounty or caprice. Man is a poetical animal, and delights in fiction. We like to have scope for the exercise of our mere will. We make kings of men, and Gods of stocks and stones: we are not jealous of the creatures of our own hands. We only want a peg or loop to hang our idle fancies on, a puppet to dress up, a lay-figure to paint from. It is 'THING Ferdinand, and not KING Ferdinand,' as it was wisely and wittily observed.* We ask only for the stage effect; we do not go behind the scenes, or it would go hard with many of our prejudices! We see the symbols of majesty, we enjoy the pomp, we crouch before the power, we walk in the procession, and make part of the pageant, and we say in our secret hearts, there is nothing but accident that prevents us from being at the head of it. There is something in the mock-sublimity of thrones, wonderfully congenial to the human mind. Every man feels that he could sit there; every man feels that he could look big there; every man feels that he could bow there; every man feels that he could play the monarch there. The transition is so easy, and so delightful! The imagination keeps pace with royal state,

> And by the vision splendid
> Is on its way attended.*

The Madman in Hogarth* who fancies himself a king, is not a solitary instance of this species of hallucination. Almost every true and loyal subject holds such a barren sceptre in his hand; and the meanest of the rabble, as he runs by the monarch's side, has wit enough to think—'There goes my *royal* self!'* From the most absolute despot to the lowest slave there is but one step (no, not one) in point of real merit. As far as truth or reason is concerned, they might change situations to-morrow—nay, they constantly do so without the smallest loss or benefit to mankind! Tyranny, in a word, is a farce got up for the entertainment of poor human nature; and it might pass very well, if it did not so often turn into a tragedy.

We once heard a celebrated and elegant historian* and a hearty Whig declare, he liked a king like George III. better than such a one as Buonaparte; because, in the former case, there was nothing to over-awe the imagination but birth and situation; whereas he could not so easily brook the double superiority of the other, mental as well as adventitious. So does the spirit of independence and the levelling pride of intellect join in with the servile rage of the vulgar! This is the advantage which an hereditary has over an elective monarchy: for there is no end of the dispute about precedence while merit is supposed to determine it, each man laying claim to this in his own person; so that there is no other way to set aside all controversy and heart-burnings, but by precluding moral and intellectual qualifica-tions altogether, and referring the choice to accident, and giving the preference to a nonentity. 'A good king,' says Swift, 'should be, in all other respects, a mere cypher.'*

It has been remarked, as a peculiarity in modern criticism, that the courtly and loyal make a point of crying up Mr. Young,* as an actor, and equally running down Mr. Kean; and it has been conjectured in consequence that Mr. Kean was a *radical*. Truly, he is not a radical politician; but what is as bad, he is a radical actor. He savours too much of the reality. He is not a mock-tragedian, an automaton player—he is something besides his paraphernalia. He has 'that within which passes shew.'* There is not a particle of affinity between him and the patrons of the court-writers. Mr. Young, on the contrary, is the very thing—all assumption and strut and measured pomp, full of self-importance, void of truth and nature, the mask of the charac-ters he takes, a pasteboard figure, a stiff piece of wax-work. He fills the throne of tragedy, not like an upstart or usurper, but as a matter of course, decked out in his plumes of feathers, and robes of state, stuck into a posture, and repeating certain words by rote. Mr. Kean has a heart in his bosom, beating with human passion (a thing for the great 'to fear, not to delight in!'*) he is a living man, and not an arti-ficial one. How should those, who look to the surface, and never probe deeper, endure him? He is the antithesis of a court-actor. It is the object there to suppress and varnish over the feelings, not to give way to them. His *overt* manner must shock them, and be thought a breach of all decorum. They are in dread of his fiery humours, of coming near his Voltaic Battery*—they chuse rather to be roused gently from their self-complacent apathy by the application of Metallic Tractors.*

They dare not trust their delicate nerves within the estuary of the passions, but would slumber out their torpid existence in a calm, a Dead Sea—the air of which extinguishes life and motion!

Would it not be hard upon a little girl, who is busy in dressing up a favourite doll, to pull it in pieces before her face in order to shew her the bits of wood, the wool, and rags it is composed of? So it would be hard upon that great baby, the world, to take any of its idols to pieces, and shew that they are nothing but painted wood. Neither of them would thank you, but consider the offer as an insult. The little girl knows as well as you do that her doll is a cheat; but she shuts her eyes to it, for she finds her account in keeping up the deception. Her doll is her pretty little self. In its glazed eyes, its cherry cheeks, its flaxen locks, its finery and its baby-house, she has a fairy vision of her own future charms, her future triumphs, a thousand hearts led captive, and an establishment for life. Harmless illusion! that can create something out of nothing, can make that which is good for nothing in itself so fine in appearance, and clothe a shapeless piece of deal-board with the attributes of a divinity! But the great world has been doing little else but playing at *make-believe* all its life-time. For several thousand years its chief rage was to paint larger pieces of wood and smear them with gore and call them Gods and offer victims to them—slaughtered hecatombs, the fat of goats and oxen, or human sacrifices—shewing in this its love of shew, of cruelty, and imposture; and woe to him who should 'peep through the blanket of the dark to cry, *Hold, hold.*'*—*Great is Diana of the Ephesians,** was the answer in all ages. It was in vain to represent to them—'Your Gods have eyes but they see not, ears but they hear not, neither do they understand'*—the more stupid, brutish, helpless, and contemptible they were, the more furious, bigotted, and implacable were their votaries in their behalf.[1] The more absurd the fiction, the louder was the noise made to hide it—the more mischievous its tendency, the more did it excite all the phrensy of the passions. Superstition nursed, with peculiar zeal, her ricketty, deformed, and preposterous offspring. She passed by the nobler races of animals even, to pay divine honours to the odious and unclean—she took toads and serpents, cats, rats, dogs, crocodiles,

[1] Of whatsoe'er descent his Godhead be,
  Stock, stone, or other homely pedigree,
  In his defence his servants are as bold
  As if he had been made of beaten gold.*—DRYDEN.

goats and monkeys, and hugged them to her bosom, and dandled
them into deities, and set up altars to them, and drenched the earth
with tears and blood in their defence; and those who did not believe
in them were cursed, and were forbidden the use of bread, of fire, and
water, and to worship them was piety, and their images were held
sacred, and their race became Gods in perpetuity and by divine right.
To touch them, was sacrilege: to kill them, death, even in your own
defence. If they stung you, you must die: if they infested the land with
their numbers and their pollutions, there was no remedy. The nuisance was intolerable, impassive, immortal. Fear, religious horror,
disgust, hatred, heightened the flame of bigotry and intolerance.
There was nothing so odious or contemptible but it found a sanctuary
in the more odious and contemptible perversity of human nature. The
barbarous Gods of antiquity reigned *in contempt of their worshippers!**

   This game was carried on through all the first ages of the world,
and is still kept up in many parts of it; and it is impossible to describe
the wars, massacres, horrors, miseries and crimes, to which it gave
colour, sanctity, and sway. The idea of a God, beneficent and just, the
invisible maker of all things, was abhorrent to their gross, material
notions. No, they must have Gods of their own making, that they
could see and handle, that they knew to be nothing in themselves but
senseless images, and these they daubed over with the gaudy emblems
of their own pride and passions, and these they lauded to the skies,
and grew fierce, obscene, frantic before them, as the representatives
of their sordid ignorance and barbaric vices. TRUTH, GOOD, were
idle names to them, without a meaning. They must have a lie, a palpable, pernicious lie, to pamper their crude, unhallowed conceptions
with, and to exercise the untameable fierceness of their wills. The
Jews were the only people of antiquity who were withheld from running headlong into this abomination; yet so strong was the propensity
in them (from inherent frailty as well as neighbouring example) that
it could only be curbed and kept back by the hands of Omnipotence.[2]
At length, reason prevailed over imagination so far, that these brute
idols and their altars were overturned: it was thought too much to set
up stocks and stones, Golden Calves and Brazen Serpents, as *bona
fide* Gods and Goddesses, which men were to fall down and worship

---

   [2] They *would* have a king in spite of the devil. The image-worship of the Papists is
a batch of the same leaven. The apishness of man's nature would not let even the
Christian Religion escape.

at their peril—and Pope long after summed up the merits of the
whole mythologic tribe in a handsome distich—

> Gods partial, changeful, passionate, unjust,
> Whose attributes were rage, revenge, or lust.*

It was thought a bold stride to divert the course of our imagination,
the overflowings of our enthusiasm, our love of the mighty and
the marvellous, from the dead to the living *subject*, and there we stick.
We have got living idols, instead of dead ones; and we fancy that they
are real, and put faith in them accordingly. Oh, Reason! when will thy
long minority expire? It is not now the fashion to make Gods of wood
and stone and brass, but we make kings of common men, and are
proud of our own handy-work. We take a child from his birth, and we
agree, when he grows up to be a man, to heap the highest honours of
the state upon him, and to pay the most devoted homage to his will.
Is there any thing in the person, 'any mark, any likelihood,'* to warrant this sovereign awe and dread? No: he may be little better than an
ideot, little short of a madman, and yet he is no less qualified for
king.[3] If he can contrive to pass the College of Physicians, the Heralds'
College dub him divine. Can we make any given individual taller or
stronger or wiser than other men, or different in any respect from
what nature intended him to be? No; but we can make a king, of him.
We cannot add a cubit to the stature, or instil a virtue into the minds
of monarchs—but we can put a sceptre into their hands, a crown
upon their heads, we can set them on an eminence, we can surround
them with circumstance, we can aggrandise them with power, we can
pamper their appetites, we can pander to their wills. We can do every

---

[3] 'In fact, the argument drawn from the supposed incapacity of the people against
a representative Government, comes with the worst grace in the world from the patrons
and admirers of hereditary government. Surely, if government were a thing requiring the
utmost stretch of genius, wisdom, and virtue to carry it on, the office of King would never
even have been dreamt of as hereditary, any more than that of poet, painter, or philosopher. It is easy here "for the Son to tread in the Sire's steady steps." It requires nothing
but the will to do it. Extraordinary talents are not once looked for. Nay, a person, who
would never have risen by natural abilities to the situation of churchwarden or parish
beadle, succeeds by unquestionable right to the possession of a throne, and wields the
energies of an empire, or decides the fate of the world with the smallest possible share of
human understanding. The line of distinction which separates the regal purple from the
slabbering-bib is sometimes fine indeed; as we see in the case of the two Ferdinands. Any
one above the rank of an ideot is supposed capable of exercising the highest functions of
royal state. Yet these are the persons who talk of the people as a swinish multitude, and
taunt them with their want of refinement and philosophy.'*—*Yellow Dwarf, p.* 84.

thing to exalt them in external rank and station—nothing to lift them one step higher in the scale of moral or intellectual excellence. Education does not give capacity or temper; and the education of kings is not especially directed to useful knowledge or liberal sentiment. What then is the state of the case? The highest respect of the community and of every individual in it is paid and is due of right there, where perhaps not an idea can take root, or a single virtue be engrafted. Is not this to erect a standard of esteem directly opposite to that of mind and morals? The lawful monarch may be the best or the worst man in his dominions, he may be the wisest or the weakest, the wittiest or the stupidest: still he is equally entitled to our homage as king, for it is the place and power we bow to, and not the man. He may be a sublimation of all the vices and diseases of the human heart; yet we are not to say so, we dare not even think so. 'Fear God, and honour the King,' is equally a maxim at all times and seasons. The personal character of the king has nothing to do with the question. Thus the extrinsic is set up over the intrinsic by authority: wealth and interest lend their countenance to gilded vice and infamy on principle, and outward shew and advantages become the symbols and the standard of respect in despite of useful qualities or well-directed efforts through all ranks and gradations of society. 'From the crown of the head to the sole of the foot there is no soundness left.'* The whole style of moral thinking, feeling, acting, is in a false tone—is hollow, spurious, meretricious. Virtue, says Montesquieu,* is the principle of republics; honour of a monarchy. But it is 'honour dishonourable, sin-bred'*—it is the honour of trucking a principle for a place, of exchanging our honest convictions for a ribbon or a garter. The business of life is a scramble for unmerited precedence. Is not the highest respect entailed, the highest station filled without any possible proofs or pretensions to public spirit or public principle? Shall not the next places to it be secured by the sacrifice of them? It is the order of the day, the understood etiquette of courts and kingdoms. For the servants of the crown to presume on merit, when the crown itself is held as an heir-loom by prescription, is a kind of *lèse majesté*, an indirect attainder of the title to the succession. Are not all eyes turned to the sun of court-favour? Who would not then reflect its smile by the performance of any acts which can avail in the eye of the great, and by the surrender of any virtue, which attracts neither notice nor applause? The stream of corruption begins at the fountainhead of court-influence. The sympathy of mankind is that on which all strong feeling and opinion floats; and this sets in full in every absolute monarchy to the side of tinsel shew and iron-handed power, in contempt and defiance of right and wrong. The right and the wrong are of little consequence, compared to the *in* and the *out*. The distinction between Whig and Tory is merely nominal: neither have their country one bit at heart. Phaw! we had forgot—Our British monarchy is a mixed, and the only perfect form of government; and therefore what is here said cannot properly apply to it. But MIGHT BEFORE RIGHT is the motto blazoned on the front of unimpaired and undivided Sovereignty!——

A court is the centre of fashion; and no less so, for being the sink of luxury and vice—

> —Of outward shew
> Elaborate, of inward less exact.*

The goods of fortune, the baits of power, the indulgences of vanity, may be accumulated without end, and the taste for them increases as it is gratified: the love of virtue, the pursuit of truth, grow stale and dull in the dissipation of a court. Virtue is thought crabbed and morose, knowledge pedantic, while every sense is pampered, and every folly tolerated. Every thing tends naturally to personal aggrandisement and unrestrained self-will. It is easier for monarchs as well as other men 'to tread the primrose path of dalliance'* than 'to scale the steep and thorny road to heaven.'* The vices, when they have leave from power and authority, go greater lengths than the virtues; example justifies almost every excess, and 'nice customs curtsy to great kings.'* What chance is there that monarchs should not yield to the temptations of gallantry there, where youth and beauty are as wax? What female heart can indeed withstand the attractions of a throne—the smile that melts all hearts, the air that awes rebellion, the frown that kings dread, the hand that scatters fairy wealth, that bestows titles, places, honour, power, the breast on which the star glitters, the head circled with a diadem, whose dress dazzles with its richness and its taste, who has nations at his command, senates at his controul, 'in form and motion so express and admirable, in action how like an angel, in apprehension how like a God; the beauty of the world, the paragon of animals!'* The power of resistance is so much the less, where fashion extends impunity to the frail offender, and screens the loss of character.

Vice is undone, if she forgets her birth,
And stoops from angels to the dregs of earth;
But 'tis the fall degrades her to a whore:
Let greatness own her, and she's mean no more.
Her birth, her beauty, crowds and courts confess,
Chaste matrons praise her, and grave bishops bless.
In golden chains the willing world she draws,
And hers the Gospel is, and hers the laws.[4]*

The air of a court is not assuredly that which is most favourable to the practice of self-denial and strict morality. We increase the temptations of wealth, of power, and pleasure a thousand-fold, while we can give no additional force to the antagonist principles of reason, disinterested integrity and goodness of heart. Is it to be wondered at that courts and palaces have produced so many monsters of avarice, cruelty, and lust? The adept in voluptuousness is not likely to be a proportionable proficient in humanity. To feed on plate or be clothed in purple, is not to feel for the hungry and the naked. He who has the greatest power put into his hands, will only become more impatient of any restraint in the use of it. To have the welfare and the lives of millions placed at our disposal, is a sort of warrant, a challenge to squander them without mercy. An arbitrary monarch set over the heads of his fellows does not identify himself with them, or learn to comprehend their rights or sympathise with their interests, but looks down upon them as of a different species from himself, as insects crawling

---

[4] A lady of quality abroad, in allusion to the gallantries of the reigning Prince, being told, 'I suppose it will be your turn next?' said, 'No, I hope not; for you know it is impossible to refuse!' What a satire on the court and fashionables! If this be true, female virtue in the blaze of royalty is no more than the moth in the candle, or ice in the sun's ray. What will the great themselves say to it, in whom at this rate,

——the same luck holds,
They all are subjects, courtiers, and cuckolds!*

Out upon it! We'll not believe it. Alas! poor virtue, what is to become of the very idea of it, if we are to be told that every man within the precincts of a palace is an *hypothetical* cuckold, or holds his wife's virtue in trust for the Prince? We entertain no doubt that many ladies of quality have resisted the importunities of a throne, and that many more would do so in private life, if they had the desired opportunity: nay, we have been assured by several that a king would no more be able to prevail with them than any other man! If however there is any foundation for the above insinuation, it throws no small light on the Spirit of Monarchy, which by the supposition implies in it the *virtual* surrender of the whole sex at discretion; and at the same time accounts perhaps for the indifference shewn by some monarchs in availing themselves of so mechanical a privilege.

on the face of the earth, that he may trample on at his pleasure, or if he spares them, it is an act of royal grace——he is besotted with power, blinded with prerogative, an alien to his nature, a traitor to his trust, and instead of being the organ of public feeling and public opinion, is an excrescence and an anomaly in the state, a bloated mass of morbid humours and proud flesh! A constitutional king, on the other hand, is a servant of the public, a representative of the people's wants and wishes, dispensing justice and mercy according to law. Such a monarch is the King of England! Such was his late, and such is his present Majesty George the IVth.!——

Let us take the Spirit of Monarchy in its highest state of exaltation, in the moment of its proudest triumph—a Coronation-day.* We now see it in our mind's eye; the preparation of weeks—the expectation of months—the seats, the privileged places, are occupied in the obscurity of night, and in silence—the day dawns slowly, big with the hope of Cæsar and of Rome—the golden censers are set in order, the tables groan with splendour and with luxury—within the inner space the rows of peeresses are set, and revealed to the eye decked out in ostrich feathers and pearls, like beds of lilies sparkling with a thousand dew-drops—the marshals and the heralds are in motion—the full organ, majestic, peals forth the Coronation Anthem—every thing is ready—and all at once the Majesty of kingdoms bursts upon the astonished sight—his person is swelled out with all the gorgeousness of dress, and swathed in bales of silk and golden tissues—the bow with which he greets the assembled multitude, and the representatives of foreign kings, is the climax of conscious dignity, bending gracefully on its own bosom, and instantly thrown back into the sightless air, as if asking no recognition in return—the oath of mutual fealty between him and his people is taken—the fairest flowers of female beauty precede the Sovereign, scattering roses; the sons of princes page his heels, holding up the robes of crimson and ermine—he staggers and reels under the weight of royal pomp, and of a nation's eyes; and thus the pageant is launched into the open day, dazzling the sun, whose beams seem beaten back by the sun of royalty—there were the warrior, the statesman, and the mitred head—there was Prince Leopold,* like a panther in its dark glossy pride, and Castlereagh, clad in triumphant smiles and snowy satin, unstained with his own blood—the loud trumpet brays, the cannon roars, the spires are mad with music, the stones in the street are startled at the presence of a king:—the crowd press on, the metropolis heaves like a sea in restless motion, the air is thick with loyalty's quick pants in its monarch's arms—all eyes drink up the sight, all tongues reverberate the sound—

> A present deity they shout around,
> A present deity the vaulted roofs rebound!*

What does it all amount to? A shew—a theatrical spectacle! What does it prove? That a king is crowned, that a king is dead! What is the moral to be drawn from it, that is likely to sink into the heart of a nation? That greatness consists in finery, and that supreme merit is the dower of birth and fortune! It is a form, a ceremony to which each successor to the throne is entitled in his turn as a matter of right. Does it depend on the inheritance of virtue, on the acquisition of knowledge in the new monarch, whether he shall be thus exalted in the eyes of the people? No:—to say so is not only an offence in manners, but a violation of the laws. The king reigns in contempt of any such pragmatical distinctions. They are set aside, proscribed, treasonable, as it relates to the august person of the monarch; what is likely to become of them in the minds of the people? A Coronation overlays and drowns all such considerations for a generation to come, and so far it serves its purpose well. It debauches the understandings of the people, and makes them the slaves of sense and show. It laughs to scorn and tramples upon every other claim to distinction or respect. Is the chief person in the pageant a tyrant? It does not lessen, but aggrandise him to the imagination. Is he the king of a free people? We make up in love and loyalty what we want in fear. Is he young? He borrows understanding and experience from the learning and tried wisdom of councils and parliaments. Is he old? He leans upon the youth and beauty that attend his triumph. Is he weak? Armies support him with their myriads. Is he diseased? What is health to a staff of physicians? Does he die? The truth is out, and he is then—nothing!

There is a cant among court-sycophants of calling all those who are opposed to them, 'the *rabble*,' '*fellows*,' '*miscreants*,' &c. This shews the grossness of their ideas of all true merit, and the false standard of rank and power by which they measure every thing; like footmen, who suppose their masters must be gentlemen, and that the rest of the world are low people. Whatever is opposed to power, they think despicable; whatever suffers oppression, they think deserves it. They are ever ready to side with the strong, to insult and trample on the weak. This is with us a pitiful fashion of thinking. They are not of the mind of Pope, who was so full of the opposite conviction, that he has even written a bad couplet to express it:—

> Worth makes the man, and want of it the fellow:
> The rest is all but leather and prunella.*

Those lines in Cowper also must sound very puerile or old-fashioned to courtly ears:—

> The only amaranthine flower on earth
> Is virtue; the only lasting treasure, truth.*

To this sentiment, however, we subscribe our hearts and hands. There is nothing truly liberal but that which postpones its own claims to those of propriety—or great, but that which looks out of itself to others. All power is but an unabated nuisance, a barbarous assumption, an aggravated injustice, that is not directed to the common good: all grandeur that has not something corresponding to it in personal merit and heroic acts, is a deliberate burlesque, and an insult on common sense and human nature. That which is true, the understanding ratifies: that which is good, the heart owns: all other claims are spurious, vitiated, mischievous, false—fit only for those who are sunk below contempt, or raised above opinion. We hold in scorn all *right-lined* pretensions but those of rectitude. If there is offence in this, we are ready to abide by it. If there is shame, we take it to ourselves: and we hope and hold that the time will come, when all other idols but those which represent pure truth and real good, will be looked upon with the same feelings of pity and wonder that we now look back to the images of Thor and Woden!

Really, that men born to a throne (limited or unlimited) should employ the brief span of their existence here in doing all the mischief in their power, in levying cruel wars and undermining the liberties of the world, to prove to themselves and others that their pride and passions are of more consequence than the welfare of mankind at large, would seem a little astonishing, but that the fact is so. It is not our business to preach lectures to monarchs, but if we were at all disposed to attempt the ungracious task, we should do it in the words of an author who often addressed the ear of monarchs.

'A man may read a sermon,' says Jeremy Taylor, 'the best and most passionate that ever man preached, if he shall but enter into the sepulchres of kings. In the same Escurial where the Spanish princes live in greatness and power, and decree war or peace, they have wisely placed a cemetery where their ashes and their glory shall sleep till time shall be no more: and where *our* kings have been crowned, their ancestors lie interred, and they must walk over their grandsire's head to take his crown. There is an acre sown with royal seed, the copy of the greatest change from rich to naked, from ceiled roofs to arched coffins, from living like Gods to die like men. There is enough to cool the flames of lust, to abate the height of pride, to appease the itch of covetous desires, to sully and dash out the dissembling colours of a lustful, artificial, and imaginary beauty. There the warlike and the peaceful, the fortunate and the miserable, the beloved and the despised princes mingle their dust, and pay down their symbol of mortality, and tell all the world, that when we die our ashes shall be equal to kings, and our accounts shall be easier, and our pains for our crimes shall be less. To my apprehension, it is a sad record which is left by Athenæus concerning Ninus, the great Assyrian monarch, whose life and death is summed up in these words; "Ninus, the Assyrian, had an ocean of gold, and other riches more than the sand in the Caspian sea; he never saw the stars, and perhaps he never desired it; he never stirred up the holy fire among the Magi; nor touched his God with the sacred rod, according to the laws; he never offered sacrifice, nor worshipped the Deity, nor administered justice, nor spake to the people, nor numbered them; but he was most valiant to eat and drink, and having mingled his wines, he threw the rest upon the stones. This man is dead: behold his sepulchre, and now hear where Ninus is. *Sometime I was Ninus, and drew the breath of a living man, but now am nothing but clay. I have nothing but what I did eat, and what I served to myself in lust is all my portion: the wealth with which I was blest, my enemies meeting together shall carry away, as the mad Thyades carry a raw goat. I am gone to Hell; and when I went thither, I carried neither gold nor horse, nor a silver chariot. I that wore a mitre, am now a little heap of dust!*" * —TAYLOR'S HOLY LIVING AND DYING.

25

MY FIRST ACQUAINTANCE WITH POETS

My father was a Dissenting Minister at W—m* in Shropshire; and in the year 1798 (the figures that compose that date are to me like the 'dreaded name of Demogorgon'*) Mr. Coleridge came to Shrewsbury, to succeed Mr. Rowe* in the spiritual charge of a Unitarian Congregation there. He did not come till late on the Saturday afternoon before he was to preach; and Mr. Rowe, who himself went down to the coach in a state of anxiety and expect-ation, to look for the arrival of his successor, could find no one at all answering the description but a round-faced man in a short black coat (like a shooting-jacket) which hardly seemed to have been made for him, but who seemed to be talking at a great rate to his fellow-passengers. Mr. Rowe had scarce returned to give an account of his disappointment, when the round-faced man in black entered, and dissipated all doubts on the subject, by beginning to talk. He did not cease while he staid; nor has he since, that I know of. He held the good town of Shrewsbury in delightful suspense for three weeks that he remained there, 'fluttering the *proud Salopians* like an eagle in a dove-cote;'* and the Welch mountains that skirt the horizon with their tempestuous confusion, agree to have heard no such mystic sounds since the days of

High-born Hoel's harp or soft Llewellyn's lay!*

As we passed along between W—m and Shrewsbury, and I eyed their blue tops seen through the wintry branches, or the red rustling leaves of the sturdy oak-trees by the roadside, a sound was in my ears as of a Siren's song; I was stunned, startled with it, as from deep sleep; but I had no notion then that I should ever be able to express my admir-ation to others in motley imagery or quaint allusion, till the light of his genius shone into my soul, like the sun's rays glittering in the puddles of the road. I was at that time dumb, inarticulate, helpless, like a worm by the way-side,* crushed, bleeding, lifeless; but now, bursting from the deadly bands that 'bound them,

With Styx nine times round them,'*

my ideas float on winged words, and as they expand their plumes, catch the golden light of other years. My soul has indeed remained in its original bondage, dark, obscure, with longings infinite* and unsatisfied; my heart, shut up in the prison-house of this rude clay, has never found, nor will it ever find, a heart to speak to; but that my understanding also did not remain dumb and brutish, or at length found a language to express itself, I owe to Coleridge. But this is not to my purpose.

My father lived ten miles from Shrewsbury, and was in the habit of exchanging visits with Mr. Rowe, and with Mr. Jenkins of Whitchurch (nine miles farther on) according to the custom of Dissenting Ministers in each other's neighbourhood. A line of communication is thus established, by which the flame of civil and religious liberty is kept alive, and nourishes its smouldering fire unquenchable, like the fires in the Agamemnon of Æschylus, placed at different stations, that waited for ten long years to announce with their blazing pyramids the destruction of Troy.* Coleridge had agreed to come over to see my father, according to the courtesy of the country, as Mr. Rowe's probable successor; but in the mean time I had gone to hear him preach the Sunday after his arrival. A poet and a philosopher getting up into a Unitarian pulpit to preach the Gospel, was a romance in these degenerate days, a sort of revival of the primitive spirit of Christianity, which was not to be resisted.

It was in January, 1798,* that I rose one morning before day-light, to walk ten miles in the mud, and went to hear this celebrated person preach. Never, the longest day I have to live, shall I have such another walk as this cold, raw, comfortless* one, in the winter of the year 1798.—*Il y a des impressions que ni le tems ni les circonstances peuvent effacer. Dusse-je vivre des siècles entiers, le doux tems de ma jeunesse ne peut renaitre pour moi, ni s'effacer jamais dans ma mémoire.** When I got there, the organ was playing the 100th psalm, and, when it was done, Mr Coleridge rose and gave out his text, 'And he went up into the mountain to pray, HIMSELF, ALONE.'* As he gave out this text, his voice 'rose like a steam of rich distilled perfumes,'* and when he came to the two last words, which he pronounced loud, deep, and distinct, it seemed to me, who was then young, as if the sounds had echoed from the bottom of the human heart, and as if that prayer might have floated in solemn silence through the universe. The idea of St. John came into mind, 'of one crying in the wilderness, who had his loins girt about, and whose food was locusts and wild honey.'* The

preacher then launched into his subject, like an eagle dallying with
the wind. The sermon was upon peace and war; upon church and
state—not their alliance, but their separation—on the spirit of the
world and the spirit of Christianity, not as the same, but as opposed to
one another. He talked of those who had 'inscribed the cross of Christ
on banners dripping with human gore.' He made a poetical and pastoral excursion,—and to shew the fatal effects of war, drew a striking
contrast between the simple shepherd boy, driving his team afield, or
sitting under the hawthorn, piping to his flock, 'as though he should
never be old,'* and the same poor country-lad, crimped,* kidnapped,
brought into town, made drunk at an alehouse, turned into a wretched
drummer-boy, with his hair sticking on end with powder and pomatum, a long cue at his back, and tricked out in the loathsome finery of
the profession of blood.

> Such were the notes our once-lov'd poet sung.*

And for myself, I could not have been more delighted if I had heard the
music of the spheres. Poetry and Philosophy had met together, Truth
and Genius had embraced, under the eye and with the sanction of
Religion. This was even beyond my hopes. I returned home well satisfied. The sun that was still labouring pale and wan through the sky,
obscured by thick mists, seemed an emblem of the *good cause*; and the
cold dank drops of dew that hung half melted on the beard of the thistle,
had something genial and refreshing in them; for there was a spirit
of hope and youth in all nature, that turned every thing into good.
The face of nature had not then the brand of JUS DIVINUM* on it:

> Like to that sanguine flower inscrib'd with woe.*

On the Tuesday following, the half-inspired speaker came. I was
called down into the room where he was, and went half-hoping, half-
afraid. He received me very graciously, and I listened for a long time
without uttering a word. I did not suffer in his opinion by my silence.
'For those two hours,' he afterwards was pleased to say, 'he was conversing with W. H.'s forehead!' His appearance was different from
what I had anticipated from seeing him before. At a distance, and in
the dim light of the chapel, there was to me a strange wildness in his
aspect, a dusky obscurity, and I thought him pitted with the small-pox.
His complexion was at that time clear, and even bright—

> As are the children of yon azure sheen.*

His forehead was broad and high, light as if built of ivory, with large projecting eyebrows, and his eyes rolling beneath them like a sea with darkened lustre. 'A certain tender bloom his face o'erspread,'* a purple tinge as we see it in the pale thoughtful complexions of the Spanish portrait-painters, Murillo and Velasquez. His mouth was gross, voluptuous, open, eloquent; his chin good-humoured and round; but his nose, the rudder of the face, the index of the will, was small, feeble, nothing—like what he has done. It might seem that the genius of his face as from a height surveyed and projected him (with sufficient capacity, and huge aspiration) into the world unknown of thought and imagination, with nothing to support or guide his veering purpose, as if Columbus had launched his adventurous course for the New World in a scallop, without oars or compass. So at least I comment on it after the event. Coleridge in his person was rather above the common size, inclining to the corpulent, or like Lord Hamlet, 'somewhat fat and pursy.'* His hair (now, alas! grey) was then black and glossy as the raven's, and fell in smooth masses over his forehead. This long pendulous hair is peculiar to enthusiasts, to those whose minds tend heavenward; and is traditionally inseparable (though of a different colour) from the pictures of Christ. It ought to belong, as a character, to all who preach *Christ crucified*, and Coleridge was at that time one of those!

It was curious to observe the contrast between him and my father, who was a veteran in the cause, and then declining into the vale of years.* He had been a poor Irish lad, carefully brought up by his parents, and sent to the University of Glasgow (where he studied under Adam Smith) to prepare him for his future destination. It was his mother's proudest wish to see her son a Dissenting Minister. So if we look back to past generations (as far as eye can reach) we see the same hopes, fears, wishes, followed by the same disappointments, throbbing in the human heart; and so we may see them (if we look forward) rising up for ever, and disappearing, like vapourish bubbles, in the human breast! After being tossed about from congregation to congregation in the heats of the Unitarian controversy, and squabbles about the American war, he had been relegated to an obscure village, where he was to spend the last thirty years of his life, far from the only converse that he loved, the talk about disputed texts of Scripture and the cause of civil and religious liberty. Here he passed his days, repining but resigned, in the study of the Bible, and the perusal of the

Commentators,—huge folios, not easily got through, one of which would outlast a winter! Why did he pore on these from morn to night (with the exception of a walk in the fields or a turn in the garden to gather brocoli-plants or kidney-beans of his own rearing, with no small degree of pride and pleasure)?—Here were 'no figures nor no fantasies,'*—neither poetry nor philosophy—nothing to dazzle, nothing to excite modern curiosity; but to his lack-lustre eyes there appeared, within the pages of the ponderous, unwieldy, neglected tomes, the sacred name of JEHOVAH in Hebrew capitals: pressed down by the weight of the style, worn to the last fading thinness of the understanding, there were glimpses, glimmering notions of the patriarchal wanderings, with palm-trees hovering in the horizon, and processions of camels at the distance of three thousand years; there was Moses with the Burning Bush, the number of the Twelve Tribes, types, shadows, glosses on the law and the prophets; there were discussions (dull enough) on the age of Methuselah,* a mighty speculation! there were outlines, rude guesses at the shape of Noah's Ark and of the riches of Solomon's Temple; questions as to the date of the creation, predictions of the end of all things; the great lapses of time, the strange mutations of the globe were unfolded with the voluminous leaf, as it turned over; and though the soul might slumber with an hieroglyphic veil of inscrutable mysteries drawn over it, yet it was in a slumber ill-exchanged for all the sharpened realities of sense, wit, fancy, or reason. My father's life was comparatively a dream; but it was a dream of infinity and eternity, of death, the resurrection, and a judgment to come!

No two individuals were ever more unlike than were the host and his guest. A poet was to my father a sort of nondescript: yet whatever added grace to the Unitarian cause was to him welcome. He could hardly have been more surprised or pleased, if our visitor had worn wings. Indeed, his thoughts had wings; and as the silken sounds rustled round our little wainscoted parlour, my father threw back his spectacles over his forehead, his white hairs mixing with its sanguine hue; and a smile of delight beamed across his rugged cordial face, to think that Truth had found a new ally in Fancy!¹ Besides, Coleridge

---

¹ My father was one of those who mistook his talent after all. He used to be very much dissatisfied that I preferred his Letters to his Sermons. The last were forced and dry; the first came naturally from him. For ease, half-plays on words, and a supine, monkish, indolent pleasantry, I have never seen them equalled.

seemed to take considerable notice of me, and that of itself was enough. He talked very familiarly, but agreeably, and glanced over a variety of subjects. At dinner-time he grew more animated, and dilated in a very edifying manner on Mary Wolstonecraft and Mackintosh.* The last, he said, he considered (on my father's speaking of his *Vindiciæ Gallicæ* as a capital performance) as a clever scholastic man—a master of the topics,—or as the ready warehouseman of letters, who knew exactly where to lay his hand on what he wanted, though the goods were not his own. He thought him no match for Burke, either in style or matter. Burke was a metaphysician, Mackintosh a mere logician. Burke was an orator (almost a poet) who reasoned in figures, because he had an eye for nature: Mackintosh, on the other hand, was a rhetorician, who had only an eye to commonplaces. On this I ventured to say that I had always entertained a great opinion of Burke, and that (as far as I could find) the speaking of him with contempt might be made the test of a vulgar democratical mind. This was the first observation I ever made to Coleridge, and he said it was a very just and striking one. I remember the leg of Welsh mutton and the turnips on the table that day had the finest flavour imaginable. Coleridge added that Mackintosh and Tom. Wedgwood* (of whom, however, he spoke highly) had expressed a very indifferent opinion of his friend Mr. Wordsworth, on which he remarked to them—'He strides on so far before you, that he dwindles in the distance!' Godwin had once boasted to him of having carried on an argument with Mackintosh for three hours with dubious success; Coleridge told him—'If there had been a man of genius in the room, he would have settled the question in five minutes.' He asked me if I had ever seen Mary Wolstonecraft, and I said, I had once for a few moments,* and that she seemed to me to turn off Godwin's objections to something she advanced with quite a playful, easy air. He replied, that 'this was only one instance of the ascendancy which people of imagination exercised over those of mere intellect.' He did not rate Godwin very high[2] (this was caprice or prejudice, real or affected) but he had a great idea of Mrs. Wolstonecraft's powers of conversation, none at all of her talent for book-making. We talked a little about Holcroft.* He had

---

[2] He complained in particular of the presumption of his attempting to establish the future immortality of man, 'without' (as he said) 'knowing what Death was or what Life was'—and the tone in which he pronounced these two words seemed to convey a complete image of both.*

been asked if he was not much struck *with* him, and he said, he
thought himself in more danger of being struck *by* him. I complained
that he would not let me get on at all, for he required a definition
of every the commonest word, exclaiming, 'What do you mean by
a *sensation*, Sir? What do you mean by an *idea*?' This, Coleridge said,
was barricadoing the road to truth:—it was setting up a turnpike-gate
at every step we took. I forget a great number of things, many more
than I remember; but the day passed off pleasantly, and the next
morning Mr. Coleridge was to return to Shrewsbury. When I came
down to breakfast, I found that he had just received a letter from his
friend, T. Wedgwood, making him an offer of £150. a-year if he chose
to wave his present pursuit, and devote himself entirely to the study
of poetry and philosophy. Coleridge seemed to make up his mind to
close with this proposal in the act of tying on one of his shoes. It threw
an additional damp on his departure. It took the wayward enthusiast
quite from us to cast him into Deva's winding vales,* or by the shores
of old romance.* Instead of living at ten miles distance, of being the
pastor of a Dissenting congregation at Shrewsbury, he was hence-
forth to inhabit the Hill of Parnassus, to be a Shepherd on the
Delectable Mountains.* Alas! I knew not the way thither, and felt
very little gratitude for Mr. Wedgwood's bounty. I was presently
relieved from this dilemma; for Mr. Coleridge, asking for a pen and
ink, and going to a table to write something on a bit of card, advanced
towards me with undulating step, and giving me the precious docu-
ment, said that that was his address, *Mr. Coleridge, Nether-Stowey,
Somersetshire*; and that he should be glad to see me there in a few
weeks' time, and, if I chose, would come half-way to meet me. I was
not less surprised than the shepherd-boy (this simile is to be found
in Cassandra*) when he sees a thunder-bolt fall close at his feet.
I stammered out my acknowledgments and acceptance of this offer
(I thought Mr. Wedgwood's annuity a trifle to it) as well as I could;
and this mighty business being settled, the poet-preacher took leave,
and I accompanied him six miles on the road. It was a fine morning in
the middle of winter, and he talked the whole way. The scholar in
Chaucer is described as going

—Sounding on his way.*

So Coleridge went on his. In digressing, in dilating, in passing from
subject to subject, he appeared to me to float in air, to slide on ice.

He told me in confidence (going along) that he should have preached two sermons before he accepted the situation at Shrewsbury, one on Infant Baptism, the other on the Lord's Supper, shewing that he could not administer either, which would have effectually disqualified him for the object in view. I observed that he continually crossed me on the way by shifting from one side of the foot-path to the other. This struck me as an odd movement; but I did not at that time connect it with any instability of purpose or involuntary change of principle, as I have done since. He seemed unable to keep on in a strait line. He spoke slightingly of Hume (whose Essay on Miracles* he said was stolen from an objection started in one of South's Sermons*—*Credat Judæus Apella!**). I was not very much pleased at this account of Hume, for I had just been reading, with infinite relish, that completest of all metaphysical *choke-pears,** his *Treatise on Human Nature*, to which the *Essays*, in point of scholastic subtlety and close reasoning, are mere elegant trifling, light summer-reading. Coleridge even denied the excellence of Hume's general style, which I think betrayed a want of taste or candour. He however made me amends by the manner in which he spoke of Berkeley.* He dwelt particularly on his *Essay on Vision* as a masterpiece of analytical reasoning. So it undoubtedly is. He was exceedingly angry with Dr. Johnson for striking the stone with his foot, in allusion to this author's Theory of Matter and Spirit, and saying, 'Thus I confute him, Sir.'* Coleridge drew a parallel (I don't know how he brought about the connection) between Bishop Berkeley and Tom Paine. He said the one was an instance of a subtle, the other of an acute mind, than which no two things could be more distinct. The one was a shop-boy's quality, the other the characteristic of a philosopher. He considered Bishop Butler* as a true philosopher, a profound and conscientious thinker, a genuine reader of nature and of his own mind. He did not speak of his *Analogy*, but of his *Sermons at the Rolls' Chapel*, of which I had never heard. Coleridge somehow always contrived to prefer the *unknown* to the *known*. In this instance he was right. The *Analogy* is a tissue of sophistry, of wire-drawn, theological special-pleading; the *Sermons* (with the Preface to them) are in a fine vein of deep, matured reflection, a candid appeal to our observation of human nature, without pedantry and without bias. I told Coleridge I had written a few remarks,* and was sometimes foolish enough to believe that I had made a discovery on the same subject (the *Natural Disinterestedness of* *the Human Mind*)—and I tried to explain my view of it to Coleridge, who listened with great willingness, but I did not succeed in making myself understood. I sat down to the task shortly afterwards for the twentieth time, got new pens and paper, determined to make clear work of it, wrote a few meagre sentences in the skeleton-style of a mathematical demonstration, stopped half-way down the second page; and, after trying in vain to pump up any words, images, notions, apprehensions, facts, or observations, from that gulph of abstraction in which I had plunged myself for four or five years preceding, gave up the attempt as labour in vain, and shed tears of helpless despondency on the blank unfinished paper. I can write fast enough now. Am I better than I was then? Oh no! One truth discovered, one pang of regret at not being able to express it, is better than all the fluency and flippancy in the world. Would that I could go back to what I then was! Why can we not revive past times as we can revisit old places? If I had the quaint Muse of Sir Philip Sidney to assist me, I would write a *Sonnet to the Road between W—m and Shrewsbury*, and immortalise every step of it by some fond enigmatical conceit. I would swear that the very milestones had ears, and that Harmer-hill stooped with all its pines, to listen to a poet, as he passed! I remember but one other topic of discourse in this walk. He mentioned Paley,* praised the naturalness and clearness of his style, but condemned his sentiments, thought him a mere time-serving casuist, and said that 'the fact of his work on Moral and Political Philosophy being made a text-book in our Universities was a disgrace to the national character.' We parted at the six-mile stone; and I returned homeward pensive but much pleased. I had met with unexpected notice from a person, whom I believed to have been prejudiced against me. 'Kind and affable to me had been his condescension, and should be honoured ever with suitable regard.'* He was the first poet I had known, and he certainly answered to that inspired name. I had heard a great deal of his powers of conversation, and was not disappointed. In fact, I never met with any thing at all like them, either before or since. I could easily credit the accounts which were circulated of his holding forth to a large party of ladies and gentlemen, an evening or two before, on the Berkeleian Theory, when he made the whole material universe look like a transparency of fine words; and another story (which I believe he has somewhere told himself*) of his being asked to a party at Birmingham, of his smoking tobacco and going to sleep after dinner on a sofa, where the company found him to their no small surprise, which was increased to wonder when he started up of a sudden, and rubbing his eyes, looked about him, and launched into a three-hours' description of the third heaven, of which he had had a dream, very different from Mr. Southey's Vision of Judgment,* and also from that other Vision of Judgment,* which Mr. Murray, the Secretary of the Bridge-street Junto,* has taken into his especial keeping!

On my way back, I had a sound in my ears, it was the voice of Fancy: I had a light before me, it was the face of Poetry. The one still lingers there, the other has not quitted my side! Coleridge in truth met me half-way on the ground of philosophy, or I should not have been won over to his imaginative creed. I had an uneasy, pleasurable sensation all the time, till I was to visit him. During those months the chill breath of winter gave me a welcoming; the vernal air was balm and inspiration to me. The golden sun-sets, the silver star of evening, lighted me on my way to new hopes and prospects. *I was to visit Coleridge in the Spring.* This circumstance was never absent from my thoughts, and mingled with all my feelings. I wrote to him at the time proposed, and received an answer postponing my intended visit for a week or two, but very cordially urging me to complete my promise then. This delay did not damp, but rather increase my ardour. In the mean time, I went to Llangollen Vale, by way of initiating myself in the mysteries of natural scenery; and I must say I was enchanted with it. I had been reading Coleridge's description of England,* in his fine *Ode on the Departing Year*, and I applied it, *con amore*, to the objects before me. That valley was to me (in a manner) the cradle of a new existence: in the river that winds through it, my spirit was baptised in the waters of Helicon!*

I returned home, and soon after set out on my journey with unworn heart and untried feet. My way lay through Worcester and Gloucester, and by Upton, where I thought of Tom Jones and the adventure of the muff.* I remember getting completely wet through one day, and stopping at an inn (I think it was at Tewkesbury) where I sat up all night to read Paul and Virginia.* Sweet were the showers in early youth that drenched my body, and sweet the drops of pity that fell upon the books I read! I recollect a remark of Coleridge's upon this very book, that nothing could shew the gross indelicacy of French manners and the entire corruption of their imagination more strongly than the behaviour of the heroine in the last fatal scene, who turns away from a person on board the sinking vessel, that offers to save her life, because he has thrown off his clothes to assist him in swimming. Was this a time to think of such a circumstance? I once hinted to Wordsworth, as we were sailing in his boat on Grasmere lake, that I thought he had borrowed the idea of his *Poems on the Naming of Places* from the local inscriptions of the same kind in Paul and Virginia. He did not own the obligation, and stated some distinction without a difference, in defence of his claim to originality. Any the slightest variation would be sufficient for this purpose in his mind; for whatever *he* added or omitted would inevitably be worth all that any one else had done, and contain the marrow of the sentiment.—I was still two days before the time fixed for my arrival, for I had taken care to set out early enough. I stopped these two days at Bridgewater, and when I was tired of sauntering on the banks of its muddy river, returned to the inn, and read Camilla.* So have I loitered my life away, reading books, looking at pictures, going to plays, hearing, thinking, writing on what pleased me best. I have wanted only one thing to make me happy; but wanting that, have wanted every thing!

I arrived, and was well received. The country about Nether Stowey is beautiful, green and hilly, and near the sea-shore. I saw it but the other day, after an interval of twenty years, from a hill near Taunton. How was the map of my life spread out before me, as the map of the country lay at my feet! In the afternoon, Coleridge took me over to All-Foxden, a romantic old family-mansion of the St. Aubins, where Wordsworth lived. It was then in the possession of a friend of the poet's, who gave him the free use of it. Somehow that period (the time just after the French Revolution) was not a time when *nothing was given for nothing*.* The mind opened, and a softness might be perceived coming over the heart of individuals, beneath 'the scales that fence'* our self-interest. Wordsworth himself was from home, but his sister kept house, and set before us a frugal repast; and we had free access to her brother's poems, the *Lyrical Ballads*, which were still in manuscript, or in the form of *Sybilline Leaves*.* I dipped into a few of these with great satisfaction, and with the faith of a novice. I slept that night in an old room with blue hangings, and covered with the round-faced family-portraits of the age of George I. and II. and from the wooded declivity of the adjoining park that overlooked my window, at the dawn of day, could

———hear the loud stag speak.*

In the outset of life (and particularly at this time I felt it so) our imagination has a body to it. We are in a state between sleeping and waking, and have indistinct but glorious glimpses of strange shapes, and there is always something to come better than what we see. As in our dreams the fulness of the blood gives warmth and reality to the coinage of the brain, so in youth our ideas are clothed, and fed, and pampered with our good spirits; we breathe thick with thoughtless happiness, the weight of future years presses on the strong pulses of the heart, and we repose with undisturbed faith in truth and good. As we advance, we exhaust our fund of enjoyment and of hope. We are no longer wrapped in *lamb's-wool*, lulled in Elysium. As we taste the pleasures of life, their spirit evaporates, the sense palls; and nothing is left but the phantoms, the lifeless shadows of what *has been!*

That morning, as soon as breakfast was over, we strolled out into the park, and seating ourselves on the trunk of an old ash-tree that stretched along the ground, Coleridge read aloud with a sonorous and musical voice, the ballad of *Betty Foy.** I was not critically or sceptically inclined. I saw touches of truth and nature, and took the rest for granted. But in the *Thorn*, the *Mad Mother*, and the *Complaint of a Poor Indian Woman*, I felt that deeper power and pathos which have been since acknowledged,

> In spite of pride, in erring reason's spite,*

as the characteristics of this author; and the sense of a new style and a new spirit in poetry came over me. It had to me something of the effect that arises from the turning up of the fresh soil, or of the first welcome breath of Spring,

> While yet the trembling year is unconfirmed.*

Coleridge and myself walked back to Stowey that evening, and his voice sounded high

> Of Providence, foreknowledge, will, and fate,
> Fix'd fate, free-will, foreknowledge absolute,*

as we passed through echoing grove, by fairy stream or waterfall, gleaming in the summer moonlight! He lamented that Wordsworth was not prone enough to belief in the traditional superstitions of the place, and that there was a something corporeal, a *matter-of-fact-ness*, a clinging to the palpable, or often to the petty, in his poetry, in consequence. His genius was not a spirit that descended to him through the air; it sprung out of the ground like a flower, or unfolded itself from a green spray, on which the gold-finch sang. He said, however (if I remember right) that this objection must be confined to his descriptive pieces, that his philosophic poetry had a grand and comprehensive spirit in it, so that his soul seemed to inhabit the universe like a palace, and to discover truth by intuition, rather than by deduction. The next day Wordsworth arrived from Bristol at Coleridge's cottage. I think I see him now. He answered in some degree to his friend's description of him, but was more gaunt and Don Quixote-like. He was quaintly dressed (according to the *costume* of that unconstrained period) in a brown fustian jacket and striped pantaloons. There was something of a roll, a lounge in his gait, not unlike his own Peter Bell.* There was a severe, worn pressure of thought about his temples, a fire in his eye (as if he saw something in objects more than the outward appearance) an intense high narrow forehead, a Roman nose, cheeks furrowed by strong purpose and feeling, and a convulsive inclination to laughter about the mouth, a good deal at variance with the solemn, stately expression of the rest of his face. Chantry's bust* wants the marking traits; but he was teazed into making it regular and heavy: Haydon's head of him, introduced into the *Entrance of Christ into Jerusalem*, is the most like his drooping weight of thought and expression. He sat down and talked very naturally and freely, with a mixture of clear gushing accents in his voice, a deep guttural intonation, and a strong tincture of the northern *burr*, like the crust on wine. He instantly began to make havoc of the half of a Cheshire cheese on the table, and said triumphantly that 'his marriage with experience had not been so unproductive as Mr. Southey's in teaching him a knowledge of the good things of this life.' He had been to see the *Castle Spectre* by Monk Lewis, while at Bristol, and described it very well. He said 'it fitted the taste of the audience like a glove.' This *ad captandum** merit was however by no means a recommendation of it, according to the severe principles of the new school, which reject rather than court popular effect. Wordsworth, looking out of the low, latticed window, said, 'How beautifully the sun sets on that yellow bank!' I thought within myself, 'With what eyes these poets see nature!' and ever after, when I saw the sun-set stream upon the objects facing it, conceived I had made a discovery, or thanked Mr. Wordsworth for having made one for me! We went over to All-Foxden again the day following, and Wordsworth read us the story of Peter Bell in the open air; and the comment made upon it by his face and voice was very different from that of some later critics! Whatever might be thought of the poem, 'his face was as a book where men might read strange matters,'* and he announced the fate of his hero in prophetic tones. There is a *chaunt* in the recitation both of Coleridge and Wordsworth, which acts as a spell upon the hearer, and disarms the judgment. Perhaps they have deceived themselves by making habitual use of this ambiguous accompaniment. Coleridge's manner is more full, animated, and varied; Wordsworth's more equable, sustained, and internal. The one might be termed more *dramatic*, the other more *lyrical*. Coleridge has told me that he himself liked to compose in walking over uneven ground, or breaking through the straggling branches of a copsewood; whereas Wordsworth always wrote (if he could) walking up and down a strait gravel-walk, or in some spot where the continuity of his verse met with no collateral interruption. Returning that same evening, I got into a metaphysical argument with Wordsworth, while Coleridge was explaining the different notes of the nightingale to his sister, in which we neither of us succeeded in making ourselves perfectly clear and intelligible. Thus I passed three weeks at Nether Stowey and in the neighbourhood, generally devoting the afternoons to a delightful chat in an arbour made of bark by the poet's friend Tom Poole,* sitting under two fine elm-trees, and listening to the bees humming round us, while we quaffed our *flip*.* It was agreed, among other things, that we should make a jaunt down the Bristol-Channel, as far as Linton. We set off together on foot, Coleridge, John Chester,* and I. This Chester was a native of Nether Stowey, one of those who were attracted to Coleridge's discourse as flies are to honey, or bees in swarming-time to the sound of a brass pan. He 'followed in the chace, like a dog who hunts, not like one that made up the cry.'* He had on a brown cloth coat, boots, and corduroy breeches, was low in stature, bow-legged, had a drag in his walk like a drover, which he assisted by a hazel switch, and kept on a sort of trot by the side of Coleridge, like a running footman by a state coach, that he might not lose a syllable or sound, that fell from Coleridge's lips. He told me his private opinion, that Coleridge was a wonderful man. He scarcely opened his lips, much less offered an opinion the whole way: yet of the three, had I to chuse during that journey, I would be John Chester. He afterwards followed Coleridge into Germany, where the Kantean philosophers were puzzled how to bring him under any of their categories. When he sat down at table with his idol, John's felicity was complete; Sir Walter Scott's, or Mr. Blackwood's, when they sat down at the same table with the King, was not more so. We passed Dunster on our right, a small town between the brow of a hill and the sea. I remember eying it wistfully as it lay below us: contrasted with the woody scene around, it looked as clear, as pure, as *embrowned* and ideal as any landscape I have seen since, of Gaspar Poussin's or Domenichino's. We had a long day's march—(our feet kept time to the echoes of Coleridge's tongue)—through Minehead and by the Blue Anchor, and on to Linton, which we did not reach till near midnight, and where we had some difficulty in making a lodgment. We however knocked the people of the house up at last, and we were repaid for our apprehensions and fatigue by some excellent rashers of fried bacon and eggs. The view in coming along had been splendid. We walked for miles and miles on dark brown heaths overlooking the channel, with the Welsh hills beyond, and at times descended into little sheltered valleys close by the sea-side, with a smuggler's face scowling by us, and then had to ascend conical hills with a path winding up through a coppice to a barren top, like a monk's shaven crown, from one of which I pointed out to Coleridge's notice the bare masts of a vessel on the very edge of the horizon and within the red-orbed disk of the setting sun, like his own spectre-ship in the *Ancient Mariner*. At Linton the character of the sea-coast becomes more marked and rugged. There is a place called the *Valley of Rocks* (I suspect this was only the poetical name for it) bedded among precipices overhanging the sea, with rocky caverns beneath, into which the waves dash, and where the sea-gull for ever wheels its screaming flight. On the tops of these are huge stones thrown transverse, as if an earthquake had tossed them there, and behind these is a fretwork of perpendicular rocks, some-thing like the *Giant's Causeway*. A thunder-storm came on while we were at the inn, and Coleridge was running out bareheaded to enjoy the commotion of the elements in the *Valley of Rocks*, but as if in spite, the clouds only muttered a few angry sounds, and let fall a few refreshing drops. Coleridge told me that he and Wordsworth were to have made this place the scene of a prose-tale, which was to have been in the manner of, but far superior to, the *Death of Abel*,* but they had relinquished the design. In the morning of the second day, we breakfasted luxuriously in an old-fashioned parlour, on tea, toast, eggs, and honey, in the very sight of the bee-hives from which it had been taken, and a garden full of thyme and wild flowers that had produced it. On this occasion Coleridge spoke of Virgil's Georgics, but not well. I do not think he had much feeling for the classical or elegant. It was in this room that we found a little worn-out copy of the *Seasons*, lying in a window-seat, on which Coleridge exclaimed, '*That* is true fame!' He said Thomson was a great poet, rather than a good one; his style was as meretricious as his thoughts were natural. He spoke of Cowper as the best modern poet. He said the *Lyrical Ballads* were an experiment about to be tried by him and Wordsworth, to see how far the public taste would endure poetry written in a more natural and simple style than had hitherto been attempted; totally discarding the artifices of poetical diction, and making use only of such words as had probably been common in the most ordinary language since the days of Henry II.* Some comparison was introduced between Shakespear and Milton. He said 'he hardly knew which to prefer. Shakespear seemed to him a mere stripling in the art; he was as tall and as strong, with infinitely more activity than Milton, but he never appeared to have come to man's estate; or if he had, he would not have been a man, but a monster.' He spoke with contempt of Gray, and with intolerance of Pope. He did not like the versification of the latter. He observed that 'the ears of these couplet-writers might be charged with having short memories, that could not retain the harmony of whole passages.' He thought little of Junius as a writer; he had a dislike of Dr. Johnson; and a much higher opinion of Burke as an orator and politician, than of Fox or Pitt. He however thought him very inferior in richness of style and imagery to some of our elder prose-writers, particularly Jeremy Taylor. He liked Richardson, but not Fielding; nor could I get him to enter into the merits of *Caleb Williams*.[3] In short, he was profound and discriminating with respect to those authors whom he liked, and where he gave his judgment fair play; capricious, perverse, and prejudiced in his antipathies and distastes. We loitered on the 'ribbed sea-sands,'* in such talk as this,

---

[3] He had no idea of pictures, of Claude or Raphael, and at this time I had as little as he. He sometimes gives a striking account at present of the Cartoons at Pisa, by Buffamalco and others; of one in particular, where Death is seen in the air brandishing his scythe, and the great and mighty of the earth shudder at his approach, while the beggars and the wretched kneel to him as their deliverer. He would of course understand so broad and fine a moral as this at any time.

a whole morning, and I recollect met with a curious sea-weed, of which John Chester told us the country name! A fisherman gave Coleridge an account of a boy that had been drowned the day before, and that they had tried to save him at the risk of their own lives. He said 'he did not know how it was that they ventured, but, Sir, we have a *nature* towards one another.' This expression, Coleridge remarked to me, was a fine illustration of that theory of disinterestedness which I (in common with Butler) had adopted. I broached to him an argument of mine to prove that *likeness* was not mere association of ideas. I said that the mark in the sand put one in mind of a man's foot, not because it was part of a former impression of a man's foot (for it was quite new) but because it was like the shape of a man's foot. He assented to the justness of this distinction (which I have explained at length elsewhere, for the benefit of the curious) and John Chester listened; not from any interest in the subject, but because he was astonished that I should be able to suggest any thing to Coleridge that he did not already know. We returned on the third morning, and Coleridge remarked the silent cottage-smoke curling up the valleys where, a few evenings before, we had seen the lights gleaming through the dark.

In a day or two after we arrived at Stowey, we set out, I on my return home, and he for Germany. It was a Sunday morning, and he was to preach that day for Dr. Toulmin of Taunton.* I asked him if he had prepared any thing for the occasion? He said he had not even thought of the text, but should as soon as we parted. I did not go to hear him,—this was a fault,—but we met in the evening at Bridgewater. The next day we had a long day's walk to Bristol, and sat down, I recollect, by a well-side on the road, to cool ourselves and satisfy our thirst, when Coleridge repeated to me some descriptive lines from his tragedy of Remorse;* which I must say became his mouth and that occasion better than they, some years after, did Mr. Elliston's and the Drury-lane boards,—

> Oh memory! shield me from the world's poor strife,
> And give those scenes thine everlasting life.*

I saw no more of him for a year or two, during which period he had been wandering in the Hartz Forest in Germany; and his return was cometary, meteorous, unlike his setting out. It was not till some time after that I knew his friends Lamb and Southey. The last always appears to me (as I first saw him) with a common-place book under his arm, and the first with a *bon-mot* in his mouth. It was at Godwin's that I met him with Holcroft and Coleridge, where they were disputing fiercely which was the best—*Man as he was, or man as he is to be.* 'Give me,' says Lamb, 'man as he is *not* to be.' This saying was the beginning of a friendship between us, which I believe still continues.—Enough of this for the present.

> But there is matter for another rhyme,
> And I to this may add a second tale.*

26

ON LONDONERS AND COUNTRY PEOPLE

I DO not agree with Mr. Blackwood in his definition of the word *Cockney*.* He means by it a person who has happened at any time to live in London, and who is not a Tory—I mean by it, a person who has never lived out of London, and who has got all his ideas from it.

The true Cockney has never travelled beyond the purlieus of the Metropolis, either in the body or the spirit. Primrose-hill is the Ultima Thule* of his most romantic desires; Greenwich Park stands him in stead of the Vales of Arcady. Time and space are lost to him. He is confined to one spot, and to the present moment. He sees every thing near, superficial, little, in hasty succession. The world turns round, and his head with it, like a roundabout at a fair, till he becomes stunned and giddy with the motion. Figures glide by as in a *camera obscura*. There is a glare, a perpetual hubbub, a noise, a crowd about him; he sees and hears a vast number of things, and knows nothing. He is pert, raw, ignorant, conceited, ridiculous, shallow, contempt-ible. His senses keep him alive; and he knows, inquires, and cares for nothing farther. He meets the Lord Mayor's coach, and without cere-mony treats himself to an imaginary ride in it. He notices the people going to court or to a city-feast, and is quite satisfied with the show. He takes the wall of a Lord, and fancies himself as good as he. He sees an infinite quantity of people pass along the street, and thinks there is no such thing as life or a knowledge of character to be found out of London. 'Beyond Hyde Park all is a desert to him.'* He despises the country, because he is ignorant of it, and the town, because he is familiar with it. He is as well acquainted with St. Paul's as if he had built it, and talks of Westminster Abbey and Poets' Corner with great indifference. The King, the House of Lords and Commons are his very good friends. He knows the members for Westminster or the City by sight, and bows to the Sheriffs or the Sheriffs' men. He is hand and glove with the Chairman of some Committee. He is, in short, a great man by proxy, and comes so often in contact with fine persons and things, that he rubs off a little of the gilding, and is surcharged with a sort of second-hand, vapid, tingling, troublesome self-importance. His personal vanity is thus continually flattered and perked up into ridiculous self-complacency, while his imagination is jaded and impaired by daily misuse. Every thing is vulgarised in his mind. Nothing dwells long enough on it to produce an interest; nothing is contemplated sufficiently at a distance to excite curiosity or wonder. *Your true Cockney is your only true leveller.* Let him be as low as he will, he fancies he is as good as any body else. He has no respect for himself, and still less (if possible) for you. He cares little about his own advantages, if he can only make a jest at yours. Every feeling comes to him through a medium of levity and impertinence; nor does he like to have this habit of mind disturbed by being brought into collision with any thing serious or respectable. He despairs (in such a crowd of competitors) of distinguishing himself, but laughs heartily at the idea of being able to trip up the heels of other people's pretensions. A Cockney feels no gratitude. This is a first principle with him. He regards any obligation you confer upon him as a species of imposition, a ludicrous assumption of fancied superiority. He talks about every thing, for he has heard something about it; and understanding nothing of the matter, concludes he has as good a right as you. He is a politician; for he has seen the Parliament House: he is a critic; because he knows the principal actors by sight—has a taste for music, because he belongs to a glee-club at the West End; and is gallant, in virtue of sometimes frequenting the lobbies at half-price. A mere Londoner, in fact, from the opportunities he has of knowing something of a number of objects (and those striking ones) fancies himself a sort of privileged person; remains satisfied with the assumption of merits, so much the more unquestionable as they are not his own; and from being dazzled with noise, show, and appearances, is less capable of giving a real opinion, or entering into any subject than the meanest peasant. There are greater lawyers, orators, painters, philosophers, players in London, than in any other part of the United Kingdom: he is a Londoner, and therefore it would be strange if he did not know more of law, eloquence, art, philosophy, acting, than any one without his local advantages, and who is merely from the country. This is a *non sequitur*; and it constantly appears so when put to the test.

A real Cockney is the poorest creature in the world, the most literal, the most mechanical, and yet he too lives in a world of romance—a fairy-land of his own. He is a citizen of London; and this abstraction leads his imagination the finest dance in the world. London is the first city on the habitable globe; and therefore he must be superior to every one who lives out of it. There are more people in London than any where else; and though a dwarf in stature, his person swells out and expands into *ideal* importance and borrowed magnitude. He resides in a garret or in a two pair of stairs' back room; yet he talks of the magnificence of London, and gives himself airs of consequence upon it, as if all the houses in Portman or in Grosvenor Square were his by right or in reversion. 'He is owner of all he surveys.'* The Monument, the Tower of London, St. James's Palace, the Mansion House, White-Hall, are part and parcel of his being. Let us suppose him to be a lawyer's clerk at half-a-guinea a week: but he knows the Inns of Court, the Temple Gardens, and Gray's-Inn Passage, sees the lawyers in their wigs walking up and down Chancery Lane, and has advanced within half-a-dozen yards of the Chancellor's chair:—who can doubt that he understands (by implication) every point of law (however intricate) better than the most expert country practitioner? He is a shopman, and nailed all day behind the counter: but he sees hundreds and thousands of gay, well-dressed people pass—an endless phantasmagoria—and enjoys their liberty and gaudy fluttering pride. He is a footman—but he rides behind beauty, through a crowd of carriages, and visits a thousand shops. Is he a tailor? The stigma on his profession is lost in the elegance of the patterns he provides, and of the persons he adorns; and he is something very different from a mere country botcher. Nay, the very scavenger and nightman thinks the dirt in the street has something precious in it, and his employment is solemn, silent, sacred, peculiar to London! A *barker* in Monmouth Street,* a slop-seller in Ratcliffe-Highway, a tapster at a night cellar, a beggar in St. Giles's, a drab in Fleet-Ditch, live in the eyes of millions, and eke out a dreary, wretched, scanty, or loathsome existence from the gorgeous, busy, glowing scene around them. It is a common saying among such persons that 'they had rather be hanged in London than die a natural death out of it any where else'—Such is the force of habit and imagination. Even the eye of childhood is dazzled and delighted with the polished splendour of the jewellers' shops, the neatness of the turnery ware, the festoons of artificial flowers, the confectionery, the chemists' shops, the lamps, the horses, the carriages, the sedan-chairs: to this was formerly added a set of traditional associations—Whittington and his Cat, Guy Faux and the Gunpowder Treason, the Fire and the Plague of London, and the Heads of the Scotch Rebels that were stuck on Temple Bar in 1745. These have vanished, and in their stead the curious and romantic eye must be content to pore in Pennant* for the scite of old London-Wall, or to peruse the sentimental mile-stone that marks the distance to the place 'where Hicks's Hall formerly stood!'*

The *Cockney* lives in a go-cart of local prejudices and positive illusions; and when he is turned out of it, he hardly knows how to stand or move. He ventures through Hyde Park Corner, as a cat crosses a gutter. The trees pass by the coach very oddly. The country has a strange blank appearance. It is not lined with houses all the way, like London. He comes to places he never saw or heard of. He finds the world is bigger than he thought it. He might have dropped from the moon, for any thing he knows of the matter. He is mightily disposed to laugh, but is half afraid of making some blunder. Between sheepishness and conceit, he is in a very ludicrous situation. He finds that the people walk on two legs, and wonders to hear them talk a dialect so different from his own. He perceives London fashions have got down into the country before him, and that some of the better sort are dressed as well as he is. A drove of pigs or cattle stopping the road is a very troublesome interruption. A crow in a field, a magpie in a hedge, are to him very odd animals—he can't tell what to make of them, or how they live. He does not altogether like the accommodations at the inns—it is not what he has been used to in town. He begins to be communicative—says he was 'born within the sound of Bow-bell,' and attempts some jokes, at which nobody laughs. He asks the coachman a question, to which he receives no answer. All this is to him very unaccountable and unexpected. He arrives at his journey's end; and instead of being the great man he anticipated among his friends and country relations, finds that they are barely civil to him, or make a butt of him; have topics of their own which he is as completely ignorant of as they are indifferent to what he says, so that he is glad to get back to London again, where he meets with his favourite indulgences and associates, and fancies the whole world is occupied with what he hears and sees.

A Cockney loves a tea-garden in summer, as he loves the play or the Cider-Cellar* in winter—where he sweetens the air with the fumes of tobacco, and makes it echo to the sound of his own voice. This kind of suburban retreat is a most agreeable relief to the close and confined air of a city life. The imagination, long pent up behind a counter or between brick walls, with noisome smells, and dingy objects, cannot bear at once to launch into the boundless expanse of the country, but 'shorter excursions tries,'* coveting something between the two, and finding it at White-conduit House, or the Rosemary Branch, or Bagnigge Wells.* The landlady is seen at a bow-window in near perspective, with punch-bowls and lemons disposed orderly around—the lime-trees or poplars wave overhead to 'catch the breezy air,'* through which, typical of the huge dense cloud that hangs over the metropolis, curls up the thin, blue, odoriferous vapour of Virginia or Oronooko*—the benches are ranged in rows, the fields and hedge-rows spread out their verdure; Hampstead and Highgate are seen in the back-ground, and contain the imagination within gentle limits—here the holiday people are playing ball; here they are playing bowls—here they are quaffing ale, there sipping tea—here the loud wager is heard, there the political debate. In a sequestered nook a slender youth with purple face and drooping head, nodding over a glass of gin toddy, breathes in tender accents—'There's nought so sweet on earth as Love's young dream;'* while 'Rosy Ann' takes its turn, and 'Scots wha hae wi' Wallace bled' is thundered forth in accents that might wake the dead. In another part sit carpers and critics, who dispute the score of the reckoning or the game, or cavil at the taste and execution of the *would-be* Brahams and Durusets.* Of this latter class was Dr. Goodman, a man of other times—I mean of those of Smollett and Defoe—who was curious in opinion, obstinate in the wrong, great in little things, and inveterate in petty warfare. I vow he held me an argument once 'an hour by St. Dunstan's clock,'* while I held an umbrella over his head (the friendly protection of which he was unwilling to quit to walk in the rain to Camberwell) to prove to me that Richard Pinch* was neither a fives-player nor a pleasing singer. 'Sir,' said he, 'I deny that Mr. Pinch plays the game. He is a cunning player, but not a good one. I grant his tricks, his little mean dirty ways, but he is not a manly antagonist. He has no hit, and no left-hand. How then can he set up for a superior player? And then as to his always striking the ball against the side-wings at Copenhagen-house,* Cavanagh,* sir, used to say, "The wall was made to hit at!" I have no patience with such pitiful shifts and advantages. They are an insult upon so fine and athletic a game! And as to his setting up for a singer, it's quite ridiculous. You know, Mr. H——, that to be a really excellent singer, a man must lay claim to one of two things; in the first place, sir, he must have a naturally fine ear for music, or secondly, an early education, exclusively devoted to that study. But no one ever suspected Mr. Pinch of refined sensibility; and his education, as we all know, has been a little at large. Then again, why should he of all other things be always singing "Rosy Ann," and "Scots wha hae wi' Wallace bled," till one is sick of hearing them? It's preposterous, and I mean to tell him so. You know, I'm sure, without my hinting it, that in the first of these admired songs, the sentiment is voluptuous and tender, and in the last patriotic. Now Pinch's romance never wandered from behind his counter, and his patriotism lies in his breeches' pocket. Sir, the utmost he should aspire to would be to play upon the Jews' harp!' This story of the Jews' harp tickled some of Pinch's friends, who gave him various hints of it, which nearly drove him mad, till he discovered what it was; for though no jest or sarcasm ever had the least effect upon him, yet he cannot bear to think that there should be any joke of this kind about him, and he not in the secret: it makes against that *knowing* character which he so much affects. Pinch is in one respect a complete specimen of a *Cockney*. He never has any thing to say, and yet is never at a loss for an answer. That is, his pertness keeps exact pace with his dulness. His friend, the Doctor, used to complain of this in good set terms.—'You can never make any thing of Mr. Pinch,' he would say. 'Apply the most cutting remark to him, and his only answer is, "*The same to you, sir*." If Shakspeare were to rise from the dead to confute him, I firmly believe it would be to no purpose. I assure you, I have found it so. I once thought indeed I had him at a disadvantage, but I was mistaken. You shall hear, sir. I had been reading the following sentiment in a modern play—"The Road to Ruin," by the late Mr. Holcroft—"For how should the soul of Socrates inhabit the body of a stocking-weaver?"* This was pat to the point (you know our friend is a hosier and haberdasher). I came full with it to keep an appointment I had with Pinch, began a game, quarrelled with him in the middle of it on purpose, went upstairs to dress, and as I was washing my hands in the slop-basin (watching my opportunity) turned coolly round and said, "It's impossible there should be any sympathy between you and me, Mr. Pinch: for as the poet says, how should the soul of Socrates inhabit the body of a stocking-weaver?" "Ay," says he, "does the poet say so? *then the same to you*, sir!"

I was confounded, I gave up the attempt to conquer him in wit or argument. He would pose the Devil, sir, by his "*The same to you, sir.*" '
We had another joke against Richard Pinch, to which the Doctor was not a party, which was, that being asked after the respectability of the *Hole in the Wall*,* at the time that Randall took it, he answered quite unconsciously, 'Oh! it's a very genteel place, I go there myself some-times!' Dr. Goodman was descended by the mother's side from the poet Jago,* was a private gentleman in town, and a medical dilettanti in the country, dividing his time equally between business and pleas-ure; had an inexhaustible flow of words, and an imperturbable vanity, and held 'stout notions on the metaphysical score.' He maintained the free agency of man, with the spirit of a martyr and the gaiety of a man of wit and pleasure about town—told me he had a curious tract on that subject by A. C. (Anthony Collins*) which he carefully locked up in his box, lest any one should see it but himself, to the detriment of their character and morals, and put it to me whether it was not hard, on the principles of *philosophical necessity*, for a man to come to be hanged? To which I replied, 'I thought it hard on any terms!' A knavish *marker*, who had listened to the dispute, laughed at this retort, and seemed to assent to the truth of it, supposing it might one day be his own case.

Mr. Smith and the Brangtons, in 'Evelina,'* are the finest possible examples of the spirit of *Cockneyism*. I once knew a linen-draper in the City, who owned to me he did not quite like this part of Miss Burney's novel. He said, 'I myself lodge in a first floor, where there are young ladies in the house: they sometimes have company, and if I am out, they ask me to lend them the use of my apartment, which I readily do out of politeness, or if it is an agreeable party, I perhaps join them. All this is so like what passes in the novel, that I fancy myself a sort of second Mr. Smith, and am not quite easy at it!' This was mentioned to the fair Authoress, and she was delighted to find that her characters were so true, that an actual person fancied himself to be one of them. The resemblance, however, was only in the exter-nals; and the real modesty of the individual stumbled on the likeness to a city coxcomb!

It is curious to what a degree persons, brought up in certain occu-pations in a great city, are shut up from a knowledge of the world, and carry their simplicity to a pitch of unheard-of extravagance. London is the only place in which the child grows completely up into the man.* I have known characters of this kind, which, in the way of childish ignorance and self-pleasing delusion, exceeded any thing to be met with in Shakspeare or Ben Jonson, or the old comedy. For instance, the following may be taken as a true sketch. Imagine a person with a florid, shining complexion like a plough-boy, large staring teeth, a merry eye, his hair stuck into the fashion with curling-irons and pomatum,* a slender figure, and a decent suit of black—add to which the thoughtlessness of the school-boy, the forwardness of the thriving tradesman, and the plenary consciousness of the citizen of London—and you have Mr. Dunster before you, the fishmonger, in the Poultry.* You shall hear how he chirps over his cups, and exults in his private opinions. 'I'll play no more with you,' I said, 'Mr. Dunster—you are five points in the game better than I am.' I had just lost three half-crown rubbers at cribbage to him, which loss of mine he presently thrust into a canvass pouch (not a silk purse) out of which he had produced just before, first a few halfpence, then half a dozen pieces of silver, then a handful of guineas, and lastly, lying *perdu* at the bottom, a fifty pound bank-note. 'I'll tell you what,' I said, 'I should like to play you a game at marbles'—this was at a sort of Christmas party or Twelfth Night merry-making. 'Marbles!' said Dunster, catching up the sound, and his eye brightening with childish glee, 'What! you mean *ring-taw*?' 'Yes.' 'I should beat you at it, to a certainty. I was one of the best in our school (it was at Clapham, Sir, the Rev. Mr. Denman's, at Clapham, was the place where I was brought up)—though there were two others there better than me. They were the best that ever were. I'll tell you, Sir, I'll give you an idea. There was a water-butt or cistern, Sir, at our school, that turned with a cock. Now suppose that brass ring that the window-curtain is fastened to, to be the cock, and that these boys were standing where we are, about twenty feet off—well, Sir, I'll tell you what I have seen them do. One of them had a favourite taw (or *alley* we used to call them)—he'd take aim at the cock of the cistern with this marble, as I may do now. Well, Sir, will you believe it? such was his strength of knuckle and certainty of aim, he'd hit it, turn it, let the water out, and then, Sir, when the water had run out as much as it was wanted, the other boy (he'd just the same strength of knuckle, and the same certainty of eye) he'd aim at it too, be sure to hit it, turn it round, and stop the water from running out. Yes, what I tell you is very remarkable, but it's true. One of these boys was named Cock, and t'other Butler.' 'They might have been named Spigot and Fawcett, my dear Sir, from your account of them.' 'I should not mind playing you at fives neither, though I'm out of practice. I think I should beat you in a week: I was a real good one at that. A pretty game, Sir! I had the finest ball, that I suppose ever was seen. Made it myself,—I'll tell you how, Sir. You see, I put a piece of cork at the bottom, then I wound some fine worsted yarn round it, then I had to bind it round with some packthread, and then sew the case on. You'd hardly believe it, but I was the envy of the whole school for that ball. They all wanted to get it from me, but lord, Sir, I would let none of them come near it. I kept it in my waistcoat pocket all day, and at night I used to take it to bed with me and put it under my pillow. I couldn't sleep easy without it.'

The same idle vein might be found in the country, but I doubt whether it would find a tongue to give it utterance. Cockneyism is a ground of native shallowness mounted with pertness and conceit. Yet with all this simplicity and extravagance in dilating on his favourite topics, Dunster is a man of spirit, of attention to business, knows how to make out and get in his bills, and is far from being henpecked. One thing is certain, that such a man must be a true Englishman and a loyal subject. He has a slight tinge of letters, with shame I confess it—has in his possession a volume of the European Magazine for the year 1761, and is an humble admirer of Tristram Shandy (particularly the story of the King of Bohemia* and his Seven Castles, which is something in his own endless manner) and of Gil Blas of Santillane. Over these (the last thing before he goes to bed at night) he smokes a pipe, and meditates for an hour. After all, what is there in these harmless half-lies, these fantastic exaggerations, but a literal, prosaic, *Cockney* translation of the admired lines in Gray's Ode to Eton College:—

> What idle progeny succeed
> To chase the rolling circle's speed
> Or urge the flying ball?*

A man shut up all his life in his shop, without any thing to interest him from one year's end to another but the cares and details of business, with scarcely any intercourse with books or opportunities for society, distracted with the buzz and glare and noise about him, turns for relief to the retrospect of his childish years; and there, through the

long vista, at one bright loop-hole,* leading out of the thorny mazes
of the world into the clear morning light, he sees the idle fancies and
gay amusements of his boyhood dancing like motes in the sunshine.
Shall we blame, or should we laugh at him, if his eye glistens, and his
tongue grows wanton in their praise?

None but a Scotchman would—that pragmatical sort of personage, who thinks it a folly ever to have been young, and who, instead of
dallying with the frail past, bends his brows upon the future, and
looks only to the *mainchance*. Forgive me, dear Dunster, if I have
drawn a sketch of some of thy venial foibles, and delivered thee into
the hands of these Cockneys of the North, who will fall upon thee and
devour thee, like so many cannibals without a grain of salt!

If familiarity in cities breeds contempt, ignorance in the country
breeds aversion and dislike. People come too much in contact in
town; in other places they live too much apart, to unite cordially and
easily. Our feelings, in the former case, are dissipated and exhausted
by being called into constant and vain activity; in the latter, they
rust and grow dead for want of use. If there is an air of levity and
indifference in London manners, there is a harshness, a moroseness,
and disagreeable restraint, in those of the country. We have little
disposition to sympathy, when we have few persons to sympathise
with: we lose the relish and capacity for social enjoyment, the sel-
domer we meet. A habit of sullenness, coldness, and misanthropy,
grows upon us. If we look for hospitality and a cheerful welcome in
country places, it must be in those where the arrival of a stranger is an
event, the recurrence of which need not be greatly apprehended, or it
must be on rare occasions, on 'some high festival of once a year.'*
Then indeed the stream of hospitality, so long dammed up, may flow
without stint for a short season; or a stranger may be expected with
the same sort of eager impatience as a caravan of wild beasts, or any
other natural curiosity, that excites our wonder and fills up the craving of the mind after novelty. By degrees, however, even this last principle loses its effect: books, newspapers, whatever carries us out of
ourselves into a world of which we see and know nothing, becomes
distasteful, repulsive; and we turn away with indifference or disgust
from every thing that disturbs our lethargic animal existence, or takes
off our attention from our petty local interests and pursuits. Man, left
long to himself, is no better than a mere clod; or his activity, for want
of some other vent, preys upon himself, or is directed to splenetic,

peevish dislikes, or vexatious, harassing persecution of others. I once drew a picture of a country life: it was a portrait of a particular place, a caricature if you will, but, with certain allowances, I fear it was too like in the individual instance, and that it would hold too generally true. *See* ROUND TABLE, vol. ii. p. 116.*

If these, then, are the faults and vices of the inhabitants of town or of the country, where should a man go to live, so as to escape from them? I answer, that in the country we have the society of the groves, the fields, the brooks, and in London a man may keep to himself, or choose his company as he pleases.

It appears to me that there is an amiable mixture of these two opposite characters in a person who chances to have passed his youth in London, and who has retired into the country for the rest of his life. We may find in such a one a social polish, a pastoral simplicity. He rusticates agreeably, and vegetates with a degree of sentiment. He comes to the next post-town to see for letters, watches the coaches as they pass, and eyes the passengers with a look of familiar curiosity, thinking that he too was a gay fellow in his time. He turns his horse's head down the narrow lane that leads homewards, puts on an old coat to save his wardrobe, and fills his glass nearer to the brim. As he lifts the purple juice to his lips and to his eye, and in the dim solitude that hems him round, thinks of the glowing line—

This bottle's the sun of our table*—

another sun rises upon his imagination; the sun of his youth, the blaze of vanity, the glitter of the metropolis, 'glares round his soul, and mocks his closing eye-lids.'* The distant roar of coaches is in his ears—the pit stare upon him with a thousand eyes—Mrs. Siddons, Bannister, King, are before him—he starts as from a dream, and swears he will to London; but the expense, the length of way, deters him, and he rises the next morning to trace the footsteps of the hare that has brushed the dew-drops from the lawn, or to attend a meeting of Magistrates! Mr. Justice Shallow answered in some sort to this description of a retired Cockney and indigenous country-gentleman. He 'knew the Inns of Court, where they would talk of mad Shallow yet, and where the bona robas were, and had them at commandment: ay, and had heard the chimes at midnight!'*

It is a strange state of society (such as that in London) where a man does not know his next-door neighbour,* and where the feelings (one would think) must recoil upon themselves, and either fester or become obtuse. Mr. Wordsworth, in the preface to his poem of the 'Excursion,' represents men in cities as so many wild beasts or evil spirits, shut up in cells of ignorance, without natural affections, and barricadoed down in sensuality and selfishness.* The nerve of humanity is bound up, according to him: the circulation of the blood stagnates. And it would be so, if men were merely cut off from intercourse with their immediate neighbours, and did not meet together generally and more at large. But man in London becomes, as Mr. Burke has it, a sort of 'public creature.'* He lives in the eye of the world, and the world in his. If he witnesses less of the details of private life, he has better opportunities of observing its larger masses and varied movements. He sees the stream of human life pouring along the streets—its comforts and embellishments piled up in the shops—the houses are proofs of the industry, the public buildings of the art and magnificence of man; while the public amusements and places of resort are a centre and support for social feeling. A playhouse alone is a school of humanity, where all eyes are fixed on the same gay or solemn scene, where smiles or tears are spread from face to face, and where a thousand hearts beat in unison! Look at the company in a country theatre (in comparison), and see the coldness, the sullenness, the want of sympathy, and the way in which they turn round to scan and scrutinize one another. In London there is a *public*; and each man is part of it. We are gregarious, and affect the kind. We have a sort of abstract existence; and a community of ideas and knowledge (rather than local proximity) is the bond of society and good-fellowship. This is one great cause of the tone of political feeling in large and populous cities. There is here a visible body-politic, a type and image of that huge Leviathan the State. We comprehend that vast denomination, the *People*, of which we see a tenth part daily moving before us; and by having our imaginations emancipated from petty interests and personal dependence, we learn to venerate ourselves as men, and to respect the rights of human nature. Therefore it is that the citizens and freemen of London and Westminster are patriots by prescription, philosophers and politicians by the right of their birth-place. In the country, men are no better than a herd of cattle or scattered deer. They have no idea but of individuals, none of rights or principles—and a king, as the greatest individual, is the highest idea they can form. He is 'a species alone,'* and as superior to any single peasant, as the latter is to the peasant's dog, or to a crow flying over his head. In London the king is but as one to a million (numerically speaking), is seldom seen, and then distinguished only from others by the superior graces of his person. A country 'squire or a lord of the manor is a greater man in his village or hundred!

27

JEREMY BENTHAM

Mr. Bentham is one of those persons who verify the old adage, that 'a prophet has no honour, except out of his own country.'* His reputation lies at the circumference, and the lights of his understanding are reflected, with increasing lustre, on the other side of the globe. His name is little known in England, better in Europe, best of all in the plains of Chili and the mines of Mexico. He has offered Constitutions for the New World, and legislated for future times. The people of Westminster, where he lives,* know little of such a person; but the Siberian savage has received cold comfort from his lunar aspect, and may say to him with Caliban, 'I know thee and thy dog and thy bush'*—the tawny Indian may hold out the hand of fellowship to him across the Great Pacific. We believe that the Empress Catherine corresponded with him; and we know that the Emperor Alexander called upon him,* and presented him with his miniature in a gold snuff-box, which the philosopher, to his eternal honour, returned. Mr. Hobhouse is a greater man at the Hustings,* Lord Rolle at Plymouth-Dock; but Mr. Bentham would carry it hollow, on the score of popularity, at Paris or Pegu. The reason is, that our author's influence is purely intellectual. He has devoted his life to the pursuit of abstract and general truths, and to those studies,—'that waft a *thought* from Indus to the Pole,'*—and has never mixed himself up with personal intrigues or party-politics. He once indeed stuck up a hand-bill to say that he (Jeremy Bentham) being of sound mind, was of opinion that Sir Samuel Romilly was the most proper person to represent Westminster, but this was the whim of the moment. Otherwise, his reasonings, if true at all, are true everywhere alike: his speculations concern humanity at large, and are not confined to the hundred, or bills of mortality. It is in moral as in physical magnitude. The little is seen only near: the great appears in its proper dimensions only from a more commanding point of view, and gains strength with time, and elevation from distance!

Mr. Bentham is very much among philosophers what La Fontaine was among poets—in general habits and in all but his professional pursuits, he is a mere child. He has lived for the last forty years in a house in Westminster overlooking the Park, like an anchoret in his cell, reducing law to a system, and the mind of man to a machine. He hardly ever goes out, and sees very little company. The favoured few, who have the privilege of the *entrée*, are always admitted one by one. He does not like to have witnesses to his conversation. He talks a great deal, and listens to nothing but facts. When any one calls upon him, he invites them to take a turn round his garden with him (Mr. Bentham is an economist of his time, and sets apart this portion of it to air and exercise)—and there you may see the lively old man, his mind still buoyant with thought and with the prospect of futurity, in eager conversation with some Opposition Member, some expatriated Patriot, or Transatlantic Adventurer, urging the extinction of Close Boroughs, or planning a code of laws for some 'lone island in the watery waste,'* his walk almost amounting to a run, his tongue keeping pace with it in shrill, cluttering accents, negligent of his person, his dress, and his manner, intent only on his grand theme of UTILITY—or pausing perhaps for want of breath, and with lacklustre eye, to point out to the stranger a stone in the wall at the end of his garden, (over-arched by two beautiful cotton-trees) *Inscribed to the Prince of Poets*, which marks the house where Milton formerly lived.* To shew how little the refinements of taste or fancy enter into our author's system, he proposed at one time to grub up these beautiful trees, to convert the garden where he had breathed the air of Truth and Heaven for near half-a-century, into a paltry *Chreistomathic School*,* and to make Milton's house (the cradle of Paradise Lost) a thoroughfare, like a three-stalled stable, for all the rabble of Westminster to pass backwards and forwards to it with their cloven hoofs. Let us not, however, be getting on too fast—Milton himself taught a school!—There is something not altogether dissimilar between Mr. Bentham's appearance, and the portraits of Milton—the same silvery tone, a few dishevelled hairs, a peevish, yet puritanical expression, an irritable temperament corrected by habit and discipline. Or in modern times, he is something between Franklin and Charles Fox, with the comfortable double-chin, and sleek thriving look of the one, and the quivering lip, the restless eye, and animated acuteness of the other. His eye is quick and lively, but it glances not from object to object, but from thought to thought. He is evidently a man occupied with some train of fine and inward association. He regards the people about him no more than the flies of a summer.*

He meditates the coming age. He hears and sees only what suits his purpose, some 'foregone conclusion;'* and looks out for facts and passing occurrences only to put them into his logical machinery and grind them into the dust and powder of some subtle theory, as the miller looks out for grist to his mill! Add to this physiognomical sketch the minor points of costume, the open shirt-collar, the single-breasted coat, the old-fashioned half-boots and ribbed stockings; and you will find in Mr. Bentham's general appearance, a singular mixture of boyish simplicity and of the venerableness of age.—In a word, our celebrated jurist presents a striking illustration of the difference between the *philosophical* and the *regal* look; that is, between the merely abstracted and the merely personal. There is a lack-a-daisical *bonhommie* about his whole aspect, none of the fierceness of pride or power; an unconscious neglect of his own person, instead of a stately assumption of superiority; a good-humoured, placid intelligence, not a lynx-eyed watchfulness, as if it wished to make others its prey, or was afraid they might turn and rend him; he is a beneficent spirit, prying into the universe, not lording it over it; a thoughtful spectator of the scenes of life, or ruminator on the fate of mankind, not a painted pageant, a stupid idol set up on its pedestal of pride for men to fall down and worship with idiot fear and wonder at the thing themselves have made, and which, without that fear and wonder, would itself be nothing!

Mr. Bentham, perhaps, over-rates the importance of his own theories. He has been heard to say (without any appearance of pride or affectation) that 'he should like to live the remaining years of his life, a year at a time at the end of the next six or eight centuries, to see the effect which his writings would by that time have upon the world.' Alas! his name will hardly live so long! Nor do we think, in point of fact, that Mr. Bentham has given any new or decided impulse to the human mind. He cannot be looked upon in the light of a discoverer in legislation or morals. He has not struck out any great leading principle or parent-truth, from which a number of others might be deduced; nor has he enriched the common and established stock of intelligence with original observations, like pearls thrown into wine. One truth discovered is immortal, and entitles its author to be so: for, like a new substance in nature, it cannot be destroyed. But Mr. Bentham's *forte* is arrangement; and the form of truth, though not its essence, varies with time and circumstance. He has methodised, collated, and condensed all the materials prepared to his hand on the subjects of which he treats, in a masterly and scientific manner: but we should find a difficulty in adducing from his different works (however elaborate or closely reasoned) any new element of thought, or even a new fact or illustration. His writings are, therefore, chiefly valuable as *books of reference*, as bringing down the account of intellectual inquiry to the present period, and disposing the results in a compendious, connected, and tangible shape; but books of reference are chiefly serviceable for facilitating the acquisition of knowledge, and are constantly liable to be superseded and grow out of fashion with its progress, as the scaffolding is thrown down according as the building is completed. Mr. Bentham is not the first writer, by a great many, who has assumed the principle of UTILITY as the foundation of just laws, and of all moral and political reasoning:*—his merit is, that he has applied this principle more closely and literally, that he has brought all the objections and arguments, more distinctly labelled and ticketed, under this head, and made a more constant and explicit reference to it at every step of his progress, than any other writer. Perhaps the weak side of his conclusions also is, that he has carried this single view of his subject too far, and not made sufficient allowance for the varieties of human nature, and the caprices and irregularities of the human will. 'He has not allowed for the *wind*.'* It is not that you can be said to see his favourite doctrine of Utility glittering every where through his system, like a vein of rich, shining ore, that is not the nature of the material,—but it might be plausibly objected that he had struck the whole mass of fancy, prejudice, passion, sense, and whim, with his petrific, leaden mace,* that he had 'bound volatile Hermes,'* and reduced the theory and practice of human life to a *caput mortuum** of reason and dull, plodding, technical calculation. The gentleman is himself a capital logician; and he has been led by this circumstance to consider man as a logical animal. We fear this view of the matter will hardly hold water. If we attend to the *moral* man, the constitution of his mind will scarcely be found to be built up of pure reason and a regard to consequences: if we consider the *criminal* man (with whom the legislator has chiefly to do), it will be found to be still less so.

Every pleasure, says Mr. Bentham, is equally a good, and is to be taken into the account as such in a moral estimate, whether it be the pleasure of sense or of conscience, whether it arise from the exercise of virtue or the perpetration of a crime. We are afraid the human mind does not readily come into this doctrine, this *ultima ratio philosophorum*,* taken according to the letter. Our moral sentiments are made up of sympathies and antipathies, of sense and imagination, of understanding and prejudice. The soul, by reason of its weakness, is an aggregating and an exclusive principle; it clings obstinately to some things, and violently rejects others. And it must do so, in a great measure, or it would act contrary to its own nature. It needs helps and stages in its progress, and 'all appliances and means to boot,'* which can raise it to a partial conformity to truth and good (the utmost it is capable of), and bring it into a tolerable harmony with the universe. By aiming at too much, by dismissing collateral aids, by extending itself to the farthest verge of the remote and possible, it loses its elasticity and vigour, its impulse and its direction. The moralist can no more do without the intermediate use of rules and principles, without the 'vantage-ground of habit, without the levers of the understanding, than the mechanist can discard the use of wheels and pulleys, and perform every thing by simple motion. If the mind of man were competent to comprehend the whole of truth and good, and act upon it at once, and independently of all other considerations, Mr. Bentham's plan would be a feasible one, and *the truth, the whole truth, and nothing but the truth*, would be the best possible ground to place morality upon. But it is not so. In ascertaining the rules of moral conduct, we must have regard not merely to the nature of the object, but to the capacity of the agent, and to his fitness for apprehending or attaining it. Pleasure is that which is so in itself: good is that which approves itself as such on reflection, or the idea of which is a source of satisfaction. All pleasure is not therefore, morally speaking, equally a good; for all pleasure does not equally bear reflecting on. There are some tastes that are sweet in the mouth and bitter in the belly; and there is a similar contradiction and anomaly in the mind and heart of man. Again, what will become of the *Posthæc meminisse juvabit** of the poet, if a principle of fluctuation and reaction is not inherent in the very constitution of our nature, or if all moral truth is a mere literal truism. We are not, then, so much to inquire what certain things are abstractedly or in themselves, as how they affect the mind, and to approve or condemn them accordingly. The same object seen near strikes us more powerfully than at a distance: things thrown into masses give a greater blow to the imagination than when scattered and divided into their component parts. A number of mole-hills do not make a mountain, though a mountain is actually made up of atoms: so moral truth must present itself under a certain aspect and from a certain point of view, in order to produce its full and proper effect upon the mind. The laws of the affections are as necessary as those of optics. A calculation of consequences is no more equivalent to a sentiment, than a *seriatim* enumeration of particles touches the fancy like the sight of the Alps or Andes.

To give an instance or two of what we mean. Those who on pure cosmopolite principles, or on the ground of abstract humanity, affect an extraordinary regard for the Turks and Tartars, have been accused of neglecting their duties to their friends and next-door neighbours. Well, then, what is the state of the question here? One human being is, no doubt, as much worth in himself, independently of the circumstances of time or place, as another; but he is not of so much value to us and our affections. Could our imagination take wing, with our speculative faculties, to the other side of the globe, or to the ends of the universe, could our eyes behold whatever our reason teaches us to be possible, could our hands reach as far as our thoughts or wishes, we might then busy ourselves to advantage with the Hottentots, or hold intimate converse with the inhabitants of the MOON; but being as we are, our feelings evaporate in so large a space, we must draw the circle of our affections and duties somewhat closer, the heart hovers and fixes nearer home. It is true, the bands of private, or of local and natural affection, are often, nay in general, too tightly strained, so as frequently to do harm instead of good: but the present question is, whether we can, with safety and effect, be wholly emancipated from them? Whether we should shake them off at pleasure and without mercy, as the only bar to the triumph of truth and justice? Or whether benevolence, constructed upon a logical scale, would not be merely *nominal*,—whether duty, raised to too lofty a pitch of refinement, might not sink into callous indifference or hollow selfishness?—Again, is it not to exact too high a strain from humanity, to ask us to qualify the degree of abhorrence we feel against a murderer, by taking into our cool consideration, the pleasure he may have in committing the deed, and in the prospect of gratifying his avarice or his revenge? We are hardly so formed as to sympathise at the same moment with the assassin and his victim. The degree of pleasure the former may feel, instead of extenuating, aggravates his guilt, and shews the depth of his malignity. Now the mind revolts against this by mere natural antipathy, if it is itself well-disposed; or the slow process of reason would afford but a feeble resistance to violence and wrong. The will, which is necessary to give consistency and promptness to our good intentions, cannot extend so much candour and courtesy to the antagonist principle of evil: virtue, to be sincere and practical, cannot be divested entirely of the blindness and impetuosity of passion! It has been made a plea (half jest, half earnest) for the horrors of war, that they promote trade and manufactures—it has been said as a set-off for the atrocities practised upon the negro-slaves in the West-Indies, that without their blood and sweat, so many millions of people could not have sugar to sweeten their tea—fires and murders have been argued to be beneficial, as they serve to fill the newspapers, and for a subject to talk of:—this is a sort of sophistry, that it might be difficult to disprove on the bare scheme of contingent Utility, but on the ground that we have stated, it must pass for a mere irony. What the proportion between the good and the evil may be in any of the supposed cases, may be a question to the understanding: but to the imagination and the heart, that is, to the natural feelings of mankind, it admits of none!

Mr. Bentham, in adjusting the provisions of a penal code, lays too little stress on the co-operation of the natural prejudices of mankind, and the habitual feelings of that class of persons, for whom they are more particularly intended. Legislators (we mean writers on legislation) are philosophers, and governed by their reason: criminals, for whose control laws are made, are a set of desperadoes, governed only by their passions. What wonder that so little progress has been made towards a mutual understanding between the two parties! They are quite a different species, and speak a different language, and are sadly at a loss for a common interpreter between them. Perhaps the Ordinary of Newgate bids as fair for this office as any one. What should Mr. Bentham, sitting at ease in his arm-chair, composing his mind before he begins to write by a prelude on the organ, and looking out at a beautiful prospect when he is at a loss for an idea, know of the principles of action of rogues, outlaws, and vagabonds? No more than Montaigne* of the motions of his cat! If sanguine and tender-hearted philanthropists have set on foot an inquiry into the barbarity and the defects of penal laws, the practical improvements have been mostly suggested by reformed cut-throats, turnkeys, and thief-takers. What

even can the Honourable House, that when the Speaker has pronounced the well-known, wished-for sounds, 'That this House do
now adjourn,' retires, after voting a royal crusade or a loan of millions, to lie on down and feed on plate in spacious palaces, know of
what passes in the hearts of wretches in garrets and night-cellars,
petty pilferers and marauders who cut throats and pick pockets with
their own hands? The thing is impossible. The laws of the country
are, therefore, ineffectual and abortive, because they are made by the
rich for the poor, by the wise for the ignorant, by the respectable and
exalted in station for the very scum and refuse of the community.
If Newgate would resolve itself into a Committee of the whole Press-
yard, with Jack Ketch at its head,* aided by confidential persons from
the county-prisons or the Hulks,* and would make a clear breast,
some *data* might be found out to proceed upon; but as it is, the *criminal mind* of the country is a book sealed, no one has been able to
penetrate to the inside! Mr. Bentham, in his attempts to revise and
amend our criminal jurisprudence, proceeds entirely on his favourite
principle of Utility. Convince highwaymen and housebreakers that it
will be for their interest to reform; and they will reform and live honest lives; according to Mr. Bentham. He says 'All men act from calculation, even madmen reason.'* And in our opinion, he might as well
carry this maxim to Bedlam, or St. Luke's,* and apply it to the inhabitants, as think to coerce or overawe the inmates of a gaol, or those
whose practices make them candidates for this distinction, by the
mere dry, detailed convictions of the understanding. Criminals are not
to be influenced by reason; for it is of the very essence of crime to
disregard consequences to itself and others. You may as well preach
philosophy to a drunken man or to the dead, as to those who are under
the instigation of any ruling passion. A man is a drunkard, and you
tell him he ought to be sober; he is debauched, and you ask him to
reform; he is idle, and you recommend industry to him as his wisest
course; he gambles, and you remind him that he may be ruined; by
this foible he has lost his character, and you advise him to get into
some reputable service or lucrative situation; vice becomes a habit
with him, and you request him to rouse himself and shake it off; he is
starving, and you warn him that if he breaks the law, he will be hanged.
None of this reasoning reaches the mark it aims at. The culprit, who
violates and suffers the vengeance of the laws, is not the dupe of
ignorance, but the slave of passion, the victim of habit or necessity.

To argue with strong passion, with inveterate habit, with desperate circumstances, is to talk to the winds. Clownish ignorance may indeed be dispelled, and taught better: but it is seldom that a criminal is not aware of the consequences of his act, or has not made up his mind to the alternative. They are in general *too knowing by half.** You tell a person of this stamp what is his interest; he says he does not care about his interest, or the world and he differ on that particular; but there is one point in which he must agree with them, namely, what *they* think of his conduct, and this is the only hold you have of him. A man may be callous and indifferent to what happens to himself, but he is never indifferent to public opinion, or proof against open scorn and infamy. Shame, not fear, is the sheet-anchor of the law. He who is not afraid of being pointed at as a *thief*, will not mind a month's hard labour. He who is prepared to take the life of another, is already reckless of his own. But every one makes a sorry figure in the pillory; and the being launched from the New Drop* lowers a man in his own opinion. The lawless and violent spirit, that is hurried by headstrong self-will to break the laws, does not like to have the ground of pride and obstinacy struck from under his feet. This is what gives the *swells* of the metropolis such a dread of the *treadmill*—it makes them ridiculous. It must be confessed, that this very circumstance renders the reform of criminals nearly hopeless. It is the apprehension of being stigmatised by public opinion, the fear of what will be thought and said of them, that deters men from the violation of the laws, while their character remains unimpeached; but honour once lost, all is lost. The man can never be himself again! A citizen is like a soldier, a part of a machine; he submits to certain hardships, privations, and dangers, not for his own ease, pleasure, profit, or even conscience, but—*for shame*. What is it that keeps the machine together in either case? Not punishment or discipline, but sympathy. The soldier mounts the breach or stands in the trenches, the peasant hedges and ditches, the mechanic plies his ceaseless task, because the one will not be called a *coward*, the other a *rogue*: but let the one turn deserter and the other vagabond, and there is an end of him. The grinding law of necessity, which is no other than a name, a breath, loses its force, he is no longer sustained by the good opinion of others, and he drops out of his place, a useless clog! Mr. Bentham takes a culprit, and puts him into what he calls a *panopticon*, that is, a sort of circular prison, with open cells, like a glass beehive. He sits in the middle, and sees all he does. He gives him work to do, and lectures him if he does not do it. He takes liquor from him, and society, and liberty; but he feeds and clothes him and keeps him out of mischief, and when he has convinced him by force and reason together, that this life is for his good, turns him out upon the world, a reformed man, and as confident of the success of his handy-work, as the shoemaker of that which he has just taken off the last, or the Parisian barber in Sterne of the buckle of his wig. 'Dip it in the ocean,' said the perruquier, 'and it will stand!'* But we doubt the durability of our projector's patchwork. Will our convert to the great principle of Utility work when he is from under Mr. Bentham's eye, because he was forced to work when under it? Will he keep sober, because he has been kept from liquor so long? Will he not return to loose company, because he has had the pleasure of sitting *vis-à-vis* with a philosopher of late? Will he not steal, now that his hands are untied? Will he not take the road, now that it is free to him? Will he not call his benefactor all the names he can set his tongue to, the moment his back is turned? All this is more than to be feared. The charm of criminal life, like that of savage life, consists in liberty, in hardship, in danger, and in the contempt of death, in one word, in extraordinary excitement; and he who has tasted of it, will no more return to regular habits of life, than a man will take to water after drinking brandy, or than a wild beast will give over hunting its prey. Miracles never cease, to be sure; but they are not to be had wholesale, or *to order*. Mr. Owen,* who is another of these proprietors and patentees of reform, has lately got an American savage with him, whom he carries about in great triumph and complacency as the antithesis to his *New View of Society*, and as winding up his reasoning to what it mainly wanted, an epigrammatic point. Does the benevolent visionary of the Lanark Cotton-mills really think this *natural man* will act as a foil to his *artificial man*? Does he for a moment imagine, that his *Address to the higher and middle classes*,* with all its advantages of fiction, makes any thing like so interesting a romance as *Hunter's Captivity among the North American Indians*?* Has he any thing to shew, in all the apparatus of New Lanark and its desolate monotony, to excite the thrill of imagination like the blankets made of wreaths of snow, under which the wild-wood rovers bury themselves for weeks in winter? Or the skin of a leopard which our hardy adventurer slew, and which served him for great coat and bedding? Or the rattle-snake that he found by his side as a bedfellow? Or his rolling

himself into a ball to escape from him? Or his suddenly placing himself against a tree to avoid being trampled to death by the herd of wild
buffaloes, that came rushing on like the sound of thunder? Or his
account of the huge spiders that prey on blue-bottles and gilded flies
in green pathless forests? Or of the great Pacific Ocean, that the
natives look upon as the gulf that parts time from eternity, and that is
to waft them to the spirits of their fathers? After all this, Mr. Hunter
must find Mr. Owen and his parallelograms* trite and flat, and will
take an opportunity to escape from them.

Mr. Bentham's method of reasoning, though comprehensive and
exact, labours under the defect of most systems—it is too *topical*.
It includes every thing, but it includes every thing alike. It is rather
like an inventory than a valuation of different arguments. Every possible suggestion finds a place, so that the mind is distracted as much
as enlightened by this perplexing accuracy. The exceptions seem as
important as the rule. By attending to the minute, we overlook the
great; and in summing up an account, it will not do merely to insist
on the number of items without considering their amount. Our
author's page presents a very nicely dove-tailed mosaic pavement of
legal common-places. We slip and slide over its even surface without
being arrested any where. Or his view of the human mind resembles
a map, rather than a picture: the outline, the disposition is correct,
but it wants colouring and relief. There is a technicality of manner,
which renders his writings of more value to the professional inquirer
than to the general reader.—Again, his style is unpopular, not to say
unintelligible. He writes a language of his own that *darkens knowledge*.
His works have been translated into French—they ought to be translated into English. People wonder that Mr. Bentham has not been
prosecuted for the boldness and severity of some of his invectives. He
might wrap up High Treason in one of his inextricable periods, and it
would never find its way into Westminster Hall. He is a kind of
Manuscript author—he writes a cypher-hand, which the vulgar do
not pry into. The construction of his sentences is a curious frame-
work with pegs and hooks to hang his thoughts upon for his own use
and guidance, but quite out of the reach of any body else. It is a barbarous philosophical jargon with all the repetitions, parentheses, for-
malities, uncouth nomenclature and *verbiage* of law-Latin; and what
makes it worse, it is not mere verbiage, but has a great deal of acuteness and meaning in it, which you would be glad to pick out if you

could. In short, Mr. Bentham writes as if he had but a single sentence to express his whole view of a subject in, and as if, should he omit a single objection, circumstance, or step of the argument, it would be lost to the world for ever, like an estate by a single flaw in the title-deeds. This is overrating the importance of our own discoveries, and mistaking the nature and object of language altogether. Mr. Bentham has acquired this disability—it is not natural to him. His admirable little work *On Usury*, published forty years ago,* is clear, easy, and spirited. But Mr. Bentham has shut himself up since then 'in nook monastic,'* conversing only with followers of his own, or with 'men of Ind,'* and has endeavoured to overlay his natural humour, sense, spirit, and style, with the dust and cobwebs of an obscure solitude. The best of it is, he thinks his present mode of expressing himself perfect, and that, whatever may be objected to his law or logic, no one can find the least fault with the purity, simplicity, and perspicuity of his style.

Mr. Bentham, in private life, is an amiable and exemplary character. He is a little romantic or so; and has dissipated part of a handsome fortune in practical speculations. He lends an ear to plausible pro-jectors, and if he cannot prove them to be wrong in their premises or their conclusions, thinks himself bound *in reason* to stake his money on the venture. Strict logicians are licensed visionaries. Mr. Bentham is half-brother to the late Mr. Speaker Abbott*—*Proh pudor!** He was educated at Eton, and still takes our novices to task about a passage in Homer, or a metre in Virgil. He was afterwards at the University, and he has described the scruples of an ingenuous youthful mind about subscribing the articles, in a passage in his *Church of Englandism,** which smacks of truth and honour both, and does one good to read it in an age when 'to be honest (or not to laugh at the very idea of honesty) is to be one man picked out of ten thou-sand!'* Mr. Bentham relieves his mind sometimes, after the fatigue of study, by playing on a noble organ, and has a relish for Hogarth's prints. He turns wooden utensils in a lathe for exercise, and fancies he can turn men in the same manner. He has no great fondness for poetry, and can hardly extract a moral out of Shakspeare. His house is warmed and lighted with steam. He is one of those who prefer the artificial to the natural in most things, and think the mind of man omnipotent. He has a great contempt for out-of-door prospects, for green fields and trees, and is for referring every thing to Utility. There is a little narrowness in this, for if all the sources of satisfaction are taken away, what is to become of Utility itself? It is indeed the great fault of this able and extraordinary man, that he has concentrated his faculties and feelings too entirely on one subject and pursuit, and has not 'looked enough abroad into universality.'*

28

WILLIAM GODWIN

THE Spirit of the Age was never more fully shewn than in its treatment of this writer—its love of paradox and change, its dastard submission to prejudice and to the fashion of the day. Five-and-twenty years ago he was in the very zenith of a sultry and unwholesome popularity; he blazed as a sun in the firmament of reputation; no one was more talked of, more looked up to, more sought after, and wherever liberty, truth, justice was the theme, his name was not far off:—now he has sunk below the horizon, and enjoys the serene twilight of a doubtful immortality. Mr. Godwin, during his lifetime, has secured to himself the triumphs and the mortifications of an extreme notoriety and of a sort of posthumous fame. His bark, after being tossed in the revolutionary tempest, now raised to heaven by all the fury of popular breath, now almost dashed in pieces, and buried in the quicksands of ignorance, or scorched with the lightning of momentary indignation, at length floats on the calm wave that is to bear it down the stream of time. Mr. Godwin's person is not known, he is not pointed out in the street, his conversation is not courted, his opinions are not asked, he is at the head of no cabal, he belongs to no party in the State, he has no train of admirers, no one thinks it worth his while even to traduce and vilify him, he has scarcely friend or foe, the world make a point (as Goldsmith used to say*) of taking no more notice of him than if such an individual had never existed; he is to all ordinary intents and purposes dead and buried; but the author of *Political Justice** and of *Caleb Williams* can never die, his name is an abstraction in letters, his works are standard in the history of intellect. He is thought of now like any eminent writer a hundred-and-fifty years ago, or just as he will be a hundred-and-fifty years hence. He knows this, and smiles in silent mockery of himself, reposing on the monument of his fame—

Sedet, in eternumque sedebit infelix Theseus.*

No work in our time gave such a blow to the philosophical mind of the country as the celebrated *Enquiry concerning Political Justice*. Tom Paine was considered for the time as a Tom Fool to him; Paley an old woman; Edmund Burke a flashy sophist. Truth, moral truth, it was supposed, had here taken up its abode; and these were the oracles of thought. 'Throw aside your books of chemistry,' said Wordsworth to a young man, a student in the Temple,* 'and read Godwin on Necessity.' Sad necessity! Fatal reverse! Is truth then so variable? Is it one thing at twenty, and another at forty? Is it at a burning heat in 1793, and below *zero* in 1814? Not so, in the name of manhood and of common sense! Let us pause here a little.—Mr. Godwin indulged in extreme opinions, and carried with him all the most sanguine and fearless understandings of the time. What then? Because those opinions were overcharged, were they therefore altogether ground-less? Is the very God of our idolatry all of a sudden to become an abomination and an anathema? Could so many young men of talent, of education, and of principle have been hurried away by what had neither truth, nor nature, not one particle of honest feeling nor the least shew of reason in it? Is the *Modern Philosophy* (as it has been called) at one moment a youthful bride, and the next a withered bel-dame, like the false Duessa* in Spenser? Or is the vaunted edifice of Reason, like his House of Pride, gorgeous in front, and dazzling to approach, while 'its hinder parts are ruinous, decayed, and old?'* Has the main prop, which supported the mighty fabric, been shaken and given way under the strong grasp of some Samson; or has it not rather been undermined by rats and vermin? At one time, it almost seemed, that 'if this failed,

> The pillar'd firmament was rottenness,
> And earth's base built of stubble:'*

now scarce a shadow of it remains, it is crumbled to dust, nor is it even talked of! 'What then, went ye forth for to see, a reed shaken with the wind?'* Was it for this that our young gownsmen of the greatest expectation and promise, versed in classic lore, steeped in dialectics, armed at all points for the foe, well read, well nurtured, well provided for, left the University and the prospect of lawn sleeves, tearing asun-der the shackles of the free born spirit, and the cobwebs of school-divinity, to throw themselves at the feet of the new Gamaliel,* and learn wisdom from him? Was it for this, that students at the bar, acute, inquisitive, sceptical (here only wild enthusiasts) neglected for a while the paths of preferment and the law as too narrow, tortuous, and unseemly to bear the pure and broad light of reason? Was it for this, that students in medicine missed their way to Lecturerships and the top of their profession, deeming lightly of the health of the body, and dreaming only of the renovation of society and the march of mind? Was it to this that Mr. Southey's *Inscriptions** pointed? to this that Mr. Coleridge's *Religious Musings** tended? Was it for this, that Mr. Godwin himself sat with arms folded, and, 'like Cato, gave his little senate laws?'* Or rather, like another Prospero, uttered syllables that with their enchanted breath were to change the world, and might almost stop the stars in their courses? Oh! and is all forgot?* Is this sun of intellect blotted from the sky? Or has it suffered total eclipse? Or is it we who make the fancied gloom, by looking at it through the paltry, broken, stained fragments of our own interests and prejudices? Were we fools then, or are we dishonest now? Or was the impulse of the mind less likely to be true and sound when it arose from high thought and warm feeling, than afterwards, when it was warped and debased by the example, the vices, and follies of the world?

The fault, then, of Mr. Godwin's philosophy, in one word, was too much ambition—'by that sin fell the angels!'* He conceived too nobly of his fellows (the most unpardonable crime against them, for there is nothing that annoys our self-love so much as being complimented on imaginary achievements, to which we are wholly unequal)—he raised the standard of morality above the reach of humanity, and by directing virtue to the most airy and romantic heights, made her path dangerous, solitary, and impracticable. The author of the *Political Justice* took abstract reason for the rule of conduct, and abstract good for its end. He places the human mind on an elevation, from which it commands a view of the whole line of moral consequences; and requires it to conform its acts to the larger and more enlightened conscience which it has thus acquired. He absolves man from the gross and narrow ties of sense, custom, authority, private and local attachment, in order that he may devote himself to the boundless pursuit of universal benevolence. Mr. Godwin gives no quarter to the amiable weaknesses of our nature, nor does he stoop to avail himself of the supplementary aids of an imperfect virtue. Gratitude, promises, friendship, family affection give way, not that they may be merged in the opposite vices or in want of principle; but that the void may be filled up by the disinterested love of good, and the dictates of inflexible justice, which is 'the law of laws, and sovereign of sovereigns.'* All minor considerations yield, in his system, to the stern sense of duty, as they do, in the ordinary and established ones, to the voice of necessity. Mr. Godwin's theory and that of more approved reasoners differ only in this, that what are with them the exceptions, the extreme cases, he makes the every-day rule. No one denies that on great occasions, in moments of fearful excitement, or when a mighty object is at stake, the lesser and merely instrumental points of duty are to be sacrificed without remorse at the shrine of patriotism, of honour, and of conscience. But the disciple of the *New School* (no wonder it found so many impugners, even in its own bosom!) is to be always the hero of duty; the law to which he has bound himself never swerves nor relaxes; his feeling of what is right is to be at all times wrought up to a pitch of enthusiastic self-devotion; he must become the unshrinking martyr and confessor of the public good. If it be said that this scheme is chimerical and impracticable on ordinary occasions, and to the generality of mankind, well and good; but those who accuse the author of having trampled on the common feelings and prejudices of mankind in wantonness or insult, or without wishing to substitute something better (and only unattainable, because it is better) in their stead, accuse him wrongfully. We may not be able to launch the bark of our affections on the ocean-tide of humanity, we may be forced to paddle along its shores, or shelter in its creeks and rivulets: but we have no right to reproach the bold and adventurous pilot, who dared us to tempt the uncertain abyss, with our own want of courage or of skill, or with the jealousies and impatience, which deter us from undertaking, or might prevent us from accomplishing the voyage!

The *Enquiry concerning Political Justice* (it was urged by its favourers and defenders at the time, and may still be so, without either profaneness or levity) is a metaphysical and logical commentary on some of the most beautiful and striking texts of Scripture. Mr. Godwin is a mixture of the Stoic and of the Christian philosopher. To break the force of the vulgar objections and outcry that have been raised against the Modern Philosophy, as if it were a new and monstrous birth in morals, it may be worth noticing, that volumes of sermons have been written to excuse the founder of Christianity for not including friendship and private affection among its golden rules, but rather excluding them.[1]

---

[1] Shaftesbury made this an objection to Christianity, which was answered by Foster, Leland, and other eminent divines, on the ground that Christianity had a higher object in view, namely, general philanthropy.

Moreover, the answer to the question, 'Who is thy neighbour?'* added to the divine precept, 'Thou shalt love thy neighbour as thyself,'* is the same as in the exploded pages of our author,—'He to whom we can do most good.' In determining this point, we were not to be influenced by any extrinsic or collateral considerations, by our own predilections, or the expectations of others, by our obligations to them or any services they might be able to render us, by the climate they were born in, by the house they lived in, by rank or religion, or party, or personal ties, but by the abstract merits, the pure and unbiassed justice of the case. The artificial helps and checks to moral conduct were set aside as spurious and unnecessary, and we came at once to the grand and simple question—'In what manner we could best contribute to the greatest possible good?' This was the paramount obligation in all cases whatever, from which we had no right to free ourselves upon any idle or formal pretext, and of which each person was to judge for himself, under the infallible authority of his own opinion and the inviolable sanction of his self-approbation. 'There was the rub that made *philosophy* of so short life!'* Mr. Godwin's definition of morals was the same as the admired one of law, *reason without passion*; but with the unlimited scope of private opinion, and in a boundless field of speculation (for nothing less would satisfy the pretensions of the New School), there was danger that the unseasoned novice might substitute some pragmatical conceit of his own for the rule of right reason, and mistake a heartless indifference for a superiority to more natural and generous feelings. Our ardent and dauntless reformer followed out the moral of the parable of the Good Samaritan into its most rigid and repulsive consequences with a pen of steel, and let fall his 'trenchant blade'* on every vulnerable point of human infirmity; but there is a want in his system of the mild and persuasive tone of the Gospel, where 'all is conscience and tender heart.'* Man was indeed screwed up, by mood and figure, into a logical machine, that was to forward the public good with the utmost punctuality and effect, and it might go very well on smooth ground and under favourable circumstances; but would it work up-hill or *against the grain*? It was to be feared that the proud Temple of Reason, which at a distance and in stately supposition shone like the palaces of the New Jerusalem, might (when placed on actual ground) be broken up into the sordid styes of sensuality, and the petty huckster's shops of self-interest! Every man (it was proposed—'so ran the tenour of the bond'*) was to be a Regulus, a Codrus, a Cato, or a Brutus—every woman a Mother of the Gracchi.

> ————It was well said,
> And 'tis a kind of good deed to say well.*

But heroes on paper might degenerate into vagabonds in practice, Corinnas into courtezans. Thus a refined and permanent individual attachment is intended to supply the place and avoid the inconveniences of marriage; but vows of eternal constancy, without church security, are found to be fragile. A member of the *ideal* and perfect commonwealth of letters lends another a hundred pounds for immediate and pressing use; and when he applies for it again, the borrower has still more need of it than he, and retains it for his own especial, which is tantamount to the public good. The Exchequer of pure reason, like that of the State, never refunds. The political as well as the religious fanatic appeals from the over-weening opinion and claims of others to the highest and most impartial tribunal, namely, his own breast. Two persons agree to live together in Chambers on principles of pure equality and mutual assistance—but when it comes to the push, one of them finds that the other always insists on his fetching water from the pump in Hare-court,* and cleaning his shoes for him. A modest assurance was not the least indispensable virtue in the new perfectibility code; and it was hence discovered to be a scheme, like other schemes where there are all prizes and no blanks, for the accommodation of the enterprizing and cunning, at the expence of the credulous and honest. This broke up the system, and left no good odour behind it! Reason has become a sort of bye-word, and philosophy has 'fallen first into a fasting, then into a sadness, then into a decline, and last, into the dissolution of which we all complain!'* This is a worse error than the former: we may be said to have 'lost the immortal part of ourselves, and what remains is beastly!'*

The point of view from which this matter may be fairly considered, is two-fold, and may be stated thus:—In the first place, it by no means follows, because reason is found not to be the only infallible or safe rule of conduct, that it is no rule at all; or that we are to discard it altogether with derision and ignominy. On the contrary, if not the sole, it is the principal ground of action; it is 'the guide, the stay and anchor of our purest thoughts, and soul of all our moral being.'* In proportion as we strengthen and expand this principle, and bring our affections and subordinate, but perhaps more powerful motives of action into harmony with it, it will not admit of a doubt that we advance to the goal of perfection, and answer the ends of our creation, those ends which not only morality enjoins, but which religion sanctions. If with the utmost stretch of reason, man cannot (as some seemed inclined to suppose) soar up to the God, and quit the ground of human frailty, yet, stripped wholly of it, he sinks at once into the brute. If it cannot stand alone, in its naked simplicity, but requires other props to buttress it up, or ornaments to set it off; yet without it the moral structure would fall flat and dishonoured to the ground. Private reason is that which raises the individual above his mere animal instincts, appetites and passions: public reason in its gradual progress separates the savage from the civilized state. Without the one, men would resemble wild beasts in their dens; without the other, they would be speedily converted into hordes of barbarians or banditti. Sir Walter Scott, in his zeal to restore the spirit of loyalty, of passive obedience and non-resistance as an acknowledgment for his having been created a Baronet by a Prince of the House of Brunswick,* may think it a fine thing to return in imagination to the good old times, 'when in Auvergne alone, there were three hundred nobles whose most ordinary actions were robbery, rape, and murder,'* when the castle of each Norman baron was a strong hold from which the lordly proprietor issued to oppress and plunder the neighbouring districts, and when the Saxon peasantry were treated by their gay and gallant tyrants as a herd of loathsome swine—but for our own parts we beg to be excused; we had rather live in the same age with the author of Waverley and Blackwood's Magazine. Reason is the meter and alnager in civil intercourse, by which each person's upstart and contradictory pretensions are weighed and approved or found wanting, and without which it could not subsist, any more than traffic or the exchange of commodities could be carried on without weights and measures. It is the medium of knowledge, and the polisher of manners, by creating common interests and ideas. Or in the words of a contemporary writer, 'Reason is the queen of the moral world, the soul of the universe, the lamp of human life, the pillar of society, the foundation of law, the beacon of nations, the golden chain let down from heaven, which links all accountable and all intelligent natures in one common system—and in the vain strife between fanatic innovation and fanatic prejudice, we are exhorted to dethrone this queen of the world, to blot

out this light of the mind, to deface this fair column, to break in pieces
this golden chain! We are to discard and throw from us with loud
taunts and bitter execrations that reason, which has been the lofty theme
of the philosopher, the poet, the moralist, and the divine, whose name
was not first named to be abused by the enthusiasts of the French
Revolution, or to be blasphemed by the madder enthusiasts, the advo-
cates of Divine Right, but which is coeval with, and inseparable from
the nature and faculties of man—is the image of his Maker stamped
upon him at his birth, the understanding breathed into him with the
breath of life, and in the participation and improvement of which
alone he is raised above the brute creation and his own physical
nature!'*—The overstrained and ridiculous pretensions of monks
and ascetics were never thought to justify a return to unbridled
licence of manners, or the throwing aside of all decency. The hypocrisy, cruelty, and fanaticism, often attendant on peculiar professions
of sanctity, have not banished the name of religion from the world.
Neither can 'the unreasonableness of the reason' of some modern sciolists 'so unreason our reason,'* as to debar us of the benefit of this
principle in future, or to disfranchise us of the highest privilege of
our nature. In the second place, if it is admitted that Reason alone is
not the sole and self-sufficient ground of morals, it is to Mr. Godwin
that we are indebted for having settled the point. No one denied or
distrusted this principle (before his time) as the absolute judge and
interpreter in all questions of difficulty; and if this is no longer the
case, it is because he has taken this principle, and followed it into its
remotest consequences with more keenness of eye and steadiness of
hand than any other expounder of ethics. His grand work is (at least)
an *experimentum crucis* to shew the weak sides and imperfections of
human reason as the sole law of human action. By over-shooting the
mark, or by 'flying an eagle flight, forth and right on,'* he has pointed
out the limit or line of separation, between what is practicable and
what is barely conceivable—by imposing impossible tasks on the
naked strength of the will, he has discovered how far it is or is not in
our power to dispense with the illusions of sense, to resist the calls of
affection, to emancipate ourselves from the force of habit; and thus,
though he has not said it himself, has enabled others to say to the
towering aspirations after good, and to the over-bearing pride of
human intellect—'Thus far shalt thou come, and no farther!'* Captain
Parry would be thought to have rendered a service to navigation and

his country, no less by proving that there is no North-West Passage,* than if he had ascertained that there is one: so Mr. Godwin has rendered an essential service to moral science, by attempting (in vain) to pass the Arctic Circle and Frozen Regions, where the understanding is no longer warmed by the affections, nor fanned by the breeze of fancy! This is the effect of all bold, original, and powerful thinking, that it either discovers the truth, or detects where error lies; and the only crime with which Mr. Godwin can be charged as a political and moral reasoner is, that he has displayed a more ardent spirit, and a more independent activity of thought than others, in establishing the fallacy (if fallacy it be) of an old popular prejudice that *the Just and True were one*, by 'championing it to the Outrance,'* and in the final result placing the Gothic structure of human virtue on an humbler, but a wider and safer foundation than it had hitherto occupied in the volumes and systems of the learned.

Mr. Godwin is an inventor in the regions of romance, as well as a skilful and hardy explorer of those of moral truth. *Caleb Williams* and *St. Leon** are two of the most splendid and impressive works of the imagination that have appeared in our times. It is not merely that these novels are very well for a philosopher to have produced—they are admirable and complete in themselves, and would not lead you to suppose that the author, who is so entirely at home in human character and dramatic situation, had ever dabbled in logic or metaphysics. The first of these, particularly, is a master-piece, both as to invention and execution. The romantic and chivalrous principle of the love of personal fame is embodied in the finest possible manner in the character of Falkland;[2] as in Caleb Williams (who is not the first, but the second character in the piece) we see the very demon of curiosity personified. Perhaps the art with which these two characters are contrived to relieve and set off each other, has never been surpassed in any work of fiction, with the exception of the immortal satire of Cervantes. The restless and inquisitive spirit of Caleb Williams, in search and in possession of his patron's fatal secret, haunts the latter like a second conscience, plants stings in his tortured mind, fans the flame of his jealous ambition, struggling with agonized remorse; and the hapless but

---

[2] Mr. Fuseli* used to object to this striking delineation a want of historical correctness, inasmuch as the animating principle of the true chivalrous character was the sense of honour, not the mere regard to, or saving of, appearances. This, we think, must be an hypercriticism, from all we remember of books of chivalry and heroes of romance.

noble-minded Falkland at length falls a martyr to the persecution of that morbid and overpowering interest, of which his mingled virtues and vices have rendered him the object. We conceive no one ever began Caleb Williams that did not read it through: no one that ever read it could possibly forget it, or speak of it after any length of time, but with an impression as if the events and feelings had been personal to himself. This is the case also with the story of St. Leon, which, with less dramatic interest and intensity of purpose, is set off by a more gorgeous and flowing eloquence, and by a crown of preternatural imagery, that waves over it like a palm-tree! It is the beauty and the charm of Mr. Godwin's descriptions that the reader identifies himself with the author; and the secret of this is, that the author has identified himself with his personages. Indeed, he has created them. They are the proper issue of his brain, lawfully begot, not foundlings, nor the 'bastards of his art.'* He is not an indifferent, callous spectator of the scenes which he himself pourtrays, but without seeming to feel them. There is no look of patch-work and plagiarism, the beggarly copiousness of borrowed wealth; no tracery-work from worm-eaten manuscripts, from forgotten chronicles, nor piecing out of vague traditions with fragments and snatches of old ballads, so that the result resembles a gaudy, staring transparency, in which you cannot distinguish the daubing of the painter from the light that shines through the flimsy colours and gives them brilliancy. Here all is fairly made out with strokes of the pencil, by fair, not by factitious means. Our author takes a given subject from nature or from books, and then fills it up with the ardent workings of his own mind, with the teeming and audible pulses of his own heart. The effect is entire and satisfactory in proportion. The work (so to speak) and the author are one. We are not puzzled to decide upon their respective pretensions. In reading Mr. Godwin's novels, we know what share of merit the author has in them. In reading the *Scotch Novels*, we are perpetually embarrassed in asking ourselves this question; and perhaps it is not altogether a false modesty that prevents the editor from putting his name in the title-page—he is (for any thing we know to the contrary) only a more voluminous sort of Allen-a-Dale.* At least, we may claim this advantage for the English author, that the chains with which he rivets our attention are forged out of his own thoughts, link by link, blow for blow, with glowing enthusiasm: we see the genuine ore melted in the furnace of fervid feeling, and moulded into stately and *ideal* forms; and this is so far better than peeping into an old iron shop, or pilfering from a dealer in marine stores! There is one drawback, however, attending this mode of proceeding, which attaches generally, indeed, to all originality of composition; namely, that it has a tendency to a certain degree of monotony. He who draws upon his own resources, easily comes to an end of his wealth. Mr. Godwin, in all his writings, dwells upon one idea or exclusive view of a subject, aggrandises a sentiment, exaggerates a character, or pushes an argument to extremes, and makes up by the force of style and continuity of feeling for what he wants in variety of incident or ease of manner. This necessary defect is observable in his best works, and is still more so in Fleetwood and Mandeville;* the one of which, compared with his more admired performances, is mawkish, and the other morbid. Mr. Godwin is also an essayist, an historian—in short, what is he not, that belongs to the character of an indefatigable and accomplished author? His *Life of Chaucer** would have given celebrity to any man of letters possessed of three thousand a year, with leisure to write quartos: as the legal acuteness displayed in his *Remarks on Judge Eyre's Charge to the Jury** would have raised any briefless barrister to the height of his profession. This temporary effusion did more—it gave a turn to the trials for high treason in the year 1794, and possibly saved the lives of twelve innocent individuals, marked out as political victims to the Moloch of Legitimacy, which then skulked behind a British throne,* and had not yet dared to stalk forth (as it has done since) from its lurking-place, in the face of day, to brave the opinion of the world. If it had then glutted its maw with its intended prey (the sharpness of Mr. Godwin's pen cut the legal cords with which it was attempted to bind them), it might have done so sooner, and with more lasting effect. The world do not know (and we are not sure but the intelligence may startle Mr. Godwin himself), that he is the author of a volume of Sermons, and of a Life of Chatham.[3]*

Mr. Fawcett* (an old friend and fellow-student of our author, and who always spoke of his writings with admiration, tinctured with wonder) used to mention a circumstance with respect to the last-mentioned work, which may throw some light on the history and progress of Mr. Godwin's mind. He was anxious to make his biographical account as complete as he could, and applied for this purpose to many of his acquaintance to furnish him with anecdotes or to suggest

---

[3] We had forgotten the tragedies of Antonio and Ferdinand.* Peace be with their *manes*!*

criticisms. Amongst others Mr. Fawcett repeated to him what he thought a striking passage in a speech on *General Warrants** delivered by Lord Chatham, at which he (Mr. Fawcett) had been present. 'Every man's house' (said this emphatic thinker and speaker) 'has been called his castle. And why is it called his castle? Is it because it is defended by a wall, because it is surrounded with a moat? No, it may be nothing more than a straw-built shed. It may be open to all the elements: the wind may enter in, the rain may enter in—but the king *cannot* enter in!' His friend thought that the point was here palpable enough: but when he came to read the printed volume,* he found it thus *transposed*: 'Every man's house is his castle. And why is it called so? Is it because it is defended by a wall, because it is surrounded with a moat? No, it may be nothing more than a straw-built shed. It may be exposed to all the elements: the rain may enter into it, *all the winds of Heaven may whistle round it*, but the king cannot, &c.' This was what Fawcett called a defect of *natural imagination*. He at the same time admitted that Mr. Godwin had improved his native sterility in this respect; or atoned for it by incessant activity of mind and by accumulated stores of thought and powers of language. In fact, his *forte* is not the spontaneous, but the voluntary exercise of talent. He fixes his ambition on a high point of excellence, and spares no pains or time in attaining it. He has less of the appearance of a man of genius, than any one who has given such decided and ample proofs of it. He is ready only on reflection: dangerous only at the rebound. He gathers himself up, and strains every nerve and faculty with deliberate aim to some heroic and dazzling atchievement of intellect: but he must make a career before he flings himself, armed, upon the enemy, or he is sure to be unhorsed. Or he resembles an eight-day clock that must be wound up long before it can strike. Therefore, his powers of conversation are but limited. He has neither acuteness of remark, nor a flow of language, both which might be expected from his writings, as these are no less distinguished by a sustained and impassioned tone of declamation than by novelty of opinion or brilliant tracks of invention. In company, Horne Tooke* used to make a mere child of him—or of any man! Mr. Godwin liked this treatment,[4] and

---

[4] To be sure, it was redeemed by a high respect, and by some magnificent compliments. Once in particular, at his own table, after a good deal of *badinage* and cross-questioning about his being the author of the Reply to Judge Eyre's Charge, on Mr. Godwin's acknowledging that he was, Mr. Tooke said, 'Come here then,'—and when his guest went round to his chair, he took his hand, and pressed it to his lips, saying—'I can do no less for the hand that saved my life!'

indeed it is his foible to fawn on those who use him *cavalierly*, and to be cavalier to those who express an undue or unqualified admiration of him. He looks up with unfeigned respect to acknowledged reputation (but then it must be very well ascertained before he admits it)—and has a favourite hypothesis that Understanding and Virtue are the same thing. Mr. Godwin possesses a high degree of philosophical candour, and studiously paid the homage of his pen and person to Mr. Malthus, Sir James Macintosh, and Dr. Parr, for their unsparing attacks on him; but woe to any poor devil who had the hardihood to defend him against them! In private, the author of *Political Justice* at one time reminded those who knew him of the metaphysician engrafted on the Dissenting Minister. There was a dictatorial, captious, quibbling pettiness of manner. He lost this with the first blush and awkwardness of popularity, which surprised him in the retirement of his study; and he has since, with the wear and tear of society, from being too pragmatical, become somewhat too careless. He is, at present, as easy as an old glove. Perhaps there is a little attention to effect in this, and he wishes to appear a foil to himself. His best moments are with an intimate acquaintance or two, when he gossips in a fine vein about old authors, Clarendon's *History of the Rebellion*, or Burnet's *History of his own Times*; and you perceive by your host's talk, as by the taste of seasoned wine, that he has a *cellarage* in his understanding! Mr. Godwin also has a correct *acquired* taste in poetry and the drama. He relishes Donne and Ben Jonson, and recites a passage from either with an agreeable mixture of pedantry and *bonhommie*. He is not one of those who do not grow wiser with opportunity and reflection: he changes his opinions, and changes them for the better. The alteration of his taste in poetry, from an exclusive admiration of the age of Queen Anne to an almost equally exclusive one of that of Elizabeth, is, we suspect, owing to Mr. Coleridge, who some twenty years ago, threw a great stone into the standing pool of criticism, which splashed some persons with the mud, but which gave a motion to the surface and a reverberation to the neighbouring echoes, which has not since subsided. In common company, Mr. Godwin either goes to sleep himself, or sets others to sleep. He is at present engaged in a History of the Commonwealth of England.*—*Esto perpetua!** In size Mr. Godwin is below the common stature, nor is his deportment graceful or animated. His face is, however, fine, with an expression of placid temper and recondite thought. He is not unlike the common portraits of Locke. There is a very admirable likeness of him by Mr. Northcote, which with a more heroic and dignified air, only does justice to the profound sagacity and benevolent aspirations of our author's mind.* Mr. Godwin has kept the best company of his time, but he has survived most of the celebrated persons with whom he lived in habits of intimacy. He speaks of them with enthusiasm and with discrimination; and sometimes dwells with peculiar delight on a day passed at John Kemble's in company with Mr. Sheridan, Mr. Curran, Mrs. Wolstonecraft and Mrs. Inchbald, when the conversation took a most animated turn and the subject was of Love.* Of all these our author is the only one remaining. Frail tenure, on which human life and genius are lent us for a while to improve or to enjoy!

29

LORD BYRON

LORD BYRON and Sir Walter Scott are among writers now living[1] the two, who would carry away a majority of suffrages as the greatest geniuses of the age. The former would, perhaps, obtain the preference with the fine gentlemen and ladies (squeamishness apart)—the latter with the critics and the vulgar. We shall treat of them in the same connection, partly on account of their distinguished pre-eminence, and partly because they afford a complete contrast to each other. In their poetry, in their prose, in their politics, and in their tempers no two men can be more unlike.

If Sir Walter Scott may be thought by some to have been

> Born universal heir to all humanity,*

it is plain Lord Byron can set up no such pretension. He is, in a striking degree, the creature of his own will. He holds no communion with his kind; but stands alone, without mate or fellow—

> As if a man were author of himself,
> And owned no other kin.*

He is like a solitary peak, all access to which is cut off not more by elevation than distance. He is seated on a lofty eminence, 'cloud-capt,'* or reflecting the last rays of setting suns; and in his poetical moods, reminds us of the fabled Titans, retired to a ridgy steep, playing on their Pan's-pipes, and taking up ordinary men and things in their hands with haughty indifference. He raises his subject to himself, or tramples on it: he neither stoops to, nor loses himself in it. He exists not by sympathy, but by antipathy. He scorns all things, even himself. Nature must come to him to sit for her picture—he does not go to her. She must consult his time, his convenience, and his humour; and wear a *sombre* or a fantastic garb, or his Lordship turns his back upon her. There is no ease, no unaffected simplicity of manner, no 'golden mean.'* All is strained, or petulant in the extreme. His thoughts are sphered and crystalline; his style 'prouder than

---

[1] This Essay was written just before Lord Byron's death.*

when blue Iris bends;'* his spirit fiery, impatient, wayward, indefatigable. Instead of taking his impressions from without, in entire and almost unimpaired masses, he moulds them according to his own temperament, and heats the materials of his imagination in the furnace of his passions.—Lord Byron's verse glows like a flame, consuming every thing in its way; Sir Walter Scott's glides like a river, clear, gentle, harmless. The poetry of the first scorches, that of the last scarcely warms. The light of the one proceeds from an internal source, ensanguined, sullen, fixed; the other reflects the hues of Heaven, or the face of nature, glancing vivid and various. The productions of the Northern Bard have the rust and the freshness of antiquity about them; those of the Noble Poet cease to startle from their extreme ambition of novelty, both in style and matter. Sir Walter's rhymes are 'silly sooth'—

> And dally with the innocence of thought,
> Like the old age*—

his Lordship's Muse spurns *the olden time*, and affects all the supercilious airs of a modern fine lady and an upstart. The object of the one writer is to restore us to truth and nature: the other chiefly thinks how he shall display his own power, or vent his spleen, or astonish the reader either by starting new subjects and trains of speculation, or by expressing old ones in a more striking and emphatic manner than they have been expressed before. He cares little what it is he says, so that he can say it differently from others. This may account for the charges of plagiarism which have been repeatedly brought against the Noble Poet—if he can borrow an image or sentiment from another, and heighten it by an epithet or an allusion of greater force and beauty than is to be found in the original passage, he thinks he shews his superiority of execution in this in a more marked manner than if the first suggestion had been his own. It is not the value of the observation itself he is solicitous about; but he wishes to shine by contrast—even nature only serves as a foil to set off his style. He therefore takes the thoughts of others (whether contemporaries or not) out of their mouths, and is content to make them his own, to set his stamp upon them, by imparting to them a more meretricious gloss, a higher relief, a greater loftiness of tone, and a characteristic inveteracy of purpose. Even in those collateral ornaments of modern style, slovenliness, abruptness, and eccentricity (as well as in terseness and

significance), Lord Byron, when he pleases, defies competition and
surpasses all his contemporaries. Whatever he does, he must do in
a more decided and daring manner than any one else—he lounges
with extravagance, and yawns so as to alarm the reader! Self-will,
passion, the love of singularity, a disdain of himself and of others
(with a conscious sense that this is among the ways and means of
procuring admiration) are the proper categories of his mind: he is
a lordly writer, is above his own reputation, and condescends to the
Muses with a scornful grace!

Lord Byron, who in his politics is a *liberal*,* in his genius is haughty
and aristocratic: Walter Scott, who is an aristocrat in principle,
is popular in his writings, and is (as it were) equally *servile* to nature
and to opinion. The genius of Sir Walter is essentially imitative,
or 'denotes a foregone conclusion:'* that of Lord Byron is self-
dependent; or at least requires no aid, is governed by no law, but the
impulses of its own will. We confess, however much we may admire
independence of feeling and erectness of spirit in general or practical
questions, yet in works of genius we prefer him who bows to the
authority of nature, who appeals to actual objects, to mouldering
superstitions, to history, observation, and tradition, before him who
only consults the pragmatical and restless workings of his own breast,
and gives them out as oracles to the world. We like a writer (whether
poet or prose-writer) who takes in (or is willing to take in) the range
of half the universe in feeling, character, description, much better
than we do one who obstinately and invariably shuts himself up in
the Bastile of his own ruling passions. In short, we had rather be
Sir Walter Scott (meaning thereby the Author of Waverley) than Lord
Byron, a hundred times over. And for the reason just given, namely,
that he casts his descriptions in the mould of nature, ever-varying,
never tiresome, always interesting and always instructive, instead of
casting them constantly in the mould of his own individual impressions. He gives us man as he is, or as he was, in almost every variety of
situation, action, and feeling. Lord Byron makes man after his own
image, woman after his own heart; the one is a capricious tyrant, the
other a yielding slave; he gives us the misanthrope and the voluptu-
ary by turns; and with these two characters, burning or melting in
their own fires, he makes out everlasting centos of himself. He hangs
the cloud, the film of his existence over all outward things—sits
in the centre of his thoughts, and enjoys dark night, bright day, the

glitter and the gloom 'in cell monastic'*—we see the mournful pall, the crucifix, the death's heads, the faded chaplet of flowers, the gleaming tapers, the agonized brow of genius, the wasted form of beauty—but we are still imprisoned in a dungeon, a curtain intercepts our view, we do not breathe freely the air of nature or of our own thoughts—the other admired author draws aside the curtain, and the veil of egotism is rent, and he shews us the crowd of living men and women, the endless groups, the landscape back-ground, the cloud and the rainbow, and enriches our imaginations and relieves one passion by another, and expands and lightens reflection, and takes away that tightness at the breast which arises from thinking or wishing to think that there is nothing in the world out of a man's self!—In this point of view, the Author of Waverley is one of the greatest teachers of morality that ever lived, by emancipating the mind from petty, narrow, and bigotted prejudices: Lord Byron is the greatest pamperer of those prejudices, by seeming to think there is nothing else worth encouraging but the seeds or the full luxuriant growth of dogmatism and self-conceit. In reading the *Scotch Novels*, we never think about the author, except from a feeling of curiosity respecting our unknown benefactor: in reading Lord Byron's works, he himself is never absent from our minds. The colouring of Lord Byron's style, however rich and dipped in Tyrian dyes,* is nevertheless opaque, is in itself an object of delight and wonder: Sir Walter Scott's is perfectly transparent. In studying the one, you seem to gaze at the figures cut in stained glass, which exclude the view beyond, and where the pure light of Heaven is only a means of setting off the gorgeousness of art: in reading the other, you look through a noble window at the clear and varied landscape without. Or to sum up the distinction in one word, Sir Walter Scott is the most *dramatic* writer now living; and Lord Byron is the least so. It would be difficult to imagine that the Author of Waverley is in the smallest degree a pedant; as it would be hard to persuade ourselves that the author of Childe Harold and Don Juan is not a coxcomb, though a provoking and sublime one. In this decided preference given to Sir Walter Scott over Lord Byron, we distinctly include the prose-works of the former; for we do not think his poetry alone by any means entitles him to that precedence. Sir Walter in his poetry, though pleasing and natural, is a comparative trifler: it is in his anonymous productions that he has shewn himself for what he is!—

Intensity is the great and prominent distinction of Lord Byron's writings. He seldom gets beyond force of style, nor has he produced any regular work or masterly whole. He does not prepare any plan beforehand, nor revise and retouch what he has written with polished accuracy. His only object seems to be to stimulate himself and his readers for the moment—to keep both alive, to drive away *ennui*, to substitute a feverish and irritable state of excitement for listless indolence or even calm enjoyment. For this purpose he pitches on any subject at random without much thought or delicacy—he is only impatient to begin—and takes care to adorn and enrich it as he proceeds with 'thoughts that breathe and words that burn.'* He composes (as he himself has said*) whether he is in the bath, in his study, or on horseback—he writes as habitually as others talk or think—and whether we have the inspiration of the Muse or not, we always find the spirit of the man of genius breathing from his verse. He grapples with his subject, and moves, penetrates, and animates it by the electric force of his own feelings. He is often monotonous, extravagant, offensive; but he is never dull, or tedious, but when he writes prose. Lord Byron does not exhibit a new view of nature, or raise insignificant objects into importance by the romantic associations with which he surrounds them; but generally (at least) takes common-place thoughts and events, and endeavours to express them in stronger and statelier language than others. His poetry stands like a Martello tower by the side of his subject. He does not, like Mr. Wordsworth, lift poetry from the ground, or create a sentiment out of nothing. He does not describe a daisy or a periwinkle, but the cedar or the cypress: not 'poor men's cottages, but princes' palaces.'* His Childe Harold contains a lofty and impassioned review of the great events of history, of the mighty objects left as wrecks of time, but he dwells chiefly on what is familiar to the mind of every school-boy; has brought out few new traits of feeling or thought; and has done no more than justice to the reader's preconceptions by the sustained force and brilliancy of his style and imagery.

Lord Byron's earlier productions, *Lara*, the *Corsair*, &c. were wild and gloomy romances, put into rapid and shining verse. They discover the madness of poetry, together with the inspiration: sullen, moody, capricious, fierce, inexorable, gloating on beauty, thirsting for revenge, hurrying from the extremes of pleasure to pain, but with nothing permanent, nothing healthy or natural. The gaudy decorations and the morbid sentiments remind one of flowers strewed over the face of death! In his *Childe Harold* (as has been just observed) he assumes a lofty and philosophic tone, and 'reasons high of providence, fore-knowledge, will, and fate.'* He takes the highest points in the history of the world, and comments on them from a more commanding emi-nence: he shews us the crumbling monuments of time, he invokes the great names, the mighty spirit of antiquity. The universe is changed into a stately mausoleum:—in solemn measures he chaunts a hymn to fame. Lord Byron has strength and elevation enough to fill up the moulds of our classical and time-hallowed recollections, and to rekindle the earliest aspirations of the mind after greatness and true glory with a pen of fire. The names of Tasso, of Ariosto, of Dante, of Cincinnatus, of Cæsar, of Scipio, lose nothing of their pomp or their lustre in his hands, and when he begins and continues a strain of panegyric on such subjects, we indeed sit down with him to a banquet of rich praise, brooding over imperishable glories,

Till Contemplation has her fill.*

Lord Byron seems to cast himself indignantly from 'this bank and shoal of time,'* or the frail tottering bark that bears up modern repu-tation, into the huge sea of ancient renown, and to revel there with untired, outspread plume. Even this in him is spleen—his contempt of his contemporaries makes him turn back to the lustrous past, or project himself forward to the dim future!—Lord Byron's tragedies, Faliero,[2] Sardanapalus, &c. are not equal to his other works. They want the essence of the drama. They abound in speeches and descrip-tions, such as he himself might make either to himself or others, loll-ing on his couch of a morning, but do not carry the reader out of the poet's mind to the scenes and events recorded. They have neither action, character, nor interest, but are a sort of *gossamer* tragedies, spun out, and glittering, and spreading a flimsy veil over the face of nature. Yet he spins them on. Of all that he has done in this way the *Heaven and Earth* (the same subject as Mr. Moore's *Loves of the Angels*) is the best. We prefer it even to *Manfred*. *Manfred* is merely himself, with a fancy-drapery on: but in the dramatic fragment pub-lished in the *Liberal*,* the space between Heaven and Earth, the stage

---

[2] 'Don Juan was my Moscow, and Faliero
My Leipsic, and my Mont St. Jean seems Cain,'*
Don Juan, Canto. XI.

on which his characters have to pass to and fro, seems to fill his Lordship's imagination; and the Deluge, which he has so finely described, may be said to have drowned all his own idle humours.

We must say we think little of our author's turn for satire. His 'English Bards and Scotch Reviewers' is dogmatical and insolent, but without refinement or point. He calls people names, and tries to transfix a character with an epithet, which does not stick, because it has no other foundation than his own petulance and spite; or he endeavours to degrade by alluding to some circumstance of external situation. He says of Mr. Wordsworth's poetry, that 'it is his aversion.'* That may be: but whose fault is it? This is the satire of a lord, who is accustomed to have all his whims or dislikes taken for gospel, and who cannot be at the pains to do more than signify his contempt or displeasure. If a great man meets with a rebuff which he does not like, he turns on his heel, and this passes for a repartee. The Noble Author says of a celebrated barrister and critic, that he was 'born in a garret sixteen stories high.'* The insinuation is not true; or if it were, it is low. The allusion degrades the person who makes, not him to whom it is applied. This is also the satire of a person of birth and quality, who measures all merit by external rank, that is, by his own standard. So his Lordship, in a 'Letter to the Editor of My Grandmother's Review,'* addresses him fifty times as '*my dear Robarts*;' nor is there any other wit in the article. This is surely a mere assumption of superiority from his Lordship's rank, and is the sort of *quizzing* he might use to a person who came to hire himself as a valet to him at *Long's**—the waiters might laugh, the public will not. In like manner, in the controversy about Pope,* he claps Mr. Bowles on the back with a coarse facetious familiarity, as if he were his chaplain whom he had invited to dine with him, or was about to present to a benefice. The reverend divine might submit to the obligation, but he has no occasion to subscribe to the jest. If it is a jest that Mr. Bowles should be a parson, and Lord Byron a peer, the world knew this before; there was no need to write a pamphlet to prove it.

The *Don Juan* indeed has great power; but its power is owing to the force of the serious writing, and to the oddity of the contrast between that and the flashy passages with which it is interlarded. From the sublime to the ridiculous there is but one step.* You laugh and are surprised that any one should turn round and *travestie* himself: the drollery is in the utter discontinuity of ideas and feelings.

He makes virtue serve as a foil to vice; *dandyism* is (for want of any other) a variety of genius. A classical intoxication is followed by the splashing of soda-water, by frothy effusions of ordinary bile. After the lightning and the hurricane, we are introduced to the interior of the cabin and the contents of wash-hand basins. The solemn hero of tragedy plays *Scrub* in the farce.* This is 'very tolerable and not to be endured.'* The Noble Lord is almost the only writer who has prostituted his talents in this way. He hallows in order to desecrate; takes a pleasure in defacing the images of beauty his hands have wrought; and raises our hopes and our belief in goodness to Heaven only to dash them to the earth again, and break them in pieces the more effectually from the very height they have fallen. Our enthusiasm for genius or virtue is thus turned into a jest by the very person who has kindled it, and who thus fatally quenches the sparks of both. It is not that Lord Byron is sometimes serious and sometimes trifling, sometimes profligate, and sometimes moral—but when he is most serious and most moral, he is only preparing to mortify the unsuspecting reader by putting a pitiful *hoax* upon him. This is a most unaccountable anomaly. It is as if the eagle were to build its eyry in a common sewer, or the owl were seen soaring to the mid-day sun. Such a sight might make one laugh, but one would not wish or expect it to occur more than once![3]

In fact, Lord Byron is the spoiled child of fame as well as fortune. He has taken a surfeit of popularity, and is not contented to delight, unless he can shock the public. He would force them to admire in spite of decency and common sense—he would have them read what they would read in no one but himself, or he would not give a rush for their applause. He is to be 'a chartered libertine,'* from whom insults are favours, whose contempt is to be a new incentive to admiration. His Lordship is hard to please: he is equally averse to notice or neglect, enraged at censure and scorning praise. He tries the patience of the town to the very utmost, and when they shew signs of weariness or disgust, threatens to *discard* them. He says he will write on, whether he is read or not.* He would never write another page, if it were not to court popular applause, or to affect a superiority over it. In this respect also, Lord Byron presents a striking contrast to Sir Walter

---

[3] This censure applies to the first Cantos of DON JUAN much more than to the last. It has been called a TRISTRAM SHANDY in rhyme:* it is rather a poem written about itself.

Scott. The latter takes what part of the public favour falls to his share, without grumbling (to be sure he has no reason to complain) the former is always quarrelling with the world about his *modicum* of applause, the *spolia opima** of vanity, and ungraciously throwing the offerings of incense heaped on his shrine back in the faces of his admirers. Again, there is no taint in the writings of the Author of Waverley, all is fair and natural and *above-board*: he never outrages the public mind. He introduces no anomalous character: broaches no staggering opinion. If he goes back to old prejudices and superstitions as a relief to the modern reader, while Lord Byron floats on swelling paradoxes—

> Like proud seas under him;*

if the one defers too much to the spirit of antiquity, the other panders to the spirit of the age, goes to the very edge of extreme and licentious speculation, and breaks his neck over it. Grossness and levity are the playthings of his pen. It is a ludicrous circumstance that he should have dedicated his *Cain* to the worthy Baronet! Did the latter ever acknowledge the obligation? We are not nice, not very nice; but we do not particularly approve those subjects that shine chiefly from their rottenness: nor do we wish to see the Muses drest out in the flounces of a false or questionable philosophy, like *Portia* and *Nerissa* in the garb of Doctors of Law. We like metaphysics as well as Lord Byron; but not to see them making flowery speeches, nor dancing a measure in the fetters of verse. We have as good as hinted, that his Lordship's poetry consists mostly of a tissue of superb common-places; even his paradoxes are *common-place*. They are familiar in the schools: they are only new and striking in his dramas and stanzas, by being out of place. In a word, we think that poetry moves best within the circle of nature and received opinion: speculative theory and subtle casuistry are forbidden ground to it. But Lord Byron often wanders into this ground wantonly, wilfully, and unwarrantably. The only apology we can conceive for the spirit of some of Lord Byron's writings, is the spirit of some of those opposed to him. They would provoke a man to write any thing. 'Farthest from them is best.'* The extravagance and license of the one seems a proper antidote to the bigotry and narrowness of the other. The first *Vision of Judgment* was a set-off to the second,* though

> None but itself could be its parallel.*

Perhaps the chief cause of most of Lord Byron's errors is, that he is that anomaly in letters and in society, a Noble Poet. It is a double privilege, almost too much for humanity. He has all the pride of birth and genius. The strength of his imagination leads him to indulge in fantastic opinions; the elevation of his rank sets censure at defiance. He becomes a pampered egotist. He has a seat in the House of Lords, a niche in the Temple of Fame. Every-day mortals, opinions, things are not good enough for him to touch or think of. A mere nobleman is, in his estimation, but 'the tenth transmitter of a foolish face:'* a mere man of genius is no better than a worm. His Muse is also a lady of quality. The people are not polite enough for him: the Court not sufficiently intellectual. He hates the one and despises the other. By hating and despising others, he does not learn to be satisfied with himself. A fastidious man soon grows querulous and splenetic. If there is nobody but ourselves to come up to our idea of fancied perfection, we easily get tired of our idol. When a man is tired of what he is, by a natural perversity he sets up for what he is not. If he is a poet, he pretends to be a metaphysician: if he is a patrician in rank and feeling, he would fain be one of the people. His ruling motive is not the love of the people, but of distinction not of truth, but of singularity. He patronizes men of letters out of vanity, and deserts them from caprice, or from the advice of friends.* He embarks in an obnoxious publication to provoke censure, and leaves it to shift for itself for fear of scandal. We do not like Sir Walter's gratuitous servility: we like Lord Byron's preposterous *liberalism* little better. He may affect the principles of equality, but he resumes his privilege of peerage, upon occasion. His Lordship has made great offers of service to the Greeks—money and horses. He is at present in Cephalonia, waiting the event!*

* * * * * * *

We had written thus far when news came of the death of Lord Byron, and put an end at once to a strain of somewhat peevish invective, which was intended to meet his eye, not to insult his memory. Had we known that we were writing his epitaph, we must have done it with a different feeling. As it is, we think it better and more like himself, to let what we had written stand, than to take up our leaden shafts, and try to melt them into 'tears of sensibility'* or mould them into dull praise, and an affected shew of candour. We were not silent during the author's life-time, either for his reproof or encouragement (such as we could give, and *he* did not disdain to accept) nor can we now turn undertakers' men to fix the glittering plate upon his coffin, or fall into the procession of popular woe.—Death cancels every thing but truth; and strips a man of every thing but genius and virtue. It is a sort of natural canonization. It makes the meanest of us sacred—it installs the poet in his immortality, and lifts him to the skies. Death is the great assayer of the sterling ore of talent. At his touch the drossy particles fall off, the irritable, the personal, the gross, and mingle with the dust—the finer and more ethereal part mounts with the winged spirit to watch over our latest memory and protect our bones from insult. We consign the least worthy qualities to oblivion, and cherish the nobler and imperishable nature with double pride and fondness. Nothing could shew the real superiority of genius in a more striking point of view than the idle contests and the public indifference about the place of Lord Byron's interment, whether in Westminster-Abbey or his own family-vault. A king must have a coronation—a nobleman a funeral-procession.—The man is nothing without the pageant. The poet's cemetery is the human mind, in which he sows the seeds of never-ending thought—his monument is to be found in his works:

> Nothing can cover his high fame but Heaven;
> No pyramids set off his memory,
> But the eternal substance of his greatness.*

Lord Byron is dead: he also died a martyr to his zeal in the cause of freedom, for the last, best hopes of man. Let that be his excuse and his epitaph!

MR. WORDSWORTH'S genius is a pure emanation of the Spirit of the Age. Had he lived in any other period of the world, he would never have been heard of. As it is, he has some difficulty to contend with, the hebetude of his intellect, and the meanness of his subject. With him 'lowliness is young ambition's ladder:'* but he finds it a toil to climb in this way the steep of Fame. His homely Muse can hardly raise her wing from the ground, nor spread her hidden glories to the sun. He has 'no figures nor no fantasies, which busy *passion* draws in the brains of men:'* neither the gorgeous machinery of mythologic lore, nor the splendid colours of poetic diction. His style is vernacular: he delivers household truths. He sees nothing loftier than human hopes; nothing deeper than the human heart. This he probes, this he tampers with, this he poises, with all its incalculable weight of thought and feeling, in his hands; and at the same time calms the throbbing pulses of his own heart, by keeping his eye ever fixed on the face of nature. If he can make the life-blood flow from the wounded breast, this is the living colouring with which he paints his verse: if he can assuage the pain or close up the wound with the balm of solitary musing, or the healing powers of plants and herbs and 'skyey influences,'* this is the sole triumph of his art. He takes the simplest elements of nature and of the human mind, the mere abstract conditions inseparable from our being, and tries to compound a new system of poetry from them; and has perhaps succeeded as well as any one could. '*Nihil humani a me alienum puto*'*—is the motto of his works. He thinks nothing low or indifferent of which this can be affirmed: every thing that professes to be more than this, that is not an absolute essence of truth and feeling, he holds to be vitiated, false, and spurious. In a word, his poetry is founded on setting up an opposition (and pushing it to the utmost length) between the natural and the artificial: between the spirit of humanity, and the spirit of fashion and of the world!

It is one of the innovations of the time. It partakes of, and is carried along with, the revolutionary movement of our age: the political changes of the day were the model on which he formed and conducted his poetical experiments. His Muse (it cannot be denied, and without this we cannot explain its character at all) is a levelling one. It proceeds on a principle of equality, and strives to reduce all things to the same standard. It is distinguished by a proud humility. It relies upon its own resources, and disdains external shew and relief. It takes the commonest events and objects, as a test to prove that nature is always interesting from its inherent truth and beauty, without any of the ornaments of dress or pomp of circumstances to set it off. Hence the unaccountable mixture of seeming simplicity and real abstruseness in the *Lyrical Ballads*. Fools have laughed at, wise men scarcely understand them. He takes a subject or a story merely as pegs or loops to hang thought and feeling on; the incidents are trifling, in proportion to his contempt for imposing appearances; the reflections are profound, according to the gravity and the aspiring pretensions of his mind.

His popular, inartificial style gets rid (at a blow) of all the trappings of verse, of all the high places of poetry: 'the cloud-capt towers, the solemn temples, the gorgeous palaces,' are swept to the ground, and 'like the baseless fabric of a vision, leave not a wreck behind.'* All the traditions of learning, all the superstitions of age, are obliterated and effaced. We begin *de novo*,* on a *tabula rasa** of poetry. The purple pall, the nodding plume of tragedy are exploded as mere pantomime and trick, to return to the simplicity of truth and nature. Kings, queens, priests, nobles, the altar and the throne, the distinctions of rank, birth, wealth, power, 'the judge's robe, the marshall's truncheon, the ceremony that to great ones 'longs,'* are not to be found here. The author tramples on the pride of art with greater pride. The Ode and Epode, the Strophe and the Antistrophe, he laughs to scorn. The harp of Homer, the trump of Pindar and of Alcæus are still. The decencies of costume, the decorations of vanity are stripped off without mercy as barbarous, idle, and Gothic. The jewels in the crisped hair,* the diadem on the polished brow are thought meretricious, theatrical, vulgar; and nothing contents his fastidious taste beyond a simple garland of flowers. Neither does he avail himself of the advantages which nature or accident holds out to him. He chooses to have his subject a foil to his invention, to owe nothing but to himself. He gathers manna* in the wilderness, he strikes the barren rock for the gushing moisture. He elevates the mean by the strength of his own aspirations; he clothes the naked with beauty and grandeur from the store of his own recollections. No cypress-grove loads his verse with perfumes: but his imagination lends 'a sense of joy

> To the bare trees and mountains bare,
> And grass in the green field.'*

No storm, no shipwreck startles us by its horrors: but the rainbow lifts its head in the cloud, and the breeze sighs through the withered fern. No sad vicissitude of fate,* no overwhelming catastrophe in nature deforms his page: but the dew-drop glitters on the bending flower, the tear collects in the glistening eye.

> Beneath the hills, along the flowery vales,
> The generations are prepared; the pangs,
> The internal pangs are ready; the dread strife
> Of poor humanity's afflicted will,
> Struggling in vain with ruthless destiny.*

As the lark ascends from its low bed on fluttering wing, and salutes the morning skies; so Mr. Wordsworth's unpretending Muse, in russet guise, scales the summits of reflection, while it makes the round earth its footstool,* and its home!

Possibly a good deal of this may be regarded as the effect of disappointed views and an inverted ambition. Prevented by native pride and indolence from climbing the ascent of learning or greatness, taught by political opinions to say to the vain pomp and glory of the world,* 'I hate ye,' seeing the path of classical and artificial poetry blocked up by the cumbrous ornaments of style and turgid *commonplaces*, so that nothing more could be achieved in that direction but by the most ridiculous bombast or the tamest servility; he has turned back partly from the bias of his mind, partly perhaps from a judicious policy—has struck into the sequestered vale of humble life, sought out the Muse among sheep-cotes and hamlets and the peasant's mountain-haunts, has discarded all the tinsel pageantry of verse, and endeavoured (not in vain) to aggrandise the trivial and add the charm of novelty to the familiar. No one has shewn the same imagination in raising trifles into importance: no one has displayed the same pathos in treating of the simplest feelings of the heart. Reserved, yet haughty, having no unruly or violent passions, (or those passions having been early suppressed,) Mr. Wordsworth has passed his life in solitary musing, or in daily converse with the face of nature. He exemplifies in an eminent degree the power of *association*; for his poetry has no other source or character. He has dwelt among pastoral scenes, till each object has become connected with a thousand feelings, a link in the chain of thought, a fibre of his own heart. Every one is by habit and familiarity strongly attached to the place of his birth, or to objects that recal the most pleasing and eventful circumstances of his life. But to the author of the *Lyrical Ballads*, nature is a kind of home; and he may be said to take a personal interest in the universe. There is no image so insignificant that it has not in some mood or other found the way into his heart: no sound that does not awaken the memory of other years.—

> To him the meanest flower that blows can give
> Thoughts that do often lie too deep for tears.*

The daisy looks up to him with sparkling eye as an old acquaintance: the cuckoo haunts him with sounds of early youth not to be expressed: a linnet's nest startles him with boyish delight: an old withered thorn is weighed down with a heap of recollections: a grey cloak, seen on some wild moor, torn by the wind, or drenched in the rain, afterwards becomes an object of imagination to him: even the lichens on the rock have a life and being in his thoughts. He has described all these objects in a way and with an intensity of feeling that no one else had done before him, and has given a new view or aspect of nature. He is in this sense the most original poet now living, and the one whose writings could the least be spared: for they have no substitute elsewhere. The vulgar do not read them, the learned, who see all things through books, do not understand them, the great despise, the fashionable may ridicule them: but the author has created himself an interest in the heart of the retired and lonely student of nature, which can never die. Persons of this class will still continue to feel what he has felt: he has expressed what they might in vain wish to express, except with glistening eye and faultering tongue! There is a lofty philosophic tone, a thoughtful humanity, infused into his pastoral vein. Remote from the passions and events of the great world, he has communicated interest and dignity to the primal movements of the heart of man, and ingrafted his own conscious reflections on the casual thoughts of hinds and shepherds. Nursed amidst the grandeur of mountain scenery, he has stooped to have a nearer view of the daisy under his feet, or plucked a branch of white-thorn from the spray: but in describing it, his mind seems imbued with the majesty and solemnity of the objects around him—the tall rock lifts its head in the erectness of his spirit; the cataract roars in the sound of his verse; and in its dim and mysterious meaning, the mists seem to gather in the hollows of Helvellyn, and the forked Skiddaw hovers in the distance. There is little mention of mountainous scenery in Mr. Wordsworth's poetry; but by internal evidence one might be almost sure that it was written in a mountainous country, from its bareness, its simplicity, its loftiness and its depth!

His later philosophic productions have a somewhat different character. They are a departure from, a dereliction of his first principles. They are classical and courtly. They are polished in style, without being gaudy; dignified in subject, without affectation. They seem to have been composed not in a cottage at Grasmere, but among the half-inspired groves and stately recollections of Cole-Orton.* We might allude in particular, for examples of what we mean, to the lines on a Picture by Claude Lorraine, and to the exquisite poem, entitled *Laodamia*.* The last of these breathes the pure spirit of the finest fragments of antiquity—the sweetness, the gravity, the strength, the beauty and the languor of death—

> Calm contemplation and majestic pains.*

Its glossy brilliancy arises from the perfection of the finishing, like that of careful sculpture, not from gaudy colouring—the texture of the thoughts has the smoothness and solidity of marble. It is a poem that might be read aloud in Elysium, and the spirits of departed heroes and sages would gather round to listen to it! Mr. Wordsworth's philosophic poetry, with a less glowing aspect and less tumult in the veins than Lord Byron's on similar occasions, bends a calmer and keener eye on mortality; the impression, if less vivid, is more pleasing and permanent; and we confess it (perhaps it is a want of taste and proper feeling) that there are lines and poems of our author's, that we think of ten times for once that we recur to any of Lord Byron's. Or if there are any of the latter's writings, that we can dwell upon in the same way, that is, as lasting and heart-felt sentiments, it is when laying aside his usual pomp and pretension, he descends with Mr. Wordsworth to the common ground of a disinterested humanity. It may be considered as characteristic of our poet's writings, that they either make no impression on the mind at all, seem mere *nonsense-verses*, or that they leave a mark behind them that never wears out. They either

> Fall blunted from the indurated breast*—

without any perceptible result, or they absorb it like a passion. To one class of readers he appears sublime, to another (and we fear the largest) ridiculous. He has probably realised Milton's wish,—'and fit audience found, though few:'* but we suspect he is not reconciled to the alternative. There are delightful passages in the EXCURSION, both of natural description and of inspired reflection (passages of the latter kind that in the sound of the thoughts and of the swelling language resemble heavenly symphonies, mournful *requiems* over the grave of human hopes); but we must add, in justice and in sincerity, that we think it impossible that this work should ever become popular, even in the same degree as the *Lyrical Ballads*. It affects a system without having any intelligible clue to one; and instead of unfolding a principle in various and striking lights, repeats the same conclusions till they become flat and insipid. Mr. Wordsworth's mind is obtuse, except as it is the organ and the receptacle of accumulated feelings: it is not analytic, but synthetic; it is reflecting, rather than theoretical. The EXCURSION, we believe, fell still-born from the press.* There was something abortive, and clumsy, and ill-judged in the attempt. It was long and laboured. The personages, for the most part, were low, the fare rustic: the plan raised expectations which were not fulfilled, and the effect was like being ushered into a stately hall and invited to sit down to a splendid banquet in the company of clowns, and with nothing but successive courses of apple-dumplings served up. It was not even *toujours perdrix!**

Mr. Wordsworth, in his person, is above the middle size, with marked features, and an air somewhat stately and Quixotic. He reminds one of some of Holbein's heads, grave, saturnine, with a slight indication of sly humour, kept under by the manners of the age or by the pretensions of the person. He has a peculiar sweetness in his smile, and great depth and manliness and a rugged harmony, in the tones of his voice. His manner of reading his own poetry is particularly imposing; and in his favourite passages his eye beams with preternatural lustre, and the meaning labours slowly up from his swelling breast. No one who has seen him at these moments could go away with an impression that he was a 'man of no mark or likelihood.'* Perhaps the comment of his face and voice is necessary to convey a full idea of his poetry. His language may not be intelligible, but his manner is not to be mistaken. It is clear that he is either mad or inspired. In company, even in a *tête-à-tête*, Mr. Wordsworth is often silent, indolent, and reserved. If he is become verbose and oracular of late years, he was not so in his better days. He threw out a bold or an indifferent remark without either effort or pretension, and relapsed into musing again. He shone most (because he seemed most roused and animated) in reciting his own poetry, or in talking about it. He sometimes gave striking views of his feelings and trains of association in composing certain passages; or if one did not always understand his distinctions, still there was no want of interest—there was a latent meaning worth inquiring into, like a vein of ore that one cannot exactly hit upon at the moment, but of which there are sure indications. His standard of poetry is high and severe, almost to exclusiveness. He admits of nothing below, scarcely of any thing above himself. It is fine to hear him talk of the way in which certain subjects should have been treated by eminent poets, according to his notions of the art. Thus he finds fault with Dryden's description of Bacchus in the *Alexander's Feast*, as if he were a mere good-looking youth, or boon companion—

> Flushed with a purple grace,
> He shews his honest face*—

instead of representing the God returning from the conquest of India, crowned with vine-leaves, and drawn by panthers, and followed by troops of satyrs, of wild men and animals that he had tamed. You would think, in hearing him speak on this subject, that you saw Titian's picture of the meeting of *Bacchus and Ariadne*—so classic were his conceptions, so glowing his style. Milton is his great idol, and he sometimes dares to compare himself with him. His Sonnets, indeed, have something of the same high-raised tone and prophetic spirit. Chaucer is another prime favourite of his, and he has been at the pains to modernise some of the Canterbury Tales.* Those persons who look upon Mr. Wordsworth as a merely puerile writer, must be rather at a loss to account for his strong predilection for such geniuses as Dante and Michael Angelo. We do not think our author has any very cordial sympathy with Shakespear. How should he? Shakespear was the least of an egotist of any body in the world. He does not much relish the variety and scope of dramatic composition. 'He hates those interlocutions between Lucius and Caius.'* Yet Mr. Wordsworth himself wrote a tragedy when he was young;* and we have heard the following energetic lines quoted from it, as put into the mouth of a person smit with remorse for some rash crime:

> ————Action is momentary,
> The motion of a muscle this way or that;
> Suffering is long, obscure, and infinite!*

Perhaps for want of light and shade, and the unshackled spirit of the drama, this performance was never brought forward. Our critic has a great dislike to Gray, and a fondness for Thomson and Collins. It is mortifying to hear him speak of Pope and Dryden, whom, because they have been supposed to have all the possible excellences of poetry, he will allow to have none. Nothing, however, can be fairer, or more amusing, than the way in which he sometimes exposes the unmeaning verbiage of modern poetry. Thus, in the beginning of Dr. Johnson's *Vanity of Human Wishes*—

> Let observation with extensive view
> Survey mankind from China to Peru*—

he says there is a total want of imagination accompanying the words, the same idea is repeated three times under the disguise of a different phraseology: it comes to this—'let *observation*, with extensive *observation*, *observe* mankind;' or take away the first line, and the second,

> Survey mankind from China to Peru,

literally conveys the whole. Mr. Wordsworth is, we must say, a perfect Drawcansir* as to prose writers. He complains of the dry reasoners and matter-of-fact people for their want of *passion*; and he is jealous of the rhetorical declaimers and rhapsodists as trenching on the province of poetry. He condemns all French writers (as well of poetry as prose) in the lump. His list in this way is indeed small. He approves of Walton's Angler,* Paley, and some other writers of an inoffensive modesty of pretension. He also likes books of voyages and travels, and Robinson Crusoe. In art, he greatly esteems Bewick's wood-cuts,* and Waterloo's sylvan etchings.* But he sometimes takes a higher tone, and gives his mind fair play. We have known him enlarge with a noble intelligence and enthusiasm on Nicolas Poussin's fine landscape-compositions, pointing out the unity of design that pervades them, the superintending mind, the imaginative principle that brings all to bear on the same end; and declaring he would not give a rush for any landscape that did not express the time of day, the climate, the period of the world it was meant to illustrate, or had not this character of *wholeness* in it. His eye also does justice to Rembrandt's fine and masterly effects. In the way in which that artist works something out of nothing, and transforms the stump of a tree, a common figure into an *ideal* object, by the gorgeous light and shade thrown upon it, he perceives an analogy to his own mode of investing the minute details of nature with an atmosphere of sentiment; and in pronouncing Rembrandt to be a man of genius, feels that he strengthens his own claim to the title. It has been said of Mr. Wordsworth, that 'he hates conchology, that he hates the Venus of Medicis.'* But these, we hope, are mere epigrams and *jeux-d'esprit*, as far from truth as they are free from malice; a sort of running satire or critical clenches—

> Where one for sense and one for rhyme
> Is quite sufficient at one time.*

We think, however, that if Mr. Wordsworth had been a more liberal and candid critic, he would have been a more sterling writer. If a greater number of sources of pleasure had been open to him, he would have communicated pleasure to the world more frequently. Had he been less fastidious in pronouncing sentence on the works of others, his own would have been received more favourably, and treated more leniently. The current of his feelings is deep, but narrow; the range of his understanding is lofty and aspiring rather than discursive. The force, the originality, the absolute truth and identity with which he feels some things, makes him indifferent to so many others. The simplicity and enthusiasm of his feelings, with respect to nature, renders him bigotted and intolerant in his judgments of men and things. But it happens to him, as to others, that his strength lies in his weakness; and perhaps we have no right to complain. We might get rid of the cynic and the egotist, and find in his stead a common-place man. We should 'take the good the Gods provide us:'* a fine and original vein of poetry is not one of their most contemptible gifts, and the rest is scarcely worth thinking of, except as it may be a mortification to those who expect perfection from human nature; or who have been idle enough at some period of their lives, to deify men of genius as possessing claims above it. But this is a chord that jars, and we shall not dwell upon it.

Lord Byron we have called, according to the old proverb, 'the spoiled child of fortune:' Mr. Wordsworth might plead, in mitigation of some peculiarities, that he is 'the spoiled child of disappointment.' We are convinced, if he had been early a popular poet, he would have borne his honours meekly,* and would have been a person of great *bonhommie* and frankness of disposition. But the sense of injustice and of undeserved ridicule sours the temper and narrows the views. To have produced works of genius, and to find them neglected or treated with scorn, is one of the heaviest trials of human patience. We exaggerate our own merits when they are denied by others, and are apt to grudge and cavil at every particle of praise bestowed on those to whom we feel a conscious superiority. In mere self-defence we turn against the world, when it turns against us; brood over the undeserved slights we receive; and thus the genial current of the soul is stopped,* or vents itself in effusions of petulance and self-conceit. Mr. Wordsworth has thought too much of contemporary critics and criticism; and less than he ought of the award of posterity, and of the opinion, we do not say of private friends, but of those who were made so by their admiration of his genius. He did not court popularity by a conformity to established models, and he ought not to have been surprised that his originality was not understood as a matter of course. He has *gnawed too much on the bridle*; and has often thrown out crusts to the critics, in mere defiance or as a point of honour when he was challenged, which otherwise his own good sense would have withheld. We suspect that Mr. Wordsworth's feelings are a little morbid in this respect, or that he resents censure more than he is gratified by praise. Otherwise, the tide has turned much in his favour of late years—he has a large body of determined partisans—and is at present sufficiently in request with the public to save or relieve him from the last necessity to which a man of genius can be reduced—that of becoming the God of his own idolatry!*

ON THE PLEASURE OF HATING

THERE is a spider crawling along the matted floor of the room where I sit (not the one which has been so well allegorised in the admirable *Lines to a Spider*,* but another of the same edifying breed)—he runs with heedless, hurried haste, he hobbles awkwardly towards me, he stops—he sees the giant shadow before him, and, at a loss whether to retreat or proceed, meditates his huge foe—but as I do not start up and seize upon the straggling caitiff, as he would upon a hapless fly within his toils, he takes heart, and ventures on, with mingled cunning, impudence, and fear. As he passes me, I lift up the matting to assist his escape, am glad to get rid of the unwelcome intruder, and shudder at the recollection after he is gone. A child, a woman, a clown, or a moralist a century ago, would have crushed the little reptile to death—my philosophy has got beyond that—I bear the creature no ill-will, but still I hate the very sight of it. The spirit of malevolence survives the practical exertion of it. We learn to curb our will and keep our overt actions within the bounds of humanity, long before we can subdue our sentiments and imaginations to the same mild tone. We give up the external demonstration, the *brute* violence, but cannot part with the essence or principle of hostility. We do not tread upon the poor little animal in question (that seems barbarous and pitiful!) but we regard it with a sort of mystic horror and superstitious loathing. It will ask another hundred years of fine writing and hard thinking to cure us of the prejudice, and make us feel towards this ill-omened tribe with something of 'the milk of human kindness,'* instead of their own shyness and venom.

Nature seems (the more we look into it) made up of antipathies: without something to hate, we should lose the very spring of thought and action. Life would turn to a stagnant pool, were it not ruffled by the jarring interests, the unruly passions of men. The white streak in our own fortunes is brightened (or just rendered visible) by making all around it as dark as possible; so the rainbow paints its form upon the cloud. Is it pride? Is it envy? Is it the force of contrast? Is it weakness or malice? But so it is, that there is a secret affinity, a *hankering* after evil in the human mind, and that it takes a perverse, but a fortunate delight in mischief, since it is a never-failing source of satisfaction. Pure good soon grows insipid, wants variety and spirit. Pain is a bitter-sweet, which never surfeits. Love turns, with a little indulgence, to indifference or disgust: hatred alone is immortal.—Do we not see this principle at work every where? Animals torment and worry one another without mercy: children kill flies for sport: every one reads the accidents and offences in a newspaper, as the cream of the jest: a whole town runs to be present at a fire, and the spectator by no means exults to see it extinguished. It is better to have it so, but it diminishes the interest; and our feelings take part with our passions, rather than with our understandings. Men assemble in crowds, with eager enthusiasm, to witness a tragedy: but if there were an execution going forward in the next street, as Mr. Burke observes,* the theatre would be left empty. A strange cur in a village, an idiot, a crazy woman, are set upon and baited by the whole community. Public nuisances are in the nature of public benefits. How long did the Pope, the Bourbons, and the Inquisition keep the people of England in breath, and supply them with nick-names to vent their spleen upon! Had they done us any harm of late? No: but we have always a quantity of superfluous bile upon the stomach, and we wanted an object to let it out upon. How loth were we to give up our pious belief in ghosts and witches, because we liked to persecute the one, and frighten ourselves to death with the other! It is not the quality so much as the quantity of excitement that we are anxious about: we cannot bear a state of indifference and *ennui*: the mind seems to abhor a *vacuum* as much as ever matter was supposed to do. Even when the spirit of the age* (that is, the progress of intellectual refinement, warring with our natural infirmities) no longer allows us to carry our vindictive and headstrong humours into effect, we try to revive them in description, and keep up the old bugbears, the phantoms of our terror and our hate, in imagination. We burn Guy Faux in effigy, and the hooting and buffeting and maltreating that poor tattered figure of rags and straw makes a festival in every village in England once a year. Protestants and Papists do not now burn one another at the stake: but we subscribe to new editions of *Fox's Book of Martyrs*;* and the secret of the success of the *Scotch Novels* is much the same—they carry us back to the feuds, the heart-burnings, the havoc, the dismay, the wrongs and the revenge of a barbarous age and people—to the rooted prejudices and deadly animosities of sects and parties in politics and

religion, and of contending chiefs and clans in war and intrigue. We feel
the full force of the spirit of hatred with all of them in turn. As we
read, we throw aside the trammels of civilization, the flimsy veil of
humanity. 'Off, you lendings!'* The wild beast resumes its sway
within us, we feel like hunting-animals, and as the hound starts in his
sleep and rushes on the chase in fancy, the heart rouses itself in its
native lair, and utters a wild cry of joy, at being restored once more to
freedom and lawless, unrestrained impulses. Every one has his full
swing, or goes to the Devil his own way. Here are no Jeremy Bentham
Panopticons, none of Mr. Owen's impassable Parallelograms, (Rob
Roy would have spurned and poured a thousand curses on them), no
long calculations of self-interest—the will takes its instant way to its
object; as the mountain-torrent flings itself over the precipice, the
greatest possible good of each individual consists in doing all the mischief he can to his neighbour: that is charming, and finds a sure and
sympathetic chord in every breast! So Mr. Irving, the celebrated
preacher, has rekindled the old, original, almost exploded hell-fire in
the aisles of the Caledonian Chapel,* as they introduce the real water
of the New River at Sadler's Wells,* to the delight and astonishment
of his fair audience. *'Tis pretty, though a plague,** to sit and peep into
the pit of Tophet, to play at *snap-dragon** with flames and brimstone
(it gives a smart electrical shock, a lively fillip to delicate constitutions), and to see Mr. Irving, like a huge Titan, looking as grim and
swarthy as if he had to forge tortures for all the damned! What
a strange being man is! Not content with doing all he can to vex and
hurt his fellows here, 'upon this bank and shoal of time,'* where one
would think there were heart-aches, pain, disappointment, anguish,
tears, sighs, and groans enough, the bigoted maniac takes him to the
top of the high peak of school divinity to hurl him down the yawning
gulf of penal fire; his speculative malice asks eternity to wreak its
infinite spite in, and calls on the Almighty to execute its relentless
doom! The cannibals burn their enemies and eat them, in good-
fellowship with one another: meek Christian divines cast those who
differ from them but a hair's-breadth, body and soul, into hell-fire,
for the glory of God and the good of his creatures! It is well that the
power of such persons is not co-ordinate with their wills: indeed, it is
from the sense of their weakness and inability to control the opinions
of others, that they thus 'outdo termagant,'* and endeavour to frighten
them into conformity by big words and monstrous denunciations.

The pleasure of hating, like a poisonous mineral, eats into the heart of religion, and turns it to rankling spleen and bigotry; it makes patriotism an excuse for carrying fire, pestilence, and famine into other lands: it leaves to virtue nothing but the spirit of censoriousness, and a narrow, jealous, inquisitorial watchfulness over the actions and motives of others. What have the different sects, creeds, doctrines in religion been but so many pretexts set up for men to wrangle, to quarrel, to tear one another in pieces about, like a target as a mark to shoot at? Does any one suppose that the love of country in an Englishman implies any friendly feeling or disposition to serve another, bearing the same name? No, it means only hatred to the French, or the inhabitants of any other country that we happen to be at war with for the time. Does the love of virtue denote any wish to discover or amend our own faults? No, but it atones for an obstinate adherence to our own vices by the most virulent intolerance to human frailties. This principle is of a most universal application. It extends to good as well as evil: if it makes us hate folly, it makes us no less dissatisfied with distinguished merit. If it inclines us to resent the wrongs of others, it impels us to be as impatient of their prosperity. We revenge injuries: we repay benefits with ingratitude. Even our strongest partialities and likings soon take this turn. 'That which was luscious as locusts, anon becomes bitter as coloquintida;'* and love and friendship melt in their own fires. We hate old friends: we hate old books: we hate old opinions; and at last we come to hate ourselves.

I have observed that few of those, whom I have formerly known most intimate, continue on the same friendly footing, or combine the steadiness with the warmth of attachment. I have been acquainted with two or three knots of inseparable companions, who saw each other 'six days in the week,'* that have broken up and dispersed. I have quarrelled with almost all my old friends, (they might say this is owing to my bad temper, but) they have also quarrelled with one another. What is become of 'that set of whist-players,' celebrated by ELIA* in his notable *Epistle to Robert Southey, Esq.* (and now I think of it—that I myself have celebrated* in this very volume) 'that for so many years called Admiral Burney friend?' They are scattered, like last year's snow. Some of them are dead—or gone to live at a distance—or pass one another in the street like strangers; or if they stop to speak, do it as coolly and try to *cut* one another as soon as possible. Some of us have grown rich—others poor. Some have got places under Government—others a *niche* in the Quarterly Review. Some of us have dearly earned a name in the world; whilst others remain in their original privacy. We despise the one; and envy and are glad to mortify the other. Times are changed; we cannot revive our old feelings; and we avoid the sight and are uneasy in the presence of those, who remind us of our infirmity, and put us upon an effort at seeming cordiality, which embarrasses ourselves and does not impose upon our *quondam* associates. Old friendships are like meats served up repeatedly, cold, comfortless, and distasteful. The stomach turns against them. Either constant intercourse and familiarity breed weariness and contempt; or if we meet again after an interval of absence, we appear no longer the same. One is too wise, another too foolish for us; and we wonder we did not find this out before. We are disconcerted and kept in a state of continual alarm by the wit of one, or tired to death of the dulness of another. The *good things* of the first (besides leaving stings behind them) by repetition grow stale, and lose their startling effect; and the insipidity of the last becomes intolerable. The most amusing or instructive companion is at best like a favourite volume, that we wish after a time to *lay upon the shelf*; but as our friends are not willing to be laid there, this produces a misunderstanding and ill-blood between us.—Or if the zeal and integrity of friendship is not abated, or its career interrupted by any obstacle arising out of its own nature, we look out for other subjects of complaint and sources of dissatisfaction. We begin to criticise each other's dress, looks, and general character. 'Such a one is a pleasant fellow, but it is a pity he sits so late!' Another fails to keep his appointments, and that is a sore that never heals. We get acquainted with some fashionable young men or with a mistress, and wish to introduce our friend; but he is awkward and a sloven, the interview does not answer, and this throws cold water on our intercourse. Or he makes himself obnoxious to opinion—and we shrink from our own convictions on the subject as an excuse for not defending him. All or any of these causes mount up in time to a ground of coolness or irritation—and at last they break out into open violence as the only amends we can make ourselves for suppressing them so long, or the readiest means of banishing recollections of former kindness, so little compatible with our present feelings. We may try to tamper with the wounds or patch up the carcase of departed friendship, but the one will hardly bear the handling, and the other is not worth the trouble of embalming! The only way to be reconciled to old friends is to part with them for good: at a distance we may chance to be thrown back (in a waking dream) upon old times and old feelings: or at any rate, we should not think of renewing our intimacy, till we have fairly *spit our spite*, or said, thought, and felt all the ill we can of each other. Or if we can pick a quarrel with some one else, and make him the scape-goat, this is an excellent contrivance to heal a broken bone. I think I must be friends with Lamb again, since he has written that magnanimous Letter to Southey, and told him a piece of his mind!—I don't know what it is that attaches me to H——* so much, except that he and I, whenever we meet, sit in judgment on another set of old friends, and 'carve them as a dish fit for the Gods.'* There was L— H—,* John Scott,* Mrs. ——,* whose dark raven locks make a picturesque background to our discourse, B—,* who is grown fat, and is, they say, married, R——;* these had all separated long ago, and their foibles are the common link that holds us together. We do not affect to condole or whine over their follies; we enjoy, we laugh at them till we are ready to burst our sides, '*sans* intermission, for hours by the dial.'* We serve up a course of anecdotes, *traits*, master-strokes of character, and cut and hack at them till we are weary. Perhaps some of them are even with us. For my own part, as I once said, I like a friend the better for having faults that one can talk about. 'Then,' said Mrs. ——,* 'you will never cease to be a philanthropist!' Those in question were some of the choice-spirits of the age, not 'fellows of no mark or likelihood;'* and we so far did them justice: but it is well they did not hear what we sometimes said of them. I care little what any one says of me, particularly behind my back, and in the way of critical and analytical discussion—it is looks of dislike and scorn, that I answer with the worst venom of my pen. The expression of the face wounds me more than the expressions of the tongue. If I have in one instance mistaken this expression, or resorted to this remedy where I ought not, I am sorry for it. But the face was too fine over which it mantled, and I am too old to have misunderstood it!...I sometimes go up to ——'s;* and as often as I do, resolve never to go again. I do not find the old homely welcome. The ghost of friendship meets me at the door, and sits with me all dinner-time. They have got a set of fine notions and new acquaintance. Allusions to past occurrences are thought trivial, nor is it always safe to touch upon more general subjects. M.* does not begin as he formerly did every five minutes, 'Fawcett* used to say,' &c. That topic is something worn. The girls are grown up, and have a thousand accomplishments. I perceive there is a jealousy on both sides. They think I give myself airs, and I fancy the same of them. Every time I am asked, 'If I do not think Mr. Washington Irvine* a very fine writer?' I shall not go again till I receive an invitation for Christmas-day in company with Mr. Liston.* The only intimacy I never found to flinch or fade was a purely intellectual one. There was none of the cant of candour in it, none of the whine of mawkish sensibility. Our mutual acquaintance were considered merely as subjects of conversation and knowledge, not at all of affection. We regarded them no more in our experiments than 'mice in an air-pump:'* or like malefactors, they were regularly cut down and given over to the dissecting-knife. We spared neither friend nor foe. We sacrificed human infirmities at the shrine of truth. The skeletons of character might be seen, after the juice was extracted, dangling in the air like flies in cobwebs: or they were kept for future inspection in some refined acid. The demonstration was as beautiful as it was new. There is no surfeiting on gall: nothing keeps so well as a decoction of spleen. We grow tired of every thing but turning others into ridicule, and congratulating ourselves on their defects.

We take a dislike to our favourite books, after a time, for the same reason. We cannot read the same works for ever. Our honey-moon, even though we wed the Muse, must come to an end; and is followed by indifference, if not by disgust. There are some works, those indeed that produce the most striking effect at first by novelty and boldness of outline, that will not bear reading twice: others of a less extravagant character, and that excite and repay attention by a greater nicety of details, have hardly interest enough to keep alive our continued enthusiasm. The popularity of the most successful writers operates to wean us from them, by the cant and fuss that is made about them, by hearing their names everlastingly repeated, and by the number of ignorant and indiscriminate admirers they draw after them:—we as little like to have to drag others from their unmerited obscurity, lest we should be exposed to the charge of affectation and singularity of taste. There is nothing to be said respecting an author that all the world have made up their minds about: it is a thankless as well as hopeless task to recommend one that nobody has ever heard of. To cry up Shakespeare as the God of our idolatry,* seems like a vulgar, national prejudice: to take down a volume of Chaucer, or Spenser, or

Beaumont and Fletcher, or Ford, or Marlowe, has very much the look of pedantry and egotism. I confess it makes me hate the very name of Fame and Genius when works like these are 'gone into the wastes of time,'* while each successive generation of fools is busily employed in reading the trash of the day, and women of fashion gravely join with their waiting-maids in discussing the preference between Paradise Lost and Mr. Moore's Loves of the Angels.* I was pleased the other day on going into a shop to ask, 'If they had any of the *Scotch Novels?*' to be told—'That they had just sent out the last, Sir Andrew Wylie!'*—Mr. Galt will also be pleased with this answer! The reputation of some books is raw and *unaired*: that of others is worm-eaten and mouldy. Why fix our affections on that which we cannot bring ourselves to have faith in, or which others have long ceased to trouble themselves about? I am half afraid to look into Tom Jones, lest it should not answer my expectations at this time of day; and if it did not, I should certainly be disposed to fling it into the fire, and never look into another novel while I lived. But surely, it may be said, there are some works, that, like nature, can never grow old; and that must always touch the imagination and passions alike! Or there are passages that seem as if we might brood over them all our lives, and not exhaust the sentiments of love and admiration they excite: they become favourites, and we are fond of them to a sort of dotage. Here is one:

> ——Sitting in my window
> Printing my thoughts in lawn, I saw a God,
> I thought (but it was you), enter our gates;
> My blood flew out and back again, as fast
> As I had puffed it forth and sucked it in
> Like breath; then was I called away in haste
> To entertain you: never was a man
> Thrust from a sheepcote to a sceptre, raised
> So high in thoughts as I; you left a kiss
> Upon these lips then, which I mean to keep
> From you for ever. I did hear you talk
> Far above singing!*

A passage like this indeed leaves a taste on the palate like nectar, and we seem in reading it to sit with the Gods at their golden tables: but if we repeat it often in ordinary moods, it loses its flavour, becomes vapid, 'the wine of *poetry* is drank, and but the lees remain.'* Or, on the other hand, if we call in the aid of extraordinary circumstances to set it off to advantage, as the reciting it to a friend, or after having our feelings excited by a long walk in some romantic situation, or while we

> —play with Amaryllis in the shade,
> Or with the tangles of Neæra's hair*—

we afterwards miss the accompanying circumstances, and instead of transferring the recollection of them to the favourable side, regret what we have lost, and strive in vain to bring back 'the irrevocable hour'*—wondering in some instances how we survive it, and at the melancholy blank that is left behind! The pleasure rises to its height in some moment of calm solitude or intoxicating sympathy, declines ever after, and from the comparison and a conscious falling-off, leaves rather a sense of satiety and irksomeness behind it....... 'Is it the same in pictures?' I confess it is, with all but those from Titian's hand. I don't know why, but an air breathes from his landscapes, pure, refreshing as if it came from other years; there is a look in his faces that never passes away. I saw one the other day. Amidst the heartless desolation and glittering finery of Fonthill,* there is a portfolio of the Dresden Gallery. It opens, and a young female head looks from it; a child, yet woman grown; with an air of rustic innocence and the graces of a princess, her eyes like those of doves, the lips about to open, a smile of pleasure dimpling the whole face, the jewels sparkling in her crisped hair, her youthful shape compressed in a rich antique dress, as the bursting leaves contain the April buds! Why do I not call up this image of gentle sweetness, and place it as a perpetual barrier between mischance and me?—It is because pleasure asks a greater effort of the mind to support it than pain; and we turn, after a little idle dalliance, from what we love to what we hate!

As to my old opinions, I am heartily sick of them. I have reason, for they have deceived me sadly. I was taught to think, and I was willing to believe, that genius was not a bawd—that virtue was not a mask—that liberty was not a name—that love had its seat in the human heart. Now I would care little if these words were struck out of the dictionary, or if I had never heard them. They are become to my ears a mockery and a dream. Instead of patriots and friends of freedom, I see nothing but the tyrant and the slave, the people linked with kings to rivet on the chains of despotism and superstition. I see folly join with knavery, and together make up public spirit and public opinions. I see the insolent Tory, the blind Reformer, the coward Whig! If mankind had wished for what is right, they might have had it long ago. The theory is plain enough; but they are prone to mischief, 'to every good work reprobate.'* I have seen all that had been done by the mighty yearnings of the spirit and intellect of men, 'of whom the world was not worthy,'* and that promised a proud opening to truth and good through the vista of future years, undone by one man, with just glimmering of understanding enough to feel that he was a king, but not to comprehend how he could be king of a free people! I have seen this triumph celebrated by poets, the friends of my youth and the friends of man, but who were carried away by the infuriate tide that, setting in from a throne, bore down every distinction of right reason before it; and I have seen all those who did not join in applauding this insult and outrage on humanity proscribed, hunted down (they and their friends made a bye-word of), so that it has become an understood thing that no one can live by his talents or knowledge who is not ready to prostitute those talents and that knowledge to betray his species, and prey upon his fellow-man. 'This was some time a mystery: but the time gives evidence of it.'* The echoes of liberty had awakened once more in Spain,* and the morning of human hope dawned again: but that dawn has been overcast by the foul breath of bigotry, and those reviving sounds stifled by fresh cries from the time-rent towers of the Inquisition—man yielding (as it is fit he should) first to brute force, but more to the innate perversity and dastard spirit of his own nature, which leaves no room for farther hope or disappointment. And England, that arch-reformer, that heroic deliverer, that mouther about liberty and tool of power, stands gaping by, not feeling the blight and mildew coming over it, nor its very bones crack and turn to a paste under the grasp and circling folds of this new monster, Legitimacy! In private life do we not see hypocrisy, servility, selfishness, folly, and impudence succeed, while modesty shrinks from the encounter, and merit is trodden under foot? How often is 'the rose plucked from the forehead of a virtuous love to plant a blister there!'* What chance is there of the success of real passion? What certainty of its continuance? Seeing all this as I do, and unravelling the web of human life into its various threads of meanness, spite, cowardice, want of feeling, and want of understanding, of indifference towards others and ignorance of ourselves—seeing custom prevail over all excellence, itself giving way to infamy—mistaken as I have been in my public and private hopes, calculating others from myself, and calculating wrong; always disappointed where I placed most reliance; the dupe of friendship, and the fool of love; have I not reason to hate and to despise myself? Indeed I do; and chiefly for not having hated and despised the world enough.[1]

[1] The only exception to the general drift of this Essay (and that is an exception in theory—I know of none in practice) is, that in reading we always take the right side, and make the case properly our own. Our imaginations are sufficiently excited, we have nothing to do with the matter but as a pure creation of the mind, and we therefore yield to the natural, unwarped impression of good and evil. Our own passions, interests, and prejudices out of the question, or in an abstracted point of view, we judge fairly and conscientiously; for conscience is nothing but the abstract idea of right and wrong. But no sooner have we to act or suffer, than the spirit of contradiction or some other demon comes into play, and there is an end of common sense and reason. Even the very strength of the speculative faculty, or the desire to square things with an *ideal* standard of perfection (whether we can or no) leads perhaps to half the absurdities and miseries of mankind. We are hunting after what we cannot find, and quarrelling with the good within our reach. Among the thousands that have read *The Heart of Mid Lothian** there assuredly never was a single person who did not wish Jeanie Deans success. Even Gentle George was sorry for what he had done, when it was over, though he would have played the same prank the next day: and the *unknown* author, in his immediate character of contributor to Blackwood and the Sentinel, is about as respectable a personage as Daddy Ratton himself. On the stage, every one takes part with Othello against Iago. Do boys at school, in reading Homer, generally side with the Greeks or Trojans?

THE motto of the English nation is 'exclusion.' In this consists our happiness and our pride. If you come to a gentleman's park and pleasure-grounds, you see written up, 'Man-traps and steel-guns set here'—as if he had no pleasure in walking in them, except in the idea of keeping other people out. Having little of the spirit of enjoyment in ourselves, we seek to derive a stupid or sullen satisfaction from the privations and disappointment of others. Every thing resolves itself into an idea of *property*, that is, of something that our neighbours dare not touch, and that we have not the heart to enjoy. The invidious distinction of the *private boxes** arose out of this principle; and has done a great deal of harm. Was it to secure the best place for the best company? Are they filled with peers and peeresses eager to see the play, and enjoying it at the height? On the contrary, they are quite empty; or you see nobody there but Madame VESTRIS and her friends.* But having secured the exclusive privilege and shut others out, this is all the satisfaction we are capable of. The consequence has been, that the nobility and gentry no longer appearing in the open boxes, they have ceased to be the favourite resort of genteel and fashionable company; people no longer go for the chance of sitting in the next box to a prince or a minister of state, of seeing how a courtier smiles on hearing a countess's lisp, or with the hope of being mixed up in splendid confusion with the flower of the land. A certain disrepute is thus thrown upon the boxes, which are left to a sort of second city-company. The partitioning off the *stalls** at the Opera is a part of the same wretched system. Before, a seat in the pit of the Opera was a reputable distinction; every one there was on a footing of equality. This pleasure was envied as getting too common; and to circumscribe it the contrivance of the stalls was invented, by which an implied stigma is thrown on the rest of the pit, and where fine gentlemen and ladies, admitted under lock and key, and sitting at English ease, look back on the crowd behind them like the footmen behind their chairs. Whether it is our unsocial temper, or our system of equality and the dread of encroachment, that produces this exclusive spirit, we cannot say; but the fruit is most bitter and painful. The

other night an attempt was made to shut out *improper* people from
the theatre; did the *proper* people go the more the next night? No!
their object was to prevent others from going; and if by this under-
hand mode the doors of the theatre were finally closed, it would afford
an additional gratification to their malice and poverty of imagination.
We hope there is more genuine old English honesty and feeling, and
more of a cordial play-going humour left in the public than to allow
of such a catastrophe. There is no calculating the mischief that would
ensue. There is not a person in this great metropolis who does not rise
with a pleasanter feeling in the morning, and eat his breakfast with
a better relish, from a consciousness (whether adverted to or not) that
he may go to which of the great theatres he pleases in the evening.
There is not a chimney-sweeper who does not get his shilling's worth
of pleasure out of them once a year, which must serve him the remainder. There is not a young lady who mopes away her time in the
country who does not console herself with the thought of seeing
Mr. CHARLES KEMBLE* act when she comes up to town in the winter. The stage is become part of the vital existence of this civilised
country; and our circulation cannot go on well without it. To the real
lover of the drama, to see the fall of one of our great theatres is like
cutting off one of his hands. Our recollections of the stage, of the
master-pieces of wit and pathos that support it, of the proud or happy
names that adorn it, of the SIDDONSES, the KEMBLES, the JORDANS,
the LEWISES, the QUICKS, the MUNDENS, the COOKES, the Little
SIMMONSES, the BANNISTERS, the SUETTS—what are they but
recollections of ourselves, of our liveliest pleasures, of our youthful
hopes, 'dear as the ruddy drops that visit the sad heart?'* and shall we
close the door on all these bright visions, and let a noble pile crumble
into ruins and bury all these cherished names in common rubbish, so
that we can never think or speak of them again but with regret and
shame, and not deem it one of the greatest calamities that can happen
to us? Whoever sees a play ought to be better and more sociable for it;
for he has something to talk about, some ideas and feelings in common with his neighbours. Even the players, as they pass along the
streets, glance a light upon the day; and (sports of fortune, puppets of
opinion as they are) give us a livelier interest in humanity, of which
they are the representatives. If we meet Mrs. D——* in Cranbourn-
alley, we get up the narrow part of King-street without being jostled
by any one. It would be one of the worst signs of the times to find that

Covent-garden was no more; and would be our first approach to the state of those old and once flourishing cities in other parts of the world, where you see the skeletons of mighty theatres still standing as monuments of the past, and the magnificence that raised them mouldering in oblivion.

THE Spirit of Controversy has often been arraigned as the source of much bitterness and vexation, as productive of 'envy, malice, and all uncharitableness:'* and the charge, no doubt, is too well founded. But it is said to be *an ill wind that blows nobody good*; and there are few evils in life that have not some qualifying circumstance attending them. It is one of the worst consequences of this very spirit of controversy that it has led men to regard things too much in a single and exaggerated point of view. Truth is not one thing, but has many aspects and many shades of difference; it is neither all black nor all white; sees something wrong on its own side, something right in others; makes concessions to an adversary, allowances for human frailty, and is nearer akin to charity than the dealers in controversy or the declaimers against it are apt to imagine. The bigot and partisan (influenced by the very spirit he finds fault with) sees nothing in the endless disputes which have tormented and occupied men's thoughts but an abuse of learning and a waste of time: the philosopher may still find an excuse for so bad or idle a practice. One frequent objection made to the incessant wrangling and collision of sects and parties is, *What does it all come to?* And the answer is, *What would they have done without it?* The pleasure of the chase, or the benefit derived from it, is not to be estimated by the value of the game after it is caught, so much as by the difficulty of starting it and the exercise afforded to the body and the excitement of the animal spirits in hunting it down: and so it is in the exercises of the mind and the pursuit of truth, which are chiefly valuable (perhaps) less for their results when discovered, than for their affording continual scope and employment to the mind in its endeavours to reach the fancied goal, without its being ever (or but seldom) able to attain it. *Regard the end*, is an ancient saying, and a good one, if it does not mean that we are to forget the *beginning* and the *middle*. By insisting on the ultimate value of things when all is over, we may acquire the character of *grave* men, but not of wise ones. *Passe pour cela*.* If we would set up such a sort of fixed and final standard of moral truth and worth, we had better try to construct life over again, so as to make it a *punctum stans*,* and not a thing in progress; for as it is, every end, before it can be realised, implies a previous imagination, a warm interest in, and an active pursuit of, itself, all which are integral and vital parts of human existence, and it is a begging of the question to say that an end is only of value in itself, and not as it draws out the living resources, and satisfies the original capacities of human nature. When the play is over, the curtain drops, and we see nothing but a green cloth; but before this, there have been five acts of brilliant scenery and high-wrought declamation, which, if we come to plain matter-of-fact and history, are still something. According to the contrary theory, nothing is real but a blank. This flatters the paradoxical pride of man, whose motto is, *all or none.* Look at that pile of school divinity! Behold where the demon of controversy lies buried! The huge tomes are mouldy and worm-eaten:—did their contents the less eat into the brain, or corrode the heart, or stir the thoughts, or fill up the void of lassitude and *ennui* in the minds of those who wrote them? Though now laid aside and forgotten, if they had not once had a host of readers, they would never have been written; and their hard and solid bulk asked the eager tooth of curiosity and zeal to pierce through it. We laugh to see their ponderous dulness weighed in scales, and sold for waste paper. We should not laugh too soon. On the smallest difference of faith or practice discussed in them, the fate of kingdoms hung suspended; and not merely so (which was a trifle) but Heaven and Hell trembled in the balance, according to the full persuasion of our pious forefathers. Many a drop of blood flowed in the field or on the scaffold, from these tangled briars and thorns of controversy; many a man marched to a stake to bear testimony to the most frivolous and incomprehensible of their dogmas. This was an untoward consequence; but if it was an evil to be burnt at a stake, it was well and becoming to have an opinion (whether right or wrong) for which a man was willing to be burnt at a stake. Read BAXTER's *Controversial Works*:* consider the flames of zeal, the tongues of fire, the heights of faith, the depths of subtlety, which they unfold, as in a darkly illuminated scroll; and then ask how much we are gainers by an utter contempt and indifference to all this? We wonder at the numberless volumes of sermons that have been written, preached, and printed on the Arian and Socinian controversies, on Calvinism and Arminianism, on surplices and stoles, on infant or adult baptism, on image-worship and the defacing of images; and we forget that it employed the preacher all the week to prepare his sermon (be the subject what it

would) for the next Lord's-day, with infinite collating of texts, authorities, and arguments; that his flock were no less edified by listening to
it on the following Sunday; and how many *David Deans's* came away
convinced that they had been listening to the 'root of the matter!'*
See that group collected after service-time and poring over the grave-
stones in the churchyard, from whence, to the eye of faith, a light
issues that points to the skies! See them disperse; and as they take
different paths homeward while the evening closes in, still discoursing
of the true doctrine and the glad tidings they have heard, how 'their
hearts burn within them by the way!'* Then again, we should set
down, among other items in the account, how the school-boy is put to
it to remember the text, and how the lazy servant-wench starts up to
find herself asleep in church-time! Such is the business of human
life; and we, who fancy ourselves above it, are only so much the more
taken up with follies of our own. We look down in this age of reason
on those controverted points and nominal distinctions which formerly
kept up such 'a coil and pudder'* in the world, as idle and ridiculous,
because we are not parties to them; but if it was the *egotism* of our
predecessors that magnified them beyond all rational bounds, it is no
less egotism in us who undervalue their opinions and pursuits because
they are not ours; and, indeed, to leave egotism out of human nature,
is 'to leave the part of *Hamlet* out of the play of *Hamlet.*'* Or what are
we the better with our *Utilitarian Controversies*, Mr. TAYLOR's
discourses* (delivered in canonicals) against the evidence of the
Christian religion, or the changes of ministry and disagreements
between the Duke of WELLINGTON and the Duke of NEWCASTLE?*

> Strange! that such difference should be
> 'Twixt Tweedledum and Tweedledee!*

But the prevalence of religious controversy is reproached with
fomenting spiritual pride and intolerance, and sowing heart-burnings,
jealousies, and fears, 'like a thick scurf o'er life;'* yet, had it not been
for this, we should have been tearing one another to pieces like sav-
ages for fragments of raw flesh, or quarrelling with a herd of swine for
a windfall of acorns under an oak-tree. The world has never yet done,
and will never be able to do, without some apple of discord—some
bone of contention—any more than courts of law can do without
pleadings, or hospitals without the sick. When a thing ceases to be
a subject of controversy, it ceases to be a subject of interest. Why need

we regret the various hardships and persecutions for conscience-sake, when men only clung closer to their opinions in consequence? They loved their religion in proportion as they paid dear for it. Nothing could keep the Dissenters from going to a conventicle while it was declared an unlawful assembly, and was the high road to a prison or the plantations—take away tests and fines,* and make the road open and easy, and the sect dwindles gradually into insignificance. A thing is supposed to be worth nothing that costs nothing. Besides, there is always pretty nearly the same quantity of malice afloat in the world; though with the change of time and manners it may become a finer poison, and kill by more unseen ways. When the sword has done its worst, slander, 'whose edge is sharper than the sword,'* steps in to keep the blood from stagnating. Instead of slow fires and paper caps fastened round the heads of the victims, we arrive at the same end by the politer way of nicknames and anonymous criticism. *Blackwood's Magazine* is the modern version of Fox's *Book of Martyrs*. Discard religion and politics (the two grand topics of controversy), and people would hate each other as cordially, and torment each other as effectually about the preference to be given to MOZART or ROSSINI, to MALIBRAN or PASTA.* We indeed fix upon the most excellent things, as God, our country, and our King, to account for the excess of our zeal; but this depends much less upon the goodness of our cause than on the strength of our passions, and our overflowing gall and rooted antipathy to whatever stands in the way of our conceit and obstinacy. We set up an idol (as we set up a mark to shoot at) for others to bow down to, on peril of our utmost displeasure, let the value of it be what it may—

> Of whatsoe'er descent his Godhead be,
> Stock, stone, or other homely pedigree,
> In his defence his servants are as bold
> As if he had been born of beaten gold.*

It is, however, but fair to add, in extenuation of the evils of controversy, that if the points at issue had been quite clear, or the advantage all on one side, they would not have been so liable to be contested about. We condemn controversy, because we would have matters all our own way, and think that ours is the only side that has a title to be heard. We imagine that there is but one view of a subject that is right; and that all the rest being plainly and wilfully wrong, it is a shocking waste of speech, and a dreadful proof of prejudice and party spirit, to have a word to say in their defence. But this is a want of liberality and comprehension of mind. For in general we dispute either about things respecting which we are a good deal in the dark, and where both parties are very possibly in the wrong, and may be left to find out their mutual error; or about those points, where there is an opposition of interests and passions, and where it would be by no means safe to cut short the debate by making one party judges for the other. They must, therefore, be left to fight it out as well as they can; and, between the extremes of folly and violence, to strike a balance of common sense and even-handed justice. Every sect or party will, of course, run into extravagance and partiality; but the probability is, that there is some ground of argument, some appearance of right, to justify the grossest bigotry and intolerance. The fury of the combatants is excited because there is something to be said on the other side of the question. If men were as infallible as they suppose themselves, they would not dispute. If every novelty were well-founded, truth might be discovered by a receipt; but as antiquity does not always turn out an old woman, this accounts for the *vis inertiæ** of the mind in so often pausing and setting its face against innovation. Authority has some advantages to recommend it as well as reason, or it would long ago have been scouted. Aristocracy and democracy, monarchy and republicanism, are not all pure good or pure evil, though the abettors or antagonists of each think so, and that all the mischief arises from others entertaining any doubt about the question, and insisting on carrying their absurd theories into practice. The French and English are grossly prejudiced against each other; but still the interests of each are better taken care of under this exaggerated notion than if that vast mass of rights and pretensions, which each is struggling for, were left to the tender mercies and ruthless candour of the other side. '*Every man for himself and God for us all*' is a rule that will apply here. Controversy, therefore, is a necessary evil or good (call it which you will) till all differences of opinion or interest are reconciled, and absolute certainty or perfect indifference alike takes away the possibility or the temptation to litigation and quarrels. We need be under no immediate alarm of coming to such a conclusion. There is always room for doubt, food for contention. While we are engrossed with one controversy, indeed, we think every thing else is clear; but as soon as one point is settled, we begin to cavil and start objections to that which had before been taken for gospel. The Reformers thought only of opposing the Church of Rome, and never once anticipated the schisms and animosities which arose among Protestants: the Dissenters, in carrying their point against the Church of England, did not dream of that crop of infidelity and scepticism which, to their great horror and scandal, sprung up in the following age, from their claim of free inquiry and private judgment. The *non-essentials* of religion first came into dispute; then the essentials. Our own opinion, we fancy, is founded on a rock; the rest we regard as stubble. But no sooner is one out-work of established faith or practice demolished, than another is left a defenceless mark for the enemy, and the engines of wit and sophistry immediately begin to batter it. Thus we proceed step by step, till, passing through the several gradations of vanity and paradox, we come to doubt whether we stand on our head or our heels, alternately deny the existence of spirit and matter, maintain that black is white, call evil good and good evil, and defy anyone to prove the contrary. As faith is the prop and cement that upholds society by opposing fixed principles as a barrier against the inroads of passion, so reason is the *menstruum* which dissolves it by leaving nothing sufficiently firm or unquestioned in our opinions to withstand the current and bias of inclination. Hence the decay and ruin of states—then barbarism, sloth, and ignorance—and so we commence the circle again of building up all that it is possible to conceive out of a rude chaos, and the obscure shadowings of things, and then pulling down all that we have built up, till not a trace of it is left. Such is the effect of the ebb and flow and restless agitation of the human mind.

34

THE FREE ADMISSION

A FREE Admission is the *lotos* of the mind: the leaf in which your name is inscribed as having the privileges of the *entrée* for the season is of an oblivious quality—an antidote for half the ills of life. I speak here not of a purchased but of a gift-ticket, an emanation of the generosity of the Managers, a token of conscious desert. With the first you can hardly bring yourself to go to the theatre; with the last, you cannot keep away. If you have paid five guineas for a free-admission for the season, this *free-admission* turns to a mere slavery. You seem to have done a foolish thing, and to have committed an extravagance under the plea of economy. You are struck with remorse. You are impressed with a conviction that pleasure is not to be bought. You have paid for your privilege in the lump, and you receive the benefit in driblets. The five pounds you are out of pocket does not meet with an adequate compensation the first night, or on any single occasion—you must come again, and use double diligence to strike a balance to make up your large arrears; instead of an obvious saving, it hangs as a dead-weight on your satisfaction all the year; and the improvident price you have paid for them kills every ephemeral enjoyment, and poisons the flattering illusions of the scene. You have incurred a debt, and must go every night to redeem it; and as you do not like being tied to the oar, or making a toil of a pleasure, you stay away altogether; give up the promised luxury as a bad speculation; sit sullenly at home, or bend your loitering feet in any other direction; and putting up with the first loss, resolve never to be guilty of the like folly again. But it is not thus with the possessor of a Free Admission, truly so called. His is a pure pleasure, a clear gain. He feels none of these irksome qualms and misgivings. He marches to the theatre like a favoured lover; if he is compelled to absent himself, he feels all the impatience and compunction of a prisoner. The portal of the Temple of the Muses stands wide open to him, closing the vista of the day—when he turns his back upon it at night with steps gradual and slow, mingled with the common crowd, but conscious of a virtue which they have not, he says, 'I shall come again to-morrow!' In passing through the streets, he casts a side-long, careless glance at the playbills: he reads the papers chiefly with a view to see what is the play for the following day, or the ensuing week. If it is something new, he is glad; if it is old, he is resigned—but he goes in either case. His steps bend mechanically that way—pleasure becomes a habit, and habit a duty—he fulfils his destiny—he walks deliberately along Long-acre (you may tell a man going to the play, and whether he pays or has a free admission)—quickens his pace as he turns the corner of Bow-street, and arrives breathless and in haste at the welcome spot, where on presenting himself, he receives a passport that is a release from care, thought, toil, for the evening, and wafts him into the regions of the blest! What is it to him how the world turns round if the play goes on; whether empires rise or fall, so that Covent-Garden stands its ground? Shall he plunge into the void of politics, that volcano burnt-out with the cold, sterile, sightless lava, hardening all around? or con over the registers of births, deaths, and marriages, when he may be present at Juliet's wedding, and gaze on Juliet's tomb? or shall he wonder at the throng of coaches in Regent-street, when he can feast his eyes with the coach (the fairy-vision of his childhood) in which Cinderella rides to the ball? Here (by the help of that *Open Sessame!* a Free Admission), ensconced in his favourite niche, looking from the 'loop-holes of retreat'* in the second circle, he views the pageant of the world played before him; melts down years to moments; sees human life, like a gaudy shadow, glance across the stage; and here tastes of all earth's bliss, the sweet without the bitter, the honey without the sting, and plucks ambrosial fruits and amaranthine flowers (placed by the enchantress Fancy within his reach,) without having to pay a tax for it at the time, or repenting of it afterwards. 'He is all ear and eye, and drinks in sounds or sights that might create a soul under the ribs of death.'* 'The fly,' says Gay, 'that sips treacle, is lost in the sweets:'* so he that has a free-admission forgets every thing else. Why not? It is the cheap and enviable transfer of his being from the real to the unreal world, and the changing half his life into a dream. 'Oh! leave me to my repose,'* in my beloved corner at Covent Garden Theatre! This (and not 'the arm-chair at an inn,' though that too, at other times, and under different circumstances, is not without its charms,) is to me 'the throne of felicity.'* If I have business that would detain me from this, I put it off till the morrow; if I have friends that call in just at the moment, let them go away under pain of bearing my maledictions with them. What is there in their conversation to atone to me for the loss of one quarter of an hour at the 'witching time of night?'* If it is on indifferent subjects, it is flat and insipid; if it grows animated and interesting, it requires a painful effort, and begets a feverish excitement. But let me once reach, and fairly establish myself in this favourite seat, and I can bid a gay defiance to mischance,* and leave debts and duns, friends and foes, objections and arguments, far behind me. I would, if I could, have it surrounded with a balustrade of gold, for it has been to me a palace of delight. There golden thoughts unbidden betide me, and golden visions come to me. There the dance, the laugh, the song, the scenic deception greet me; there are wafted Shakspear's winged words, or Otway's plaintive lines; and there how often have I heard young Kemble's voice,* trembling at its own beauty, and prolonging its liquid tones, like the murmur of the billowy surge on sounding shores! There I no longer torture a sentence or strain a paradox: the mind is full without an effort, pleased without asking why. It inhales an atmosphere of joy, and is steeped in all the luxury of woe. To show how much sympathy has to do with the effect, let us suppose any one to have a free admission to the rehearsals of a morning, what mortal would make use of it? One might as well be at the bottom of a well, or at the top of St. Paul's for any pleasure we should derive from the finest tragedy or comedy. No, a play is nothing without an audience, it is a satisfaction too great and too general not to be shared with others. But reverse this cold and comfortless picture—let the eager crowd beset the theatre-doors 'like bees in spring-time, when the sun with Taurus rides'*—let the boxes be filled with innocence and beauty like beds of lilies on the first night of Isabella or Belvidera,* see the flutter, the uneasy delight of expectation, see the big tear roll down the cheek of sensibility as the story proceeds—let us listen to the deep thunder of the pit, or catch the gallery's shout at some true master-stroke of passion; and we feel that a thousand hearts are beating in our bosoms, and hail the sparkling illusion reflected in a thousand eyes. The stage has, therefore, been justly styled 'a discipline of humanity;'* for there is no place where the social principle is called forth with such strength and harmony, by a powerful interest in a common object. A crowd is everywhere else oppressive; but the fuller the play-house, the more intimately and cordially do we sympathize with every individual in it. Empty benches have as bad an effect on the spectator as on the players. This is one reason why so many mistakes are made with respect to plays and players, ere they come before the public. The taste is crude and uninformed till it is ripened by the blaze of lighted lamps and the sunshine of happy faces: the cold, critical faculty, the judgment of Managers and Committees asks the glow of sympathy and the buzz of approbation to prompt and guide it. We judge in a crowd with the sense and feelings of others; and from the very strength of the impression, fancy we should have come to the same unavoidable conclusion had we been left entirely to ourselves. Let any one try the experiment by reading a manuscript play, or seeing it acted—or by hearing a candidate for the stage rehearse behind the scenes, or *top* his part after the orchestra have performed their fatal prelude. Nor is the air of a playhouse favourable only to social feel-ing—it aids the indulgence of solitary musing. The brimming cup of joy or sorrow is full; but it runs over to other thoughts and subjects. We can there (nowhere better) 'retire, the world shut out, our thoughts call home.'* We hear the revelry and the shout, but 'the still, small voice'* of other years and cherished recollections is not wanting. It is pleasant to hear Miss Ford* repeat *Love's Catechism*, or Mrs. Humby¹* sing 'I cannot marry Crout:' but the ear is not therefore deaf to Mrs. Jordan's laugh in Nell;* Mrs. Goodall's Rosalind* still haunts the glades of Arden, and the echo of Amiens' song, 'Blow, blow, thou win-ter's wind,' lingers through a lapse of thirty years. A pantomime (the Little Red Riding-Hood) recalls the innocence of our childish thoughts: a dance (the Minuet de la Cour) throws us back to the gor-geous days of Louis XIV. and tells us that the age of chivalry is gone for ever.* Who will be the Mrs. Siddons of a distant age? What future Kean shall 'strut and fret his hour upon the stage,'* full of genius and free from errors? What favourite actor or actress will be taking their farewell benefit a hundred years hence? What plays and what players will then amuse the town? Oh, many-coloured scenes of human life! where are ye more truly represented than in the mirror of the stage? or where is that eternal principle of vicissitude which rules over ye, the painted pageant and the sudden gloom, more strikingly exemplified than here? At the entrance to our great theatres, in large capitals over the front of the stage, might be written MUTABILITY! Does not the curtain that falls each night on the pomps and vanities it was with-drawn awhile to reveal (and the next moment all is dark) afford a fine moral lesson? Here, in small room, is crowded the map of human life;

¹ This lady is not, it is true, at Covent-Garden: I wish she were!

the lengthened, varied scroll is unfolded like rich tapestry with its quaint and flaunting devices spread out; whatever can be saved from the giddy whirl of ever-rolling time and of this round orb, which moves on and never stops,[2] all that can strike the sense, can touch the heart, can stir up laughter or call tears from their secret source, is here treasured up and displayed ostentatiously—here is Fancy's motley wardrobe, the masks of all the characters that were ever played—here is a glass set up clear and large enough to show us our own features and those of all mankind—here, in this enchanted mirror, are represented, not darkly, but in vivid hues and bold relief, the struggle of Life and Death, the momentary pause between the cradle and the grave, with charming hopes and fears, terror and pity in a thousand modes, strange and ghastly apparitions, the events of history, the fictions of poetry (warm from the heart); all these, and more than can be numbered in my feeble page, fill that airy space where the green curtain rises, and haunt it with evanescent shapes and indescribable yearnings.

> See o'er the stage the ghost of Hamlet stalks,
> Othello rages, Desdemona mourns,
> And poor Monimia pours her soul in love.*

Who can collect into one audible pulsation the thoughts and feelings that in the course of his life all these together have occasioned; or what heart, if it could recall them at once, and in their undiminished power and plenitude, would not burst with the load? Let not the style be deemed exaggerated, but tame and creeping, that attempts to do justice to this high and pregnant theme, and let tears blot out the unequal lines that the pen traces! Quaffing these delights, inhaling this atmosphere, brooding over these visions, this long trail of glory, is the possessor of a Free Admission to be blamed if 'he takes his ease'* at the play; and turning theatrical recluse, and forgetful of himself and his friends, devotes himself to the study of the drama, and to dreams of the past? By constant habit (having nothing to do, little else to think of), he becomes a tippler of the dews of Castaly*—a dram-drinker on Mount Parnassus. He tastes the present moment, while a rich sea of pleasure presses to his lip and engulfs him round. The noise, the glare, the warmth, the company, produce a sort of listless intoxication, and clothe the pathos and the wit with a bodily sense. There is a weight, a closeness even, in the air, that makes it difficult to breathe out of it. The custom

---

[2] 'Mais vois la rapidité de cet astre qui vole et ne s'arrête jamais.'—*New Eloise.*

of going to the play night after night becomes a relief, a craving, a necessity—one cannot do without it. To sit alone is intolerable, to be in company is worse; we are attracted with pleasing force to the spot where 'all that mighty heart is beating still.'* It is not that perhaps there is any thing new or fine to see—if there is, we attend to it—but at any time, it kills time and saves the trouble of thinking. O, Covent Garden! 'thy *freedom* hath made me effeminate!'* It has hardly left me power to write this description of it. I am become its slave, I have no other sense or interest left. There I sit and lose the hours I live beneath the sky, without the power to stir, without any determination to stay. 'Teddy the Tiler'* is become familiar to me, and, as it were, a part of my existence: 'Robert the Devil'* has cast his spell over me. I have seen both thirty times at least, (no offence to the Management!) and could sit them out thirty times more. I am bed-rid in the lap of luxury; am grown callous and inert with perpetual excitement.

>   ——What avails from iron chains
>   Exempt, if rosy fetters bind as fast?*

I have my favourite box too, as Beau Brummell had his favourite leg;* one must decide on something, not to be always deciding. Perhaps I may have my reasons too—perhaps into the box next to mine a Grace enters; perhaps from thence an air divine breathes a glance (of heaven's own brightness), kindles contagious fire;—but let us turn all such thoughts into the lobbies. These may be considered as an Arabesque border round the inclosed tablet of human life. If the Muses reign within, Venus sports heedless, but not unheeded without. Here a bevy of fair damsels, richly clad, knit with the Graces and the Hours in dance, lead on 'the frozen winter and the pleasant spring!'* Would I were allowed to attempt a list of some of them, and Cowley's *Gallery** would blush at mine! But this is a licence which only poetry, and not even a Free Admission can give. I can now understand the attachment to a player's life, and how impossible it is for those who are once engaged in it ever to wean themselves from it. If the merely witnessing the bustle and the splendour of the scene as an idle spectator creates such a fascination, and flings such a charm over it, how much more must this be the case with those who have given all their time and attention to it—who regard it as the sole means of distinction—with whom even the monotony and mortifications must please—and who, instead of being passive, casual votaries, are the dispensers of the bounty of the gods, and the high-priests at the altar?

35

THE LETTER-BELL

COMPLAINTS are frequently made of the vanity and shortness of human life, when, if we examine its smallest details, they present a world by themselves. The most trifling objects, retraced with the eye of memory, assume the vividness, the delicacy, and importance of insects seen through a magnifying glass. There is no end of the brilliancy or the variety. The habitual feeling of the love of life may be compared to 'one entire and perfect chrysolite,'* which, if analyzed, breaks into a thousand shining fragments. Ask the sum-total of the value of human life, and we are puzzled with the length of the account, and the multiplicity of items in it: take any one of them apart, and it is wonderful what matter for reflection will be found in it! As I write this, the *Letter-Bell* passes: it has a lively, pleasant sound with it, and not only fills the street with its importunate clamour, but rings clear through the length of many half-forgotten years. It strikes upon the ear, it vibrates to the brain, it wakes me from the dream of time, it flings me back upon my first entrance into life, the period of my first coming up to town, when all around was strange, uncertain, adverse— a hubbub of confused noises, a chaos of shifting objects—and when this sound alone, startling me with the recollection of a letter I had to send to the friends I had lately left,* brought me as it were to myself, made me feel that I had links still connecting me with the universe, and gave me hope and patience to persevere. At that loud-tinkling, interrupted sound (now and then), the long line of blue hills* near the place where I was brought up waves in the horizon, a golden sunset hovers over them, the dwarf-oaks rustle their red leaves in the evening-breeze, and the road from —— to ——,* by which I first set out on my journey through life, stares me in the face as plain, but from time and change not less visionary and mysterious, than the pictures in the *Pilgrim's Progress.* I should notice, that at this time the light of the French Revolution circled my head like a glory, though dabbled with drops of crimson gore: I walked confident and cheerful by its side—

And by the vision splendid
Was on my way attended.*

It rose then in the east: it has again risen in the west.* Two suns in one day, two triumphs of liberty in one age, is a miracle which I hope the Laureate* will hail in appropriate verse. Or may not Mr. Wordsworth give a different turn to the fine passage, beginning—

> What, though the radiance which was once so bright,
> Be now for ever vanished from my sight;
> Though nothing can bring back the hour
> Of glory in the grass, of splendour in the flower?*

For is it not brought back, 'like morn risen on mid-*night*;'* and may he not yet greet the yellow light shining on the evening bank with eyes of youth, of genius, and freedom, as of yore? No, never! But what would not these persons give for the unbroken integrity of their early opinions—for one unshackled, uncontaminated strain—one *Io pæan** to Liberty—one burst of indignation against tyrants and sycophants, who subject other countries to slavery by force, and prepare their own for it by servile sophistry, as we see the huge serpent lick over its trembling, helpless victim with its slime and poison, before it devours it! On every stanza so penned would be written the word RECREANT! Every taunt, every reproach, every note of exultation at restored light and freedom, would recal to them how their hearts failed them in the Valley of the Shadow of Death.* And what shall we say to *him**—the sleep-walker, the dreamer, the sophist, the word-hunter, the craver after sympathy, but still vulnerable to truth, accessible to opinion, because not sordid or mechanical? The Bourbons being no longer tied about his neck, he may perhaps recover his original liberty of speculating; so that we may apply to him the lines about his own *Ancient Mariner*—

> And from his neck so free
> The Albatross fell off, and sank
> Like lead into the sea.*

This is the reason I can write an article on the *Letter-Bell*, and other such subjects; I have never given the lie to my own soul. If I have felt any impression once, I feel it more strongly a second time; and I have no wish to revile and discard my best thoughts. There is at least a thorough *keeping* in what I write—not a line that betrays a principle or disguises a feeling. If my wealth is small, it all goes to enrich the same heap; and trifles in this way accumulate to a tolerable sum.—Or if the Letter-Bell does not lead me a dance into the country, it fixes me in the thick of my town recollections, I know not how long ago. It was a kind of alarm to break off from my work when there happened to be company to dinner or when I was going to the play. *That* was going to the play, indeed, when I went twice a year, and had not been more than half a dozen times in my life. Even the idea that any one else in the house was going, was a sort of reflected enjoyment, and conjured up a lively anticipation of the scene. I remember a Miss D——,* a maiden lady from Wales (who in her youth was to have been married to an earl), tantalized me greatly in this way, by talking all day of going to see Mrs. Siddons' 'airs and graces' at night in some favourite part; and when the Letter-Bell announced that the time was approaching, and its last receding sound lingered on the ear, or was lost in silence, how anxious and uneasy I became, lest she and her companion should not be in time to get good places—lest the curtain should draw up before they arrived—and lest I should lose one line or look in the intelligent report which I should hear the next morning! The punctuating of time at that early period—every thing that gives it an articulate voice—seems of the utmost consequence; for we do not know what scenes in the *ideal* world may run out of them: a world of interest may hang upon every instant, and we can hardly sustain the weight of future years which are contained in embryo in the most minute and inconsiderable passing events. How often have I put off writing a letter till it was too late! How often had to run after the postman with it—now missing, now recovering, the sound of his bell—breathless, angry with myself—then hearing the welcome sound come full round a corner—and seeing the scarlet costume which set all my fears and self-reproaches at rest! I do not recollect having ever repented giving a letter to the postman, or wishing to retrieve it after he had once deposited it in his bag. What I have once set my hand to, I take the consequences of, and have been always pretty much of the same humour in this respect. I am not like the person who, having sent off a letter to his mistress, who resided a hundred and twenty miles in the country, and disapproving, on second thoughts, of some expressions contained in it, took a post-chaise and four to follow and intercept it the next morning. At other times, I have sat and watched the decaying embers in a little *back* painting-room (just as the wintry day declined), and brooded over the half-finished copy of a Rembrandt, or a landscape by Vangoyen,* placing it where it might catch a dim gleam of light from the fire; while the Letter-Bell was the only sound that drew my thoughts to the world without, and reminded me that I had a task to perform in it. As to that landscape, methinks I see it now—

> The slow canal, the yellow-blossomed vale,
> The willow-tufted bank, the gliding sail.*

There was a windmill, too, with a poor low clay-built cottage beside it:—how delighted I was when I had made the tremulous, undulating reflection in the water, and saw the dull canvas become a lucid mirror of the commonest features of nature! Certainly, painting gives one a strong interest in nature and humanity (it is not the *dandy-school* of morals or sentiment)—

> While with an eye made quiet by the power
> Of harmony and the deep power of joy,
> We see into the life of things.*

Perhaps there is no part of a painter's life (if we must tell 'the secrets of the prison-house'*) in which he has more enjoyment of himself and his art, than that in which after his work is over, and with furtive sidelong glances at what he has done, he is employed in washing his brushes and cleaning his pallet for the day. Afterwards, when he gets a servant in livery to do this for him, he may have other and more ostensible sources of satisfaction—greater splendour, wealth, or fame; but he will not be so wholly in his art, nor will his art have such a hold on him as when he was too poor to transfer its meanest drudgery to others—too humble to despise aught that had to do with the object of his glory and his pride, with that on which all his projects of ambition or pleasure were founded. 'Entire affection scorneth nicer hands.'* When the professor is above this mechanical part of his business, it may have become a *stalking-horse* to other worldly schemes, but is no longer his *hobby-horse* and the delight of his inmost thoughts—

> His shame in crowds, his solitary pride!*

I used sometimes to hurry through this part of my occupation, while the Letter-Bell (which was my dinner-bell) summoned me to the fraternal board, where youth and hope

> Made good digestion wait on appetite
> And health on both*—

or oftener I put it off till after dinner, that I might loiter longer and with more luxurious indolence over it, and connect it with the thoughts of my next day's labours.

The dustman's-bell, with its heavy, monotonous noise, and the brisk, lively tinkle of the muffin-bell, have something in them, but not much. They will bear dilating upon with the utmost license of inventive prose. All things are not alike *conductors* to the imagination. A learned Scotch professor found fault with an ingenious friend and arch-critic* for cultivating a rookery on his grounds: the professor declared 'he would as soon think of encouraging a *froggery.*' This was barbarous as it was senseless. Strange, that a country that has produced the Scotch Novels and Gertrude of Wyoming* should want sentiment!

The postman's double-knock at the door the next morning is 'more germain to the matter.'* How that knock often goes to the heart! We distinguish to a nicety the arrival of the Two-penny or the General Post. The summons of the latter is louder and heavier, as bringing news from a greater distance, and as, the longer it has been delayed, fraught with a deeper interest. We catch the sound of what is to be paid—eight-pence, nine-pence, a shilling—and our hopes generally rise with the postage. How we are provoked at the delay in getting change—at the servant who does not hear the door! Then if the postman passes, and we do not hear the expected knock, what a pang is there! It is like the silence of death—of hope! We think he does it on purpose, and enjoys all the misery of our suspense. I have sometimes walked out to see the Mail-Coach pass, by which I had sent a letter, or to meet it when I expected one. I never see a Mail-Coach, for this reason, but I look at it as the bearer of glad tidings—the messenger of fate. I have reason to say so.—The finest sight in the metropolis is that of the Mail-Coaches setting off from Piccadilly. The horses paw the ground, and are impatient to be gone, as if conscious of the precious burden they convey. There is a peculiar secrecy and despatch, significant and full of meaning, in all the proceedings concerning them. Even the outside passengers have an erect and supercilious air, as if proof against the accidents of the journey. In fact, it seems indifferent whether they are to encounter the summer's heat or winter's cold, since they are borne through the air in a winged chariot. The Mail-Carts drive up; the transfer of packages is made; and, at a signal given, they start off, bearing the irrevocable scrolls that give wings to thought, and that bind or sever hearts for ever. How we hate the Putney and Brentford stages that draw up in a line after they are gone! Some persons think the sublimest object in nature is a ship launched on the bosom of the ocean: but give me, for my private satisfaction, the Mail-Coaches that pour down Piccadilly of an evening, tear up the pavement, and devour the way before them to the Land's-End!

In Cowper's time, Mail-Coaches were hardly set up;* but he has beautifully described the coming in of the Post-Boy:—

> Hark! 'tis the twanging horn o'er yonder bridge,
> That with its wearisome but needful length
> Bestrides the wintry flood, in which the moon
> Sees her unwrinkled face reflected bright:—
> He comes, the herald of a noisy world,
> With spattered boots, strapped waist, and frozen locks;
> News from all nations lumbering at his back.
> True to his charge, the close-packed load behind,
> Yet careless what he brings, his one concern
> Is to conduct it to the destined inn;
> And having dropped the expected bag, pass on.
> He whistles as he goes, light-hearted wretch!
> Cold and yet cheerful; messenger of grief
> Perhaps to thousands, and of joy to some;
> To him indifferent whether grief or joy.
> Houses in ashes and the fall of stocks,
> Births, deaths, and marriages, epistles wet
> With tears that trickled down the writer's cheeks
> Fast as the periods from his fluent quill,
> Or charged with amorous sighs of absent swains
> Or nymphs responsive, equally affect
> His horse and him, unconscious of them all.*

And yet, notwithstanding this, and so many other passages that seem like the very marrow of our being, Lord Byron denies* that Cowper was a poet!—The Mail-Coach is an improvement on the Post-Boy; but I fear it will hardly bear so poetical a description. The picturesque and dramatic do not keep pace with the useful and mechanical. The telegraphs that lately communicated the intelligence of the new revolution* to all France within a few hours, are a wonderful contrivance; but they are less striking and appalling than the beacon-fires (mentioned by Æschylus),* which, lighted from hill-top to hill-top, announced the taking of Troy and the return of Agamemnon.

EXPLANATORY NOTES

The density of allusion in Hazlitt's prose presents a challenge in terms of anno-tation. These notes are greatly indebted to Hazlitt's previous editors, and espe-cially to the editions of A. R. Waller and Arnold Glover, P. P. Howe, George Sampson, Jon Cook, Tom Paulin and David Chandler, and Duncan Wu. In keeping with the spirit of the present selection, we have placed equal emphasis on Hazlitt's literary allusions and his references to people and contemporary events. Hazlitt usually quoted from memory and with some degree of liberty. For this reason, we follow Wu in using 'from' to signal direct quotations, 'see' for freer allusions, and 'a recollection of' for significant departures from the source.

Where Hazlitt's essays exist in multiple versions, we have departed from most previous editions by taking as our copy text the earliest publication, direct from the pages of the newspaper or periodical in which it first appeared. For further details, please see the Introduction and Note on the Text.

The following editions and abbreviations are used in the notes:

Chaucer	*The Riverside Chaucer*, gen. ed. Larry D. Benson (Oxford, 1988)
Cowper	*The Poems of William Cowper*, ed. John D. Baird and Charles Ryskamp, 3 vols (Oxford, 1980–95)
Gray	*The Complete Poems of Thomas Gray*, ed. H. W. Starr and J. R. Hendrikson (Oxford, 1966)
Howe	*The Complete Works of William Hazlitt*, ed. P. P. Howe, 21 vols (London, 1930–4)
Jones	Stanley Jones, *Hazlitt: A Life, from Winterslow to Frith Street* (London, 1989)
Memoirs	W. Carew Hazlitt, *Memoirs of William Hazlitt*, 2 vols (London, 1867)
Milton	*The Poems of Milton*, ed. John Carey and Alastair Fowler (Harlow, 1968)
Pope	*Alexander Pope: The Major Works*, ed. Pat Rogers (Oxford, 2006)
SW	*The Selected Writings of William Hazlitt*, ed. Duncan Wu, 9 vols (London, 1998)
Thomson	James Thomson, *The Seasons and The Castle of Indolence*, ed. James Sambrook (Oxford, 1972)
Wordsworth	*William Wordsworth: The Major Works*, ed. Stephen Gill (Oxford, 1984)
Wu	Duncan Wu, *William Hazlitt: The First Modern Man* (Oxford, 2008)

All references to Shakespeare are to Stanley Wells and Gary Taylor (general eds), *William Shakespeare: The Complete Works* (2nd edn; Oxford, 2005). All references to the Bible are to the King James Version.

1. REPLY TO MALTHUS

Published on 23 May 1807 in *Cobbett's Weekly Political Register*, under the heading 'Poor Laws. Being the Third Letter of A.O.'. Hazlitt republished the letters in *A Reply to the Essay on Population, By the Rev. T. R. Malthus* (1807) and *Political Essays* (1819).

3 *'A swaggering paradox . . . common-place'*: possibly a reference to *Reflections on the Revolution in France* (1790), 252: 'I believe, that were Rousseau alive, and in one of his lucid intervals, he would be shocked at the practical phrenzy of his scholars, who in their paradoxes are servile imitators; and even in their incredulity discover an implicit faith.'

Essay on Population: Thomas Robert Malthus's (1766–1834) *Essay on the Principle of Population* was published anonymously in 1798. Malthus refuted the perfectibilist theories of Condorcet and Godwin, arguing that the rate of population growth would always outstrip increases in food supply.

his octavo book: the first edition of Malthus's essay appeared as a slim octavo volume.

4 *checked by vice and misery*: Malthus argued that the population principle could only be countered by 'vice', which he defined as contraception, abortion and prostitution, and 'misery', or the postponement of marriage.

a large quarto: a second, expanded edition of Malthus's *Essay* was published in quarto in 1803.

moral restraint: in the second edition, Malthus emphasized the role of late marriage, now labelled 'moral restraint', in checking population growth.

the reply of the author of the Political Justice: William Godwin, *Thoughts occasioned by the Perusal of Dr. Parr's Spital Sermon* (London, 1801).

5 *'But, Mr. Godwin says . . . with very inconsiderable force'*: from Malthus, *Essay on the Principle of Population* (1803), 383–4.

Condorcet: Nicolas de Condorcet (1743–94), French political economist and mathematician.

6 *'false, sophistical, unfounded in the extreme'*: unidentified.

old political receipt-book . . . one Wallace: Robert Wallace (1697–1771), *Various Prospects of Mankind, Nature and Providence* (1761).

7 *'What conjuration . . . magic'*: from *Othello*, I.iii.92.

'chusing among them . . . loathe': see Miguel de Cervantes, *Don Quixote*, translated by Tobias Smollett (1755): 'there are so many masters, graduates, and divines, in the convent, among whom your ladyship may choose, as one picks pears, saying, "This I like, that I loath"' (I.169).

8 *as Trim . . . busy in besieging*: see Laurence Sterne, *The Life and Opinion of Tristram Shandy* (1759–67). Hazlitt is referring to an episode in book VI, chapter xxiii.

9 *'These three bear record . . . Population'*: see 1 John 5:7.

stage maxim: see George Villiers, 2nd Duke of Buckingham, *The Rehearsal* (1671), I.i.

10 *'Tis as easy as lying . . . stops'*: see *Hamlet*, III.ii.345–8.

Mr. Whitbread's Poor Bill: Samuel Whitbread (1758–1815), Whig politician, introduced a Poor Law Bill on 19 February 1807, influenced by Malthus's ideas. His proposals included changes to the law of settlement, a national system of free education, a cottage-building programme financed out of the parish rates, and a system of badges to distinguish the deserving from the undeserving poor.

2. WHY THE ARTS ARE NOT PROGRESSIVE?

Published as two articles in *The Morning Chronicle* for 11 and 15 January 1814, under the heading 'Fragments on Art. Why the Arts Are Not Progressive?'. Revised and reprinted in *The Round Table* (1817).

11 *tricks of galvanism*: the application of pulses of electric current to stimulate the contraction of muscular tissue, as performed by Luigi Galvani (1737–98).

Antaeus: in Greek mythology, the giant Antaeus received new strength each time he touched his mother, Gaia, the earth, but was defeated when Hercules held him aloft; see Milton, *Paradise Regained*, IV.563–8.

13 *'Now tired with pomp . . . accomplished excellence'*: see Northcote's 'Varieties on Art (The Dream of a Painter)' in his *Memoirs of Sir Joshua Reynolds* (1813), pp. xvi–xvii.

14 *'There is no shuffling . . . faults'*: see *Hamlet*, III.iii.61–4.

To use the distinction . . . the mind: a distinction established in Antoine Arnauld and Pierre Nicole's *Port-Royal Logic* (1662).

15 *'the human face divine'*: from Milton, *Paradise Lost*, III.44.

'And made a sunshine . . . shady place': from Edmund Spenser, *The Faerie Queene*, I.iii.4:8.

Prince of Painters: Raphael.

patient sorrow of Griselda: see Chaucer's *The Clerk's Tale*.

delight . . . knows no ebb: an allusion to *The Floure and the Leafe*, a fifteenth-century poem no longer attributed to Chaucer.

the divine story of the Hawk: see Boccaccio's *The Decameron*, Fifth Day, Novel IX.

Isabella . . . Basile: see Boccaccio's *The Decameron*, Fourth Day, Novel V.

16 *Lear . . . like him*: see King Lear, II.ii.362–5.

Titian . . . in the Louvre: Titian's *Man with a Glove*.

St. Peter Martyr: Titian's *The Death of St Peter Martyr*. Hazlitt saw the painting at the Louvre in 1802, and again in Venice in 1825.

Nicolas Poussin . . . Arcadian!': Poussin, *Et in Arcadia Ego*.

Mr. Rogers's 'Pleasures of Memory' . . . Sir James Macintosh's History: Samuel Rogers, *The Pleasures of Memory* (1792); Thomas Campbell, *The*

Pleasures of Hope (1799); Richard Westall (1765–1836) staged his own exhibition in Pall Mall in 1814; Benjamin West (1738–1820), history painter; Frances Burney, *The Wanderer* (1814), Maria Edgeworth, *Tales from Fashionable Life* (1809, 1812); Francis Jeffrey reviewed Germaine de Staël's *De la littérature* in the *Edinburgh Review*, 21 (February 1813), 1–50, James Mackintosh reviewed de Staël's *De l'Allemagne* in the *Edinburgh Review*, 22 (October 1813), 198–238; Mackintosh planned to write a history of England.

3. MR. KEAN'S SHYLOCK

Published in the *Morning Chronicle* for 27 January 1814, the day after Edmund Kean's London debut. Reprinted in *A View of the English Stage* (1818).

18 *Miss Smith*: Sarah Smith, later Bartley (1783?–1850), actress and rival of Sarah Siddons, who refused to perform alongside Siddons in secondary parts.

Rae: Alexander Rae (1782–1820), actor, superseded in lead roles at Drury Lane by Kean.

4. ON IMITATION

Published in the *Examiner* for 18 February 1816; reprinted in *The Round Table* (1817).

19 *Jennerian Professor*: Edward Jenner (1749–1823) pioneered vaccination against smallpox through cowpox inoculation from 1796.

the new Spurtzheim principles: Johann Gaspar Spurzheim (1776–1832), pioneer of phrenology, which claimed to reveal character through measurements of the skull.

20 *Vanhuysum*: Jan van Huysum (1682–1749), Dutch painter, who specialized in still lifes.

21 *'pansy freak'd with jet'*: from Milton, *Lycidas*, 144.

22 *'a pleasure in art which none but artists feel'*: an allusion to Cowper, *The Task*, ii.285–6, 'There is a pleasure in poetic pains | Which only poets know'.

Titian's Schoolmaster: Giovanni Battista Moroni, *Titian's Schoolmaster*, once thought to be by Titian himself.

Raphael's Galatea: Raphael, *The Triumph of Galatea*.

23 *Werter*: Johann Wolfgang von Goethe, *The Sorrows of Young Werther* (1774).

Robbers: Friedrich Schiller's play *The Robbers* (1781).

'without form and void': see Genesis 1:2.

British Institution: founded in 1805, the British Institution put on exhibitions of contemporary artists and Old Masters at its gallery in Pall Mall.

Unlike the Royal Academy, membership was dominated by aristocratic connoisseurs.

5. ON GUSTO

Published in the *Examiner* for 26 May 1816; reprinted in *The Round Table* (1817).

24 *morbidezza*: lifelike delicacy in flesh tints (*OED*).

Albano's is like ivory: Francesca Albano (1578–1660), painter of the Bolognese School and pupil of Ludovico Carracci.

25 *This may seem . . . great want of gusto*: Hazlitt deleted this Shandean footnote when the essay was republished in *The Round Table*.

the Orleans Gallery: exhibition of Italian old masters placed on sale in Pall Mall from December 1798 to July 1799. The bulk of the collection had belonged to the Regent Orléans in Paris.

Acteon hunting: Titian's *Diana and Actaeon*.

Mr. West: Benjamin West succeeded Joshua Reynolds as President of the Royal Academy in 1792.

27 *'by their beauty they are deified*: see Wordsworth, 'Resolution and Independence', 47, 'By our own spirits are we deified'.

'Or where Chineses drive . . . bliss': from *Paradise Lost*, III.438–9; V.297.

Prior's tales: Matthew Prior (1664–1721), poet and diplomat.

Beggar's Opera: 1728 ballad opera by John Gay (1685–1732), with music by Johann Christoph Pepusch.

6. ON THE ELGIN MARBLES

Published as two articles in the *Examiner* for 16 and 30 June 1816 under the heading *Report from the Select Committee of the House of Commons on the Elgin Marbles*. Hazlitt returned to the subject and recycled some of the material in the *London Magazine* for February and May 1822.

28 *the Elgin Marbles*: Lord Elgin removed the collection of classical sculptures now known as the Parthenon Marbles from Athens between 1801 and 1812. Following the report of a House of Commons select committee charged with establishing the legality of his actions and value of the collection, the Elgin Marbles were bought for the nation at a cost of £35,000 and deposited in the British Museum.

Sir Joshua Reynolds's Discourses: Joshua Reynolds, *Discourses on Art*, a series of lectures delivered to students at the Royal Academy between 1769 and 1790, collected for publication in 1797.

Mr. Chauntry: Sir Francis Chantrey (1781–1841), sculptor.

Sir Thomas Laurence: Sir Thomas Lawrence (1769–1830), portrait painter.

28 *Mr. Flaxman*: John Flaxman (1755–1826), sculptor, decorative designer, and illustrator.

Mr. Payne Knight's: Richard Payne Knight (1751–1824), art collector and writer.

Phidias: Greek sculptor (*c*.480–430 BC), who supervised the construction of the Parthenon and created the lost statue of the Athena Parthenon.

29 *Gallery of the Louvre*: following the French Revolution, the National Assembly turned the Louvre Palace into a museum of the nation's master-pieces. The collection was opened in 1793, later renamed Musée Napoléon, and expanded through artworks looted on Napoleon's Italian campaigns. Hazlitt visited the Louvre in 1802, during the Peace of Amiens; while there he saw Bonaparte and met Fox.

'stood the statue . . . world': the Venus de' Medici. Hazlitt quotes from James Thomson, *The Seasons* (1730): 'So stands the statue that enchants the world' ('Summer', 1347).

30 *'There was old Proteus . . . horn'*: see Wordsworth, 'The World Is Too Much With Us', 13–14, 'Have sight of Proteus rising from the sea; | Or hear old Triton blow his wreathèd horn.'

to strut and fret: see Macbeth, V.v.24.

32 *'Who to the life . . . eye and motion of his hand'*: from Abraham Cowley, 'To the Royal Society', 79–88.

33 *'To learn . . . taste her style'*: from Cowper, *The Task*, iii.227–8, 'Acknowledges with joy | His manner, and with rapture tastes his stile'.

34 *'alternate action and repose'*: see Sir Thomas Lawrence's testimony: 'There is in them that variety that is produced in the human form, by the alternate action and repose of the muscles, that strikes one particularly' (*Report from the Select Committee*, 91).

36 *'When the last . . . I was present'*: Lord Byron, *Childe Harold's Pilgrimage*, II.xii.

7. MRS. SIDDONS

Published in the *Examiner* for 16 June 1816; reprinted in *A View of the English Stage* (1818). Sarah Siddons returned to the stage at Covent Garden on 31 May 1816 to play Katherine in *Henry VIII* for a benefit performance for Mr and Mrs Charles Kemble, and on 8 June 1816 to play Lady Macbeth, her most celebrated role, in a command performance for Princess Charlotte. She continued to make occasional performances in benefits for members of her family until 1819.

37 *Mrs. Siddons retired once from the stage*: Siddons retired at the end of the 1811–12 season, closing with a benefit performance as Lady Macbeth on 29 June 1812 at Covent Garden.

38 *'the baby of a girl'*: from *Macbeth*, III.iv.105.

'Rather than so . . . utterance': see *Macbeth*, III.i.72–3.

Gil Blas: see Alain-René Lesage, *Gil Blas* (1715–35), book VII, chapter 4, in which the hero tells the Archbishop of Granada what he thought of his sermon.

the Princess Charlotte: Princess Charlotte Augusta (1796–1817), only child of the ill-fated marriage of the Prince Regent and Caroline of Brunswick. A hugely popular figure, she married Prince Leopold of Saxe-Coburg on 2 May 1816 and died in childbirth on 5 November 1817.

'*Leave me to my repose*': see Thomas Gray, 'The Descent of Odin', 50, 'Leave me, leave me to repose'.

'*The line . . . move slow*': from Pope, *Essay on Criticism*, 371.

'*I tell you he cannot rise from his grave*': see *Macbeth*, V.i.60–1.

39 '*Go, go*': a recollection of the banquet scene of *Macbeth*, III.iv.118–19.

Mr. Horace Twiss: Twiss (1787–1849), a nephew of Mrs Siddons, who wrote the address she delivered on taking her farewell from the stage in 1812.

'*himself again*': see *Richard III*, adapted by Colley Cibber (London, 1818), V.v, 'Conscience avaunt! Richard's himself again.'

'*To-morrow and to-morrow*': from *Macbeth*, V.v.18.

printed by a steam-engine: *The Times* moved to printing by steam-powered press in November 1814. Hazlitt spent eight months on the staff of the paper, edited by his brother-in-law John Stoddart, in 1817, but retained this sentence when he reprinted the essay the following year.

8. MR. KEMBLE'S KING JOHN

Published in the *Examiner* for 8 December 1816; reprinted in *A View of the English Stage* (1818). John Philip Kemble (1757–1823) opened in *King John* at Covent Garden on 3 December 1816, reprising the role on 5 and 7 December. He retired from the stage six months later.

40 '*when we waked, have cried to dream again*': from *The Tempest*, III.ii.145–6.

41 '*man delight not us, nor women neither*': from *Hamlet*, II.ii.310–11.

42 *Miss O'Neill*: Eliza O'Neill (1791–1872), actress.

Mr. Charles Kemble: Charles Kemble (1775–1854), actor, theatre manager, and playwright. Brother of John Philip Kemble and Sarah Siddons.

'*the bulk . . . the spirit*': see *2 Henry IV*, III.ii.255–6.

'*Could Sir Robert make this leg?*': see *King John*, I.i.240.

9. CORIOLANUS

Published in the *Examiner* for 15 December 1816, following performances of *Coriolanus* at Covent Garden on 19, 28, and 30 November. Reprinted in *Characters of Shakespeare's Plays* (1817), with several additional paragraphs, and in *A View of the English Stage* (1818).

43 *'no jutting frieze . . . procreant cradle in'*: see *Macbeth*, I.vi.6–8.

44 *'it carries noise . . . tears'*: from *Coriolanus*, II.i.156.

'Carnage is its daughter!': see Wordsworth, 'Ode. The Morning of the Day Appointed for a General Thanksgiving. January 18, 1816', 279–82:

> But thy most dreaded instrument
> In working out a pure intent,
> Is Man – arrayed for mutual slaughter,—
> Yea, Carnage is thy daughter!

'poor rats': see *Coriolanus*, I.i.249.

'as if he were a God . . . infirmity': from *Coriolanus*, III.i.85–6.

'Mark you his absolute shall?': from *Coriolanus*, III.i.92–3.

45 *'cares . . . fears'*: see *Coriolanus*, III.i.138–40:

> Thus we debase
> The nature of our seats, and make the rabble
> Call our cares fears

'Now the red pestilence . . . perish': from *Coriolanus*, IV.i.14–15.

Mrs. Hunn: Mrs Hunn, the Irish actress Mary Ann Costello (1747–1827), was the mother of George Canning (1770–1827), president of the Board of Control and future prime minister. Political opponents constantly used the fact his mother was an actress against Canning: see Cobbett, *Political Register*, 13 November 1819, 369.

Spa-fields meeting: on 2 December 1816, the second of two mass meetings at Spa Fields, Islington, organized by the ultra-radical Spenceans and addressed by Henry Hunt, was followed by rioting. The organizers hoped to seize control of the Tower of London and Bank of England and overthrow the government. They were charged with high treason but the trials collapsed and the only person to be convicted was John Cashman, an Irish sailor, for looting a gunsmiths. He was hanged at the scene of the crime, the last time this punishment was carried out. Hazlitt deleted this sentence when he came to reprint the essay.

those who have little shall have less: an ironic parody of Luke 6:20–2.

46 *poetical justice*: an ironic allusion to William Godwin's *Political Justice* (1793).

what is sport to the few, is death to the many: Hazlitt recycles this line in 'On Living to One's-Self' (*Table Talk*, 1821), 'Poor Keats! What was sport to the town, was death to him.'

Simmons: Samuel Simmons (*c*.1777–1819), actor.

47 *Mr. H—*: farce by Charles Lamb, booed off the stage at Drury Lane in December 1806

10. ON ACTORS AND ACTING

Published in the *Examiner* for 5 January 1817; expanded and reprinted in two parts in *The Round Table* (1817).

48 *'the abstracts and brief chronicles of the time'*: from *Hamlet*, II.ii.527–8.

49 *George Barnwell*: 1731 play by George Lillo (1693–1739).

the Ordinary's Sermon: the Ordinary of Newgate, the prison chaplain, charged with the spiritual care of condemned prisoners. The Ordinary published his sermons, together with accounts of the lives, crimes, confessions, and last dying speeches of the prisoners, as the Ordinary's Accounts.

the Inconstant: 1702 comedy by George Farquhar.

Mr. Liston: John Liston (*c*.1776–1846), actor.

50 *Etherege*: Sir George Etherege (1636–1691/2), playwright and diplomat.

Pierre: character—and conspirator against the state—in Thomas Otway's *Venice Preserved* (1682).

the Stranger: play by August von Kotzebue, translated by Benjamin Thompson and first performed in 1798, with Kemble in the title role.

'a tale of other times!': see the opening of James Macpherson's *Ossian*, 'A tale of the times of old!', and Sophia Lee's Gothic historical novel *The Recess; or, A Tale of Other Times* (1783–5). In *The Round Table* text, Hazlitt interpolates here a passage from his 'Theatrical Examiner' column for 4 June 1815 to close the first part of the essay:

> One of the most affecting things we know is to see a favourite actor take leave of the stage. We were present not long ago when Mr Bannister quitted it. We do not wonder that his feelings were overpowered on the occasion: ours were nearly so too. We remembered him in the first heyday of our youthful spirits, in the *Prize*, in which he played so delightfully with that fine old croaker Suett, and Madame Storace,—in the farce of *My Grandmother*, in the *Son-in-law*, in *Autolycus*, and in *Scrub*, in which our satisfaction was at its height. At that time, King and Parsons, and Dodd, and Quick, and Edwin were in the full vigour of their reputation, who are now all gone. We still feel the vivid delight with which we used to see their names in the play-bills, as we went along to the Theatre. Bannister was one of the last of these that remained; and we parted with him as we should with one of our oldest and best friends. The most pleasant feature in the profession of a player, and which, indeed, is peculiar to it, is that we not only admire the talents of those who adorn it, but we contract a personal intimacy with them. There is no class of society whom so many persons regard with affection as actors. We greet them on the stage; we like to meet them in the streets; they almost always recal to us pleasant associations; and we feel our gratitude excited, without the uneasiness of a sense of obligation. The very gaiety and popularity, however, which surround the life of a favourite performer, make the retiring from it a very serious business. It glances a mortifying reflection on the shortness of human life, and the vanity of human pleasures. Something reminds us, that 'all the world's a stage, and all the men and women merely players.'

'leaving the world no copy': see *Twelfth Night*, I.v.232.

50 *Colley Cibber's account . . . the stage*: see Cibber's *Apology* (1740), chapter IV.

51 *British Gallery*: also known as the British Institution; see note to p. 23.

Betterton and Booth . . . Shuter: Thomas Betterton (1635?–1710), actor and theatre manager; Barton Booth (1681–1733), actor; Robert Wilks (*c*.1665–1732), actor and theatre manager; Samuel Sandford (*fl.* 1661–98), actor; James Noakes (d. 1692), actor; Anthony Leigh (d. 1692), actor; William Pinkethman (*c*.1660x65–1725), actor and theatre manager; William Bullock (*c*.1667–1742), actor; Richard Estcourt (1668?–1712), actor; Thomas Dogget (*c*.1640–1721), actor; Elizabeth Barry (1658–1713), actress and theatre manager; Susanna Mountfort (*c*.1666–1703), actress; Anne Oldfield (1683–1730), actress; Anne Bracegirdle (*c*.1671–1748), actress and singer; Susannah Maria Cibber (1714–66), actress and singer; Colley Cibber (1671–1757), actor, writer, and theatre manager; Charles Macklin (1699?–1797), actor and playwright; James Quin (1693–1766), actor; Margaret [Peg] Woffington (1720?–1760), actress; Catherine [Kitty] Clive (1711–85), actress; Hannah Pritchard (1709–68), actress and theatre manager; Frances Abington (1737–1815), actress; Thomas Weston (1737–76), actor; Edward Shuter (1728?–76), actor and singer.

'gladdened life . . . nations!': see Samuel Johnson on the death of Garrick: 'one who has gladdened life . . . I am disappointed by that stroke of death, which has eclipsed the gaiety of nations, and impoverished the publick stock of harmless pleasure' (*Lives of the Poets* [1783], II.253).

hundred days: the period between Napoleon's arrival in Paris on 20 March 1815, after returning from exile on Elba, and his final defeat at Waterloo.

52 *Betterton's Hamlet . . . Belvidera*: Cibber describes Betterton's performances in these roles (*Apology*, chapter 4), Booth's 1713 Cato (chapter 14), and Mrs Barry's Monimia and Belvidera in Thomas Otway's *The Orphan* and *Venice Preserved* (chapter 5).

Penkethman's manner . . . the Tatler: see *Tatler*, 188 (22 June 1710), 'Penkethman devours a cold Chick with great Applause; Bullock's Talent lies chiefly in Sparagrass'.

Dowton: William Dowton (1764–1851), actor.

Wilks: Robert Wilks (*c*.1665–1732), actor and theatre manager

Sir Harry Wildair: 1701 comedy by George Farquhar.

Macklin . . . Shakespear drew: an exclamation (attributed to Pope) overheard at one of Macklin's performances as Shylock.

as often as we pleased!: in *The Round Table*, Hazlitt interpolates here the following passage, drawing on his 'Theatrical Examiner' columns for 14 January 1816 and 31 March 1816:

> Players, after all, have little reason to complain of their hard-earned, short-lived popularity. One thunder of applause from pit, boxes, and gallery, is equal to a whole immortality of posthumous fame: and when we hear an actor, whose modesty is equal to his merit, declare, that he

would like to see a dog wag his tail in approbation, what must he feel when he sets the whole house in a roar! Besides, Fame, as if their reputation had been entrusted to her alone, has been particularly careful of the renown of her theatrical favourites: she forgets one by one, and year by year, those who have been great lawyers, great statesmen, and great warriors in their day; but the name of Garrick still survives with the works of Reynolds and of Johnson.

Actors have been accused, as a profession, of being extravagant and dissipated. While they are said to be so as a piece of common cant, they are likely to continue so. But there is a sentence in Shakespeare which should be stuck as a label in the mouths of our beadles and whippers-in of morality. 'The web of our life is of a mingled yarn, good and ill together: our virtues would be proud if our faults whipped them not: and our vices would despair if they were not cherished by our virtues.' With respect to the extravagance of actors, as a traditional character, it is not to be wondered at. They live from hand to mouth: they plunge from want into luxury; they have no means of making money *breed*, and all professions that do not live by turning money into money, or have not a certainty of accumulating it in the end of parsimony, spend it. Uncertain of the future, they make sure of the present moment. This is not unwise. Chilled with poverty, steeped in contempt, they sometimes pass into the sunshine of fortune, and are lifted to the very pinnacle of public favour; yet even there cannot calculate on the continuance of success; but are, 'like the giddy sailor on the mast, ready with every blast to topple down into the fatal bowels of the deep!' Besides, if the young enthusiast, who is smitten with the stage, and with the public as a mistress, were naturally a close *hunks*, he would become or remain a city clerk, instead of turning player. Again, with respect to the habit of convivial indulgence, an actor, to be a good one, must have a great spirit of enjoyment in himself, strong impulses, strong passions, and a strong sense of pleasure: for it is his business to imitate the passions, and to communicate pleasure to others. A man of genius is not a machine. The neglected actor may be excused if he drinks oblivion of his disappointments; the successful one if he quaffs the applause of the world, and enjoys the friendship of those who are the friends of the favourites of fortune, in draughts of nectar. There is no path so steep as that of fame: no labour so hard as the pursuit of excellence. The intellectual excitement, inseparable from those professions which call forth all our sensibility to pleasure and pain, requires some corresponding physical excitement to support our failure, and not a little to allay the ferment of the spirits attendant on success. If there is any tendency to dissipation beyond this in the profession of a player, it is owing to the prejudices entertained against them, to that spirit of bigotry which in a neighbouring country would deny actors Christian burial after their death, and to that cant of criticism, which, in our own, slurs over their characters, while living, with a half-witted jest.

52 *Coleridge . . . Lay Sermon*: in December 1816, Coleridge published his first *Lay Sermon*, *The Statesman's Manual*, which Hazlitt reviewed for the *Edinburgh Review*. Hazlitt cut the final three sentences of this paragraph, including the swipe at Coleridge, when he reprinted the essay.

53 *'consummation devoutly to be wished'*: from *Hamlet*, III.i.65–6.

'The wine of life . . . lees remain': see *Macbeth*, II.iii.94–5.

54 *'Hurried from . . . more fierce'*: see *Paradise Lost*, II.598–9:

> and feel by turns the bitter change
> Of fierce extremes, extremes by change more fierce

the strolling player in Gil Blas: see Lesage, *Gil Blas*, book II, chapter 8.

11. MACBETH

First published in *Characters of Shakespeare's Plays* (1817).

55 *'The poet's eye . . . name'*: from *A Midsummer Night's Dream*, V.i.12–17.

the rapidity of the action: cf. Coleridge, 'Lecture on Hamlet' (1818), 'this tragedy presents a direct contrast to that of *Macbeth*; the one proceeds with the utmost slowness, the other with a crowded and breathless rapidity.'

'your only tragedy-maker': see *Hamlet*, III.ii.119, 'your only jig-maker.'

'the air smells wooingly': see *Macbeth*, I.vi.5–6, 'the heavens' breath | Smells wooingly here.'

'the temple-haunting martlet builds': see *Macbeth*, I.vi.4.

'the blasted heath': from *Macbeth*, I.iii.75.

'air-drawn dagger': from *Macbeth*, III.iv.61.

'gracious Duncan': from *Macbeth*, III.i.67.

'blood-boultered Banquo': from *Macbeth*, IV.i.139.

56 *'What are these . . . on't?'*: from *Macbeth*, I.iii.37–40.

'bends up each corporal instrument . . . feat': from *Macbeth*, I.vii.79–80.

'The deed . . . confounds him': a recollection of *Macbeth*, II.ii.10–11, 'Th'attempt and not the deed | Confounds us.'

'preternatural solicitings': a recollection of *Macbeth*, I.iii.129–30, 'This supernatural soliciting | Cannot be ill, cannot be good.'

57 *'Bring forth men children . . . males!'*: from *Macbeth*, I.vii.72–4.

'screw his courage to the sticking-place': from *Macbeth*, I.vii.60.

'lost so poorly in himself': see *Macbeth*, II.ii.69–70, 'Be not lost | So poorly in your thoughts.'

'a little water . . . deed': from *Macbeth*, II.ii.65.

'the sides of his intent': from *Macbeth*, I.vii.26.

'for their future days . . . masterdom': see *Macbeth*, I.v.68–9.

'his fatal entrance . . . battlements': see *Macbeth*, I.v.37–9, 'The raven himself is hoarse | That croaks the fatal entrance of Duncan | Under my battlements.'

58 '*Come all you spirits . . . hold!*': from *Macbeth*, I.v.39–53.

   '*Duncan comes . . . mad to say it*': see *Macbeth*, I.v.30.

   '*Hie thee hither . . . withal*': from *Macbeth*, I.v.24–9.

59 '*There is no art . . . upon me*': see *Macbeth* I.iv.11–16.

   '*How goes the night . . . repose*': see *Macbeth*, II.i.1–9.

60 '*Light thickens . . . inn*': from *Macbeth*, III.ii.51–2; III.iii.6–7.

   '*So fair and foul . . . seen*': from *Macbeth*, I.iii.36.

   '*Such welcome and unwelcome news together*': see *Macbeth*, IV.iii.139, 'Such welcome and unwelcome things at once'.

   '*Men's lives . . . sickens*': see *Macbeth*, IV.iii.172–4.

   '*Look like . . . under it*': from *Macbeth*, I.v.64–5.

   '*To him and all . . . quit my sight*': from *Macbeth*, III.iv.90–2.

   '*himself again*': see *Richard III* adapted by Cibber, V.v, 'Conscience avaunt! Richard's himself again.'

   '*he may sleep . . . thunder*': see *Macbeth*, IV.i.102.

61 '*Then be thou jocund . . . note*': see *Macbeth*, III.ii.41–5.

   '*Had he not resembled . . . done 't*': from *Macbeth*, II.ii.12–13.

   '*rejoice when good kings bleed*': from a song in William Davenant's adaptation of *Macbeth* (*c*.1664), 'We should rejoice when good kings bleed' (II.ii).

   '*they should be women . . . forbid it*': a recollection of *Macbeth*, I.iii.43–5.

   in deeper consequence: see *Macbeth*, I.iii.124.

   '*Why stands Macbeth thus amazedly?*': from *Macbeth*, IV.i.141–2.

   '*the milk of human kindness*': from *Macbeth*, I.v.16.

62 '*himself alone*': see *3 Henry VI*, V.vi.84, 'I am myself alone', and John 6:15: 'When Jesus therefore perceived that they would come and take him by force, to make him a king, he departed again into a mountain himself alone.' This was the text that Hazlitt heard Coleridge preach on at Shrewsbury in January 1798; see 'My First Acquaintance with Poets'.

   '*For Banquo's issue . . . kings*': from *Macbeth*, III.i.66–7, 71.

   '*Duncan is in his grave . . . sleeps well*': from *Macbeth*, III.ii.24–5.

   '*direness . . . slaughterous thoughts*': see *Macbeth*, V.v.14.

   '*troubled . . . her rest*': see *Macbeth*, V.iii.40–1.

63 '*subject to all the skyey influences*': a recollection of *Measure for Measure*, III.i.9.

   '*My way of life . . . dare not*': a recollection of *Macbeth*, V.iii.24–30.

   Lillo's murders: George Lillo, dramatist (1693–1739), author of *Fatal Curiosity* and *George Barnwell*.

   '*Though some resemblance . . . o'er life*': from Charles Lamb's notes in *Specimens of English Dramatic Poets* (1808), appended to an extract from Middleton's *The Witch* (174).

63 *the Witch of Middleton*: Thomas Middleton (*c*.1580–1627). It is now thought that *The Witch* dates from *c*.1615, *Macbeth* from 1605–6.

64 *They raise jars . . . thick scurf o'er life'*: from Middleton, *The Witch*, I.ii.171–3, 'Well may we raise jars, | Jealousies, strifes and heart-burning disagreements, | Like a thick scurf o'er life'.

12. HAMLET

First published in *Characters of Shakespeare's Plays* (1817).

65 *'this goodly frame . . . vapours'*: a recollection of *Hamlet*, II.ii.299–304.

'man delighted not, nor woman neither': from *Hamlet*, II.ii.310–11.

'too much i' th' sun': from *Hamlet*, I.ii.67.

'the pangs of despised love . . . unworthy takes': see *Hamlet*, III.i.74–6.

66 *'the outward pageants and the signs of grief'*: a recollection of *Hamlet*, I.ii.86, 'These but the trappings and the suits of woe.'

'we have that within which passes shew': from *Hamlet*, I.ii.85.

The character of Hamlet: the next three paragraphs draw loosely on Hazlitt's review of Kean's Hamlet (*Morning Chronicle*, 14 March 1814).

67 *'that has no relish of salvation in it'*: from *Hamlet*, III.iii.92.

'He kneels and prays . . . in a rage': a recollection of *Hamlet*, III.iii.73–9, 88–9.

68 *'How all occasions . . . or be nothing worth'*: from *Hamlet*, IV.iv.23–57.

'that noble and liberal casuist': from one of Hazlitt's favourite passages in Lamb's *Specimens*:

> A puritanical obtuseness of sentiment, a stupid infantile goodness, is creeping among us, instead of the vigorous passions, and virtues clad in flesh and blood, which the old dramatists present us. Those noble and liberal casuists could discern in the differences, the quarrels, the animosities of man, a beauty and truth of moral feeling, no less than in the iterately inculcated duties of forgiveness and atonement. (136)

69 *The Whole Duty of Man*: Richard Allestree's ethical treatise *The Whole Duty of Man* (1657).

The Academy of Compliments: a handbook for courting couples by 'Philomusus', first published in 1640.

'his father's spirit was in arms': from *Hamlet*, I.ii.254.

'I loved Ophelia . . . sum': from *Hamlet*, V.i.266–8.

'Sweets to the sweet . . . thy grave': from *Hamlet*, V.i.239–42.

Oh rose of May . . . faded: from *Hamlet* IV.v.158. The *Quarterly* failed to catch the allusion, attributing the exclamation to Hazlitt: 'The variety of Mr. Hazlitt's style is as striking as his phraseology. Sometimes he would seem, from his gorgeous accumulation of emblematical terms, which leave all meaning far behind, to have formed himself upon the model of Samuel

Johnson—not the author of the Rambler—but, of Hurlothrumbo the Supernatural. Sometimes he breaks forth into a poetical strain, as, at the mention of Ophelia, "O rose of May! O, flower too soon faded!"' (*Quarterly Review*, 18 (January 1818), 459).

70 '*a wave o' th' sea*': from *The Winter's Tale*, IV.iv.141.

13. CHARACTER OF MR. BURKE

First published as part of the article 'Coleridge's Literary Life', in the *Edinburgh Review*, August 1817. Reproduced without the final paragraph in the *Champion*, 5 October 1817, and reprinted in *Political Essays* (1819).

73 *received his pension*: after resigning from his parliamentary seat in 1794, Burke received a government pension.

75 *his speech on the Begum's affairs*: Burke was one of the leaders of the attempt to impeach Warren Hastings (1732–1818), governor-general of India, for corruption. One of many charges against Hastings was that he stole property owned by the mother and grandmother of the Nawab of Oudh. Burke discussed this episode at his opening speech at the trial on 18 February 1788. Hastings was finally acquitted in 1795.

Nor did he care . . . attract admiration: Hazlitt revised this line for *Political Essays*, to become, 'Nor did he care one jot who caused the famine he described, so that he described it in a way no one else could'.

he represents the French priests . . . notorious facts: see Burke, *Reflections on the Revolution in France*, 199–222.

puts an interpretation on the word abdication: see Burke, *Reflections*, 38. Burke argued that the abdication of James II and the 'Glorious Revolution' of 1688 was 'a parent of settlement, and not a nursery of future revolutions'. Radicals like Hazlitt claimed that it confirmed the right of a people to cashier their rulers.

lamentation over the age of chivalry: see Burke, *Reflections*, 112–13.

Salvator Rosa: Italian landscape painter (1615–73).

those newspaper paragraphs . . . to our political philosophy: in *Biographia Literaria* (1817), Coleridge had written, 'the essays and leading paragraphs of our journals are so many remembrances of EDMUND BURKE' (ch. 10).

76 '*Never so sure . . . of all we hate*': a recollection of Pope, 'Epistle to a Lady', 51–2:

> Yet ne'er so sure our passion to create,
> As when she touched the brink of all we hate.

Jeremy Taylor: Church of Ireland bishop of Down and Connor and religious writer (bap. 1613–1667).

14. WHAT IS THE PEOPLE?

Published in the *Champion* for 12, 19, and 26 October 1817. Reprinted in two parts in the *Yellow Dwarf* for 7 and 14 March 1818, and afterwards in *Political Essays* (1819).

77 *'a vile jelly'*: from *King Lear*, III.vii.81.

Legitimacy: 'the legal right to govern or to sovereignty; specifically the fact or principle of strict hereditary succession to a throne' (*OED*). This term seems to have been put into circulation in 1817 after the defeat of Napoleon and restoration of the Bourbons to the French throne. 'Legitimacy' was viewed by radicals as an attempt to re-establish the doctrine of the divine right of kings. See note to p. 83.

'the unbought grace of life': from Burke's lament for the age of chivalry in *Reflections on the Revolution in France*, 113; first of many ironic allusions to Burke in this essay.

78 *'resemble the flies of a summer'*: from Burke, *Reflections*, 141.

without remorse!: in *Political Essays*, Hazlitt adds a note: 'This passage is nearly a repetition of what was said before; but as it contains the sum and substance of all I have ever said on such subjects, I have let it stand.'

'Fine word, Legitimate!': from *King Lear*, I.ii.18. In the *Yellow Dwarf*, Hazlitt adds a note: 'The *word* is not even to be found in Waverly, nor would Miss Flora MacIvor have known what it meant.'

the Right-Liners . . . Sir Robert Filmer's: Sir Robert Filmer (d. 1653), a royalist in the English Civil War. Filmer's *Patriarcha* is a defence of absolute royal authority and the target of John Locke's criticism in the first of his *Two Treatises on Civil Government* (1690).

Latter Lammas: a day that will never come.

'Miratur novos . . . non sua poma': a recollection of Virgil, *Georgics*, ii.82, 'miratastque novas frondes et non sua poma' ('marvels at its strange leafage and fruits not its own', Loeb edition, trans. H. R. Fairclough).

79 *a certain author*: John Stoddart (1773–1856), leader writer and editor of *The Times*. Hazlitt's brother-in-law.

eyeless drudge of despotism: 'infatuated drudge' in the *Yellow Dwarf* and *Political Essays*.

'Louis XVIII . . . estate at Holkham': *Yellow Dwarf* and *Political Essays* add the following note, referring to Arthur Elphinstone, Lord Balmerino, and Simon Fraser, Lord Lovat, who were executed for their part in the Jacobite rising of 1745:

> What is the amount of this right of Mr. Coke's? It is not greater than that of the Lords Balmerino and Lovatt to their estates in Scotland, or to the heads upon their shoulders, the one of which however were forfeited, and the other stuck upon Temple Bar, for maintaining, in theory and practice, that James II. had the same right to the throne of these realms, independently of his merits or conduct, that Mr. Coke has to his estate at Holkham. So thought they. So did not think George II.

'Mr. Cobbett . . . suffered his confinement!': in June 1810, Cobbett was convicted on a charge of seditious libel for publishing an article on flogging in the military. He made and then withdrew an offer to the government to

discontinue the *Political Register* in order to escape punishment. He was sentenced to two years' imprisonment and fined £1,000, but continued to publish from Newgate. See *The Times*, 14 November 1816.

80 *'the professional gentleman'*: apparently Stoddart's self-description.

the Delphin edition of Ovid's Metamorphoses: the Delphin edition of classical authors, issued by A. and J. Valpy.

'Gods to punish . . . men of our infirmity': from *Coriolanus*, III.i.85–6.

81 *In spite of Mr. Malthus*: on Malthus's population theory, see note to p. 3.

the description of Gargantua in Rabelais: François Rabelais, *Gargantua and Pantagruel* (*c*.1534).

compagnons du lys: in 'Definition of Wit', Hazlitt explains, '*Compagnons du lys*, may mean either the *companions of the order of the flower-de-luce*, or the *companions of Ulysses*—who were transformed into swine—according as you lay the emphasis' (Howe, xx.355).

naturals and non-naturals: in ancient medicine, non-naturals are 'the six external factors (air, diet, sleep, exercise, excretion, and emotion) regarded as necessary to health, but which may through abuse, accident, etc., become a cause of disease' (*OED*).

'Why, what a fool . . . God!': see *The Tempest*, V.i.299–300.

82 *'Because men suffer it, their toy, the world'*: from Cowper, *The Task*, v.192.

'cribbed . . . cabin'd in': from *Macbeth*, III.iv.23.

'the right divine of kings to govern wrong': from Pope, *Dunciad*, IV.188.

'broad and casing . . . the rock': see *Macbeth* III.iv.21–2, 'Whole as the marble, founded as the rock, | As broad and general as the casing air'.

'Like the lightning's . . . gone for ever!': a recollection of Robert Burns, 'Tam o' Shanter', 61–6:

> Or like the snow falls in the river,
> A moment white—then melts for ever;
> Or like the borealis race,
> That flit ere you can point their place;
> Or like the rainbow's lovely form,
> Evanishing amid the storm.

83 *'enthroned in the hearts of kings'*: from *Merchant of Venice*, IV.i.191.

mild paternal sway: see Hazlitt's use of the phrase in 'Sketch of the History of the Good Old Times', for *The Examiner* 6, 13, and 20 April 1817: 'whoever after this sketch shall have the face to talk of "the good old times," of mild paternal sway, and the blessings of Legitimacy, that is, of power restrained only by its own interests, follies, vices, and passions, and therefore necessarily sacrificing to them the rights, liberties, and happiness of nations, we shall pronounce to be either a consummate hypocrite or a "fool indeed"' (Howe, xix.196).

'and levy cruel . . . the earth': from *Paradise Lost*, II.501–2.

83 '_steeped in poverty to the very lips_': from _Othello_, IV.ii.52.

'_to betray the cause of the people_': from Robespierre's speech of 28 December 1792 at the trial of Louis XVI, rejecting any suggestion that the king's fate should be determined by a referendum: 'Citizens, to betray the cause of the people and our own conscience, to hand over the nation to the chaos that the slow pace of such a trial would cause, that is the only danger we have to fear.'

84 '_punish the last successful example . . . rebellion_': from Stoddart in _The Times_.

'_large heart . . . confined in too narrow room_': an ironic adaptation of _Paradise Lost_, VII.484–8, 'First crept | The Parsimonious emmet, provident | Of future, in small room large heart enclosed, | Pattern of just equality perhaps | Hereafter'. Hazlitt substitutes 'narrow' for 'small', 'narrow room' being a common metaphor for the grave.

un people serf . . . misericorde: 'A servile people, liable to forced labour and exploitation, at the mercy of others' (Cook's translation).

'_king's castle_': see Burke, _Reflections_, 307, 'They have not forgot the taking of the King's castles in Paris'.

The Government of Ovando . . . History of the Buccaneers: see James Burney's (1750–1821) _Buccaneers of America_, vol. IV of his _Chronological History of the Discoveries in the south Sea or Pacific Ocean_ (1816): 'On her death bed she earnestly recommended to King Ferdinand to recal Ovando. Ovando, however, sent home much gold, and Ferdinand referred to a distant time the fulfilment of her dying request.'

lettres de cachet: documents signed by the king and sealed with the royal seal, used for various purposes but most notoriously to sentence a subject to indefinite imprisonment without trial.

corvees: rents paid in labour.

menus plaisirs: 'small pleasures', or pocket money.

85 _Mr. C—— or Lord C——_: George Canning and Lord Castlereagh (1769–1822).

Count Fathom or Jonathan Wild: anti-heroes of Tobias Smollett's _Adventures of Ferdinand Count Fathom_ (1753) and Fielding's _Jonathan Wild_ (1743).

'_O silly sheep . . . here of the wolf?_': see _Measure for Measure_, V.i.294–5, 'But O, poor souls, | Come you to seek the lamb here of the fox'.

'_any faction . . . sword into its hands_': from Burke, _An Appeal from the New to the Old Whigs_ (1791): 'These doctrines concerning the _people_ (a term which they [the new Whigs] are far from accurately defining, but by which, from many circumstances, it is plain enough they mean their own faction, if they should grow by early arming, by treachery, or violence, into the prevailing force)...' (56–7). See also Southey's review of pamphlets on parliamentary reform in the _Quarterly_, 16 (October 1816, actually published 11 February 1817), 225–78: 'By the _people_, of course, the discontented faction is meant—the deceivers and the deceived—according to that figure of speech by which a part is put for the whole—a political synecdoche' (262).

86 *Vox populi vox dei*: 'The voice of the people is the voice of God' (proverbial).

Hobbes's Leviathan: see the introduction to Thomas Hobbes's *Leviathan*, 'by art is created that great LEVIATHAN called a COMMONWEALTH, or STATE.'

87 *Lord Bacon*: Francis Bacon (1561–1626), lord chancellor and natural philosopher.

'tried wisdom': from the Prince Regent's reply to the 'Address of the Corporation of London' on the national distresses of the winter of 1816, as reported in the *Examiner* for 15 December 1816:

> Deeply as I deplore the prevailing distress and difficulties of the Country, I derive consolation from the persuasion, that the great body of his Majesty's subjects, notwithstanding the various attempts which have been made to irritate and mislead them, are well convinced, that the SEVERE TRIALS which they sustain with such exemplary patience and fortitude, are chiefly to be attributed to UNAVOIDABLE CAUSES . . . I shall resort, with the utmost confidence, to the TRIED WISDOM OF PARLIAMENT.

except the income-tax: the House of Commons rejected the government's proposal for a 5% property (income) tax on 19 March 1816.

88 *'If they had not ploughed . . . our riddle'*: from Judges 14:18.

Franklin, Howard, Clarkson and Bentham: Benjamin Franklin (1706–90), natural philosopher, writer, and American revolutionary; John Howard (1726?–1790), philanthropist and prison reformer; Thomas Clarkson (1760–1846), abolitionist; Jeremy Bentham (1748–1832), philosopher, jurist, and reformer. This sentence was cut from *Political Essays*.

How long . . . our state-jugglers: the Roman Catholic Emancipation Act was passed in 1829.

See Coleridge's Friend, No. 15: see *The Friend* for 30 November 1809.

89 *'left his wife . . . Lamb and Southey'*: this attack on Coleridge, Lamb, and Southey by John Gifford (1758–1818), editor of *The Anti-Jacobin Review and Magazine*, was published as a note to the poem 'The New Morality' in *The Beauties of the Anti-Jacobin* (1799), 306. William Gifford (no relation) was the editor of another Tory publication, the *Quarterly Review*.

'the universal Spanish nation': Canning used the phrase in a speech in the House of Commons on 31 January 1809: 'the universal Spanish nation in arms against the usurpation of Joseph Buonaparté, who neither had right to their throne nor possession of their monarchy.'

ode, elegy, or sonnet: see Johnson, 'Lines Written in Ridicule of Thomas Warton's Poems', 8.

'make him a willow . . . night!': from *Twelfth Night*, I.v.257–60.

90 *'the most popular . . . carried on'*: from Southey's article in the *Quarterly*: 'no object could be more rational than that for which the war was persisted in, no object more just, more necessary, more popular' (239).

He indeed assures us . . . twenty-five years?: see Southey's review of pamphlets on parliamentary reform in the *Quarterly* (October 1816):

> How often have we heard that the voice of the people is the voice of God, from demagogues who were labouring to deceive the people, and who despised the wretched instruments of whom they made use! But it is the Devil whose name is Legion. *Vox Populi, vox Dei!* When or where has it been so? Was it in England during the riots in 1780? Has it been in France during the last six and twenty years? Or was it in Spain when the people restored the Inquisition?—for it *was* the people who restored that accursed tribunal, spontaneously and tumultuously—*not* the government, which only ratified what the people had done . . . Or was it so at Jerusalem when they cried, Crucify Him! crucify Him! (276)

'persecuted, insulted . . . and fortune': see Southey in the *Quarterly*: 'The principle of loyalty was triumphant even to intolerance; in most parts of England the appellations of republican and jacobin were sufficient to mark a man for public odium, perhaps for personal danger, persecution and ruin' (228).

Mr. Locke has observed: see John Locke, *An Essay Concerning Human Understanding* (1689), IV.xx, section 18.

91 *the dispute between Mr. Epps . . . for himself*: in *Political Essays*, Mr. Epps goes from being 'the ham-shop keeper in the Strand' to just 'the angry shopkeeper in the Strand'.

like Orlando's eldest brother . . . 'stying us': see *As You Like It*, I.i.8, 'He sties me here at home' (Warburton's emendation of the Folio text).

a Reading Public: see Coleridge's contemptuous passage on 'The Reading Public' (117–18).

Bell and Lancaster's plans: the educational systems of Andrew Bell (1753–1832) and Joseph Lancaster (1778–1838).

92 *Mr. Vansittart . . . in 'Change-alley*: Nicholas Vansittart (1766–1851), chancellor of the exchequer; see Burke, *Reflections*, 156: 'The Jews in Change Alley have not yet dared to hint their hopes of a mortgage on the revenues belonging to the see of Canterbury'.

Joanna Southcott and the Millennium: Joanna Southcott (1750–1814) had prophesied Christ's Second Coming.

When the sky falls: see Matthew 16:1–3, 'O ye hypocrites, ye can discern the face of the sky; but can ye not discern the signs of the times?'; also Rabelais, *Gargantua and Pantagruel*, I.xi: 'By robbing Peter he payed Paul, he kept the Moon from the wolves, and hoped to catch Larks if ever the Heavens should fall'.

the proverb is somewhat musty: see *Hamlet*, III.ii.330–1.

'hold a barren ... unlineal hand!': from *Macbeth*, III.i.63–4.

93 *'for the Son ... steady steps'*: see Robert Southey, *The Lay of the Laureate: Carmen Nuptiale* (1816), 307–8:

> Look to thy Sire, and in his steady way,
> As in his Father's he, learn thou to tread ...

the two Ferdinands: Ferdinand I (1751–1825), King of the Two Sicilies, and Ferdinand VII (1784–1833), King of Spain.

swinish multitude: a famous phrase from Burke's *Reflections*, 117: 'Along with its natural protectors and guardians, learning will be cast into the mire, and trodden down under the hoofs of a swinish multitude.'

'It is the cause, it is the cause, my soul': from *Othello*, V.ii.1. This quotation provided the epigraph to the third part of the essay in the *Champion* but was replaced by asterisks in *Political Essays*.

'that complex constable': see Thomas Heywood, *The second part of King Edward the fourth*, 'the Constable', 'the great Constable', 'the treacherous Constable', 'our cunning Constable', etc.

For a people ... will to be free: see Voltaire, *Brutus*, II.i (1730), 'L'homme est libre au moment qu'il veut l'être' ('Man is free at the instant he wants to be').

94 *'Liceat, quæso ... mittat'*: from Milton, *Pro Populo Anglicano Defensio* ('Defence of the People of England', 1658): 'A people that has felt the yoke of slavery heavy on its neck may well be allowed to be wise and learned and noble enough to know what should be done to its oppressor, though it send not to ask either foreigners or grammarians' (I.i).

Mr. Burke's Sublime and Beautiful: see Burke's *Philosophical Enquiry into the Origin of our Ideas of the Sublime and Beautiful* (1757).

poor Evans ... politics: Thomas Evans (1763–*c*.1831), leader of the agrarian-radical Society of Spencean Philanthropists, was arrested in February 1817 under the Habeas Corpus Suspension Act and imprisoned in Horsemonger Lane Gaol. According to a petition presented to parliament on his behalf, he was 'removed to a condemned cell of the most wretched description, and a flute, his only amusement, taken from him' (*Hansard*, 27 June 1817). He was eventually released without charge.

Mr. Hiley Addington: John Hiley Addington (1759–1818), brother of Lord Sidmouth, the Home Secretary, told the House, 'Much stress had been laid on depriving Mr. Evans of his flute; it was, however, the rule of the prison not to allow music, as it disturbed others, but Mr. Evans might have had his flute if he did not make use of it' (*Hansard*, 2 July 1817).

nor out of his arcade: this phrase is not included in the *Yellow Dwarf* or *Political Essays*.

'forsooth': quoting John Stoddart's account of Evans's story in *The Day and New Times*.

Mr. Cobbett himself ... quit the country: William Cobbett fled to America in March 1817, fearing arrest after the suspension of habeas corpus. He spent over two years on Long Island, continuing to publish the *Political Register* before returning to Britain after the Peterloo massacre.

95 *Lisbon Job*: George Canning had been sent to Lisbon in 1814 as ambassador extraordinary to receive the King of Portugal on his return from Brazil. The appointment carried a salary of £14,000; when the King did not return the appointment was denounced by the Opposition as a fake job.

'*duller . . . Lethe's wharf*': from *Hamlet*, I.v.32–3.

96 '*the dim suffusion . . . no dawn*': see *Paradise Lost*, III.22–6:

> but thou
> Revisitst not these eyes, that roll in vain
> To find thy piercing ray, and find no dawn;
> So thick a drop serene hath quenched their orbs,
> Or dim suffusion veiled.

'*making Ossa like a wart*': from *Hamlet*, V.i.280.

'*as gross as ignorance made drunk*': from *Othello*, III.iii.409–10.

97 *Wat Tyler*: Wat Tyler, leader of the Peasants' Revolt, was killed in 1381 when his rebel bands met Richard II at Smithfield. Robert Southey's radical play *Wat Tyler* was written in 1794, but remained unpublished until pirated in 1817 to embarrass Southey. Lord Eldon rejected Southey's application for an injunction on publication.

'*a necessity . . . to anarchy*': from Burke, *Reflections*, 144.

98 '*too foolish fond and pitiful*': a recollection of *King Lear*, IV.vi.53, 'I am a very foolish, fond old man'.

John Ball's: chaplain in the Peasants' Revolt, executed 1381.

written in very choice blank verse: see *Hamlet*, III.ii.250–1, 'writ in choice Italian'.

'*did never wrong but with just cause*': see *Julius Caesar*, III.i.47, 'Know Caesar doth not wrong but with just cause'.

99 *Reform in old government . . . to quit*: John Nash's (1752–1835) plans to connect Carlton House, in Pall Mall, with the Regent's Park through the creation of Regent Street were approved by parliament in 1813. The project involved the destruction of many older streets.

Exit by Mistake: play by Robert Francis Jameson, performed at the Haymarket in July 1816.

15. ON COURT INFLUENCE

Published in the *Yellow Dwarf* for 3 and 10 January 1818. Reprinted in *Political Essays* (1819).

101 '*To be honest . . . out of ten thousand*': from *Hamlet*, II.ii.180–1.

102 '*But still the world and its dread laugh prevails!*': see Thomson, *The Seasons*, 'Autumn', 233, 'For still the world prevailed, and its dread laugh'.

a book . . . ought to read: George III reportedly told Burke at a levee (3 February 1791), 'I know that there is no Man who calls himself a Gentleman that must not think himself obliged to you, for you have supported the cause of the Gentlemen.' See *Correspondence of Edmund Burke*, ed. Thomas W. Copeland et al., 10 vols (Cambridge, 1958–78), VI.239.

103 *'a certificate of merit'*: from Burke, *A Letter to a Noble Lord* (1796), 29: 'At every step of my progress in life (for in every step was I traversed and opposed), and at every turnpike I met, I was obliged to shew my passport, and again and again to prove my sole title to the honour of being useful to my Country, by a proof that I was not wholly unacquainted with its laws, and the whole system of its interests both abroad and at home.'

'Thou hast it now, king, Cawdor, Glamis, all!': from *Macbeth*, III.i.1.

104 *'swept and garnished'*: from Luke 11:25.

Indignatio facit versus: from Juvenal, *Satires*, I.79, 'facit indignatio versum' ('indignation makes poetry').

The Letters of William Burke . . . not desert his cause: *The Works of James Barry* (2 vols, London, 1809) contains ten letters from William Burke (a distant relative of Edmund) to Barry. Here Hazlitt recollects Burke's letter to Barry of 3 December 1766:

> Our friend E.B. has acted all along with so unwearied a worthiness, that the world even does him the justice to know, that in his public conduct, he has no one view but the public good; and indeed, Barry, there is a satisfaction in thinking, that to a friend intimate as you are, to whom we might trust our faults even, we have no single motive of our conduct to state, but the one which is visible and apparent, that is, a real disinterested desire and determination of acting strictly right. (i.77)

105 *'And with it words . . . more rare'*: see *Hamlet*, III.i.100–1: 'And with them words of so sweet breath composed | As made the things more rich.'

'escap'd from Pyrrho's maze, and Epicurus' sty': from James Beattie, *The Minstrel* (1771), I.357.

'Britain's warriors, her statesmen, and her fair': from Southey, *Lay of the Laureate*, 215–16:

> Of Britain's Court . . . a proud assemblage there,
> Her statesmen, and her Warriors, and her Fair.

'Rich gifts wax poor, when givers prove unkind': from *Hamlet*, III.i.103.

106 *'In their Livery . . . from their Pockets'*: from *Antony and Cleopatra*, V.ii.89–91.

That sweet smile that hangs on princes' favours: as Howe notes, this is a good example of the composite or synthetic quotation, from *Henry VIII*, III.ii.367–70:

> O, how wretched
> Is that poor man that hangs on princes' favours!

> There is betwixt that smile we would aspire to,
> That sweet aspect of princes...

107 '*Soul-killing lies, and truths that work small good*': from Lamb, *John Woodvil*, II.ii.

'*pierces through the body of the city, country, court*': from *As You Like It*, II.i.58–9.

'*Whosoever shall stumble . . . grind him to powder*': from Matthew 21:44.

108 '*scorn to point his slow and moving finger at*': from *Othello*, IV.ii.56–7.

the hardest stone . . . at a man: see Sir Thomas Browne, *Hydriotaphia* (1658), ch. 4: 'It is the heaviest stone that melancholy can throw at a man, to tell him he is at the end of his nature; or that there is no further state to come' (67).

'*a consummation devoutly to be wished*': from *Hamlet*, III.i.65–6.

a certain distinguished character: Lord Castlereagh.

Walcheren: a disastrous British military expedition to the Low Countries in July 1809, during which four thousand soldiers died, mainly of disease.

109 *Reynolds*: Thomas Reynolds (1771–1836), informer in the Irish Rebellion of 1798 and one of the grand jury who returned a true bill against James Watson and others for high treason following the Spa Fields meetings. Francis Burdett denounced him in the Commons as 'a notorious spy' in receipt of a government pension (16 June 1817) and the government, embarrassed by this revelation, shipped him out of the country to take up the post of British consul in Iceland.

the Attorney-General: Sir Samuel Shepherd MP (1760–1840) succeeded Sir William Garrow as attorney-general in spring 1817 with mixed success in his prosecution of radicals.

Mr. Coleridge, in his Literary Biography: a reference to the note at the end of *Biographia Literaria*, ch. 3, which Hazlitt reviewed for the *Edinburgh Review* in August 1817, the month after its publication.

his present friend and associate in the Quarterly Review: William Gifford (1756–1826), editor of *The Anti-Jacobin or Weekly Examiner* (1797–8) and the *Quarterly* (1809–24).

'*the cynosure of longing eyes*': see Milton, *L'Allegro*, 80, 'The cynosure of neighbouring eyes'.

110 *In an article in the Quarterly Review . . . life*: see Southey's review of the pamphlets on parliamentary reform (*Quarterly*, October 1816), quoted in note to p. 90.

The same consistent writers . . . in this country: see Coleridge's attack on Unitarianism in *The Statesman's Manual*, the first of his *Lay Sermons* (reviewed by Hazlitt in the *Edinburgh* for December 1816) and Southey's article in the *Quarterly*.

'the single-heartedness of the Spanish nation': Southey claimed that 'the Spaniards were devotedly attached' to their royal family before Napoleon detained Ferdinand VII; see *Quarterly Review* (October 1816), 241.

in discharge of an old debt: Hazlitt picks up here from a footnote at the end of *The Round Table* essay 'On the Tendency of Sects': 'We shall some time or other give the reverse of the picture' (Howe, iv.51).

'at the peril . . . their lives': another paraphrase of the lines from Southey's *Quarterly* article.

112 *'Or if severe . . . is in fault'*: see Oliver Goldsmith, *The Deserted Village* (1770), 205–6:

> or if severe in aught,
> The love he bore to learning was in fault.

safest partizans . . . in spite of opposition: recycled from the final paragraph of 'On the Tendency of Sects'.

'the hortus siccus of dissent': from Burke, *Reflections on the Revolution in France*, 15: 'It would certainly be a valuable addition of nondescripts to the ample collection of known classes, genera and species, which at present beautify the *hortus siccus* [dried garden] of dissent.'

Non ex quovis lingo fit Mercurius: from Erasmus, *Adagiorum Chiliades*, II.v.47: 'A Mercury is not made out of any piece of wood.'

But we have known some such: Hazlitt is thinking here of his father, who he had recently visited in his retirement at Bath.

113 *Book of Martyrs*: John Foxe's account of the martyrdoms of John Huss (1415) and Jerome of Prague (1416) in *Actes and Monuments* (1563).

Neale's History of the Puritans: Daniel Neal (1648–1743), *History of the Puritans* (1732–8).

Calamy's Account . . . Ejected Ministers: Edmund Calamy (1671–1732), *The Nonconformist's Memorial*, edited by Samuel Palmer (London, 1802).

silver-tongued Bates . . . old honest Howe: William Bates (1625–99) and John Howe (1630–1705), two of the ejected ministers.

Lardner's Credibility of the Gospel History: by Nathaniel Lardner (1684–1768), published 1727–57.

the Fratres Poloni: The *Bibliotheca Fratrum Polonorum* (8 vols, 1656) was in Hazlitt's father's library.

'time-rent': from Coleridge, 'To the Author of *The Robbers*' (1796), 3: 'From the dark dungeon of the tower time-rent'.

'Glory to God . . . good will to man': from Luke 2:14.

114 *'hurt by the archers'*: from Cowper, *The Task*, iii.113.

the poisoned shirt of Nessus: in Greek mythology, the poisoned tunic of the centaur Nessus who killed Heracles.

114 *Happy are they . . . about them*: this paragraph was a favourite of Hazlitt's and became a touchstone in his writing, first appearing as the peroration to *A Reply of Malthus* and then at the end of a 'Round Table' essay in the *Examiner* (9 April 1815), which was republished in 1839 as 'Mind and Motive'. See the Introduction, pp. xxx–xxxi.

a dream and a glory is ever about them: see Wordsworth, 'Ode: Intimations of Immortality', 57, 'Where is it now, the glory and the dream?'

16. ON FASHION

Published in the *Edinburgh Magazine* for September 1818.

115 *'Born of nothing, begot of nothing'*: see *Othello*, III.iv.159, 'Begot upon itself, born on itself.'

'His garment . . . there': from Spenser, *The Faerie Queene*, III.xii.8.

'the great vulgar and small': from Cowley, *Horace's Odes*, III.i.2.

116 *'The fashion of an hour old mocks the wearer'*: unidentified.

117 *virtù*: 'appreciation or taste for, or expertise in, the fine arts' (*OED*).

pomatum: 'an ointment for the skin or hair' (*OED*).

Lord Foppington: a character in Vanbrugh's play *The Relapse* (1696).

'the sign of an inward and invisible grace': part of the Catechism from the *Book of Common Prayer*.

118 *'and are, when unadorned . . . the most'*: see Thomson, *The Seasons*, 'Autumn', 206.

authentic Memoirs of the Fudge Family: Thomas Moore, *The Fudge Family in Paris* (1818).

Niobe head: figure from Greek mythology and popular subject in eighteenth-century sculpture.

poke bonnet: a women's bonnet with a small crown and wide and projecting brim.

marchands des modes: fashion merchants.

'the city madam . . . unworthy shoulders': see *As You Like It*, II.vii.75–6.

'In the grand carnival of this our age': see Burke, *A Letter to a Noble Lord*, 'in the masquerades of the grand carnival of our age, whimsical adventures happen' (8).

'the age . . . his kibe': see *Hamlet*, V.i.135–7.

to take the wall: to walk next to the wall, away from the road, and hence to take precedence.

119 *petit-maitre*: 'an effeminate man; a dandy, a fop' (*OED*).

the story in Peregrine Pickle: see Smollett, *Peregrine Pickle*, ch. 87.

'lisping, and ambling . . . creatures': see *Hamlet*, III.i.147–8.

120 *'in a high or low degree'*: see Pope, 'Epilogue to the Satires: Dialogue I', 137.

'*And thin partitions . . . divide*': from Dryden, *Absalom and Achitophel*, 164.

Mr Smith and the Brangtons: in Burney's *Evelina* (1778), the Branghtons are the city cousins of the heroine. Mr Smith is their lodger.

'*Kings are naturally lovers of low company*': an oft-quoted line from Burke's 'Speech on Economical Reform' (11 February 1780).

17. MINOR THEATRES

Published in the *London Magazine* as Hazlitt's monthly column on 'The Drama' for March 1820.

121   *Theatre-Royal*: the royal patent theatres of Covent Garden, Drury Lane, and (during the summer months) the Haymarket held an exclusive licence on 'legitimate' or spoken drama until the Theatres Act of 1843. As a way around this monopoly, the 'minor' or 'illegitimate' theatres incorporated music, mime, and dance into their productions.

'*ample scope and verge enough*': see Thomas Gray, 'The Bard', 51–2, 'Give ample room, and verge enough | The characters of hell to trace.'

'*this I like . . . as one picks pears*': Cervantes, *Don Quixote*, see note to p. 7.

the Surry theatre: the Surrey Theatre, south of the Thames on Blackfriars Road.

snatch a grace . . . reach of art: from Pope, *Essay on Criticism*, 155.

Miss Dennetts at the Adelphi: the three Dennett sisters were regular performers at the Adelphi Theatre on the Strand.

Devil upon Two Sticks: a reference to Alain-René Lesage's 1707 comic novel, *The Devil upon Two Sticks* (*Le Diable Boiteux*).

Mr. Booth at the Cobourg: Junius Brutus Booth (1796–1852), playing at the Royal Coburg Theatre (now the Old Vic).

Mr. Rae and the East London: Alexander Rae (1782–1820) had recently taken over the management of the East London Theatre, also known as the Royalty, in Wellclose Square, Whitechapel.

Mrs. Gould . . . the Furies: Mrs Gould performed the title role of William Thomas Moncrieff's 'operatic extravaganza' *Giovanni in London; or, The Libertine Reclaimed* (1817) in breeches.

'*constrained by mastery*': from Chaucer, *Canterbury Tales*, 'The Franklin's Tale', 36.

'*speculative and officed instruments*': from *Othello*, I.iii.270.

'*clappeth his wings . . . is gone*': see Robert Blair, *The Grave*, 767, 'Then claps his well-fledg'd wings, and bears away.'

122   '*There he arriving . . . wretchedness!*': from Spenser, 'Muiopotmos, or the Fate of the Butterflie', stanzas 22 and 27.

'*like greyhound on the slip*': from *Henry V*, III.i.31.

'*the full eyes . . . childhood*': see Jeremy Taylor, *Holy Dying* (1651), I.ii.

123 *'embalmed with odours'*: from *Paradise Lost*, II.842–3.

'a wide O': see 'this wooden O', *Henry V*, Prologue, 13.

'Come, let me clutch thee!': from *Macbeth*, II.i.34.

'those gay creatures . . . clouds!': from Milton, *Comus*, 299–301.

W——m in S——shire: Wem, Shropshire.

124 *W——ch*: Whitchurch, nine miles from Wem.

the Rev. Mr. J——s: in 'My First Acquaintance with Poets', Hazlitt describes how his father 'was in the habit of exchanging visits . . . with Mr. Jenkins of Whitchurch'.

the West-Indian: Richard Cumberland, *The West Indian* (1771).

No Song No Supper: Stephen Storace's 1790 English opera, to a libretto by Prince Hoare.

125 *like Nebuchadnezzar's image*: see Daniel 2.

'of imagination all compact': from *A Midsummer Night's Dream*, V.i.8.

'Their mind to them a kingdom is': from Sir Edward Dryer's 'My mynde to me a kyngdome is,' set to music by William Byrd in 1588.

'of all earth's bliss . . . loving': the concluding lines of Lamb's translation of Thekla's song from Schiller, *The Piccolomini*, printed at the end of *John Woodvil* (1802).

Fortunatus's Wishing Cap: from Giovanni Francesco Straparola's *The Nights of Straparola* (1550–3).

aurum potabile: 'drinkable gold'.

126 *'by his so potent art'*: from *The Tempest*, V.i.50.

'happy alchemy of mind': from Matthew Green, *The Spleen* (1737), 610–11, 'By happy alchymy of mind | They turn to pleasure all they find'.

who once overtook us: as Howe suggests, surely a memory of Hazlitt's journey to Nether Stowey to visit Coleridge in May 1798, described in 'My First Acquaintance with Poets'.

'Severn's sedgy side': see *1 Henry IV*, I.iii.97, 'gentle Severn's sedgy bank'.

'The beggars are . . . in velvet gowns': from the nursery rhyme, 'Hark, hark! the dogs do bark'.

'Alas! how changed . . . whim!': from Pope, 'An Epistle to Allen Lord Bathurst', 305–6.

127 *'pleasure's finest point'*: cf. 'Thoughts on Taste' (*Edinburgh Magazine*, July 1819), in reference to Angelica Catalani: 'he who has an ear attuned to the trembling harmony, and a heart "pierceable" by pleasure's finest point, is the best judge of music'.

cheveux-de-fris: an anti-cavalry defence, consisting of a timber frame with projecting spikes (literally, 'Frisian horse', the Frisians having few cavalry).

'made of penetrable stuff': from *Hamlet*, III.iv.35.

128 *'see the puppets dallying'*: from *Hamlet*, III.ii.235.

'*not the men you took them for*': from *Much Ado About Nothing*, III.iii.46.

Mr. Stanley: Hazlitt reviewed his Drury Lane debut for *The Times* (12 September 1817).

129 *Panopticon*: Jeremy Bentham's prison design, in which an individual in a central tower can observe all the prisoners or workers in their cells, without them knowing whether they are being watched (*Panopticon, or The Inspection-House*, 1791).

Mr. H. Kemble: Henry Kemble (1789–1836), son of Stephen Kemble and nephew of Mrs Siddons, performing in the minor theatres after a disastrous season under his father's management at Drury Lane.

'*My soul turn . . . survey*': from Oliver Goldsmith, *The Traveller* (1764), 163.

we believe has been said: by Hazlitt himself in the *Examiner* (27 October 1816).

'*Her lovely Venus . . . bore*': from Milton, *L'Allegro*, 14–16.

Columbines, and figurantes: Columbina is a character in the *commedia dell'arte*, the mistress of Harlequin, transferred to English pantomime or harlequinade; a figurante is a ballet dancer or a supernumerary character (*OED*).

'*vernal airs . . . leaves*': from *Paradise Lost*, IV.264–6.

'*four red roses on a stalk*': from *Richard III*, IV.iii.12.

'*the witchery of the soft blue sky*': from Wordsworth, *Peter Bell*, 235.

the Count Stendhal, who speaks so feelingly: see Stendhal, *Rome, Naples et Florence en 1817*.

130 *Mr. Reeve*: John Reeve (1799–1838), mimic and comedian.

Matthews: Charles Mathews (1776–1835), comic actor and mimic, celebrated for his 'At Home' one-man shows.

Farren . . . Harley: William Farren (1786–1861) and John Pritt Harley (1786–1858), both actors at the patent theatres.

131 *Haymarket and Lyceum*: the Haymarket Theatre was licensed to stage spoken or legitimate drama in the summer months while the Lyceum, or English Opera House, adjacent to Exeter Change on the Strand, held a summer licence to stage musical farces and ballad operas.

'*our hint to speak*': from *Othello*, I.iii.141.

Mr. Dibdin: Thomas John Dibbin (1771–1841), playwright and actor, took over the Surrey Theatre in 1816.

Mr. Peter Moore: Peter Moore (1753–1828), politician and formerly a director of Drury Lane.

Mr. Elliston: Robert William Elliston (1774–1831), actor and manager of Drury Lane.

the Antiquary: an adaptation of Scott's novel by Isaac Pocock and Daniel Terry, first performed 25 January 1820.

131 *admirable portrait of Dominie Sampson*: from Scott's *Guy Mannering* (1815).

Emery: John Emery (1777–1822), actor.

'warbled': see *As You Like It*, II.v.34: 'Come, warble, come.'

Miss Stephens: Catherine (Kitty) Stephens (1794–1882), singer and actress.

132 *in the words of a contemporary journal*: Hazlitt quotes from his own review of Kean's Othello in *The Times* (27 October 1817).

18. ON THE PLEASURE OF PAINTING

Hazlitt's father died on 16 June 1820. Invited to write an obituary, Hazlitt wrote this essay instead, published in the *London Magazine* for December 1820 and reprinted in the first volume of *Table Talk* (1821).

134 *'There is a pleasure in painting which none but painters know'*: see Cowper, *The Task*, ii.285–6, 'There is a pleasure in poetic pains | Which only poets know', and behind this Dryden, *The Spanish Friar* (1681), II.i, 'There is a pleasure, sure, | In being mad, which none but madmen know!'

'no juggling here': see *Troilus and Cressida*, II.iii.70–1, 'Here is such patchery, such juggling and such knavery', also Kane O'Hara, *April-Day* (1777), II, 'This is past coz'nage, no juggling here'.

'study with joy . . . her style': see Cowper, *The Task*, iii.227–8.

spolia opima: 'ultimate spoils', the armour of an enemy commander killed in single combat, offered to Jupiter.

a passage in Werter: see Goethe's *Die Leiden des Jungen Werthers* ('The Sorrows of Young Werther') (1774), Letter viii. Hazlitt quotes from the first English translation, by Daniel Malthus (1779).

135 *'more tedious than a twice-told tale'*: see *King John*, III.iv.108.

'My mind to me a kingdom is': first line of a poem on contentment first published in William Byrd's *Psalmes, Sonets, & Songs* (1588), once attributed to Edward Dryer (1543–1607), more probably by Edward de Vere, earl of Oxford (1550–1604).

'to set a throne . . . other men': see Bacon, *Advancement of Learning*, I.viii.3: 'For there is no power on earth which setteth up a throne or chair of estate in the spirits and souls of men, and in their cogitations, imagination, opinions, and beliefs, but knowledge and learning'.

'Pure in the last recesses of the mind': from Dryden, *Satires of Aulus Persius Flaccus*, ii.133.

136 *'palpable to feeling as to sight'*: cf. *Othello*, I.ii.77, 'palpable to thinking', and *Macbeth*, II.i.36–41:

> Art thou not, fatal vision, sensible
> To feeling as to sight? . . .
> I see thee yet, in form as palpable
> As this which now I draw.

'fleecy fools': see Charles Lamb, *The Adventures of Ulysses* (1808), 1, or alternatively, Cobbett, 'Mr. Cobbett's Taking Leave of his Countrymen' (March 1817), 11.

'light thickened': see *Macbeth*, III.ii.51, 'light thickens'.

137 *Wilson said*: Richard Wilson (1714–82). As Cook suggests, Hazlitt's source for these stories was probably James Northcote; see *Conversations of James Northcote, Esq, RA* (1830).

It was not so Claude . . . distant hills!: Claude returned to Rome in 1627, remaining there until his death in 1682.

The first head I ever tried to paint: Hazlitt's son relates that, 'This person the writer met with in the vicinity of Manchester in 1803 (I believe)'; the painting is now in Maidstone Museum.

to see good in every thing: see *As You Like It*, II.i.17.

If art was long . . . too: a reworking of the Latin proverb *ars longa, vita brevis* ('art is long, life is short'), a translation by Seneca (*Dialogi*, X.i) from the first of the *Aphorismi* of Hippocrates.

138 *with Sir Joshua . . . individual details*: an argument Hazlitt expanded in his *Table Talk* essays 'On Certain Inconsistencies in Sir Joshua Reynolds's Discourses'.

139 *'as in a glass darkly, but now face to face'*: see 1 Corinthians, 13:12.

'sees into the life of things': from Wordsworth, 'Tintern Abbey', 50.

Jan Steen or Gerard Dow: Jan Havicksz Steen (*c.*1626–79) and Gerard Dou (1613–75), Dutch Old Masters.

'mist, the common gloss of theologians': from *Paradise Lost*, V.435–6.

140 *Richardson . . . accordingly*: see *The Works of Jonathan Richardson* (1792 edition), 209. The original story is in Vasari's *Lives of the Artists*.

The famous Schiller . . . duty: the source for this supposed remark is untraced.

141 *'That you might almost say his picture thought!'*: see Donne, 'Of the Progress of the Soul. The Second Anniversary', 245–6, 'so distinctly wrought, | That one might almost say, her body thought'.

'he took no other . . . painting-room': again, the likely source is Hazlitt's conversations with Northcote.

'the source . . . to him': see James Northcote, *Memoirs of Sir Joshua Reynolds* (1813), 370: 'I have been fortunate in an uninterrupted share of good health and success for thirty years of my life: therefore, whatever ills may attend on the remainder of my days, I shall have no right to complain'.

a picture of my father: now in Maidstone Museum. Hazlitt's grandson relates that this was 'taken in 1804; the Rev. W. Hazlitt was then sixty-eight' (*Table Talk*, 1869 edition, 11).

142 *Gribelin's etchings*: in the second (1714) and subsequent editions of Shaftesbury's *Characteristics*.

142 *'riches fineless'*: from *Othello*, III.iii.177.

'ever in the haunch of winter sings': from *2 Henry IV*, IV.iii.92.

'I also am a painter!': on standing before a painting by Raphael, Correggio is supposed to have said, 'Anch'io son pittore'.

It was an idle thought, a boy's conceit: Wu identifies this as a quotation from Schiller, *Die Räuber*, tr. A. F. Tyler (1792), III.ii, 'Twas an idle thought, a boy's conceit!' (108).

to the Exhibition: Hazlitt's 'Portrait of his father' was in the Royal Academy exhibition of 1802 at Somerset House.

Mr. Skeffington: Sir Lumley St. George Skeffington (1771–1850), play-wright and fop, who succeeded his father as baronet in 1815. The portrait was by John James Masquerier (1778–1855).

the battle of Austerlitz: Napoleon's victory over the Austrian and Russian armies on 2 December 1805.

the evening star set over a poor man's cottage: Hazlitt reprises an image from his letter to the *Morning Chronicle* (28 January 1814), part of a combative exchange with John Stoddart, his brother-in-law and editor of *The Times*: 'He who has seen the evening star set over a poor man's cottage, or has connected the feeling of hope with the heart of man, and who, though he may have lost the feeling, has never ceased to reverence it—he, Sir, with submission, and without a nickname, is the *true Jacobin*.' See Matthew 2:9–10 for the messianic overtones; also Wordsworth, 'Michael', 485–6, 'The Cottage which was named The Evening Star | Is gone'.

the great Platonic year: the mythical period in which the heavenly bodies will return to their original positions; see Plato's *Timaeus*, 38b–40d.

the window . . . the chapel: the presbytery in Noble Street, Wem still stands, now named Hazlitt House; the chapel has been converted into the garage of the White Horse Hotel.

143 *'Whate'er Lorraine . . . Poussin drew'*: from Thomson, *The Castle of Indolence* (1748), I.xxxviii.8–9.

Lord Radnor's Park: Longford Castle, Wiltshire. See Hazlitt's *Sketches of the Principal Picture Galleries in England* (1824) for this and other collections referred to here.

'embowered deep in tufted trees': see Milton, *L'Allegro*, 78, 'Bosomed high in tufted trees'. Unusually, Hazlitt corrected the quotation when he republished the essay.

the Orleans Gallery: see note to p. 25.

the scales fell off: see Acts 9:18.

144 *'hands that the rod of empire had swayed'*: from Thomas Gray, 'Elegy Written in a Country Churchyard', 47.

'a forked mountain . . . with air': from *Antony and Cleopatra*, IV.xv.5–7.

'signifying nothing': from *Macbeth*, V.v.27.

the Provoked Husband: Vanbrugh's unfinished comedy, completed by Cibber (1728).

when I went to the Louvre: see note to p. 29.

which a friend lent me: Wu suggests Robert Freebairn (1794/5–1846), landscape painter and pupil of Richard Wilson.

Titian's Mistress: in the Louvre; in fact a portrait of Alphonso of Ferrara and Laura Dianti.

'A young Nobleman with a glove': Hazlitt's copy of Titian's painting is now in the Maidstone Museum.

145 *un beau jour*: Jean Sylvain Bailly's description of 6 October 1789, when Louis XVI was forced from Versailles to Paris, ironically quoted by Burke in *Reflections on the Revolution in France*, 103.

the Transfiguration . . . Hippolito de Medici: after Waterloo, Raphael's *Transfiguration* and Domenichino's *Communion of St. Jerome* were restored to Rome; Titian's *St. Peter Martyr* to Venice, and his *Hippolito de Medici* to Florence.

'if thou has not seen . . . damned!': see *As You Like It*, III.ii.34.

which I have been forced to part with: Hazlitt sold his copies to Haydon during financial difficulties in 1819. He later recovered them at the sale of Haydon's belongings after his bankruptcy in 1823.

'hard money': see Kite's speech in George Farquhar, *The Recruiting Officer* (1706), IV.ii: 'your Mother has an hundred Pound in hard Money lying at this Minute in the hands of a Mercer, not forty Yards from this Place'.

experimentum crucis: 'decisive experiment'.

146 *'number, numberless'*: from *Paradise Regained*, III.310.

'casual fruition, joyless, unendeared': see *Paradise Lost*, IV.766–7.

147 *W——*: possibly Richard Wilson or David Wilkie.

a friend of mine: Benjamin Robert Haydon, whose *Christ's Entry into Jerusalem* was exhibited in March 1820.

praise of the Edinburgh Review: Hazlitt himself praised the painting in his review of Farington's *Life of Reynolds* for the *Edinburgh* (August 1820).

Mrs. Siddons's . . . sublime: see the description of the work's reception in George Paston, *B.R. Haydon and his Friends* (1905), 102–3:

> Keats and Hazlitt were rejoicing in a corner . . . The only doubt expressed by the polite throng was on the subject of the head of Christ . . . in swept Mrs. Siddons with all the dignity of her majestic presence. A silence fell on the crowd as she contemplated the picture. At length Sir George Beaumont timidly inquired, 'How do you like the Christ?' Everybody listened for her reply. After a moment she said in a deep, loud, tragic voice, 'It is completely successful. The paleness gives it a supernatural look.'

149 *Richardson, in his Essays*: see *Works of Jonathan Richardson*, 249–51, 152–3.

151 *Gandy*: William Gandy (d. 1729). See *Conversations of Northcote*, 'Conversation the Third'. A memoir of Gandy is included in Northcote's *Life of Reynolds*.

The best known . . . that city: a possible reference to Gandy's portrait of the Reverend Tobias Langdon on display in the college hall at Exeter.

Dan. Stringer: Daniel Stringer (1754–1808), RA.

'swallowing the tailor's news': from *King John*, IV.ii.196.

'bastards of his genius, not his children': see Milton, *Comus*, 727, 'And live like Nature's bastards, not her sons', also Shakespeare, *A Lover's Complaint*, 174–5, 'Thought characters and words merely but art, | And bastards of his foul adulterate heart.'

19. CHARACTER OF COBBETT

Published in the first volume of *Table Talk* (1821). Included in the Paris and second London editions of *The Spirit of the Age* (1825).

152 *Cribb*: Tom Cribb (1781–1848), champion pugilist and proprietor of the King's Arms, St James's, and afterwards the Union Arms, Haymarket.

'fillips the ear . . . a three-man beetle': see *2 Henry IV*, I.ii.229, 'fillip me with a three-man beetle'.

'lays waste': see Dryden, *The Hind and the Panther*, i.158, 'Lay waste thy woods, destroy thy blissfull bow'r.'

fourth estate: possibly the earliest application of the phrase to a single individual or to the press in general. As the *OED* notes, there is no evidence for the earlier instance cited by Carlyle: 'Burke said there were Three Estates in Parliament; but, in the Reporters' Gallery . . . there sat a Fourth Estate more important far than they all.'

153 *'damnable iteration in him'*: from *1 Henry IV*, I.ii.90.

pestering Erskine . . . Baron Clackmannan: Thomas Erskine, first Baron Erskine (1750–1823), lord chancellor.

'to clear it from all controversy, past, present, and to come': possibly a recollection of *Measure for Measure*, IV.ii.144–6, 'A man that apprehends death no more dreadfully but as a drunken sleep; careless, reckless, and fearless of what's past, present, or to come'.

154 *The Reformers read him . . . to the Whigs*: Cobbett was a staunch anti-Jacobin during the 1790s, before his conversion to radicalism. Hazlitt alludes to the Shakespearean commonplace that caviar is unpalatable to the ignorant; see *Hamlet*, II.ii.439 ('"Twas caviare to the general').

The late Lord Thurlow . . . political reasoner: Edward Thurlow, first Baron Thurlow (1731–1806), twice lord chancellor. The comment is untraced.

nunquam sufflaminandus erat: 'there was no stopping him'; see Ben Jonson's description of Shakespeare in *Timber, or Discoveries* (1641): 'He was, indeed, honest and of an open and free nature; had an excellent fantasy, brave notions, and gentle expressions; wherein he flowed with that facility that sometime it was necessary he should be stopped. "*Sufflaminandus erat*", as Augustus said of Haterius. His wit was in his own power; would the rule of it had been so too.' *Cambridge Edition of the Works of Ben Jonson*, 7 vols (Cambridge, 2012), VII.522.

'full of matter': from *As You Like It*, II.i.68.

'weary, stale, and unprofitable': from *Hamlet*, I.ii.133.

155 *Barmecide*: in 'The Story of the Barber's Sixth Brother'.

What a noble account . . . America!: see Cobbett's 'To the People of England, Scotland and Ireland', written from Long Island, in *Political Register* (12 July 1817), 468: 'We have smoaked fish, chops, butter, and eggs, for breakfast, with bread (the very finest I ever saw), crackers, sweet cakes . . . in *loads*. Not *an egg*, but a dish full of eggs. Not a snip of meat or of fish; but a plate full. Lump Sugar for our tea and coffee; not broke into little bits the size of a hazle-nut; but in good thumping pieces.'

'live in this description . . . look green': see Pope, 'Windsor Forest', 7–8, 'The groves of Eden, vanished now so long, | Live in description, and look green in song'.

in the manner of Bewick: Thomas Bewick (1753–1828), wood engraver.

the curls of Dr. Parr's wig: Samuel Parr (1747–1825), schoolmaster, writer, and clergyman, famous for his large powdered wig. Hazlitt may be remembering a satirical letter on classical learning that alludes to Parr in *Cobbett's Weekly Political Register* (28 March 1807, around the time he contributed his own letters on Malthus): 'Consider, Sir, I beseech you, the woeful plight in which you would see the possessors of these heads and perriwigs'.

Mr.——: Henry Brougham.

His Grammar: Cobbett published *Grammar of the English language, in a Series of Letters* (1818) during his exile in America.

156 *the Yanguesian carriers*: see Cervantes, *Don Quixote*, translated Smollett, I.80.

'He has the back-trick . . . in Illyria': see *Twelfth Night*, I.iii.118–19, 'I think I have the back-trick simply as strong as any man in Illyria'.

'arrowy sleet': see *Paradise Regained*, III.323–5: 'flying behind them shot | Sharp sleet of arrowy showers against the face | Of their pursuers'.

an Ishmaelite: see John 1:47: 'Behold an Israelite indeed', and the description of Ishmael, Genesis 16:12.

157 *Boroughmongers*: traders in parliamentary seats.

cudgel-playing or single-stick: Cobbett was a vocal supporter of traditional sports such as single-stick, in which two contestants competed to be the first to draw an inch of blood from their opponent's head. He organized single-stick tournaments in Botley between 1805 and 1808.

158 '*deliberately or for money*': see Gay, *The Beggar's Opera*, I.viii, 'deliberately for Honour or Money'.

the two-penny trash: in November 1816 Cobbett exploited a loophole in the stamp duty laws and began to issue each week's leading article as a separate pamphlet which, as commentary rather than news, did not require a stamp and could be sold for twopence. Cobbett later claimed that 'Stewart of the Courier, Walter of the Times, William Gifford and Southey of the Quarterly Review . . . Corruption's forlorn-hope, came, at last, about a month before the Parliament met to call for *new laws* to protect the Constitution against the "Two-penny *Trash*". New Laws to protect a Constitution against *trash!*' (*Cobbett's Weekly Political Pamphlet*, 16 August 1817, 616).

till a Bill passed the House: at the end of 1819, Cobbett's *Political Register* was taxed after the fifth of the Six Acts, raising the price to sixpence.

'*the gentleman and scholar*': from Burns, 'The Twa Dogs', 14.

Paine said on some occasion: Hazlitt may have heard this from Godwin. These are also Pilate's words in John 19:22.

159 '*ample scope and verge enough*': see note to p. 121.

he tosses and tumbles about his unwieldy bulk: see Burke's *Letter to a Noble Lord*: 'The Duke of Bedford is the Leviathan among all the creatures of the Crown. He tumbles about his unwieldy bulk; he plays and frolicks in the ocean of the Royal bounty' (37).

'*He pours out . . . Montaigne*': from Pope, 'The First Satire of the Second Book of Horace Imitated', 51–2.

like pancakes, hot and hot: an ironic and unknowing echo of Southey's warning to Lord Liverpool that radical newspapers like the *Political Register* were 'daily and weekly issued, fresh and fresh, and read aloud in every alehouse'. *Life and Administration of Robert Banks, Second Earl of Liverpool*, 3 vols (London, 1868), II.298.

160 *Antipholis of Ephesus . . . Syracuse*: see *Comedy of Errors*, V.i.297–331.

the relics of Mr Thomas Paine: Cobbett disinterred Tom Paine's remains from New Rochelle, New York in September 1819 and brought them to England as a rallying point for reform in the wake of the Peterloo Massacre. His scheme to raise a memorial failed to take off and by the 1840s the whereabouts of the bones were unknown.

'*his canonised bones*': from *Hamlet*, I.iv.28.

161 *a Big Ben in politics*: Benjamin Bryan (1753–94), nicknamed Big Ben, celebrated pugilist and champion of England 1791–4.

The Edinburgh Review: Francis Jeffrey's article on 'Cobbett's *Political Register*' was published in the *Edinburgh* for July 1807. Cobbett's response appeared in the *Political Register* for 29 August 1807.

The only time I ever saw him: It is not known when this was. It may have been in connection with Hazlitt's contributions to the *Register* in 1807 on

Malthus; alternatively, he may (like Godwin) have visited Cobbett during his imprisonment in Newgate (1810–12), or heard him speak at a public meeting.

20. THE INDIAN JUGGLERS

Published in the first volume of *Table Talk* (1821). The concluding section had previously appeared as Hazlitt's obituary for John Cavanagh in the *Examiner* for 7 February 1819.

162 *the Indian Jugglers*: performing at the Olympic Theatre, off the Strand, in the winter of 1815.

thy ways past finding out!: see Romans 11:33, 'his ways past finding out!'.

163 *rolling a stone up a hill*: an allusion to the story of Sisyphus in Homer's *Odyssey*, XI.593–600.

164 *I was at that time . . . Sir Joshua Reynolds's*: Hazlitt's copy 'appears to have been made in 1803' (William Carew Hazlitt's 1869 edition of *Table Talk*, 107) and is included on the list of his paintings in *Memoirs*, I.xvi.

165 *'In argument they own'd . . . argue still'*: see Goldsmith, *The Deserted Village*, 211–12.

under the wheels of the Jaggernaut: a likeness of the Hindu god Krishna, annually dragged in procession, under which devotees threw themselves to be crushed.

166 *'to allow for the wind'*: from Scott, *Ivanhoe* (1819), xiii.

'human face divine': from *Paradise Lost*, III.44.

H——s and H——s: Wu records that the manuscript reads 'H—s and Hiltons' (William Hilton, 1786–1839). Suggestions for the first name have included Hayman, Highmore, Hudson, and Hoppner, all portrait painters and contemporaries of Reynolds.

'in tones and gestures hit': see *Paradise Regained*, IV.255, 'harmony in tones and numbers hit'.

To snatch this grace: see Pope, *Essay on Criticism*, 155, 'And snatch a grace beyond the reach of art'.

167 *'commercing with the skies'*: from Milton, *Il Penseroso*, 39.

the winter's flaw: from *Hamlet*, V.i.211.

as true as touch: from Spenser, *The Faerie Queene*, I.iii.2:5.

'And visions, . . . every bough': a verse fragment by Thomas Gray, included in a letter to Horace Walpole (August 1736), later published as 'Lines on Beech Trees', 7–8.

'Thrills . . . the line': a composite quotation, from Addison, 'Milton's Style Imitated', 124, 'Ran through each nerve, and thrill'd in every vein', and Pope, *Essay on Man*, I.218, 'Feels at each thread, and lives along the line'.

168 *'half flying, half on foot'*: see *Paradise Lost*, II.941–2.

168 *I know an individual*: Leigh Hunt (1784–1859), poet, essayist, and editor of the *Examiner*.

nugæ canoræ: from Horace, *Ars Poetica*, 322, 'sonorous trifles'.

169 *Themistocles*: Themistocles (528–462 BC) was an Athenian statesman and naval commander. The anecdote is from Plutarch's *Life of Themistocles*, though Hazlitt's likely source is Francis Bacon's *Advancement of Learning*, I.

170 *Jedediah Buxton*: farm labourer and mathematical genius (1707–72).

Napier's bones: a calculator devised by John Napier (1550–1617), who invented algorithms. See also Ezekiel 37:3.

'he dies and leaves the world no copy?': see *Twelfth Night*, I.v.232.

John Hunter: surgeon (1728–93).

Sir Humphry Davy: chemist (1778–1829).

171 *'great scholar's memory outlives him half a century'*: see *Hamlet*, III.ii.125–6, 'Then there's hope a great man's memory may outlive his life half a year.'

become a Wolsey: Thomas Wolsey (1475–1530), cardinal and statesman under Henry VIII.

the late John Cavanagh: John [Jack] Cavanagh (d. 1819), Irish fives player, 'a game in which a ball is struck by the hand against the front wall of a three-sided court' (*OED*).

an article in the Examiner: without signature, and with the following motto: 'And is old Double dead? See, see, he drew a good bow; and dead! He shot a fine shoot. John of Gaunt loved him well and betted much money on his head. Dead! he would have clapt in the clout at twelve score, and carried you a forehead shaft a fourteen and fourteen and a half, that it would have done a man's heart good to see' (see *2 Henry IV*, III.ii.39–47).

172 *'Care mounted . . . skirts'*: from Horace, *Odes*, III.40, 'post equitem sedet atra cura'.

'in the instant': see *Macbeth*, I.v.56–7, 'I feel now | The future in the instant.'

'domestic treason . . . further': see *Macbeth*, III.ii.26–8, 'Nor steel nor poison, | Malice domestic, foreign levy, nothing | Can touch him further.'

Junius: pseudonym for the writer of a series of letters on political conduct and corruption in the *Public Advertiser* (1769–72).

173 *Rosemary Branch*: a tavern at Peckham.

Copenhagen-house: a tavern, tea-garden, and site of political meetings in Islington, located on what is now Caledonian Park.

Goldsmith consoled himself: see Northcote's *Life of Reynolds*.

Mr. Powell: Howe cites Pierce Egan's *Book of Sports* (1832), 226: 'It is now eight or ten years since old one-eyed Powell's establishment (so designated from having lost one of his eyes by a ball while playing a game at rackets) was broken up by his Court being broken down. All who have an acquaintance with rackets recollect him, in his day, a first-rate player, and, after his day, competent to cool the consequence of many who fancied themselves good performers.'

174 *Mr. Murray the bookseller*: John Murray (1778–1843), publisher of Byron. Murray lost the sight in his right eye as a child.

the late John Davies: Hazlitt describes Davies as the 'finest player in the world' in *Conversations of Northcote* (Howe, xi.305). See also the letter from Thomas Pittman (All England rackets champion, 1825–34) to Hazlitt of 16 July 1821, inviting him to play at Canterbury (*Memoirs*, II.3–5): 'One of the old racket-players here says: "Jack Davies was the finest player I ever saw; and, by God, there is nobody can come near him." '

The four best racket-players . . . Church: for Jack Spines, see *Conversations of Northcote*, as above, and Thomas Pittman's letter. The other players are unknown.

the Fleet or King's Bench: Fleet Prison in Farringdon Street and the King's Bench Prison in Southwark (both debtor's prisons), where there were open-air racket courts.

'Who enters here . . . his friends': a recollection of Pope's *Dunciad*, IV.518–19: 'Which whoso tastes, forgets his former friends, | Sire, ancestors, himself.'

175 *Mr. Manners Sutton*: Charles Manners Sutton, first Viscount Canterbury (1780–1845), elected speaker of the House of Commons in 1817.

'Let no rude hand . . . Jacet': see Wordsworth, 'Ellen Irwin', 55–6: 'May no rude hand deface it, | And its forlorn *hic jacet*!'

21. ON A LANDSCAPE OF NICOLAS POUSSIN

Published in the *London Magazine* for August 1821. Reprinted in the second volume of *Table Talk* (1822).

176 *this landscape*: Poussin's 'Landscape with Orion', or 'Blind Orion Searching for the Rising Sun' (1658), shown at the annual exhibition of Old Masters at the British Institution, June and July 1821. The painting is now in the Metropolitan Museum of Art, New York.

'a hunter of shadows, himself a shade': see Pope's translation of Homer's *Odyssey*, XI.703–4, 'There huge Orion, of portentous size, | Swift through the gloom a giant-hunter flies.' Odysseus describes how he saw Orion in the underworld pursuing the shades of beasts he had slain.

having lost an eye: after assaulting Merope, Orion was blinded by her father Oenopion.

'the grey dawn and the Pleiades before him dance': from *Paradise Lost*, VII.373–4.

'a forerunner of the dawn': see James Montgomery, 'Departed Days: A Rhapsody', 87, 'Forerunner of the day'.

'shadowy sets off': from *Paradise Lost*, V.43.

Sir Joshua has: see Reynolds, *Discourses*, V.

176 'denote a foregone conclusion': from *Othello*, III.iii.433.

'take up the isles . . . balance': from Isaiah 40:15 and 40:12.

177 *high and palmy state*: from *Hamlet*, I.i.112.

'so potent art': from *The Tempest*, V.i.50.

'more than natural': from *Hamlet*, II.ii.368.

'gives to airy nothing . . . a name': from *A Midsummer Night's Dream*, V.i.16–17.

178 '*Blind Orion hungry for the morn*': from Keats, *Endymion*, II.198.

I have often admired . . . lately published: from Maria Graham (Lady Callcott), *Memoirs of the Life of Nicholas Poussin*, 2 vols (London, 1820), i.5–6.

179 *his Plague of Athens*: 'The Plague of Ashdod' (1630), in the Louvre.

His picture of the Deluge: *Winter* or *The Deluge*, from *The Four Seasons* (1660–4), also in the Louvre.

'o'er informed': from Dryden, *Absalom and Achitophel*, 158, 'And o'er-informed the tenement of clay.'

'the very stones prate of their whereabout': from *Macbeth*, II.i.58.

a picture of Aurora: 'Cephalus and Aurora' (*c*.1630), now in the National Gallery.

180 '*Leaping like wanton kids in pleasant spring*': from Spenser, *The Faerie Queene*, I.vi.14:4.

his picture of the shepherds: *Et in Arcadia Ego* (1637–8), in the Louvre.

ET EGO IN ARCADIA VIXI: 'And I too have dwelt in Arcadia'.

'the valleys low, where the mild zephyrs use': see Milton, *Lycidas*, 136.

'within the book . . . baser matter!': see *Hamlet*, I.v.103–4.

181 '*the sober certainty of waking bliss*': from Milton, *Comus*, 263.

'he who knows . . . not unwise!': a recollection of Milton, *Sonnet* 17, 13–14:

> He who of those delights can judge, and spare
> To interpose them oft, is not unwise.

'Old Genius the porter . . . out to wend': from Spenser, *The Faerie Queene*, III.vi.31–2.

'there were propagation too!': as Wu notes, from Bell's acting edition of *Shakespeare* (1774), *Macbeth*, II.iv:

> Dread horrors still abound
> And ev'ry place surround,
> As if in death were found
>   Propagation too.

stray gifts: from Wordsworth, 'Stray Pleasures', 27–8, 'Thus pleasure is spread through the earth | In stray gifts to be claimed by whoever shall find'.

at Blenheim, at Burleigh . . . and others: see Hazlitt's *Sketches of the Principal Picture Galleries in England* (1824).

182 *since the Louvre is stripped*: after Waterloo, many of the works in the Louvre were restored to the countries they had been taken from.

hunter of greatness . . . shade: Napoleon died on 5 May 1821.

22. THE FIGHT

Published in the *New Monthly Magazine* for February 1822, signed 'Phantastes'. The fight between Tom Hickman, the 'Gas-man', and Bill Neate took place on 11 December 1821 at Hungerford in Berkshire.

183 *'The fight . . . the conscience of the king'*: a reworking of *Hamlet*, II.ii.606–7.

Jack Randall's: 'The Hole in the Wall' in Chancery Lane, kept by Jack Randall, the pugilist.

where the fight the next day was to be: major bouts of this kind were often held out of London, advertised at short notice and by word of mouth, to avoid being shut down by the authorities.

'the proverb . . . musty': from *Hamlet*, III.ii.330–1.

the FANCY!: the art of boxing; pugilism.

blue ruin: low-grade gin.

184 *Jo. Toms*: Joseph Parkes (1796–1865), one of Hazlitt's sporting acquaintances, articled to a London solicitor, follower of Bentham, later an influential reformer.

alter idem: '[each] another self'.

'so carelessly did we fleet the time': see *As You Like It*, I.i.112–13.

Jack Pigott: P. G. Patmore (1786–1855), writer and journalist.

'What more felicity . . . delight with liberty?': from Spenser, 'Muiopotmos', 209–10.

to start from Tom Belcher's: Tom Belcher (1783–1854), younger brother of the prize-fighter James Belcher, kept the Castle tavern in Holborn.

'Well, we meet at Philippi!': see *Julius Caesar*, IV.ii.337.

185 *'I follow Fate, which does too hard pursue!'*: see Dryden, *The Indian Emperor*, IV.iii.3–5:

> As if the cares of human life were few,
> > We seek out new:
> And follow fate, which would too fast pursue.

Jehu: slang for a driver, derived from 2 Kings 9:12.

186 *Tom Turtle*: identified by Hazlitt's son and the evidence of the manuscript (see *SW*, 9.227) as John Thurtell (1794–1824), trainer, fight promoter, and tavern owner, who was tried and executed in 1824 for murdering his gambling companion William Weare.

186 '*quite chap-fallen*': see *Hamlet*, V.i.188.

a word to throw at a dog: from *As You Like It*, I.iii.2–3.

Martin: Jack Martin, known as 'The Master of the Rolls'.

Mr. Richmond: Bill Richmond (1763–1829), former slave, pugilist, and owner of the Horse and Dolphin in Westminster. Hazlitt later refers to him as 'my old master', suggesting Richmond taught him to fight.

187 '*where good digestion . . . health on both*': from *Macbeth*, III.iv.37–8.

social chat and native glee: a recollection of Burns, 'Address to the Unco Guid', 33, 'See Social Life and Glee sit down.'

'*Follows so . . . profitable ardour*': from *Henry V*, IV.i.273–4, 'And follows so the ever-running year | With profitable labour to his grave.'

Is not this life more sweet than mine?: see *As You Like It*, II.i.2–3, 'Hath not old custom made this life more sweet | Than that of painted pomp?'

bitter as coloquintida: from *Othello*, I.iii.348–9; the colocynth or bitter-apple is used as a purgative.

'*more figures and more fantasies*': see *Julius Caesar*, II.i.230, 'Thou hast no figures nor no fantasies'.

He had faith in surgery: see *1 Henry IV*, V.i.133, 'Honor hath no skill in surgery, then?'

'*his dream . . . foregone conclusion*': from *Othello*, III.iii.432–3.

'*seriously inclined*': from *Othello*, I.iii.145.

d'un beau jour: see note to p. 145.

envious showers: see *The Taming of the Shrew*, Induction 2, 64, 'envious floods'; similarly *Richard III*, I.iv.37.

188 *Gilpin*: eponymous hero of Cowper's 'Diverting History of John Gilpin'.

something like Mathews: see note to p. 130.

'*A lusty man to ben an abbot able*': see Chaucer, *General Prologue to the Canterbury Tales*, 167, 'A manly man, to been an abbot able.'

189 *standing like greyhounds*: from *Henry V*, III.i.31.

oaken towel: slang for a cudgel.

'*he moralized into a thousand similes*': from *As You Like It*, II.i.44–5.

firebrand like Bardolph's: see *2 Henry IV*, II.ii.83.

'*loud and furious fun*': from Burns, 'Tam o' Shanter', 144, 'The mirth and fun grew fast and furious.'

190 *Cribb's beating Jem*: Cribb defeated Jem Belcher twice, in 1807 and 1809. Belcher lost an eye in 1803 through an accident playing rackets.

Gully: John Gully (1783–1863), prize-fighter, racehorse owner, and later colliery owner and politician.

'*there are three things . . . Impudence!*': an allusion to Danton's famous statement of 1792, 'De l'audace, encore de l'audace, toujours de l'audace, et la France est sauvée.'

'Alas! the Bristol man was not so tamed!': see Cowper, *The Task*, ii.322, 'Alas! Leviathan is not so tamed.'

191 *the Fives Court*: a venue for bare-knuckle fights in London.

Achilles surveyed Hector: see Homer, *Iliad*, XXII.

Game Chicken: Henry Pearce (1777–1809), prize-fighter.

'That man was made to mourn': see Matthew Prior, 'Solomon on the Vanity of the World', iii.240, 'Who breathes, must suffer; and who thinks, must mourn', and Burns, 'Man Was Made to Mourn'.

192 *'Between the acting . . . hideous dream'*: from *Julius Caesar*, II.i.63–5.

my fairest hopes: an allusion to his failed love affair with Sarah Walker.

swells: fashionably dressed people.

193 *'with Atlantean shoulders, fit to bear'*: from *Paradise Lost*, II.306.

the scratch: 'the line drawn across a ring to which boxers are brought for an encounter' (*OED*).

'grinned horrible a ghastly smile': from *Paradise Lost*, II.846.

194 *'like two clouds over the Caspian'*: see *Paradise Lost*, II.714–16.

195 *Scroggins*: Jack Scroggins, prize-fighter.

'In doleful . . . upon his stumps': see 'The Ancient Ballad of Chevy-Chase', 119–22.

Jackson: 'Gentleman' John Jackson (1769–1845), prize-fighter, whose pupils included Byron.

Mais au revoir, as Sir Fopling Flutter says: see Dorimant in George Etherege, *The Man of Mode* (1676), III.ii.305, 'A revoir, as Sir Fopling says.'

196 *O procul este profani*: see Virgil, *Aeneid*, vi.258, 'You who are profane, stand at a distance.'

a cross: slang for a rigged fight.

sans intermission by the dial: from *As You Like It*, II.vii.32–3.

New Eloise: Rousseau, *La Nouvelle Héloïse* (1761).

Ned Turner: Ned Turner (1791–1826), conqueror of Scroggins.

197 *Mr. Windham*: William Windham (1750–1810), Whig politician, committed pugilist and sometime ally of Cobbett.

Broughton and George Stevenson: the fight between Jack Broughton (1704–89) and George Stevenson, 'The Coachman' (*c.*1720–41) took place in 1741 and resulted in Stevenson's death.

23. ON FAMILIAR STYLE

Published in the second volume of *Table Talk* (1822).

200 *'tall, opaque words'*: see Sterne, *Tristram Shandy*, III.xx, 'I hate set dissertations,—and above all things in the world, 'tis one of the silliest things in one of them, to darken your hypothesis by placing a number of tall, opake

words, one before another, in a right line, betwixt your own and your reader's conception'.

200 *'first row of the rubric'*: see *Hamlet*, II.ii.422.

cum grano salis: 'with a grain of salt'.

201 *the term impersonal applied to feelings*: see *An Essay on the Principles of Human Action* (1805).

I have been (I know) loudly accused: the *Quarterly*'s review of the first volume of *Table Talk* described Hazlitt as a 'Slang-Whanger' (October 1821).

Mr. Cobbett . . . the best: see *A Grammar of the English Language* (1818), Letter XXIII, 'Use the first words that occur to you, and never attempt to alter a thought; for, that which has come of itself into your mind is likely to pass into that of another more readily and with more effect than any thing which you can, by reflection invent.'

202 *his papers under the signature of Elia*: Hazlitt and Lamb were engaged in a friendly rivalry across the pages of the *London Magazine*. Hazlitt's first 'Table Talk', 'On the Qualifications Necessary to Success in Life', appeared in June 1820; Lamb's first Elia essay, 'Recollections of the South Sea House', two months later.

Mrs. Battle's Opinions on Whist: published in the *London Magazine* (February 1821).

'A well of native English undefiled': see Spenser, *The Faerie Queene*, IV.ii.32:8, 'Dan Chaucer, well of English undefiled'.

Erasmus's Colloquies: The *Colloquia* (1519).

203 *'What do you read? . . . What is the matter?'*: from *Hamlet*, II.ii.193–6.

florilegium: a collection of flowers, or a literary anthology.

tulippomania: 'craze for tulips', referring to the seventeenth-century bubble; Howe suggests a specific allusion to *Tatler*, No. 218: 'a Person of good Sense, had not his Head been touched with . . . the *Tulippomania*.'

Sermo humi obrepens: a recollection of Horace, *Epistles*, II.i.250–1, 'nec sermones ego mallem | repentis per humum quam res componere gestas'.

'ambition is more lowly': see *The Tempest*, I.ii.484–6, 'My affections | Are then most humble. I have no ambition | To see a goodlier man.'

'unconsidered trifles': from *The Winter's Tale*, IV.iii.26.

'That strut . . . the stage': from *Macbeth*, V.v.24.

204 *'And on their pens . . . plumed'*: see *Paradise Lost*, IV.988–9, 'and on his crest | Sat horror plumed'.

'nature's own sweet . . . laid on': from *Twelfth Night*, I.v.229.

205 *Cowper's description . . . it was cold!*: see *The Task*, v.173–6:

> 'Twas transient in its nature, as in show
> 'Twas durable. As worthless as it seemed
> Intrinsically precious. To the foot
> Treach'rous and false, it smiled and it was cold.

24. ON THE SPIRIT OF MONARCHY

Published in the *Liberal* for January 1823.

206 *'As for politics . . . the Dutch'*: from William Shenstone (1714–63) to William Graves, 6 April 1746; see Marjorie Williams (ed.), *Letters of William Shenstone* (Oxford, 1939), 101. Hazlitt omits the sentence that follows: 'The Tories, on the other hand, are taken mightily with that shewy, ostentatious nation the French.'

207 *wisely and wittily observed*: by Leigh Hunt; see Howe, xx.440.

'And by the vision . . . attended': see Wordsworth, 'Ode: Intimations of Immortality', 73–4.

The Madman in Hogarth: see *The Rake's Progress*, Plate VIII.

'There goes my royal self': cf. 'On the Spirit of Partisanship', Howe, xvii.43.

208 *a celebrated . . . historian*: William Roscoe, whose portrait Hazlitt painted.

'A good king . . . cypher': unidentified; cf. 'The Lex Talionis Principle', Howe, xix.124, 'It was remarked by Swift that a perfect king should be a figure stuffed with straw.'

Mr. Young: Charles Mayne Young (1777–1856), actor.

'that within which passes shew': see *Hamlet*, I.ii.85.

'to fear, not to delight in!': see *Othello*, I.ii.72.

Voltaic Battery: the first electric battery, invented by Alessandro Volta (1745–1826) in the 1790s.

Metallic Tractors: 'a device invented by Elisha Perkins, an American physician (died 1799), consisting of a pair of pointed rods of different metals, as brass and steel, which were believed to relieve rheumatic or other pain by being drawn or rubbed over the skin' (*OED*).

209 *'peep through . . . Hold, hold'*: from *Macbeth*, I.v.52–3.

Great is Diana of the Ephesians: Acts 19:28.

'Your Gods . . . understand': see Matthew 13:13; the broader allusion is to Elijah and the prophets of Baal: see 1 Kings 18:27.

'Of whatsoe'er descent . . . beaten gold': from Dryden, *Absalom and Achitophel*, 100–3.

210 *in contempt of their worshippers*: cf. Burke, *Reflections on the Revolution in France*, 19, 'he holds his crown in contempt of the choice of the Revolution Society, who have not a single vote for a king amongst them'.

211 *'God's partial . . . or lust'*: from Pope, *Essay on Man*, III.257–8.

'any mark, any likelihood': see *1 Henry IV*, III.ii.45.

'In fact, the argument . . . philosophy': from Hazlitt's own 'What is the People?', see p. 93.

212 *'From the crown . . . soundness left'*: see Isaiah 1:6.

Virtue, says Montesquieu: in *Espirit de Lois* (1748), III.vi.

'honour dishonourable, sin-bred': from *Paradise Lost*, IV.314–15.

213 *'Of outward shew . . . less exact'*: from *Paradise Lost*, VIII.538–9.

   'to tread the . . . dalliance': see *Hamlet*, I.iii.50.

   'to scale the . . . to heaven': see *Hamlet*, I.iii.48.

   'nice customs . . . great kings': from *Henry V*, V.ii.267.

   'in form . . . of animals!': from *Hamlet*, II.ii.306–9.

214 *'Vice is undone . . . the laws'*: from Pope, 'Epilogue to the Satires: Dialogue I', 141–8.

   'the same luck . . . cuckolds!': see Byron, *Don Juan*, II.1647–8, 'the same luck holds, | They all were heroes, conquerors, and cuckolds.'

215 *a Coronation-day*: the coronation of George IV took place on 19 July 1821. The general acclaim contrasted with the new king's deep unpopularity during the Queen Caroline affair.

   Prince Leopold: Prince Leopold of Saxe-Coburg (1790–1865), husband of Princess Charlotte, first King of the Belgians after the country came into being in 1831.

216 *'A present deity . . . rebound!'*: from Dryden, 'Alexander's Feast; or, The Power of Music', 35–6.

217 *'Worth makes . . . prunella'*: from Pope, *Essay on Man*, IV.203–4.

   'The only amaranthine . . . truth': from Cowper, *The Task*, iii.268–9.

218 *'A man may read . . . heap of dust!'*: from Jeremy Taylor, *Holy Dying*, I.ii.

25. MY FIRST ACQUAINTANCE WITH POETS

Published in *The Liberal* for April 1823.

219 *W—m*: Wem, Shropshire, where Hazlitt's family moved in 1787.

   'dreaded name of Demogorgon': from *Paradise Lost*, II.964–5, invoking both the French Revolution of 1789 and the Irish Rebellion of 1798.

   Mr. Rowe: John Rowe (1764–1832), Unitarian minister.

   'fluttering the proud Salopians . . . dove-cote': see *Coriolanus*, V.vi.115–16. A Salopian is a person from Shropshire.

   'High-born Hoel's harp . . . lay!': from Thomas Gray, 'The Bard', 28.

   like a worm by the way-side: see Chaucer, *The Clerk's Tale*, 879–80, 'wherefore I yow preye, | Lat me nat lyk a worm go by the weye.'

   'bound them . . . round them': from Pope, 'Ode for Music on St. Cecilia's Day', 90–1.

220 *with longings infinite*: from Wordsworth, 'The Affliction of Margaret', 63, 'With love and longings infinite.'

   like the fires . . . destruction of Troy: see Clytemnestra's speech in Aeschylus, *Agamemnon*, 281–316.

   It was in January, 1798: this paragraph—the germ of this essay—had appeared in a short letter on Coleridge's *Lay Sermon* in the *Examiner* (12 January 1817), reprinted in *Political Essays* (1819).

cold, raw, comfortless: see William Godwin, *Things as They Are; or, The Adventures of Caleb Williams* (1794), II.44, where Caleb tells Falkland 'I am foolish, raw, inexperienced'.

Il y a des impressions . . . memoire: one of Hazlitt's favourite quotations, adapted from Rousseau, *Julie, ou La Nouvelle Héloïse* (6 vols, Amsterdam, 1761), vi.57–8 ('There are impressions that neither time nor circumstances can erase. Should I live for centuries, the sweet period of my youth would not be reborn for me, nor ever effaced from my memory').

'And he went . . . ALONE': a conflation of Matthew 14:23 and John 6:15.

'rose like a steam of rich distilled perfumes': from Milton, *Comus*, 556.

'of one crying . . . honey': Matthew 3:3–4 and Mark 1:3.

221 *'as though he should never be old'*: from Sir Philip Sidney, *The Countess of Pembroke's Arcadia*, I.2.

crimped: coerced into the army.

'Such were the notes . . . sung': from Pope, 'Epistle to Robert Earl of Oxford', 1.

JUS DIVINUM: 'Divine Right [of Kings]'.

'Like to that sanguine . . . with woe': the hyacinth; see Milton, *Lycidas*, 106.

'As are the children . . . sheen': see James Thomson, *The Castle of Indolence*, II.xxxiii.7.

222 *'A certain tender bloom . . . o'erspread'*: see James Thomson, *The Castle of Indolence*, I.lvii.3, 'A certain tender gloom o'erspread his face'.

'somewhat fat and pursy': Hazlitt conflates *Hamlet*, III.iv.144, 'For in the fatness of these pursy times', and V.ii.240, 'He's fat and scant of breath'.

declining into the vale of years: see Cowper, *The Task*, ii.725–6, 'But Discipline, a faithful servant long, | Declined at length into the vale of years'.

223 *'no figures nor no fantasies'*: from *Julius Caesar*, II.i.230.

the age of Methuselah: 969 in Genesis 5:27, oldest of the patriarchs.

224 *Mackintosh*: James Mackintosh (1765–1832), writer and politician, author of *Vindiciae Gallicae* (1791), an early defence of the French Revolution.

Tom. Wedgwood: Thomas Wedgwood (1771–1805), chemist and son of the potter Josiah Wedgwood.

I had once for a few moments: Hazlitt probably met Wollstonecraft in London in autumn 1796.

attempting to establish . . . image of both: Godwin speculates on the possibility of immortality in *Political Justice* (1793), VIII.vii.

Holcroft: Thomas Holcroft (1745–1809), playwright, whose autobiography Hazlitt completed after his death.

225 *Deva's winding vales*: see Milton, *Lycidas*, 55, 'where Deva spreads her wizard stream'.

225 *the shores of old romance*: see Wordsworth, 'A narrow girdle of rough stones and crags', 40, 'Sole-sitting by the shores of old romance'.

the Delectable Mountains: in John Bunyan's *Pilgrim's Progress*, Christian and Hopeful escape from Doubting Castle and the Giant Despair to the Delectable Mountains.

this simile . . . Cassandra: from Gauthier de Costes de la Calprenède, *Cassandra* (1644–50), II.v.

'Sounding on his way': a recollection of the *General Prologue to the Canterbury Tales*, where the Merchant is 'Sownynge alwey th'encrees of his wynnyng' (275) and the Clerk, 'Sownyne in moral vertu was his speech' (307), filtered through Wordsworth's *Excursion*, iii.701, 'Went sounding on, a dim and perilous way', which Coleridge alludes to at the end of *Biographia Literaria*, ch. 5.

226 *Essay on Miracles*: David Hume (1711–76), philosopher and historian, author of *A Treatise of Human Nature* (1739) and *Essays Moral and Political* (1741–2).

South's Sermons: Robert South (1634–1716), preacher at the court of Charles II.

Credat Judæus Apella!: see Horace, *Satires*, I.v.100: 'Apella the Jew may believe it, not I'.

choke-pears: as Sampson notes, 'Literally a fruit difficult to swallow because of its rough, astringent nature, and so, metaphorically, anything hard to understand.'

Berkeley: George Berkeley (1685–1753), philosopher and bishop of Cloyne, whose *Essay Towards a New Theory of Vision* was published in 1709.

'Thus I confute him, Sir': see Boswell, *Life of Johnson*, i.471.

Bishop Butler: Joseph Butler (1692–1752), philosopher and bishop of Durham; *Fifteen Sermons*, preached at the Rolls Chapel, was published in 1726 and his *Analogy of Religion* ten years later.

I had written a few remarks: the kernel of Hazlitt's *Essay on the Principles of Human Action* (1805).

227 *Paley*: William Paley (1743–1805), theologian and philosopher, whose *Principles of Moral and Political Philosophy* (1785) Coleridge and Wordsworth would have encountered at Cambridge.

'Kind and affable . . . regard': see Adam's words to Raphael in *Paradise Lost*, VIII.648–50:

> Gentle to me and affable hath been
> Thy condescension, and shall be honoured ever
> With grateful memory

has somewhere told himself: in *Biographia Literaria*, ch. 10, Coleridge provides a different account of the story.

228 *Mr. Southey's Vision of Judgment*: Southey's laureate poem, published in 1821, describing George III's ascent to heaven.

that other Vision of Judgment: Byron's satire on Southey's poem, published in *The Liberal* (1822).

the Bridge-street Junto: Charles Murray, solicitor to the Constitutional Association for Opposing Disloyal and Seditious Principles, whose offices were at 6 New Bridge Street, Blackfriars, prosecuted the publishers of Byron's poem for libel.

description of England: see Coleridge, 'Ode to the Departing Year' (1796), st. 7.

the waters of Helicon: in Greek mythology, the springs of Aganippe and Hippocrene, sacred to the Muses, flow out of Mount Helicon.

Tom Jones and the adventure of the muff: see Joseph Fielding, *Tom Jones* (1749), X.5–7.

Paul and Virginia: a translation of Jacques-Henri Bernardin de Saint-Pierre's novel *Paul et Virginie* (1788).

229 *Camilla*: 1796 novel by Frances Burney.

nothing was given for nothing: see *King Lear*, I.iv.131, 'Nothing can be made out of nothing.'

softness . . . scales that fence: a possible recollection of Acts 9:18; see *Lectures on the Dramatic Literature of the Age of Elizabeth* (1820), Lecture I, 'in the Christian religion, "we perceive a softness coming over the heart of a nation, and the iron scales that fence and harden it, melt and drop off" ' (Howe, vi.184).

form of Sybilline Leaves: 'in loose sheets'; the title of Coleridge's 1817 collection.

'hear the loud stag speak': from Ben Johnson, 'To Sir Robert Wroth, lulled in Elysium', 22.

230 *ballad of Betty Foy*: i.e. Wordsworth's 'The Idiot Boy', published in *Lyrical Ballads* (1798) with the other poems listed here.

'In spite of pride . . . spite': from Pope, *Essay on Man*, I.293.

'While yet the trembling . . . unconfirmed': from Thomson, *The Seasons*, 'Spring', 18.

'Of Providence . . . foreknowledge absolute': from *Paradise Lost*, II.559–60.

231 *his own Peter Bell*: the eponymous hero of Wordsworth's *Peter Bell* (1819; written 1798) has a 'long and slouching . . . gait' (282).

Chantry's bust: Sir Francis Chantry (1781–1841) exhibited a bust of Wordsworth at the Royal Academy in 1821.

ad captandum: proverbial; in full 'ad captandum vulgus', 'to catch the rabble'.

232 *'his face was a book . . . strange matters'*: from *Macbeth* I.v.61–2.

Tom Poole: Thomas Poole (1765–1836), neighbour of Coleridge at Nether Stowey.

232 *flip*: 'a mixture of beer and spirit sweetened with sugar and heated with a hot iron' (*OED*).

John Chester: a local farmer, who accompanied Coleridge to Germany in 1798.

'followed in the chace . . . up the cry': see *Othello*, II.iii.354–5.

233 *scene of a prose-tale . . . the death of Abel*: see Salomon Gessner's *Der Tod Abels* (1758). The 'prose-tale' Coleridge referred to was the *Wanderings of Cain* (1828).

234 *He said the Lyrical Ballads . . . of Henry II*: see Wordsworth, Advertisement to *Lyrical Ballads* (1798): 'The majority of the following poems are to be considered as experiments. They were written chiefly with a view to ascertain how far the language of conversation in the middle and lower classes of society is adapted to the purposes of poetic pleasure.'

'ribbed sea-sands': from Coleridge, 'The Rime of the Ancient Mariner', 219.

235 *Dr Toulmin of Taunton*: Joshua Toulmin (1740–1815), Unitarian minister and historian.

his tragedy of Remorse: Coleridge wrote the first draft of this play in 1797; it was first performed at Drury Lane in January 1813.

'Oh memory! . . . everlasting life': not in fact from Coleridge's *Remorse* but the final lines of an ode by Robert Bloomfield, 'On revisiting the place of my Nativity', inserted into the second edition of *The Farmer's Boy* (1800). See Susan Wolfson, *Romantic Shades and Shadows* (Baltimore, 2018), 94–7.

236 *'But there is matter . . . tale'*: see Wordsworth, 'Hart-Leap Well', 95–6. Hazlitt never wrote a sequel.

26. ON LONDONERS AND COUNTRY PEOPLE

Published in the *New Monthly Magazine* for August 1823. Reprinted in *The Plain Speaker* (1826).

237 *I do not agree with Mr. Blackwood . . . Cockney*: the author of 'Hazlitt Cross-Questioned' in *Blackwood's Edinburgh Magazine* (August 1818) calls Hazlitt a 'hard-hearted Cockney' (551).

Ultima Thule: the northernmost place in ancient Greek and Roman literature and cartography.

'Beyond Hyde Park . . . to him': in Sir George Etherege's *The Man of Mode*, Harriet says to Dorimant: 'I know all beyond Hyde Park is a desert to you, and that no gallantry can draw you farther' (V.ii).

239 *'He is owner of all he surveys'*: see Cowper, 'Verses supposed to be written by Alexander Selkirk', 1: 'I am monarch of all I survey'.

A barker in Monmouth Street: a shop-tout or sham auctioneer, in Monmouth Street, St Giles, known in this period for its second-hand clothes shops.

240 *Pennant*: Thomas Pennant (1726–98), *Some Account of London* (1790).

'where Hicks's Hall formerly stood!': in St John Street, Clerkenwell.

the Cider-Cellar: a tavern and 'midnight concert room' at 10 Maiden Lane, Covent Garden.

241 *'shorter excursions tries'*: from Pope, *Essay on Criticism*, 738.

White-conduit House . . . Bagnigge Wells: White Conduit House was a tavern and pleasure garden in Islington; the Rosemary Branch, Islington was an alehouse and tea-gardens; Bagnigge Wells was a spa on King's Cross Road.

'catch the breezy air': from Wordsworth, 'Lines Written in Early Spring', 18.

Virginia or Oronooko: varieties of tobacco.

'There's nought . . . dream': one of Thomas Moore's *Irish Melodies*.

Brahams and Durusets: John Braham and J. B. Durusett were the two leading tenors of the day.

'an hour by St. Dunstan's clock': see *1 Henry IV*, V.iv.144–5, 'we rose both at an instant, and fought a long hour by Shrewsbury clock.'

Richard Pinch: in 'The Fight', he appears as James Simpkins, hosier in the Strand.

Copenhagen-house: see note to p. 173.

Cavanagh: see note to p. 171.

242 *'For how . . . stocking-weaver'*: from Thomas Holcroft, *The Road to Ruin*, III.ii.

243 *Hole in the Wall*: see note to p. 183.

the poet Jago: Richard Jago (1715–81), author of *Edge Hill* (1767).

Anthony Collins: (1676–1729), philosopher and freethinker, whose *A Discourse of Free-Thinking* (1713) was publicly burnt by the common hangman.

Mr. Smith and the Brangtons, in 'Evelina': see note to p. 120. Howe suggests that Hazlitt's anecdote was related to Burney by the Lambs.

244 *the child grows completely up into the man*: see Wordsworth, 'My heart leaps up when I behold', 7: 'The Child is Father of the Man'.

pomatum: see note to p. 117.

Mr. Dunster . . . fishmonger, in the Poultry: identified by Hazlitt's grandson as 'a poulterer in Duke Street, and Mr Hazlitt met him at some Christmas Party or Twelfth-Night celebration . . . Fisher was a man of some literary taste, and an admirer of Sterne and Le Sage. He was a true Cockney' (*Memoirs*, II.310).

245 *the story of the King of Bohemia*: from Sterne, *Tristram Shandy*, VIII.xix.

'What idle progeny . . . flying ball?': from Thomas Gray, 'Ode on a Distant Prospect of Eton College', 28–30.

246 *at one bright loop-hole*: see Cowper, *The Task*, iv.88–9: "Tis pleasant through the loop-holes of retreat | To peep at such a world.'

246 *'some high festival of once a year'*: from Goldsmith, *The Traveller*, 222.

247 *See Round Table, vol. ii. p. 116*: Hazlitt refers to the passage in his essay 'On Mr. Wordsworth's *Excursion*' beginning 'All country people hate each other' (Howe, iv.122).

'This bottle's the sun of our table': from Sheridan, *The Duenna*, III.v.1.

'glares round his soul . . . eye-lids': Stanley Jones identifies the quotation as from Coleridge, *Remorse* (1813), III.ii: 'An inward day, that never, never sets, | Glares round his soul, and mocks the closing eyelids!'

'knew the Inns of Court . . . midnight!': a conflation of *2 Henry IV*, III. ii.12–14, 22–3, 211.

where a man does not know his next-door neighbour: see Wordsworth, *The 1805 Prelude* (unpublished in his lifetime), VII.117–20:

> Above all, one thought
> Baffled my understanding, how men lived
> Even next-door neighbours, as we say, yet still
> Strangers, and knowing not each other's names.

248 *Mr Wordsworth . . . selfishness*: in his Prospectus to 'The Recluse', published in the Preface to *The Excursion* (1814), xiii:

> must hang
> Brooding above the first confederate storm
> Of sorrow, barricaded evermore
> Within the walls of Cities

'public creature': in *A Letter to a Noble Lord*, Burke writes of his late son Richard, 'He was made a publick creature; and had no enjoyment whatever, but in the performance of some duty' (50).

'a species alone': see Cowley, 'The Praise of Pindar', 2, 'The Phoenix Pindar is a vast species alone.'

27. JEREMY BENTHAM

First published in the *New Monthly Magazine* for January 1824; reprinted in *The Spirit of the Age* (1825).

250 *'a prophet . . . country'*: see Matthew 13:57, 'A prophet is not without honour, save in his own country, and in his own house.'

Westminster, where he lives: in Queen Square Place, now Queen Anne's Gate.

'I know thee . . . thy bush': see *The Tempest*, II.ii.140, 'My mistress showed me thee, and thy dog and thy bush.'

the Emperor Alexander called upon him: in 1814 when the Allied sovereigns visited London.

Mr. Hobhouse is a greater man at the Hustings: John Cam Hobhouse (1786–1869), returned to parliament in 1820 as a radical MP for the seat of Westminster.

'*that waft . . . to the Pole*': see Pope, *Eloisa to Abelard*, 58, 'And waft a sigh from Indus to the Pole.'

251 '*lone island in the watery waste*': from Pope, *Essay on Man*, I.106, 'Some happier island in the watery waste.'

a stone in the wall . . . formerly lived: according to his son, Hazlitt placed the stone there himself: 'In the spring of 1811 my father removed to London, and tenanted of Mr Bentham the house in York street, Westminster, once honoured in the occupation of Milton, a circumstance which is commemorated on a small tablet, in the yard at the back of the house, placed there by my father in his veneration for the Poet and the Patriot.' See *Literary Remains of the Late William Hazlitt*, 2 vols (1836), I.lix.

Chreistomathic School: Bentham's *Chrestomathia* (1818) argued for the monitorial system pioneered by Joseph Lancaster and the exclusion of religion in education.

the flies of a summer: see note to p. 78.

252 '*foregone conclusion*': from *Othello*, III.iii.433.

253 *Mr. Bentham is not the first writer . . . political reasoning*: the argument from utility had been made by Francis Hutcheson (*Enquiry concerning Moral Good and Evil*, 1764), Cesare Beccaria (*On Crimes and Punishment*, 1764), and Joseph Priestley (*Essay on Government*, 1768).

'*He has not allowed for the wind*': from Scott, *Ivanhoe* (1819), p. xiii.

his petrific, leaden mace: from *Paradise Lost*, X.294: 'Death with his mace petrific'.

'*bound volatile Hermes*': from *Paradise Lost*, III.602–3.

caput mortuum: 'worthless remains'.

254 *ultima ratio philosophorum*: 'the last argument of philosophers', a play on Cardinal Richelieu's maxim, *ultima ratio regum* ('the last argument of kings', i.e. war).

'*all appliances and means to boot*': from *2 Henry IV*, III.i.29.

Posthæc meminisse juvabit: from Virgil, *Aeneid*, i.203, 'Afterwards we will delight in remembering.'

256 *No more than Montaigne*: see Michel de Montaigne, *An Apology for Raymond Sebond*, 'When I play with my cat, how do I know that she is not passing time with me rather than I with her?' (*The Complete Essays*, trans. M. A. Screech (London, 2003), 505).

257 *the whole Press-yard, with Jack Ketch at its head*: a yard at Newgate from which condemned prisoners were led to their execution; Jack Ketch (d. 1686), infamous public executioner.

Hulks: boats serving as prisons.

'*All men act . . . madmen reason*': see Bentham, *Introduction to the Principles of Morals and Legislation* (London, 1789), p. clxxxv: 'Men calculate, some with less exactness, indeed, some with more: but all men calculate. I would not say, that even a madman does not calculate.'

257 *Bedlam, or St. Luke's*: Bethlem Royal Hospital and St Luke's Hospital, insane asylums in London.

258 *too knowing by half*: see Sheridan, *The Rivals*, III.iv.13, 'That's too civil by half.'

the New Drop: a scaffold introduced at Newgate for public executions in 1783.

259 *'Dip it in the ocean . . . stand!'*: see Sterne, *A Sentimental Journey*, 'The Wig'.

Mr. Owen: Robert Owen (1771–1858), whose *A New View of Society* was published in 1813–14.

Address to the higher and middle classes: a sardonic allusion to the second of Coleridge's *Lay Sermons* (1817), 'addressed to the higher and middle classes'.

Hunter's Captivity . . . Indians: see John Dunne Hunter, *Memoirs of a Captivity Among the Indians of North America* (London, 1823).

260 *Mr. Owen and his parallelograms*: Owen's *Report to the Committee for the Relief of the Manufacturing Poor* (1817) proposed to house the poor in squares of 'public buildings, which divide them into parallelograms'.

261 *His admirable little work On Usury . . . forty years ago*: see Bentham's *Defence of Usury*, written 1787, but not published until 1816.

'in nook monastic': see *As You Like It*, III.ii.404–5, 'forswear the full stream of the world and to live in a nook merely monastic'.

'men of Ind': from *The Tempest*, II.ii.58.

the late Mr. Speaker Abbot: Charles Abbot (1757–1829), Speaker of the Commons, 1802–17. His mother was Bentham's stepmother.

Proh pudor!: 'for shame!'

Church of Englandism: Bentham's *Church-of-Englandism and its Catechism Examined* (1818), a critical analysis of the Anglican establishment.

'to be honest . . . ten thousand!': see *Hamlet*, II.ii.180–1, 'To be honest, as this world goes, is to be one man picked out of ten thousand.'

262 *'looked enough abroad into universality'*: from Bacon, *Advancement of Learning*, 'the corrupter sort of mere politiques, that have not their thoughts established by learning in the love and apprehension of duty, nor never look abroad into universality', quoted by Hazlitt in *Lectures on the Dramatic Literature of the Age of Elizabeth* (Howe, vi.329).

28. WILLIAM GODWIN

Published in *The Spirit of the Age* (1825).

263 *as Goldsmith used to say*: see Boswell, *Life of Johnson*, iii.252: 'Whenever I write any thing, the public make a point to know nothing about it.'

Political Justice: Godwin's *Enquiry Concerning Political Justice* was published in 1793.

'*Sedet, in eternumque . . . Theseus*': from Virgil, *Aeneid*, vi.617–18, 'Unlucky Theseus sits, and will sit for eternity.'

264 *a young man, a student in the Temple*: probably Basil Montagu (1770–1851), an early disciple of Godwin's, who temporarily abandoned his legal studies under the influence of *Political Justice*.

like the false Duessa: see Spenser, *The Faerie Queene*, I.iv, where Duessa leads the Red Cross Knight into the House of Pride.

'*its hinder parts are ruinous, decayed, and old*': see Spenser, *The Faerie Queene*, I.iv.5:8–9, 'And all the hinder partes, that few could spie, | Were ruinous and old, but painted cunningly.'

'*if this failed . . . stubble*': from Milton, *Comus*, 597–9.

'*What then . . . the wind?*': see Matthew 11:7, 'What went ye out into the wilderness to see? A reed shaken with the wind?'

the new Gamaliel: see Acts 22:3.

265 *Mr. Southey's Inscriptions*: Southey published eight 'Inscriptions' in his *Poems* (1797).

Mr. Coleridge's Religious Musings: published in *Poems on Various Subjects* (1796) as 'Religious Musings: A Desultory Poem, Written on Christmas' Eve, 1794'.

'*like Cato ! . . . senate laws?*': from Pope, 'Epistle to Dr Arbuthnot', 209.

Oh! and is all forgot?: see *Midsummer Night's Dream*, III.ii.202.

'*by that sin fell the angels!*': from *Henry VIII*, III.ii.442.

'*the law of laws, and sovereign of sovereigns*': Burke's phrase for God's will in *Reflections on the Revolution in France* (146), echoing Revelations 17:14.

267 '*Who is thy neighbour?*': see Luke 10:29; Jesus responds with the parable of the Good Samaritan.

'*Thou shalt love thy neighbour as thyself*': from Luke 10:27.

'*There was the rub . . . short life!*': see *Hamlet*, III.i.67, 70–1, 'Ay, there's the rub . . . There's the respect | That makes calamity of so long life'.

'*trenchant blade*': from Samuel Butler, *Hudibras*, I.i.357.

'*all is conscience and tender heart*': see Chaucer, *General Prologue to the Canterbury Tales*, 150, 'And al was conscience and tendre herte.'

268 '*so ran the tenour of the bond*': see *The Merchant of Venice*, IV.i.231–2.

'*It was well said . . . to say well*': see *Henry VIII*, III.ii.153–4.

Hare-court: the pump in Hare Court, Temple, a well-known London landmark.

'*fallen first into a fasting . . . we all complain!*': see *Hamlet*, II.ii.148–52.

'*lost the immortal . . . beastly*': from *Othello*, II.iii.257–8.

'*the guide, the stay . . . moral being*': see Wordsworth, 'Tintern Abbey', 110–12:

> The anchor of my purest thoughts, the nurse,
> The guide, the guardian of my heart, and soul
> Of all my moral being.

269 *created a Baronet by a Prince of the House of Brunswick*: George IV made Scott a baronet on 30 March 1820.

'*when in Auvergne . . . murder*': see Scott, *Quentin Durward* (1823), I.4–5.

270 '*Reason is the queen . . . physical nature!*': Hazlitt quotes from his own 'Illustrations of Vetus' (*Morning Chronicle*, 5 January 1814).

'*the unreasonableness . . . our reason*': from the book on knight-errantry that Don Quixote reads: 'The reason of the unreasonable usage my reason has met with, so unreasons my reason, that I have reason to complain of your beauty' (Cervantes, translated by Smollett, I.2).

'*flying an eagle . . . right on*': see *Timon of Athens*, I.i.49.

'*Thus far . . . no farther!*': from Job 38:11.

271 *Captain Parry . . . North-West Passage*: Sir William Edward Parry (1790–1855), naval officer and Arctic explorer, who from 1818 led several expeditions to locate the north-west passage to the Pacific, publishing accounts of his voyages in 1821 and 1824.

'*championing it to the Outrance*': see *Macbeth*, III.i.73, 'champion me to th'utterance'.

St. Leon: Godwin's novel *St. Leon: A Tale of the Sixteenth Century* was published in 1799.

Mr. Fuseli: Henry Fuseli (1741–1825), painter and writer.

272 '*bastards of his art*': see Shakespeare, *A Lover's Complaint*, 174–5, 'Thought characters and words merely but art, | And bastards of his foul adulterate heart.'

Allen-a-Dale: one of Robin Hood's Merry Men, and 'northern minstrel' in Scott's *Ivanhoe*.

273 *Fleetwood and Mandeville*: novels by Godwin, published 1805 and 1817 respectively.

Life of Chaucer: Godwin's four-volume *Life of Geoffrey Chaucer* was published in 1803.

Remarks on Judge Eyre's Charge to the Jury: Godwin's *Cursory Strictures on the Charge Delivered by Lord Chief Justice Eyre*, a forensic examination of the prosecution case in the Treason Trials of 1794, which helped to secure the acquittals.

skulked behind a British throne: see *A Letter to William Gifford*: 'Mr. Sheridan once spoke of certain politicians in his day who "skulked behind the throne, and made use of the sceptre as a conductor to carry off the lightning of national indignation which threatened to consume them"' (Howe, ix.26). The allusion is to a speech Sheridan made in the Commons on 3 December 1795 on the Seditious Meetings Act, one of the so-called 'Gagging Acts'.

a volume of Sermons, and of a Life of Chatham: Godwin, *Sketches of History, in Six Sermons*, published anonymously in 1784; his *History of the Life of William Pitt, Earl of Chatham* (1783) was his first publication, also anonymous.

tragedies of Antonio and Ferdinand: Godwin's tragedy *Antonio* was performed at Drury Lane on 13 December 1800; *Faulkner* (not *Ferdinand*) on 16 December 1807. Both were poorly received.

manes: the deified dead in ancient Roman religion.

Mr. Fawcett: Joseph Fawcett (*c.*1758–1804), Presbyterian minister and poet, whom Godwin described as one of his four 'principal oral instructors'.

274 *speech on General Warrants*: the speech was in fact on the Cider Bill of 1763. When the House of Commons debated the issuing of general arrest warrants for those suspected of sedition during the John Wilkes controversy, Chatham declared 'General Warrants are always wrong'.

the printed volume: Godwin's *History of the Life of William Pitt, Earl of Chatham* (1783), p. v.

Horne Tooke: John Horne Tooke (1736–1812), radical and philologist.

275 *History of the Commonwealth of England*: a four-volume history published 1824–8.

Esto perpetua: 'let it endure for ever'.

276 *a very admirable likeness . . . our author's mind*: now in the National Portrait Gallery, London.

He speaks of them with enthusiasm . . . Love: an occasion also described in the *Plain Speaker* essay, 'On the Conversation of Authors' (Howe, xii.41).

29. LORD BYRON

Published in *The Spirit of the Age* (1825).

277 *This Essay . . . Lord Byron's death*: Byron died at Missolonghi in Greece on 19 April 1824; news reached England on 14 May.

'Born universal heir to all humanity': see John Fletcher, *The Faithful Shepherdess* (1679), I.iv:

> Thy manners are as gentle and as fair
> As his, who brags himself born only heir
> To all humanity.

'As if a man . . . no other kin': see *Coriolanus*, V.iii.36–7.

'cloud-capt': from *The Tempest*, IV.i.152.

'golden mean': from Horace's 'auream mediocritatem', *Odes*, II.x.5.

278 *'prouder than when blue Iris bends'*: from *Troilus and Cressida*, I.iii.373.

'silly sooth . . . old age': from *Twelfth Night*, II.iv.45–7, Hazlitt substituting 'thought' for 'love'.

279 *in his politics is a liberal*: a new term in politics at this time, associated with the more radical element of the Whig party who supported revolutionary Liberal parties in Europe.

'denotes a foregone conclusion': from *Othello*, III.iii.433.

280 *'in cell monastic'*: see *As You Like It*, III.ii.404–5.

dipped in Tyrian dyes: see Dryden, *Secular Masque*, 56, 'The sprightly green has drunk the Tyrian dye.'

281 *'thoughts that breathe and words that burn'*: from Thomas Gray, 'The Progress of Poesy', 110.

as he himself has said: see Byron's letter to John Hunt of 17 March 1823, which Hunt may have shown to Hazlitt: 'I continue to compose for the same reason that I ride, or read, or bathe, or travel—it is a habit' (*Letters and Journals*, ed. Leslie A. Marchand, x.123).

'poor men's cottages, but princes' palaces': from *The Merchant of Venice*, I.ii.13–14.

282 *'reasons high of providence, fore-knowledge will, and fate'*: from *Paradise Lost*, II.558–9.

'Till Contemplation has her fill': from John Dryer, 'Grongar Hill', 26.

'this bank and shoal of time': from *Macbeth*, I.vii.6.

'Don Juan was my Moscow . . . seems Cain': from *Don Juan*, XI.441–2.

published in the Liberal: Byron's fragment *Heaven and Earth* appeared in the second number of *The Liberal*; see Hazlitt's review in the *Edinburgh* for April 1823 (Howe, xvi.411–15).

283 *'it is his aversion'*: see *Don Juan*, III.848–9:

> A drowsy frowzy poem, call'd the 'Excursion,'
> Writ in a manner which is my aversion.

'born in a garret sixteen stories high': from *English Bards* and *Scotch Reviews* (1809), 478–82:

> The Tolbooth felt defrauded of his charms,
> If Jeffrey died, except within her arms:
> Nay, last not least, on that portentous morn
> The sixteenth story where himself was born,
> His patrimonial garret fell to ground . . .

'Letter to the Editor . . . Review': Byron's 'A Letter to the Editor of "My Grandmother's Review"', addressed from Wortley Clutterbuck to William Roberts, editor of the *British Review*, appeared in the first number of *The Liberal* (1822), responding to criticisms of *Don Juan*.

Long's: Long's Hotel, New Bond Street.

controversy about Pope: William Lisle Bowles (1762–1850), clergyman and poet. Critical comments in his 1806 edition of Pope in 1806 provoked Byron's *Letter to John Murray, Esq.* Hazlitt wrote about the controversy in the *London Magazine* for June 1821 (Howe, xix.62–84).

From the sublime . . . but one step: attributed to Napoleon on his retreat from Moscow in 1812; see also Paine, *The Age of Reason* (1795): 'The sublime and the ridiculous are often so nearly related, that it is difficult to class them separately. One step above the sublime, makes the ridiculous; and one step above the ridiculous, makes the sublime again' (II.20).

284 *Scrub in the farce*: in George Farquhar's *The Beaux' Stratagem* (1707).

'very tolerable and not to be endured': see *Much Ado About Nothing*, III. iii.35.

a TRISTRAM SHANDY in rhyme: see Byron's letter to Douglas Kinnaird of 14 April 1823: 'You must not mind occasional rambling I mean it for a poetical T. Shandy—or Montaigne's Essays—with a story for a hinge' (*Letters and Journals*, x.150).

'a chartered libertine': from *Henry V*, I.i.49.

He says he will write on . . . not: see *Don Juan*, XV.475, 'I write the world, nor care if the world read.'

285 *spolia opima*: see note to p. 134.

'Like proud seas under him': from *Two Noble Kinsmen*, II.ii.19–20, 'feel our fiery horses | Like proud seas under us'.

'Farthest from them is best': from *Paradise Lost*, I.247.

The first Vision of Judgment . . . second: Southey's *Vision of Judgment* (1821) described George III's ascent into heaven; Byron published his satire on it the following year.

'None but itself could be its parallel': from Lewis Theobald, *Double Falshood, or, The Distrest Lovers* (1728), III.i.

286 *'the tenth transmitter of a foolish face'*: see Richard Savage, *The Bastard* (1728), 8, 'No tenth transmitter of a foolish face'.

from the advice of friends: Thomas Moore wrote to Byron in January 1822, attempting to dissuade him from working with Shelley and Hunt on *The Liberal*.

He is at present in Cephalonia, waiting the event!: Byron arrived on Cephalonia on 2 August 1823, remaining there until 29 December.

'tears of sensibility': generic, although Hazlitt may have in mind the series of novels by François-Thomas-Marie de Baculard D'Arnaud, translated into English under this title in 1773.

287 *'Nothing can cover . . . greatness'*: from Beaumont and Fletcher, *The False One*, II.i.153–5.

30. MR. WORDSWORTH

Published in *The Spirit of the Age* (1825).

288 *'lowliness is young ambition's ladder'*: from *Julius Caesar*, II.i.22.

'no figures . . . men': from *Julius Caesar*, II.i.230–1, Hazlitt substituting 'passion' for 'care'.

288 *'skyey influences'*: from *Measure for Measure*, III.i.9.

 'Nihil humani . . . puto': from Terence, *Heautontimorumenos*, I.i.77, 'I consider nothing pertaining to humanity foreign to me'.

289 *'the cloud-capt towers . . . behind'*: see *The Tempest*, IV.i.151–6.

 de novo: 'anew'.

 tabula rasa: 'clean slate'.

 'the judge's robe . . . 'longs': see *Measure for Measure*, II.ii.61–3.

 jewels in the crisped hair: from William Collins, 'The Manners. An Ode', 55.

 He gathers manna: see the description of Moses in Exodus 16:11–15 and 17:3–6.

290 *'a sense of joy . . . green field'*: from Wordsworth, 'Lines written at a Small Distance from my House', 6–8.

 sad vicissitude of fate: the phrase 'sad vicissitude of things' appears in Richard Gifford's poem *Contemplation* and is quoted by Johnson in Boswell's *Life* (v.117–18); it also appears in Laurence Sterne's *Sermons* (XVI). Cf. Edward Young, *Night Thoughts*, i.189, 'Sheds sad vicissitude on all beneath.'

 'Beneath the hills . . . ruthless destiny': see Wordsworth, *The Excursion*, vi.553–7.

 the round earth its footstool: see Isaiah 66:1.

 the vain pomp and glory of the world: from *Henry VIII*, III.ii.366.

291 *'To him the meanest flower. . . tears'*: see Wordsworth, 'Ode: Intimations of Immortality', 205–6.

292 *Cole-Orton*: Sir George Beaumont's country house in Leicestershire, where Wordsworth frequently stayed.

 the exquisite poem, entitled Laodamia: composed 1814 and published in *Poems* (1815).

 'Calm contemplation and majestic pains': see Wordsworth, 'Laodamia', 72, 'Calm pleasures there abide—majestic pains.'

293 *'Fall blunted from the indurated breast'*: see Goldsmith, *The Traveller*, 230–1, 'Fall blunted from each indurated heart, | Some sterner virtues o'er the mountain's breast'.

 'and fit audience found, though few': see *Paradise Lost*, VII.31, quoted by Wordsworth in his Prospectus to 'The Recluse', published in the Preface to *The Excursion* (xi).

 fell still-born from the press: see Pope, 'Epilogue to the Satires: Dialogue II', 226, 'All, all but truth, drops dead-born from the press'.

 toujours perdrix: 'always partridge', a comment made by the confessor to Henry VI of France when the king ordered partridge for every course at dinner.

'man of no mark or likelihood': see *1 Henry IV*, III.ii.45.

294 *'Flushed with a purple grace . . . honest face'*: from Dryden, 'Alexander's Feast', 51–2.

to modernise some of the Canterbury Tales: Hazlitt refers to Wordsworth's re-tellings of Chaucer, which he probably saw in manuscript in 1803, of which only *The Prioress's Tale* had been published, in *Poems* (1820).

295 *'He hates those interlocutions between Lucius and Caius'*: a misremembering of *Cymbeline* by Hazlitt or Wordsworth—there are no dialogues between Lucius and Caius.

Mr. Wordsworth . . . when he was young: *The Borderers*, a five-act blank verse drama, written 1796–7, not published until 1842.

'Action is momentary . . . obscure, and infinite!': see Wordsworth, *The Borderers*, III.v.60–5:

> Action is transitory—a step, a blow,
> The motion of a muscle—this way or that—
> 'Tis done, and in the after-vacancy
> We wonder at ourselves like men betrayed:
> Suffering is permanent, obscure and dark,
> And shares the nature of infinity.

'Let observation . . . China to Peru': the periphrasis of these lines had become a critical commonplace; Hazlitt first attributed the analysis of Johnson's poem to Wordsworth in conversation with John Payne Collier in 1811 (Jones, 65).

Drawcansir: a character in George Villiers, Duke of Buckingham, *The Rehearsal* (1671), who enters a battle and kills soldiers on both sides.

Walton's Angler: Izaak Walton's *The Compleat Angler* (1653).

Bewick's wood-cuts: Thomas Bewick (1753–1828), wood engraver.

Waterloo's sylvan etchings: Antoine Waterloo (1609–76), painter, engraver from Lille.

296 *'he hates conchology . . . Venus of Medicis'*: in Hazlitt's own *Lectures on the English Poets* (1818); see Howe, v.163–4.

'Where one for sense . . . at one time': from Samuel Butler, *Hudibras*, II.i. 29–30.

'take the good the Gods provide us': see Dryden, 'Alexander's Feast', 106.

297 *he would have borne his honours meekly*: see *Macbeth*, I.vii.16–17, 'this Duncan | Hath borne his faculties so meek'.

the genial current of the soul is stopped: see Thomas Gray, 'Elegy Written in a Country Churchyard', 52, 'And froze the genial current of the soul'.

the God of his own idolatry: in David Garrick's *Ode Upon Dedicating a Building, and Erecting a Statue, to Shakespeare* (1769) Shakespeare is 'The god of our idolatry!' (14).

31. ON THE PLEASURE OF HATING

Published in *The Plain Speaker* (1826).

298   *Lines to a Spider*: see Leigh Hunt, 'To a Spider Running Across a Room', published in the third number of *The Liberal* (April 1823).

      'the milk of human kindness': from *Macbeth*, I.v.16.

299   *Mr. Burke observes*: in *A Philosophical Enquiry into the Origin of our Ideas of the Sublime and Beautiful*.

      the spirit of the age: although not published until 1826, this essay was composed at the end of 1823, around the time that Hazlitt was working on the 'Spirits of the Age' series, which launched with the essay on Bentham in the *New Monthly Magazine* for January 1824.

      new editions of Fox's Book of Martyrs: a new folio edition was published by subscription in 1811.

300   *'Off, you lendings!'*: from *King Lear*, III.iv.102.

      Mr. Irving . . . Caledonian Chapel: Edward Irving (1792–1834), preacher and theologian, took up the position of minister of the Caledonian Chapel, Hatton Garden in 1822. Hazlitt wrote about Irving in 'Pulpit Oratory' (*The Liberal*, July 1823) and in *The Spirit of the Age*.

      real water of the New River at Sadler's Wells: the New River was an artificial waterway that flowed from Hertfordshire to supply London with fresh drinking water. It terminated in a reservoir just south of Sadler's Wells, allowing the theatre to pump it into an enormous tank in the arena, used for naval melodramas and other aquatic spectacles.

      'Tis pretty, though a plague: from *All's Well that Ends Well*, I.i.91.

      snap-dragon: a Christmas game, where raisins are snatched out of a bowl of burning brandy and eaten while still alight.

      'upon this bank and shoal of time': from *Macbeth*, I.vii.6.

      'outdo termagant': see *Hamlet*, III.ii.13–14.

301   *'That which was luscious as locusts . . . coloquintida'*: see *Othello*, I.iii.347–9.

      'six days in the week': from Richardson, *Clarissa*, Letter 529.

      celebrated by ELIA: in Lamb's *Letter of Elia to Robert Southey, Esquire*, published in the *London Magazine* for October 1823. See the Introduction, p. xi.

      that I myself have celebrated: see 'On the Conversation of Authors', another *Plain Speaker* essay (Howe, xii.24–44).

303   *H——*: [William] Hone (1780–1842), political writer and publisher. This identification and the ones that follow are suggested by William Carew Hazlitt in *Memoirs* (II.241–2).

      'carve them . . . the Gods': from *Julius Caesar*, II.i.173.

      L— H—: Leigh Hunt.

      John Scott: John Scott (1783–1821), editor of the *London Magazine*, who died from injuries sustained in a duel with Jonathan Christie, London agent for the editor of *Blackwood's Edinburgh Magazine* John Gibson Lockhart.

Mrs. ——: [Mary Sabilla] Novello (1789–1854).

B—: [Thomas] Barnes (1785–1841), newspaper editor and essayist.

R——: [John] Rickman (1771–1840), statistician and civil servant.

'sans intermission, for hours by the dial': see *As You Like It*, II.vii.32–3.

Mrs. ——: Novello.

'fellows of no mark or likelihood': from *1 Henry IV*, III.ii.45.

——'s: Basil Montagu.

M: Montagu.

Fawcett: see note to p. 273.

304   *Mr. Washington Irvine*: Washington Irving (1783–1859).

Mr. Liston: John Liston (*c.*1776–1846), actor.

'mice in an air-pump': from Burke's *Letter to a Noble Lord*: 'These philosophers, consider men in their experiments, no more than they do mice in an air pump' (62). See also Anna Laetitia Barbauld's poem to Joseph Priestley, 'The Mouse's Petition'.

the God of our idolatry: see note to p. 297.

305   *'gone into the wastes of time'*: see *Shakespeare*, 'Sonnet 12', 10, 'That thou among the wastes of time must go'.

Mr. Moore's Loves of the Angels: Thomas Moore's poem was published in January 1823.

Sir Andrew Wylie: 1822 novel by John Galt.

'Sitting in my window . . . Far above singing!': from Francis Beaumont and John Fletcher, *Philaster*, V.i.156–67.

'the wine of poetry is drank, but the lees remain': see *Macbeth*, II.iii.94–5, 'The wine of life is drawn, and the mere lees | Is left this vault to brag of.'

306   *'play with Amaryllis . . . hair'*: see Milton, *Lycidas*, 68–9.

'the irrevocable hour': see Wordsworth, 'Ode: Intimations of Immortality', 180, 'Though nothing can bring back the hour'.

Fonthill: Wiltshire home of William Beckford, author of *Vathek*. Hazlitt went to see the gallery there, and refers to the picture known as 'Titian's Mistress'.

307   *'to every good work reprobate'*: from Titus 1:16.

'of whom the world was not worthy': from Hebrew 11:38.

'This was some time . . . evidence of it': see *Hamlet*, III.i.116–17, 'This was sometime a paradox, but now the time gives it proof.'

awakened once more in Spain: in March 1820, revolutionaries seized control from Ferdinand VII and suppressed the Inquisition, marking the beginning of the *Trienio Liberal*, a three-year period of liberal government.

307 *'the rose plucked . . . blister there!'*: see *Hamlet*, III.iv.41–3.

308 *The Heart of Mid Lothian*: 1818 novel by Walter Scott.

32. OUR NATIONAL THEATRES

Published in the *Atlas* for 11 October 1829.

309 *private boxes*: in 1809, John Philip Kemble introduced a new tier of subscription boxes to Covent Garden theatre, one of the changes that provoked the 'Old Price riots'.

Madame Vestris and her friends: Lucia Elizabeth Vestris, née Bartolozzi (1797–1856), actress and singer, whose series of romantic liaisons in the 1820s was public knowledge.

partitioning off the stalls: Hazlitt refers to the new practice of placing rows of expensive, individual seats in the front of the pit, traditionally the cheapest ticket in the house.

310 *'dear as . . . sad heart?'*: from *Julius Caesar*, II.i.288–9.

Mrs. D——: probably Mary Ann Davenport, née Harvey (1759–1843), acting the Nurse to Fanny Kemble's Juliet in her last season on the stage.

33. THE SPIRIT OF CONTROVERSY

Published in the *Atlas* for 31 January 1830, under the heading 'Specimens of a Dictionary of Definitions, No. III'.

312 *'envy, malice, and all uncharitableness'*: see the Litany in the *Book of Common Prayer*, 'from envy, hatred, and malice, and all uncharitablness'.

Passe pour cela: 'let that be'.

punctum stans: 'eternal moment'.

313 *Baxter's Controversial Works*: Richard Baxter (1615–91), ejected minister and religious writer.

314 *David Deans's . . . of the matter!*: see Scott's *The Heart of Mid-Lothian*, ch. xliii: 'of a surety I would deem it my duty to gang to the root o' the matter'.

'their hearts burn within them by the way!': see Luke 24:32, 'And they said to one another, Did not our heart burn within us, while he talked with us by the way, and while he opened to us the scriptures?'

'a coil and pudder': see Pope's text of *King Lear*, III.ii.49–50, 'Let the great gods, | That keep this dreadful pudder o'er our heads'.

'to leave the part of Hamlet out of the play of Hamlet': the phrase 'Hamlet without the Prince' goes back to an account in the *Morning Post* (21 September 1775) of a theatrical company in which the actor playing the lead ran off with an innkeeper's daughter. When the play was announced, the audience was told 'the part of Hamlet to be left out, for that night'.

Mr. Taylor's discourses: Robert Taylor (1784–1844) had recently been sentenced to a year's imprisonment for blasphemy. He was tried in full canonicals, i.e. clerical dress.

Duke of NEWCASTLE: the fourth duke of Newcastle (1785–1851), leader of the Tory 'ultras' and violent opponent of Catholic Emancipation.

'Strange . . . Tweedledee!': see John Byrom (1692–1763), 'On the Feuds Between Handel and Bononcini' (1727): 'Strange! that such high dispute should be | 'Twixt Tweedledum and Tweedledee.'

'like a thick scurf o'er life': from Thomas Middleton, *The Witch*, I.ii.174.

315 *Nothing could keep the Dissenters . . . tests and fines*: the 1828 Repeal of the Test and Corporation Acts removed the seventeenth-century legislation restricting the civil rights of Protestant dissenters from the Church of England.

'whose edge is sharper than the sword': from *Cymbeline*, III.iv.34.

Malibran or Pasta: Maria Felica Malibran (1808–36) and Giuditta Pasta (1797–1865), Spanish and Italian sopranos respectively. Malibran first appeared as an understudy to Pasta in June 1825 at Covent Garden, but soon became her principal rival.

Of whatsoe'er descent . . . beaten gold: from Dryden, *Absalom and Achitophel*, 100–3.

316 *vis inertiæ*: 'force of inactivity'.

34. THE FREE ADMISSION

Published in the *New Monthly Magazine* for July 1830.

319 *'loop-holes of retreat'*: from Cowper, *The Task*, iv.88.

'He is all ear . . . ribs of death': see Milton, *Comus*, 560–2, 'I was all ear, | And took in strains that might create a soul | Under the ribs of death'.

'The fly . . . lost in the sweets': from Gay, *The Beggar's Opera*, II.viii.

'Oh! leave me to my repose': see Thomas Gray, 'The Descent of Odin', 50.

'the arm-chair at an inn . . . throne of felicity': from Boswell's *Life of Johnson*, 'I have heard him assert that a tavern chair was the throne of human felicity' (ii.452).

320 *'witching time of night'*: from *Hamlet*, III.ii.377.

bid a gay defiance to mischance: see Leigh Hunt, *The Story of Rimini* (1816), IV.8, 'Strike up a blithe defiance to mischance'.

young Kemble's voice: Frances Anne (Fanny) Kemble (1809–93), actress and author, daughter of Charles Kemble and Maria Theresa De Camp, and niece of Sarah Siddons. She made a sensational stage debut in the 1829–30 season.

'like bees in spring-time, when the sun with Taurus rides': from *Paradise Lost*, I.768–9.

320 *Isabella or Belvidera*: Kemble made her debut in Garrick and Southerne's *Isabella; or the Fatal Marriage* and as Belvidera in Otway's *Venice Preserved*—both famous parts of Sarah Siddons—on 9 December 1829 and 28 April 1830.

'*a discipline of humanity*': from Francis Bacon, 'Of Marriage and Single Life': 'Certainly, Wife and Children are a kinde of Discipline of Humanity'. Hazlitt himself had described the stage as 'a test and school of humanity' in the *London Magazine* (January 1820).

321 '*retire, the world shut out, our thoughts call home*': from Young, *Night Thoughts*, ix.1441.

'*the still, small voice*': from 1 Kings 19:12.

Miss Ford: Miss Forde played Cherry in *The Beaux' Stratagem* at Covent Garden on 31 December 1828. Hazlitt described the dialogue between Cherry and Archer in Act II, Scene 2 as a 'love catechism' in *Lectures on the Comic Writers*.

Mrs. Humby: Mrs Humby played Luise in Planché's *The Green-Eyed Monster* at the Haymarket, 18 August 1828.

Mrs. Jordan's laugh in Nell: Dorothy Jordan (1761–1816) first played Nell in Charles Coffey's *The Devil to Pay* in the 1788–9 season.

Mrs. Goodall's Rosalind: Charlotte Goodall (1765–1830) made her first appearance in London as Rosalind, at Drury Lane on 2 October 1788.

the age of chivalry is gone for ever: see note to p. 75.

'*strut and fret his hour upon the stage*': from *Macbeth*, V.v.24.

322 '*See o'er the stage . . . pours her soul in love*': see Thomson, *The Seasons*, 'Winter', 646–8.

'*he takes his ease*': see *1 Henry IV*, III.iii.80.

the dews of Castaly: from Spenser, *The Ruines of Time*, 431, 'With verses, dipt in deaw of Castalie'.

323 '*all that mighty heart is beating still*': see Wordsworth, 'Composed Upon Westminster Bridge', 14, 'And all that mighty heart is lying still!'

'*thy freedom hath made me effeminate!*': see *Romeo and Juliet*, III.i.114, 'Thy beauty hath made me effeminate'.

'*Teddy the Tiler*': a farce by G. H. B. Rodwell (1800–52), performed at Covent Garden, 8 February 1830.

'*Robert the Devil*': a 'musical romance' by Raymond, performed at Covent Garden, 2 February 1830.

'*What avails . . . bind as fast?*': from Sneyd Davies, 'To Frederick Cornwallis, now Archbishop of Canterbury' (1782), 79–80.

as Beau Brummell had his favourite leg: see Hazlitt's 'Brummelliana' (Howe, xx.152–4).

knit with the Graces . . . pleasant spring!: see *Paradise Lost*, IV.266–8:

> while universal Pan
> Knit with the Graces and the Hours in dance
> Led on the eternal spring.

Cowley's Gallery: see Abraham Cowley's *The Chronicle. A Ballad.*

35. THE LETTER-BELL

Hazlitt's final essay, posthumously published in the *Monthly Magazine* for March 1831.

324 *'one entire and perfect chrysolite'*: from *Othello*, V.ii.152.

the friends I had lately left: i.e. his father, mother, and sister.

the long line of blue hills: Wem is within sight of the Welsh mountains; cf. 'Why Distant Objects Please': 'When I was a boy, I lived within sight of a range of lofty hills, whose blue tops blending with the setting sun had often temped my longing eyes and wandering feet' (Howe, viii.256).

the road from —— to ——: from Wem to Shrewsbury.

'And by the vision splendid . . . attended': see Wordsworth, 'Ode: Intimations of Immortality', 73–4.

325 *again risen in the west*: in France, with the July Revolution, *les trois glorieuses* of 27–9 July 1830, which was triggered by the suspension of the freedom of the press. It led to the abdication of Charles X and installment of Louis Phillipe, the duc d'Orléans, as a constitutional monarch or 'citizen king'. Hazlitt heard the news during his final illness and apparently replied, 'Ah! I am afraid . . . things will go back again' (Wu, 427–8). It was engraved on his tombstone in St Anne's Church, Soho, that he had lived 'To see the downfall of the Bourbons'.

Laureate: Robert Southey.

'What, though the radiance . . . flower?': from Wordsworth, 'Ode: Intimations of Immortality', 178–81.

'like morn risen on mid-night': see *Paradise Lost*, V.310–11, 'another morn | Risen on mid-noon'.

Io pæan: 'hymn of praise'; Burke uses the phrase in *Reflections*, 108, describing the response of the Revolution Society to events in France.

the Valley of the Shadow of Death: see Psalm 23:4, 'Yea, though I walk through the valley of the shadow of death, I will fear no evil'.

And what shall we say to him: Coleridge.

'And from his neck . . . into the sea': from Coleridge, 'The Rime of the Ancient Mariner', 289–91.

326 *Miss D——*: unidentified.

Vangoyen: Jan van Goyen (1596–1656), Dutch landscape painter.

327 *'The slow canal . . . the gliding sail'*: from Goldsmith, *The Traveller*, 291–2.

'While with an eye . . . life of things': from Wordsworth, 'Tintern Abbey', 48–50.

327 *'the secrets of the prison-house'*: see *Hamlet*, I.v.14; also Wordsworth, 'Ode: Intimations of Immortality', 67, 'Shades of the prison-house'.

'Entire affections scorneth nicer hands': see Spenser, *The Faerie Queene*, I.viii.40:3, 'Entire affection hateth nicer hands'.

'His shame in crowds, his solitary pride!': see Goldsmith, *The Deserted Village*, 412.

'Made good digestion . . . health on both': from *Macbeth*, III.iv.37–8.

328 *an ingenious friend and arch-critic*: probably Francis Jeffrey.

Gertrude of Wyoming: poem by Thomas Campbell (1809).

'more germain to the matter': from *Hamlet*, V.ii.120.

329 *In Cowper's time . . . hardly set up*: the national mail coach system was introduced in 1784.

'Hark! 'tis the twanging . . . unconscious of them all': from Cowper, *The Task*, iv.1–22.

Lord Byron denies: in his *Letter to John Murray Esq.* (1821) Byron declared 'Cowper is no poet.'

telegraphs . . . new revolution: news of the July Revolution was communicated across France by Claude Chappe's mechanical semaphore system, or telegraph, mounted on a series of towers across the country.

the beacon-fires (mentioned by Æschylus): see note to p. 220.

The Oxford World's Classics Website

www.worldsclassics.co.uk

- Browse the full range of Oxford World's Classics online

- Sign up for our monthly e-alert to receive information on new titles

- Read extracts from the Introductions

- Listen to our editors and translators talk about the world's greatest literature with our Oxford World's Classics audio guides

- Join the conversation, follow us on Twitter at OWC_Oxford

- Teachers and lecturers can order inspection copies quickly and simply via our website

www.worldsclassics.co.uk

American Literature

British and Irish Literature

Children's Literature

Classics and Ancient Literature

Colonial Literature

Eastern Literature

European Literature

Gothic Literature

History

Medieval Literature

Oxford English Drama

Philosophy

Poetry

Politics

Religion

The Oxford Shakespeare

A complete list of Oxford World's Classics, including Authors in Context, Oxford English Drama, and the Oxford Shakespeare, is available in the UK from the Marketing Services Department, Oxford University Press, Great Clarendon Street, Oxford OX2 6DP, or visit the website at www.oup.com/uk/worldsclassics.

In the USA, visit www.oup.com/us/owc for a complete title list.

Oxford World's Classics are available from all good bookshops. In case of difficulty, customers in the UK should contact Oxford University Press Bookshop, 116 High Street, Oxford OX1 4BR.

TROLLOPE IN   OXFORD WORLD'S CLASSICS

ANTON CHEKHOV	**About Love and Other Stories**
	Early Stories
	Five Plays
	The Princess and Other Stories
	The Russian Master and Other Stories
	The Steppe and Other Stories
	Twelve Plays
	Ward Number Six and Other Stories
FYODOR DOSTOEVSKY	**Crime and Punishment**
	Devils
	A Gentle Creature and Other Stories
	The Idiot
	The Karamazov Brothers
	Memoirs from the House of the Dead
	Notes from the Underground and
	The Gambler
NIKOLAI GOGOL	**Dead Souls**
	Plays and Petersburg Tales
MIKHAIL LERMONTOV	**A Hero of Our Time**
ALEXANDER PUSHKIN	**Boris Godunov**
	Eugene Onegin
	The Queen of Spades and Other Stories
LEO TOLSTOY	**Anna Karenina**
	The Kreutzer Sonata and Other Stories
	The Raid and Other Stories
	Resurrection
	War and Peace
IVAN TURGENEV	**Fathers and Sons**
	First Love and Other Stories
	A Month in the Country

GUY DE MAUPASSANT	A Day in the Country and Other Stories
	A Life
	Bel-Ami
PROSPER MÉRIMÉE	Carmen and Other Stories
MOLIÈRE	Don Juan and Other Plays
	The Misanthrope, Tartuffe, and Other Plays
BLAISE PASCAL	Pensées and Other Writings
ABBÉ PRÉVOST	Manon Lescaut
JEAN RACINE	Britannicus, Phaedra, and Athaliah
ARTHUR RIMBAUD	Collected Poems
EDMOND ROSTAND	Cyrano de Bergerac
MARQUIS DE SADE	The Crimes of Love
	Justine
	The Misfortunes of Virtue and Other Early Tales
GEORGE SAND	Indiana
MME DE STAËL	Corinne
STENDHAL	The Red and the Black
	The Charterhouse of Parma
PAUL VERLAINE	Selected Poems
JULES VERNE	Around the World in Eighty Days
	Journey to the Centre of the Earth
	Twenty Thousand Leagues under the Seas
VOLTAIRE	Candide and Other Stories
	Letters concerning the English Nation
	A Pocket Philosophical Dictionary